D1351964

In the Eyes of the Beholder

Critical Issues
for Diversity
in Gifted Education

In the
Eyes
of the
Beholder

Critical Issues
for Diversity
in Gifted Education

edited by

Diane Boothe and
Julian C. Stanley

PRUFROCK PRESS, INC.

ISBN-13: 978-1-59363-004-1
ISBN-10: 1-59363-004-2

At the time of this book's publication, all facts and figures cited are the most current available. All telephone numbers, addresses, and Web site URLs are accurate and active. All
publications, organizations, Web sites, and other resources exist as described in the book,
and all have been verified. The authors and Prufrock Press, Inc., make no warranty or
guarantee concerning the information and materials given out by organizations or content
found at Web sites, and we are not responsible for any changes that occur after this book's
publication. If you find an error, please contact Prufrock Press, Inc. We strongly recommend to parents, teachers, and other adults that you monitor children's use of the Internet.

Prufrock Press, Inc.
P.O. Box 8813
Waco, Texas 76714-8813
(800) 998-2208
Fax (800) 240-0333
http://www.prufrock.com

To my mother, Bette Louise West,
and in memory of my grandmothers,
Beulah Ann Cooksey and Ruth Kelley West,
three inspirational role models
who enriched my life
with diverse learning opportunities.

—D.B.

For
Dot, Suzy, and Lestina

—J.C.S.

[Table of Contents]

[Part I: Cultural Considerations]

[Part III: Pertinent Perspectives on the Challenges of Giftedness]

Introduction:
New Approaches to Giftedness and Talent

by Julian C. Stanley

This is not like the usual book or textbook about gifted and talented boys and girls. All of its authors are specialists on the topic for which we invited them to submit one of the chapters. Only four or five of the authors, however, might be termed gifted-child specialists, but each knows a great deal about gifted children in his or her specialty.

Even in 20 chapters, it was not possible to cover all kinds of diversity among the gifted and talented. Blacks, Hispanics, Native Americans, Indians, and Chinese each have a chapter. Visual art does, but not music, drama, dance, or athletics specifically. The distinctively different points of view of Donna Ford, Howard Gardner, Linda Gottfredson, and Robert Sternberg are well represented. So are those of Linda Brody, Paula Olszewski-Kubilius, Joseph Renzulli and Sally Reis, and Joyce VanTassel-Baska, all of whose main work for many years has been with a wide variety of gifted and talented students. Other approaches round out the treatment of diversity of identification and educational facilitation of high-ability or highly talented youth.

Here are fascinating additions to better known viewpoints: Judy Rance-Roney on second culture/second language acquisition, Arthur Jensen on mental chronometry, Marie Jackson and Brent Snow on counseling, Margarete Parrish on the deleterious effects of urban poverty and homelessness on academic achievement, Robert Lerner and Althea Nagai's almost unique quantitative approach to affirmative-action in higher education (probabilities of being admitted to highly selective universities will astound you), Clifton Wickstrom with an in-depth historical and legal review of U.S. national policy on education for the highly capable, and Diane Boothe's treatment of gender differences among the gifted.

The three chapter divisions (Cultural Considerations, Views From the Core Education Community, and Pertinent Perspectives on the Challenges of Giftedness) provide coherence. Among them, however, there are subgroups of chapters worth reading together, such as those by Ford, Gottfredson, Jensen, and Lerner and Nagai and the ones by Kornhaber (representing Howard Gardner's multiple intelligences) and Sternberg and Kwaitkowski (presenting Sternberg's alternative theory of intelligences). Perhaps the greatest contrast occurs in the chapter by Ford versus that by Gottfredson, augmented independently by the extensive quantitative analyses of Lerner and Nagai.

All in all, we are proud of this collection. The manuscripts, expertly prepared initially, were studied carefully by us. We made some suggestions, chiefly stylistic, for improving them so that what you have in print is a revision of the originals. We did not tamper with the substantive views of the authors because each of them knows much more about his or her area than we do.

The extensive citations of important work are a treasure-trove for readers interested in knowing more about a topic than can be included in a brief chapter. All of the references have been gathered together in a single long list at the end of the book. The name index, also at the end, will make finding the chapter citation of a reference easy. The cumulative references and the name index help indicate some of the main thrusts of the book.

Perhaps diversity discussions can now rest on a broader, more fundamental basis than the usual rhetoric. Maybe educators and gifted-child specialists can come away from reading the book with somewhat greater sensitivity to the needs of these special populations. If so, assembling this collection will have been worth the effort involved.

Part I

Cultural Considerations

Empowering and Serving Hispanic Students in Gifted Education

by Jaime Castellano

Gifted education continues to be one of the most hotly debated programs in the U.S. public school system. In some schools, giftedness is viewed broadly. In other schools, gifted education has a much narrower, more exclusive meaning. While educators in gifted education may disagree about identification procedures and the meaning of giftedness, they usually agree that the primary purpose of gifted education is to meet students' special talents or the unique educational needs of either exceptionally bright or highly talented students to the maximum degree possible (U.S. Department of Education, 1998).

This chapter will explore empowering and serving Hispanic students in gifted education, their curricular and instructional needs, and methods for balancing their home, school, and community worlds. Assessment alternatives for determining mastery of skills and content will also be provided. This chapter is written with the understanding that the changing demographics of the United States is readily seen in its public schools, and this diversity permeates every school-based program that exists, with the exception, perhaps, of gifted education.

According to the U.S. Department of Education, between 1978 and 1997, Hispanic students identified as gifted increased from 5.2% to 8.6% nationally. The overall Hispanic student population went from 6.8% to 14.3% (Gonzalez, 2000). The Census 2000 data suggests that the "browning" of U.S. schools will continue. Deduction suggests that, over the next few years, the number of Hispanic students eligible for gifted education will increase steadily (Castellano, 2003). Hispanics are the majority student group in school districts in California, Florida, Texas, Illinois, and New York, among other states.

Raul Yzaguirre, executive director of the National Council of La Raza, maintains that, if we equip Latino children (and all other children) with high-quality education and ensure their well-being, we will have a tremendous pool of talent ready to lead the nation forward and every American will benefit (Yzaguirre, 2001). There should be no gatekeepers in gifted education. Rather, we should acknowledge that there is no other program best suited to represent diversity in terms of intelligence, language, and ethnicity than gifted education programs.

Attempting to describe and discuss the wide range of concerns regarding gifted education for Hispanic students is both challenging and far-reaching. The combination of relevant cultural, linguistic, socioeconomic, political, personal, and other variables unique to each individual exacerbates the discussion of the issue (Diaz, 1999). Although Hispanics share a common origin and linguistic base, the groups that make up the Hispanic population are not monolithic. According to Bean and Tienda (1987), Hispanics living in the United States come from 22 different countries or territories. Their unique experiences have influenced them both before and after immigration to the U.S., and these differences are crucial when we consider the identification and development of giftedness among Hispanic students.

Curricular Options for Gifted Hispanic Students

To meet the special needs of gifted Hispanic students, a curriculum that recognizes their advanced academic strengths should be offered. There is a general feeling among experts in gifted education that what is taught to gifted students must include how a subject is presented, the process used in teaching, alternative products that show mastery, and the pace with which content, processes, and products are completed. Pace, depth, and complexity lay the curricular foundation for any gifted student, including those who are Hispanic.

In addition, any curriculum must be modified to accommodate the unique characteristics that students bring to the classroom. For gifted Hispanic students, variables that immediately come to mind include language, culture, and ethnicity. According to Granada (2002), curricula for gifted Hispanic learners should be conceptual in content emphasis and should allow the development of a learning environment in which students can freely use English or Spanish to help define the concepts and generalizations they are learning. Students need to be able to communicate more complex thinking in whatever manner they can. If this emphasis is not built into the curriculum, gifted Hispanic students may run up against false ceilings based on language-usage limitations (Granada, 2002, p. 139). In any case, a curriculum for gifted Hispanic students should be based on sound theory that is developed within a structured framework and is reflective of state and national standards. Infused in the curricular design are multicultural and linguistic components reflective of the cultures and languages of the students being served. The curriculum must also align with the model or models in place for the delivery of gifted services (Granada, 2003).

It is important to realize that students who are gifted and Hispanic have varied strengths. The curriculum with which they are provided must build on these strengths and further validate that gifted Hispanic students can be producers of knowledge, not just consumers. The content should include a multicultural interdisciplinary approach, higher level thinking skills, and abstract concepts. The learning environment should also be student-centered and open-ended, and it should promote creative and divergent thinking. In other words, a curriculum for gifted Hispanic students will be influenced by the demographics of the classroom, delivery model of the program, teacher interests and knowledge, and the characteristics of participating students.

Objectives and Outcomes

In order to demonstrate that mastery of the basic curriculum is occurring, accompanying objectives or outcomes must be defined. Typically, the state education agency (SEA) develops a structured framework of standards that all public schools are required to include in the daily curricular experiences of the students they serve, including those being served in gifted education programs. Demonstrating mastery of the basic curricular emphasis is critical for Hispanic and other historically underrepresented students because ability to master course content with ease is one consideration in placing students at an appropriate instructional level emphasizing a more complex curriculum. Equally important is the necessity to offer alternative learning activities that reflect advanced curricular content and that speak to the unique demographic characteristics students bring to the classroom.

Balancing Home, School, and Community Worlds

How students balance their home, school, and community worlds is crucial to their daily classroom experiences. Teachers and administrators who are aware of the real-life circumstances surrounding their students—including socioeconomic, linguistic, and cultural conditions—and are proactive and sensitive can identify a course of study that is empowering and challenging. Table 1.1 outlines the curricular, instructional, and assessment considerations for empowering and serving gifted Hispanic students and gifted English language learners who are at different stages in balancing home, school, and community worlds.

Living Traditions

Living Traditions is an interdisciplinary curricular model that draws from a community's natural and cultural heritage. Developed by a trio of Vermont educa-

Table 1.1

Balancing Home, School, and Community Worlds: Considerations for Empowering and Serving Gifted Hispanic Students and Gifted English Language Learners

	Curriculum	Instruction	Assessment
Conflicting Worlds Crossings between family, peer group, and school are difficult. Values, beliefs, and expectations are discordant.	• Content must be culturally and linguistically sensitive. • Builds positive cultural identity.	• Forming collaborative work groups. • Opportunities for learning the history and background of who they are. • Use of resources within community; building partnerships.	• Students participate as cross-cultural leaders responsible for helping bridge home, school, and community worlds. • Create opportunities to be engaged in their community.
Merging Worlds Students are able to move between family, peer group, and school. However, crossings are not always easy.	• Living Traditions • Democratic Core Curriculum • Collaborative Curriculum	• Use a multicultural and interdisciplinary approach. • Enrichment • Acceleration • Bibliotherapy • Storytelling	• Project-Based Learning • Performance Assessment • Pretesting
Congruent Worlds Students have mastered the crossings between family, peer group, and school. Crossings are easily manageable.	• Aligned with program delivery model. • Conceptual foundation • Abstract concepts	• Design instruction based on cognitive demands. • Pace-complexity-depth.	• Based on analyzing a test's cognitive demands. • Mastery of course content/state-mandated content standards.

Note. The considerations provided in each cell are appropriate recommendations for any gifted student, regardless of where their "World" is.

tors (Mark Skelding, Martin Kemple, and Joseph Keifer), this model shows teachers how to help forge the connection between students and their community. Skelding maintains that, even in highly transient areas, students can explore the connection between their cultural and natural heritage. He further states that it makes particular sense to include local residents because, ultimately, they drive the curriculum; they're not add-ons (Pellett, 2002). This model is consistent with accommodating the student's skills and talents. Furthermore, this curriculum uses oral histories and other local resources to teach students about their world. This is especially significant for gifted Hispanic students, as more and more school districts across the United States are beginning to discover the importance of matching the needs of the students to the most appropriate delivery model while maintaining the integrity of and respect for their ethnic, cultural, and linguistic diversity. The Living Traditions interdisciplinary curriculum allows this to occur.

The Democratic Core Curriculum

The Democratic Core Curriculum is a model that embraces not only common knowledge, but also the values and processes of the democratic way of life. It essentially asks two questions: (1) What questions or concerns do you have about yourself? and (2) What questions or concerns do you have about the world? Strengths of this model include the following points:

- integrating self-interest and the common good;
- valuing diversity;
- asking powerful questions;
- doing real work;
- meeting rigorous standards; and
- focusing on the affective dimension of education.

It is particularly important that teachers and students develop this curricular model collaboratively. Thus, the buy-in is immediate. In addition, young people are brought together in situations in which they experience the democratic way of life. Significant issues and multiple sources of knowledge are addressed. Students are involved in activities in which people in a democracy engage in order to understand themselves, one another, and the world around them.

Collaborative Curriculum

Collaborative Curriculum planning allows for school districts to band together to write standards-based curriculum and assessments. For districts that venture across boundaries, the collaborative process has turned into a high-level professional development tool that brings outstanding teachers together to reflect on their practices as they help to redefine curriculum in an era of adherence to standards (Allen, 2002). Cornerstones of this planning include (1) standards as the glue, (2) high-level professional development, and (3) the extension of limited resources. The impact a model such as this has on gifted Hispanic students is that it creates a more demanding curriculum, allows for greater articulation among teachers across a given geographic area, and serves as a form of accountability, ensuring access to a deeper curriculum.

Instructional Considerations
When Working With Gifted Hispanic Students

Providing differentiated instruction for high-ability students is a given in gifted education. According to Granada (2003), instruction for gifted Hispanic students must be well-designed and purposeful. Teachers of these students must avoid instruction that consists of loosely connected "gifted activities" gleaned from commercial resources and staff-development workshops. Cumulative learning experiences are a necessity, particularly those that are student-centered and that integrate depth and complexity in content learning and language development. The most exemplary curriculum will be rendered ineffective when paired with poor instruction. Learning experiences that allow gifted Hispanic students the opportunity to grow cognitively and linguistically, that celebrate diversity, and that establish an atmosphere conducive to risk taking should be the prioritized instructional goal.

Qualitatively different instruction refers to those learning experiences that reflect the development of critical and creative thinking skills, content acceleration, and affective education. There may be lessons where one area is emphasized; but, generally, the variables are correlated into a comprehensive program. To the extent possible, gifted Hispanic students should be allowed to participate by speaking and writing in the language with which they feel most comfortable. This is certainly consistent with maintaining ethnic identity, accommodating learning-style differences, and providing an accelerated and enriched curriculum. Furthermore, empowering this population of students is not only important to their personal success, but to the success of the overall program. Providing support systems that focus on social, academic, and familial issues are also equally important and should be a justifiable part of their program focus.

Enrichment and Acceleration

Enrichment and acceleration are two avenues for ensuring that the cognitive and academic needs of gifted students are being met. Enrichment refers to the curriculum, as well as program delivery of services to students and includes richer, more varied educational experiences that have been modified or added to in some way. These modifications or additions may be in content or teaching strategies and are ideally based on the characteristics of the learner(s) for whom they are designed. The enriched curriculum and instruction offers greater depth or breadth than that generally provided and includes a systematic plan for student learning (White, 2002).

Acceleration can also be used to denote both service delivery and curriculum and may include a variety of sources (White, 2002). Acceleration as a service delivery may include grade skipping, subject skipping, and part-time acceleration (entering a higher grade for part of a day) to receive instruction in one or more subjects. Acceleration as a curricular model involves speeding up the pace at which material is presented, expected to be mastered, or both. Both enrichment and acceleration are defensible means of accommodating the needs of high-ability students. In practice, meeting the needs of gifted students as determined by their learning characteristics requires that abstract or complex concepts be taught (enrichment) and that students proceed at a pace that is more rapid than that of the average learner (acceleration). As evidenced by practice and the literature, enrichment and acceleration are complementary components of a comprehensive curricular and instructional plan for students enrolled in gifted education programs.

Adjusting Instructional Time

Adjusting instructional time for students to demonstrate mastery of course goals and objectives is also consistent with principles of acceleration and enrichment. However, for those students enrolled in gifted education programs who have not mastered particular course objectives, providing small-group or individualized instruction is appropriate. The pace of instruction also allows teachers to condense content material.

To be successful with gifted Hispanic students, teachers must expand their vision and use a variety of teaching techniques to ensure that the student is actively involved in the learning process. This is of particular importance to teachers of gifted students at the secondary level who are more academic or content-area specialists. In addition, validating the language and culture of each Hispanic student enrolled in a gifted education program is critical to developing an interactive classroom where all students are engaged and motivated and where their individuality and self-esteem are supported and nurtured.

Bibliotherapy

According to Delisle (1992), bibliotherapy is the use of reading materials to help solve emotional problems and promote mental health. With gifted students, bibliotherapy can include reading about the predicaments and benefits of being gifted as a route to self-understanding and reassurance. This is especially important to gifted Hispanic and other students who must often balance their home, school, and community worlds.

Using bibliotherapy as an instructional strategy is an effective way to involve students in their own learning. It can take into account the demographic make-up of participating students, thus offering a multicultural perspective to teaching. Bibliotherapy also has the potential to combine many of the guiding principles that make up a gifted education program that honors diversity and is committed to equity and excellence. That is, it can target particular problem-solving skills, knowledge, cognitive development, creative thinking, affective development, and personal stories.

Storytelling

Closely related to the idea of bibliotherapy is the use of storytelling to foster cultural diversity and academic opportunities. Table 1.2 offers practitioners a look at how this can be done. Storytelling is a powerful learning tool that addresses the lives of students and offers an opportunity to involve family and community. It also allows them to examine their own feelings and beliefs in a safe, nurturing environment.

The Hispanic community is filled with a long history of rich storytelling traditions. Weaving this fact into the curriculum and instruction makes sense; it's a real-life connection for them. Storytelling can be a fun part of a student's curricular experiences and still meet the challenge of addressing standards and benchmarks mandated by local and state policymakers. Storytelling can meet the cognitive, academic, creative, and social/emotional needs of gifted students. Infusing the use of music that students listen to can be a starting point for the telling of stories because that is what musicians do: They tell stories. Storytelling transcends culture, race, religion, and language, and it serves as a logical and natural springboard to validate students' personal existence. The telling of a story is a social event. This is evidenced in cultural groups around the world. The processes used address the curricular and instructional issues that accommodate those policymakers who are student-performance-oriented and test-oriented. In short, storytelling is a win-win strategy.

Assessing and Evaluating the Work of Gifted Hispanic Students

While the strategies presented here are appropriate for any gifted student, there will be occasional references that speak to the characteristics Hispanic students bring to their school experiences and the potential impact that they have on evaluation, assessment, or both.

Project-Based Learning

Project-based learning brings a decidedly different dimension to the concept of projects (Diffily, 2002). They help students relate the work of school to work outside the classroom. Students select an area of interest and work collaboratively to research the topic using as many different types of information as possible. Using a competent model and a specific audience, they create a real-world product to share what they have learned.

Table 1.2

Using Storytelling to Foster Cultural Diversity and Academic Achievement

Foster Cultural Diversity	Foster Academic Achievement
• Storytelling transcends culture, race, religion, and language. • It is a logical and natural springboard to validate personal identity and existence. • The demographics specific to local student populations should be considered in how a teacher approaches this process. • Storytelling is a social event. This is evidenced in cultural groups around the world and from the beginning of human existence. • Match the teaching style to the learning styles of students. • In cultures where people do a lot of reading, stories tend to be organized around a beginning, middle, and end. • In cultures that rely on an oral tradition, stories follow different patterns, sometimes starting with the most exciting event, for example, then working their way back to the beginning before swinging back around to the end. • One of the best things is for children to hear as wide a range of stories from different cultures as possible. • Emphasis is on the deep elements of culture.	• Cognitively, gifted students easily grasp the mechanics and rationale for telling stories. • Intellectually, they understand that, for example, stories in the form of fables, legends, and fairy tales, have a beginning, middle, and end, and include a conflict of some sort. • Storytelling can be fun while still meeting the challenge of addressing standards and benchmarks. • Through the use of storytelling, the cognitive, academic, creative, and social/emotional needs of gifted students can be met. • The process of putting together a story includes the use of critical thinking, problem-solving, and creative thinking, all hallmarks of gifted education. • At the heart of each story is a problem to be solved. • Students pick up a great deal of specific information from stories. • Parents and teachers use stories specifically to teach children lessons. • Honors the ideas of content-process-product and pace-complexity-depth.

The content and processes of learning are connected to the world outside the classroom, rather than being prescribed by textbooks. Textbooks are not completely abandoned in project classrooms, but they serve as only one resource and do not dictate what knowledge and skills will be learned at a particular time. Students consult the Internet and print and human resources in their project work. Observation is also a key source of information when topics lend themselves to personal observation. Students learn academic skills to accomplish something that is part of their work. Unlike more traditional learning experiences, projects are conducted over several days or several weeks, and each project ends with students sharing what they have learned with a real audience outside their own classroom. Diffily (2002) summarized the idea of projects as an assessment tool in the following way. They are:

1. student-directed;
2. connected to the real world;
3. informed by multiple sources;
4. research-based;
5. embedded with knowledge and skills;
6. conducted over time; and
7. concluded with an end product fashioned after an adult model.

Project-based learning complements the nature of cooperative work groups, a strategy often recommended for use with Hispanic students due to their preference for working together toward a common goal. In addition, making real-world connections personalizes the process and product and requires students to think critically by analyzing, synthesizing, and evaluating the research-based information they have acquired from multiple sources.

Performance Assessment

Closely related to project-based learning is the idea of performance assessment. Performance assessments can be defined as those tasks that require students to demonstrate their synthesized knowledge, understanding, and skills by addressing several objectives, sometimes across multiple disciplines, all without teacher assistance. Common to all performance assessments is the fundamental notion that students are engaged in conceptualized academic exercises where they are comparing, contrasting, summarizing, and predicting (Moon, 2002). For gifted Hispanic students, performance assessment allows them to capitalize on their cognitive and academic strengths while honoring their preferred learning style. This also allows students the opportunity to apply real-life situations to what they have learned or are learning, using an array of resources within and outside the community.

Although teachers face many educational stresses in the classroom, performance assessment is one viable option to assist them in addressing their students' academic diversity while staying focused on state-mandated content standards. When appropriately constructed, performance assessments can ensure that students know what to expect, encounter learning that they come to value as useful because of its real-life application, and achieve the goal of making connections among different disciplines (Moon & Callahan, 2001).

Pretesting

It makes good sense to pretest students enrolled in gifted education programs to determine their content area knowledge and skill level before instruction begins. Pretesting provides teachers with exact information on which objectives have been mastered and those that have yet to be attained. For gifted Hispanic students, this strategy allows for the identification of content knowledge gaps that are preventing them from mastering the basic curriculum. The hope is that, once identified, the gaps can be quickly filled by implementing those teaching strategies (compacting, differentiated curriculum, pace) that speak to a student's learning strengths. Once the student has caught up, more challenging content can be offered. Subsequently, opportunities for self-directed learning are provided.

Pretesting is a simple, yet powerful tool. Related cut scores, or level of mastery, should be decided before the pretest is administered, and this information should be shared with students. The expectation is that they will do their best. They also need to know that they will not be penalized for what they don't know. Rather, they should be told that teaching and learning experiences will be tailored to meet individual needs, a win-win strategy for both teacher and students.

The Truth About Testing

In his book *The Truth About Testing: An Educator's Call to Action*, W. James Popham (2001) identified four rules for classroom assessment that are appropriate for the gifted education classroom.

1. Use only a modest number of major classroom tests, but make sure these tests measure learner outcomes of indisputable importance. For students enrolled in gifted education programs, this speaks to the use of curriculum compacting weaved with state-mandated content area standards. To draw valid inferences about students, we need to use tests that representatively sample an intended learning outcome. Obviously, it is better to measure a small number of learning outcomes representatively than it is to measure a large number of outcomes unrepresentatively (p. 106).

2. Use diverse types of classroom assessments to clarify the nature of any learning outcome you seek. The cognitive demands that tests place on students should occupy a teacher's attention and drive a teacher's instruction. Teachers who spend even a modest amount of time analyzing a test's cog-

nitive demands will have a better idea about how to design instruction that will satisfy requirements of a worthwhile test and promote the desired major learning outcomes (p. 111).

3. Make students' responses to classroom assessments central to your instructional decision making. This strategy speaks to the core of curriculum compacting and differentiated curriculum and instruction. Pretesting in the content area assists the teacher with planning appropriately. The objectives that frame the decision-making process are what is tested.

4. Regularly assess educationally significant students' affect, but only to make inferences about groups of students, not individual students. When collected on a group basis, students' affect regarding their own capabilities can offer teachers useful insight regarding the degree to which students actually possess the skills (p. 123). Perception of their own cognitive and academic strengths and areas needing development further provides the gifted education teacher with direction in planning relevant instruction.

Summary and Conclusion

Programs including gifted Hispanic students should be designed to nurture individual giftedness and provide a classroom climate that encourages them to use their talents in productive ways. The United States is a country in transition, with considerable demographic changes taking place (Diaz, 2002). It also poses serious challenges to deeply rooted habits of the mind, to assumptions, and to conduct. An example of this is the educational challenge posed by increasing numbers of Hispanic and other culturally and linguistically diverse students in schools. A better understanding of these students calls for a type of education that capitalizes on the growing diversity of students in the United States by helping them to tap their potential sources of talent.

This chapter acknowledges that the information presented is appropriate for any group of students enrolled in a gifted education program. However, there are cultural and linguistic considerations specific to Hispanic students that must be taken into account when planning curriculum, instruction, and assessment. This chapter does not begin to cover the complexities in serving a group of students who have historically been on the outside looking in. Rather, this chapter serves as a catalyst to promote further dialogue and research. The Census 2000 data suggest that the number of Hispanic students will continue to increase, thus increasing the talent pool considered for gifted education.

Finally, identifying, recruiting, and retaining Hispanic students in gifted education can provide them with a brighter future and increase their opportunity for securing a postsecondary education. This is especially important, considering that the difference between a high school diploma and a medical degree is about $3.2

million. Graduating from college and earning advanced degrees translates into much higher lifetime earnings—an estimated $4.4 million for doctors, lawyers, and others with professional degrees; $2.5 million for those with a master's degree; and $2.1 million for college graduates (Armas, 2002). Keeping our best and brightest Hispanic students in school should be a priority, not only to increase their lifetime earnings, but also because it is the right thing to do.

2

Underachievement Among Gifted African American Students:
Cultural, Social, and Psychological Considerations

by Donna Y. Ford, Tarek C. Grantham, and H. Richard Milner

For more than 50 years, reports have highlighted the reality that African American students are consistently underrepresented in gifted education programs nationally. In 1978, for example, African Americans were underrepresented in gifted programs by 33%; in 1992, their underrepresentation had increased to 41% (see Ford & Harris, 1999); in 1993, their underrepresentation was 50% (U.S. Department of Education, 1993); and more recent data indicate that African American students are underrepresented by 60% (Ford & Harris).

Many explanations have been advanced to explain this persistent underrepresentation problem. Frasier, Garcia, and Passow (1995) proposed three reasons: (1) test bias; (2) underreferrals by teachers; and (3) deficit-based paradigms. Ford (1995a, 1996) and Ford, Harris, Tyson, and Frazier Trotman (2002) also noted these issues as barriers, as well as additional ones such as underachievement and negative peer pressure. In particular, Ford et al. proposed that deficit thinking is the underlying factor that contributes to diverse students being underrepresented in gifted education programs. They argued that educators who are not prepared to work with and understand culturally diverse students fail to see strengths and potential in diverse learners.

In this chapter, three areas around underachievement are discussed: cultural factors, social factors, and psychological factors. One of the most pressing and promising means of addressing underachievement among gifted African American students is to "look at giftedness in cultural context" (see Ford & Harris, 1999; Frasier et al., 1995). To understand, prevent, or reverse underachievement in gifted African American students, we must look at their underachievement from a cultural lens paradigm—one that considers and centralizes culture in our thinking about underachievement.

When discussing gifted African American students, it is helpful to think of a Venn diagram. As Figure 2.1 illustrates, these students are gifted *and* African American. Therefore, educators must understand and address their needs as gifted students and as African American (or culturally diverse) students. In terms of their needs as gifted students, educators should focus on their cognitive, academic, affective, psychological, cultural, and social needs and development. We must be concerned about challenging gifted students cognitively and academically; we must also address students' needs for identity, friends, belonging, and safety.

Similarly, when students are culturally diverse, we ought to address their needs in these same areas, but pay particular attention to the needs associated with being culturally different. Three questions are central here: (1) How do cultural beliefs and values affect students' achievement? (2) How do the social needs of gifted diverse students affect their achievement? (3) How do psychological needs affect the achievement of gifted diverse students? As will be discussed in more detail later, Ford (1995b, 1996) and Fordham and Ogbu (1986) maintain that social needs and issues may be different for African American and White students. Their research points to a consistent and persistent pattern of high-achieving African American students facing negative peer pressures. Many high-achieving or gifted African American students are accused of "acting White" when they do well in school or participate in gifted programs. This accusation has a profoundly negative impact on the psyche of African American students, many of whom succumb to the negative peer pressures and underachieve. Ford and others also contend that, when students are culturally diverse, educators must consider how racial identity, not just self-esteem and self-concept, affect achievement.

In this chapter, it is proposed that, in order to prevent or reverse underachievement among gifted African American students, we must pay considerable attention to their needs and development as cultural beings and the unique social and psychological issues they face.

Cultural Issues, Needs, and Achievement

In focusing on cultural needs and issues, we must address two phenomena: deficit thinking and cultural diversity. Later, in discussing social and psychological needs, we address peer pressures, racial identity, and concerns experienced by African American students in school settings.

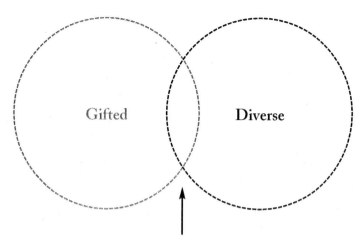

Cultural needs and development
Psychological needs and development
Social needs and development
Academic needs and development

Figure 2.1. Gifted and diverse: Dual needs and developmental issues

Deficit Thinking and Cultural Misunderstanding

Start where you are, but don't stay there.
—African Proverb

According to Frasier et al. (1995), manifestations of characteristics associated with giftedness may be different in culturally diverse students, yet teachers are seldom formally prepared in identifying those characteristics and associated behaviors. As a result, teachers may not recognize giftedness in culturally diverse students. This lack of recognition can manifest itself in several ways: (a) teachers may not refer these students for gifted education screening, so students may go unchallenged and become bored in school; and (b) teachers may not understand the learning and cultural styles of African American students, thus, students' learning styles and teachers' teaching styles may not match. In both instances, gifted African American students may underachieve.

Teachers enter classrooms lacking multicultural preparation; that is, they seldom have significant experiences with students from different cultural backgrounds (Banks, 1999; Milner, 2002) and, consequently, these teachers often lack the competencies to address the academic, cognitive, psychological, and cultural needs of African American students. When teachers do not understand the cultural experiences that students bring into the classroom, it may be difficult for them to understand, teach, and promote achievement among gifted African

American students. To illustrate, many teachers have never attended schools with individuals of a different culture or lived in cross-cultural neighborhoods, and their knowledge and understanding of culturally diverse students may be vague and prejudicial (Ford, 1996; Milner). Given this lack of knowledge, exposure, and understanding, teachers may rely on stereotypical conceptions and beliefs of African American students—perceptions they may extract from television programming, media coverage, or even family biases that still prevail in teachers' thinking about diverse groups (Ford et al., 2002; Milner). Unfortunately, these stereotypical beliefs may force teachers to perceive, make curricular decisions, and teach culturally diverse students through deficit models, consciously or unconsciously. They may equate creativity and risk taking as defiance or eagerness and energy as hyperactivity or attention-deficit disorder. Because teachers may rely on stereotypical beliefs or overly simplistic notions of difference where diverse students are concerned, it may be difficult for them to "see the genius" that culturally diverse or other marginalized students, and particularly African American students, bring into the learning environment.

While it is logical to assume that every teacher who pursues coursework in gifted education will learn about the characteristics of gifted students, it is not safe to assume that they will learn about the characteristics of culturally diverse students (Ford & Harris, 1999) and the affective, psychological, cultural, and social issues often associated with African American students. As Figure 2.1 suggests, educators must learn about the characteristics and needs of students who are gifted *and* culturally diverse.

Textbooks in gifted education often contain one chapter on culturally diverse populations, but other chapters virtually ignore these students. Hence, a chapter focusing on identifying gifted students may not even mention culturally diverse students, thus placing issues of culture on the fringes of teachers' minds and suggesting that matters of cultural diversity are not important. Likewise, a chapter on teaching gifted students may not address culturally different learning styles or multicultural curricula. As a result, teachers learn little about culturally diverse gifted students, and teacher-training institutions—directly and indirectly—create, maintain, or reinforce stereotypes about characteristics of gifted students. Moreover, teachers are given the opportunity to see cultural diversity as a separate issue, a topic that is not central to their goals of learning to teach. Thus, teachers may leave their courses with no or very limited knowledge about African American and other culturally diverse gifted students. Accordingly, teachers may consider gifted students to be a homogeneous group in terms of characteristics and needs.

Since the 1980s, there has been an increase in research and scholarship on culturally diverse students. This work has attempted to change the perceptions educators might hold of African American students from being "culturally deprived or disadvantaged" to being "culturally different and culturally diverse" (Ford et al., 2002). The notion of cultural deprivation is negative and educationally harmful. To be culturally deprived implies that one does not have a culture; to be culturally disadvantaged implies that one (and one's culture) is inferior to another. It is more proactive and advantageous for students if teachers believe that they are culturally different and culturally diverse, rather than culturally disadvantaged or deficient.

Cultural Needs and Underachievement

The body is the hardware. Culture is the software.
—Anonymous

Many definitions of culture can be found in the literature. In this chapter, culture is defined as beliefs, values, dispositions, traditions, customs, and habits that are specific to a group. These beliefs, values, and traditions serve as a filter through which a group of people view and respond to the world (thus, informing a person's paradigmatic thinking). For example, in "teen culture," one finds shared values, beliefs, behaviors, and traditions that are thought to characterize the period of adolescence (e.g., increased concerns for popularity, anxiety about physical characteristics, temperament). These characteristics are common with each group, representing modal characteristics, but they must not be used as stereotypes.

More specifically, cultural characteristics can be visible or invisible (see Figure 2.2). Visible or obvious characteristics include foods, holidays, dress, and music preference shared by a cultural group. Less visible cultural characteristics, referred to as "deep culture," relate to such variables as beliefs, values, and ways of perceiving and thinking. That is, different groups have different beliefs and values about cooperation versus competition, matriarchal versus patriarchal households, nuclear versus extended family structures, communicating verbally versus nonverbally, being monochronic versus polychronic, and so forth. Individuals from different cultural backgrounds may share different beliefs about a number of variables, including showing respect to elders or those in authority, showing emotions, asking questions or asking for help, handling conflict, solving problems, touching, and personal space (Shade, Kelly, & Oberg, 1998; Storti, 1989, 2001). Clearly, understanding how one's culture operates and the relation of that culture to an individual's orientations and choices may help us understand how culturally diverse students approach learning and achievement.

Cultural Characteristics of African Americans

Boykin (1994), Shade et al. (1998), and other scholars have conducted research exploring cultural styles among African American students.

In his Afro-centric model, Boykin identified nine cultural styles commonly found among African Americans: spirituality, harmony, oral tradition, affect, verve, communalism, movement, social-time perspective, and expressive individualism. Boykin's model provides educators with a framework from which to begin understanding and teaching African American students. Some African American students will display all or a majority of these characteristics; some may display just

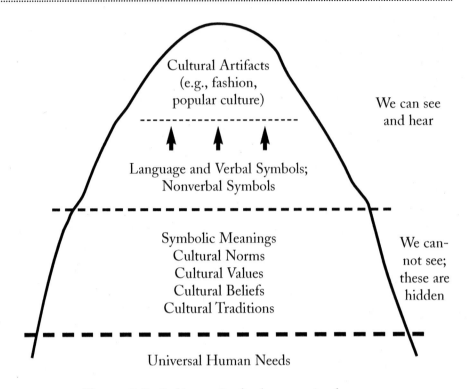

Figure 2.2. Culture: An iceberg metaphor

Note. From *Communication Across Culture* (p. 10), by S. Ting-Toomey, 1999, New York: Guilford Press. Copyright ©1999 by Guilford Press. Reprinted with permission.

a few. Thus, teachers must be careful not to stereotype and categorize all students in the same manner based on any model of cultural diversity. Teachers should not perceive these characteristics as prescriptive or predictive of all African American students. Teachers should use these characteristics as a place to start to become learners in their particular contexts.

Movement refers to African Americans being tactile and kinesthetic learners who show a preference for being involved in learning experiences. They are active learners who are engaged when they are physically and psychologically involved; otherwise, they may be easily distracted and off-task. Harmony refers to an ability to read the environment well, to read nonverbal behaviors proficiently. Thus, students who feel unwelcome in their classes may become unmotivated and uninterested in learning. Communalism refers to a cooperative, interdependent style of living and learning such that competition (especially with friends) is devalued. Hence, students with this learning preference may be unmotivated in highly individualistic and competitive classrooms, preferring instead to learn in groups. Harmony and communalism may explain why an increasing number of African American students (especially middle school and high school students) are choosing not to be in gifted programs. They recognize that such programs are primarily comprised of White students and, thus, express concerns about alienation and isolation (Ford, 1996). Further, communalism may result in some African American students shunning participation in gifted programs and equating high achievement with "acting White" (Fordham, 1988; Fordham & Ogbu, 1986).

Educators who take the time to get to know culturally diverse students and their families can avoid what we refer to as "drive-by teaching": driving into culturally diverse communities, teaching the students who are strangers, and driving out of the community immediately after school. Drive-by teaching is counterproductive to students and the educational process in general; it does not give educators time to get to know and understand their students, their parents, and the community, and it fails to give students opportunities to know educators.

Accordingly, teachers should learn to modify their teaching styles to accommodate different learning styles. For example, to accommodate African American students' preference for communalism, teachers can use cooperative learning strategies and place students in groups. To accommodate oral tradition, verve, and movement, teachers can give students opportunities to write and perform skits, to give oral presentations, and to participate in debates. More examples appear in Ford and Harris (1999) and Shade et al. (1998).

How does culture impact achievement? Research and theory suggest that teachers who understand and integrate the cultural needs and styles of African Americans into the curriculum promote and enhance achievement among these students (e.g., Ford & Harris 1999; Hale, 2002; Ladson-Billings, 1994; Milner, 2002, 2003; Shade et al., 1998). Table 2.1 presents teaching strategies that align with the cultural styles proposed by Boykin (1984).

We cannot, however, end the discussion here. As discussed earlier, in addition to addressing the cultural needs and development of African American students, other areas that must be addressed are their psychological and social needs.

Psychological Needs and Underachievement

In this section, we discuss racial identity development that contributes to underachievement among gifted African American students.

Racial Identity Issues

Race and racial identity affect one's socioemotional and psychological health in significant ways. The issue of race may be more salient for African Americans than White Americans. For instance, White Americans are much less likely to experience the chronic stress and problems associated with race because the color of their skin is not viewed with a deficit orientation and, thus, is not a barrier to academic and social success.

Racism, prejudice, and discrimination can negatively affect the extent to which African Americans identify with their racial background and heritage; it

Table 2.1

Culturally Responsive Teaching Strategies: Applying Boykin's Model

Afrocentric Expressions	Teaching Strategies and Products
Movement Harmony Verve Expressive Individualism	• Creative movement (mime, drama, dance, tableau techniques — body used to communicate) • Hands-on thinking; manipulatives (e.g., sculpting) • Role plays, simulations, theatre • Field trips • Physical activity • Sports and games • Learning centers • Singing, humming whistling, chanting • Curriculum songs (creating melodies, songs, rap, cheers, jingles, etc.) • Background music • Playing instruments • Poetry/poems • Drama
Social Time Perspective Harmony	• Environmental issues • Social issues • Outdoor activities • Flexible assignments
Social Time Perspective Spirituality	• Graphic-rich environment (visuals and graphic organizers, pictures, posters, charts, graphs, diagrams) • Mind mapping (webbing) • Puzzles and games (e.g., Chess) • Patterns • Painting, collages, visual arts
Oral Tradition	• Lectures • Socratic questioning • Scientific investigations & experiments • Logical-sequential assignments (reports, experiments, research) • Problem solving; problem-based lessons • Logical puzzles and games

	• Competitions
	• Analogies
	• Independent study projects
Oral Tradition	• Lectures
Verve	• Seminars
Expressive Individualism	• Discussions/dialogues
	• Oral presentations & speeches; debates
	• Guest speakers
	• Word games (e.g., idioms, jokes, puns, riddles, homonyms, homophones, anagrams, mnemonics)
	• Poetry; proverbs, puns
	• Storytelling and drama
	• Reading (choral, peer, individual)
	• Journal writing
Spirituality	• Visualizations
Harmony	• Proverbs, poetry
	• Self-paced, independent instruction/assignments
	• Choices and options; interest-based assignments
	• Reflection time/opportunity (e.g., journals, poetry)
Communalism	• Social and cooperative learning
Affective	• Opportunity to help others (e.g., tutoring, mentoring)
	• Service and community involvement
	• Conflict-mediation lessons
	• Simulations

can affect their racial identity. As with self-concept and self-esteem, racial identity influences students' motivation, persistence, and achievement (Ford, 1996).

In his revised model of racial identity, entitled Nigrescence Theory (Cross & Vandiver, 2001), which is also referred to as the process of becoming Black, Cross presented eight identity types clustered into three major stages: (1) pre-encounter; (2) immersion-emersion; and (3) internalization.

In the first stage, pre-encounter, there are three identity types. *Pre-encounter assimilation* describes the Black person whose social identity is organized around his or her sense of being an American and an individual. This person places little emphasis on racial group identity, affiliation, or salience, and, consequently, he or she is not engaged in the Black community and culture. *Pre-encounter miseducation* depicts a Black person who accepts without question the negative images, stereotypes, and historical misinformation about Black people. This person sees little strength in the African American community and hesitates to engage in solving or resolving issues in the Black community. Further, he or she often holds the attitude "That's the way *they* act, but *I* am different." The final pre-encounter type is called *pre-encounter racial self-hatred*. This person experiences profoundly negative feelings and severe self-loathing because of being Black. Vandiver and Cross (2001) contend that this dysfunctional and group hatred limits the person's positive engagement of Black problems and Black culture.

The next stage of identity, immersion-emersion, is characterized by two identity types. In *immersion-emersion anti-White*, the person is nearly consumed by a hatred of White people and society and all that it represents. He or she engages in Black problems and culture, but is frequently full of fury and pent-up rage. In *immersion-emersion intense Black involvement*, the person often holds a simplistic, romanticized, and obsessive dedication to all things Black. He or she engages in Blackness in nearly a cult-like fashion and is subject to "blacker-than-thou" social interactions with other Blacks.

The final racial identity stage, internalization, is comprised of three identity types. In *internalization nationalist*, the individual stresses an Africentric perspective about him- or herself, other African Americans, and the world. Without question, this individual engages in the Black community and Black problems. *Internalization biculturalist* is an African American who gives equal importance to being an African American and an American. He or she is able to celebrate being both Black and an American and is able to engage in both cultures without identity conflicts, doubt, and self-questioning. Finally, *internalization multiculturalist* is an exemplar of a Black person whose identity fuses between two or more social categories or frames of reference. He or she is interested in resolving issues that address multiple oppressions and is confident and comfortable in multiple groups.

Although Nigrescence Theory is a stage model, it acknowledges that individuals can regress or get stuck at one stage. Whether one regresses, becomes stuck, or progresses through the stages of racial identity depends, in large part, on the individual's personality, support base, resources, and experiences. For example, African American children and adults in predominantly White settings may experience more negative encounters based on race than those in predominantly African American settings. They may also experience such encounters at an earlier age than African Americans in predominantly African American settings. Relative to gifted African American students, their perceptiveness, insightfulness, and keen sense of justice may push them through the racial identity stages at an earlier age and faster pace (Ford, 1996). The achievement of students in the first five stages of identity is in jeopardy as these students grapple with their uncertain identity, allegiance issues, anger issues, and working within mainstream society.

Social Issues and Underachievement

Allegiance issues and peer pressures can have a negative influence on African Americans. High-achieving African Americans may experience conflict relative to supporting the beliefs, values, and norms of the dominant culture as opposed to their parent culture. Consequently, they show ambivalence about their abilities and consider them as being envied by others, yet personally undesirable. W.E.B. DuBois described this phenomenon when he wrote about two warring souls fighting with each other to be accepted in White America (Weis, 1985).

Leanita McClain, the first African American female elected to the board of directors of the *Chicago Tribune*, was subsequently perceived by many as acting White. She described the dilemma of bicultural stress most poignantly in a newspaper column:

> I run a gauntlet between two worlds, and I am cursed and blessed by both. I travel, observe and take part in both; I can also be used by both. I am a rope in a tug of war. If I am a token in my downtown office, so am I at my cousin's tea. I assuage white guilt. . . . I have a foot in each world, but I cannot fool myself about either. . . . Whites won't believe that I remain culturally different; African Americans won't believe that I remain culturally the same. (McClain, 1983, p. C4)

McClain described this identity issue as "hellish confusion" whereby successful African Americans feel guilty and stressful about their success. Success sometimes leads African Americans to ask themselves, as did McClain, "I have made it, but where?" (see Campbell, 1984, p. 74). McClain eventually committed suicide. This frustration, confusion, and anger was more recently discussed in *The Rage of a Privileged Class* (Cose, 1993). With success comes a unique set of issues for African Americans.

Not surprisingly, therefore, many educators have noted a significant change in the aspirations of African Americans toward academic achievement and social mobility. Specifically, while previous generations had defined success for one African American person as success for all African Americans, more recently, African Americans are less apt to view the achievements of individual African Americans as progress for *all* African Americans. The "all for one and one for all" collective sense of success has all but disappeared for some African Americans and has been replaced by the perception that successful African Americans have "sold out" and are "acting White" when they achieve (Corwin, 2001; Fordham, 1988; Suskind, 1998).

Smith (1989) argued that race serves to create a common referent of peoplehood such that individuals tend to define themselves in terms of membership in a particular group. Thus, this collective identity represents the sense of belonging that is psychologically important for people of color. To reinforce the belief that they are still legitimate members of the African American community, African

Americans may sabotage any chance they have of succeeding outside of it. With this antiachievement ethic, African Americans may underachieve, drop out, refuse to participate in gifted programs, refuse to accept certain positions, and otherwise fail to reach their academic potential in school and in life (Corwin, 2001; Ford, 1996; Fordham, 1988; Suskind, 1998).

In short, detachment from one's race, whether perceived or real, threatens the survival of the African American community and its culture and creates suspicion among African Americans about member loyalty. Hence, the African American community may reject successful African Americans not because they have achieved, but because they appear removed and detached from their indigenous community. The African American community may reject those who identify with the dominant culture, desire to join it, and accept its behaviors as paradigms worth copying. Which culture, then, should African Americans emulate when trying to fulfill their potential? Which belief and value system should they incorporate?

Stereotype Threat

Stereotype threat is a situational threat—a threat in the air—that, in general form, can affect the members of a group about whom a negative stereotype exists. Where African Americans are concerned, stereotype threat is a social psychological predicament rooted in the prevailing image of African Americans as intellectually inferior (e.g., Aronson, Lustina, Good, Keough, Steele, & Brown, 1999). The idea is that, when stereotyped individuals are in situations where the stereotype applies, they bear an extra emotional, psychological, and cognitive burden. The burden that African Americans face concerns the possibility of confirming the stereotype in the eyes of others or in their own eyes. Thus, when females are asked to solve complicated mathematics problems, for example, they are at risk of confirming widely held stereotypes that females are inferior to males in mathematics. It is not necessary that the individual even believes the stereotype. All that matters is that the person is *aware* of the stereotype and *cares about performing* well enough to disprove its unflattering implications (Aronson et al.).

The most immediate effect of stereotype threat can be anxiety that undermines performance (Osborne, 2001). In a series of experiments, Claude Steele, Josh Aronson, and their colleagues demonstrated that, when African American or Latino college students are put in situations that induce stereotype threat, their performance suffers (Aronson & Salinas, 1998; Steele & Aronson, 1995). For example, African American and White undergraduate students in an experiment at Stanford University were told that the test they were about to take would precisely measure their verbal ability. A similar group of students was told that the purpose of the test was to understand the psychology of verbal problem solving and not to assess individual ability. When the test was presented as diagnostic of verbal ability, the African American students solved about half as many problems as the White students. In the nonthreat situation, the two groups solved about the same number of problems. Anxiety and distraction were the main problems cited. The

African American students were more likely to be thinking about the stereotypes as they tried to work (Osborne; Steele, 1997; Steele & Aronson). Thus, gifted students, and culturally diverse students in general, may operate in classrooms where they are concerned about confirming stereotypes. Psychologically, students carry the burden of being a representative of their group. Attempting to demystify or change negative stereotypes also carries enormous burdens for students.

Recommendations and Promising Practices

There are a myriad of factors affecting the achievement and potential of gifted African American students, as we have just discussed. Albeit quite complex, there are promising practices for addressing underachievement among gifted African American students, many of which have been described elsewhere by Ford (1996). In this chapter, we concentrate on three major categories of recommendations: (1) teacher education and professional development; (2) multicultural gifted curricula; and (3) counseling.

Teacher Education and Professional Development

It goes without saying that all gifted education teachers must pursue and receive training to work with culturally diverse students. Teacher education programs and professional development programs must focus on such issues and topics as we have discussed in this chapter (e.g., understanding cultural diversity, appreciating cultural differences, eliminating deficit thinking, and raising expectations for diverse students). Ford (1996), Ford and Frasier Trotman (2001), and Ford and Harris (1999) have outlined specific suggestions for education and training.

Multicultural Gifted Curricula

A student's culture must be considered not only relative to teaching styles and strategies, but also relative to the curriculum. In one study (see Ford, 1996) of gifted African American students who were underachieving, students reported a lack of interest in school because they could not relate to what was being taught. These students expressed a lack of interest and boredom because of the content of the curriculum. Many of these students provided such insightful comments as "I would be more interested in school if I were learning about my culture," "School is more interesting when we learn about African Americans and what they have done for this nation," and "I like being in school more when we talk about my heritage." Ford concluded that a culturally irrelevant curriculum contributes to underachievement among gifted African American students. She recommended, as we do here, the need for curricula to be multicultural as one way to increase students' interest and, thus, achievement in school.

Banks (1999) presented a four-level model for infusing multicultural content into the curriculum. The lowest level of curricular integration is the contributions approach. Here, the curriculum focuses extensively, sometimes exclusively, on culturally diverse heroes, holidays, and discrete cultural elements. Students study, for example, pyramids of ancient Egypt, tepees of Native Americans, Kwanzaa for African Americans, and so forth. Students exposed to this low level of curricular integration acquire a superficial understanding of culturally diverse groups; they may even adopt stereotypes about these groups.

At the second level, the additive level, some multicultural content, concepts, themes, and perspectives are added to the curriculum without changing the curriculum's basic structure. Multicultural topics, issues, and events are *added* to the curriculum on a temporary basis, such as during Black History Month. Further, controversial issues and people are avoided. Consequently, students fail to understand how the predominant culture interacts with and is related to culturally diverse groups, and they fail to get exposure to substantive topics and persons of diversity.

At the transformation level, the structure of the curriculum is changed to enable students to view concepts, issues, events, and themes from the perspectives of diverse racial and cultural groups. Further, unlike the additive level, every effort is made to ensure that all content areas, topics, and materials are diverse. Everyday, every subject area and topic can be analyzed from different points of view.

At the social action level, students make decisions on important social issues and take actions to help solve them. Thus, if students perceive stereotypes in a book they are reading, they might contact the publisher to share their concerns and recommend changes. Essentially, students become empowered to make meaningful contributions to the resolution of social issues and problems with multiculturalism as a frame.

Ford and Harris (1999) created a framework using Bloom's taxonomy (Bloom, 1985) and Banks' (1999) multicultural education model to assist educators of gifted students in developing learning experiences that are multicultural *and* challenging. The result is a 24-cell matrix. The Ford-Harris model (also known as the Bloom-Banks model) is presented in Table 2.2. Four of the 24 levels are described below (see Ford & Harris for a more complete application of the model).

At the knowledge-contributions level, students are provided information and facts about cultural heroes, holidays, events, and artifacts. For example, students might be taught about Martin Luther King, Jr., and then asked to regurgitate three facts about him on a test. They might be introduced to Cinco de Mayo and be required to recite the year when it became a holiday.

At the comprehension-transformation level, students are required to explain what they have been taught, but from the perspective of another group or individual. For instance, students might be asked to explain events leading up to slavery in America and then to talk about how slaves might have felt being held captive. They might talk about the Trail of Tears from the perspective of a Native American child living during that time.

At the analysis-social action level, students are asked to analyze an event from more than one point of view. Students in this case might be asked to compare and contrast events during slavery with events associated with the current-day child labor infractions. Following these comparisons, students could be asked to develop a plan for eliminating illegal child labor.

At the evaluation-social action level, students might be asked to conduct a study or survey about prejudice in their local stores. This information would be given to store owners, along with a plan of action for change (such as developing a culturally sensitive training program).

A primary rationale for multicultural education is the promise that it holds for engaging students and giving them opportunities to identify with, connect with, and relate to the curriculum. A multicultural curriculum is composed of deliberate, ongoing, planned, and systematic opportunities that avoid drive-by teaching; they make learning meaningful and relevant to students and give culturally diverse students mirrors in order to see themselves reflected in the curriculum. Multicultural gifted education challenges students culturally, affectively, academically, and cognitively, all of which hold promise to promote student achievement.

Counseling Development

Not only must teachers learn about themselves and how their attitudes and perceptions affect culturally diverse students, students must also learn about themselves. Gifted African American students who are underachieving may need to work with a counselor on such areas and issues as (a) coping with negative peer pressures; (b) working and living in mainstream society and schools; and (c) developing a positive and strong racial identity, as exemplified by holding an internalization identity (see Cross & Vandiver, 2001). We advocate that all culturally diverse students become, at minimum, bicultural in order to work and live—to thrive—in their own culture and mainstream society.

One of the most effective ways to help diverse students cope with negative peer pressures is to involve them in mentoring programs where they have an opportunity to work with a mentor and role model. This relationship gives students opportunities to learn from someone who faced similar problems and overcame them. Older students, college students, and adult professionals from the Black community would be ideal mentors and role models. Likewise, students should be introduced to successful heroes and sheroes from their cultural group through books, for example, and related bibliotherapeutic and biographical techniques.

Diverse students may also need anger management and conflict resolution training in order to develop effective coping skills when faced with negative peer pressures and social injustices of any kind (prejudice and discrimination, in particular). Students who can cope effectively with social ills are likely to be resilient and, consequently, achieve.

Table 2.2

Ford-Harris Multicultural Gifted Education Framework: Description of Levels

	Knowledge	Comprehension	Application	Analysis	Synthesis	Evaluation
Contributions	Students are taught and know facts about cultural artifacts, events, groups, and other cultural elements.	Students show understanding of information about cultural artifacts, groups, etc.	Students are asked to and can apply information learned on cultural artifacts, events, etc.	Students are taught to and can analyze (e.g., compare and contrast) information about cultural artifacts, groups, etc.	Students are required to and can create a new product from the information on cultural artifacts, groups, etc.	Students are taught to and can evaluate facts and information based on cultural artifacts, groups, etc.
Additive	Students are taught and know concepts and themes about cultural groups.	Students are taught and can understand cultural concepts and themes.	Students are required to and can apply information learned about cultural concepts and themes.	Students are taught to and can analyze important cultural concepts and themes.	Students are asked to and can syntheize important information on cultural concepts and themes.	Students are taught to and can critique cultural concepts and themes.

Transformation	Students are given information on important cultural elements, groups, etc., and can understand this information from different perspectives.	Students are taught to understand and can demonstrate understanding of important cultural concepts and themes from different perspectives.	Students are asked to and can apply their understanding of important concepts and themes from different perspectives.	Students are taught to and can examine important cultural concepts and themes from more than one perspective.	Students are required to and can create a product based on their new perspective or the perspective of another group.	Students are taught to and can evaluate or judge important cultural concepts and themes from different viewpoints (e.g., minority group).
Social Action	Based on information on cultural artifacts, etc., students make recommendations for social action.	Based on their understanding of important concepts and themes, students make recommendations for social action.	Students are asked to apply their understanding of important social and cultural issues; they make recommendations for and take action on these issues.	Students are required to and can analyze social and cultural issues from different perspectives; they take action on these issues.	Students create a plan of action to address one or more social and cultural issues; they seek important social change.	Students critique important social and cultural issues and seek to make national and/or international change.

Note. Actions taken on the social action level can range from immediate and small scale (e.g., classroom and school level) to moderate (e.g., community or regional level) to large scale (state, national, and international levels). Likewise, students can make recommendations for action or actually take social action. Source: Ford & Harris (1999).

3

Individual Differences and Cultural Diversity in the Art Forms of Children Talented in the Visual Arts

by Claire Golomb

Precocious talent in the visual arts, how to account for its emergence in childhood, and how to foster its development have been topics of considerable interest to psychologists and educators. It has also engaged the imagination of artists, especially those who, at the beginning of the 20th century, rejected the time-honored conventions of realism in art and turned to children's drawings for inspiration and authenticity (Fineberg, 1997; Golomb, 2002).

A relatively early reference to the gifted child artist can be found in Vasari's (1559/1959) history of art, *The Life of the Most Eminent Painters, Sculptors, and Architects*, in which he recounts how the gifted child Giotto was "discovered." According to Vasari, on one of his walks in the country, the great artist Cimabue came across the amazing drawings of a simple shepherd boy, and, being astounded by his gifts, he invited the child to live with him. In this account, the boy was completely self-taught, a natural genius, and, under the tutelage of his master, he soon equaled him in his drawing from nature.

Despite this early interest in artistic giftedness and the fascination of many modern artists with the drawings of the young child that were hailed as having the mark of genius, research devoted to the identification of children gifted in the arts is sparse. Reports of early writers on this topic tend to be anecdotal (Baumgarten, 1930) or limited to the description of a single case, for example, the author's child (Wulff, 1927). It is of interest that

Lewis M. Terman's sample of gifted, high-IQ children whose development was studied over their full lifecycle did not include any of the children identified as having a special artistic ability (Winner, 1996).

An early search for talented or gifted children[1] initiated by Georg Kerschensteiner (1905) had only limited success in the identification of such youngsters. On the basis of his massive study of the drawings of public school children in the city of Munich at the beginning of the 20th century, he singled out the horse drawings of an 8-year-old boy. They are remarkable for the vitality of line, the dramatic use of foreshortening, the depiction of motion, and the facility with which different orientations are represented. However, according to Kerschensteiner, the drawings of this child were unique among the horse drawings he obtained from 58,000 children ranging in age from 6 to 13 years. Similarly, Goodenough (1926), who launched an extensive search for gifted drawers, found such talent to be exceedingly rare. Underlying some of the difficulty of identifying talent or giftedness in the visual arts is the problem of how to define these terms, which in subsequent years has led to the adoption of a more comprehensive and diverse set of criteria.

There is now a considerable consensus concerning the identification of children talented in the visual arts whose drawings are considered more advanced than those made by their regular agemates. Giftedness is viewed within a developmental framework, and children are most likely singled out on the basis of their more mature use of representational techniques, especially their facility to draw naturalistically. A child who at an early age employs sophisticated techniques, for example, partial overlapping of forms, elimination of lines hidden from view, foreshortening, rotation of figures, oblique drawing systems, and modeling, all of which suggest the solidity of an object extended in space, clearly calls attention to special abilities. However, under the influence of the modernist revolution in the arts and the respect accorded child art by some of the major art educators and artists of the beginning of the 20th century (e.g., Britsch, 1926; Cizek, 1935, cited in Viola, 1936; Kandinsky, 1912/1977; Klee, 1964; Werckmeister, 1977), originality and an aesthetic that is reminiscent of folk art have also been singled out as a mark of talent (Golomb, 1992b, 2002). Thus, precocity in the accelerated acquisition of technical drawing skills and an early awareness of artistic form and quality have been identified as signs of talent (Clark, 1993; Clark & Zimmerman, 1992; Duncum, 1981, 1984, 1986; Golomb, 1992a, 1992b, 1995; Lark-Horovitz, Lewis, & Luca, 1967; Milbrath, 1995, 1998; Rostan, Pariser, & Gruber, 2000; Wilson, 1974, 1976; Wilson & Wilson, 1976, 1977; Winner, 1996, 2000).

Most talented children go beyond the confines of the schematic child art style in one of the following ways: (1) They retain the schematic vocabulary of the child art style, but develop their own vision that imposes an order on the composition, reminiscent of folk art. In this case, the aesthetic quality does not depend on an approximation to photographic realism, but resides totally within the child-art style. (2) Children may develop a rich graphic vocabulary and an ability to depict spatial relations clearly, which makes their work in conception and execution akin to that of the adult. (3) A third group of child artists, identified by Wilson and Wilson (1976, 1977) and Duncum (1981, 1986), chronicle the cartoon style of prolific drawers who create expressive narratives on themes of competition and extraterrestrial warfare. Such drawings, initially based on the copying of well-known cartoon figures, can attain a high level of mastery, and the prolific drawers can develop an original pictorial narrative that is quite effective in getting its message across.

With access to a wider set of developmental studies and in line with the changing conceptions of modern and postmodern art, we are in a better position to identify children who are talented in the visual arts and for whom art making continues to be a priority throughout the childhood years. With the information that has become available, we can now address a number of central questions:

1. Does the course of pictorial development in talented children follow the general patterns documented for ordinary children, and is this development mostly defined by a precocious rate at which they acquire the representational conventions of this domain? This question touches on the role of universal versus more local factors that underlie artistic development, at least in its early phases.
2. Is artistic development more than the accelerated acquisition of skills, involving originality and uniqueness of expression?
3. Is artistic development geared toward pictorial realism as a natural and desired endpoint in the evolution of the young artist's competence?
4. What is the role of culture and training in the representational development of young artists?
5. Does precocity, originality, and motivation during the childhood years predict the future choice of an artistic career and its likely success?

Fortunately, we now have a growing number of studies that provide longitudinal accounts of talented child artists and their development (Beck, 1928; Golomb, 1992a, 1992b, 1995; Goldsmith, 1992; Matthews, 1999; Milbrath, 1995, 1998; Pariser, 1987, 1991, 1995; Winner, 1996; Zimmerman, 1995), and cross-sectional studies that focus on prodigious drawers who derive their inspiration from the youth culture of comic strips and cartoon characters (Duncum, 1981, 1986; Wilson & Wilson, 1977, 1979).

Artistic Development in Talented Children

In general, the evidence suggests that individuals who pursue a career in the visual arts and gain entry to art schools have been avid drawers since their childhood years, usually dating from ages 6 to 8 (Beck, 1928; Bloom, 1985; Duncum, 1984, 1986; Csikszentmihalyi, Rathunde, & Whalen, 1993; Getzels &

Csikszentmihalyi, 1976; Golomb, 1992a, 1992b, 1995; Gordon, 1987; MacKinnon, 1962; Matthews, 1999; Milbrath, 1995, 1998; Paine, 1981; Pariser, 1987, 1995; Winner, 1996, 2000; Zimmerman, 1995). As children, some pursued early instruction, while others insisted on being in charge of their own path of discoveries by teaching themselves all they thought they needed to know.

Not surprisingly, the individual characteristics of artistically gifted children differ markedly in terms of style, preferred subject matter, temperament, sociability, and intelligence. Some gifted children, enthralled by the visual appearance of interesting objects and sights, desire to capture their essence with fidelity and singularity of purpose. These children will teach themselves many, if not most, of the techniques to depict the three-dimensional character of objects and scenes. Other children are colorists and adopt a more painterly style. By their nature and inclination, they tend to use dramatic, rather than naturalistic, forms, and they relish the expressive and decorative attributes of color, texture, and design. Their colorful and richly ornamental works are strikingly appealing, reminiscent of various forms of folk art. Their aesthetic is of a different order than that of the realists, as seen in figures drawn without regard for anatomically correct proportions; colors used expressively, rather than naturalistically; and the flatness of the composition. In the eyes of the modern beholder, their appeal is as powerful as the drawings of the young realists.

There are, however, characteristics that many of the gifted children have in common. They are incessant drawers, seemingly compelled to translate their experiences into pictorial form. Thus, in addition to their natural talent and intrinsic motivation, they gain immensely from the interaction with their chosen medium and from the ongoing problem seeing and solving. There seems to be a consensus that these children are highly observant; attuned to the visual world; endowed with a superior visual memory and a visual-spatial motor precocity that, in the case of the realists, foster the creation of fluid lines that capture the natural contours of figures; and, in the case of the colorists, yield richly ornamental and expressive designs. Their special gifts suggest heightened visual attentiveness, perceptual dominance, and a related brain organization that, according to Winner (1996), is associated with a greater incidence of left-handedness and an increased frequency of dyslexia.

I now turn to a series of case studies that provide us with more detailed information about the developmental trajectories of artistically talented children, their motivation, style of drawing and painting, preferred subject matter, and the goals they pursue. What can we learn from their development during the childhood years? Does it follow the same sequence of stages that is typical for ordinary children, but shows greatly accelerated acquisition of drawing skills, or are there qualitative differences in the perception and production of artistically gifted children? Can we perceive continuities over time in the style and the themes of these artists? Lastly, is the development of artistically talented children geared toward a specific endpoint and does it culminate in the achievement of photographic realism?

Selected Case Studies of Artistically Gifted Children

This section reports on the development of three artistically gifted children and their adult status. Two of these children, Varda and Eitan, come from a similar Western cultural background, but present radically different developmental trajectories. The third child artist, Yani, represents the precocious work of a child steeped in the cultural traditions of China.

Varda

Varda is the third of four children in her family, born and raised on an Israeli kibbutz. All her siblings showed a talent for and love of drawing and painting. On her mother's side there are many artists in the family, and there is the general expectation that the children will be talented in the arts. The record of her childhood drawings is extensive, with drawings made daily from age 2 to 18. Until Varda entered art school, she was essentially self-taught.

The earliest drawings in the collection I studied date from the age of 2-0^2 and consist of dots, loops, open circles, continuous and discontinuous lines, and lines drawn as parallels. They are dispersed across the page, but they stay within the border of the paper space, an indication of careful visual-motor inspection and control. Over the next few months, Varda experimented with lines and shapes (see Figures 3.1a and b), with mixing colors, and with creating tonal gradations. Just before she turned 4, she created her first human. What sets her work apart from that of her agemates is the care and thoughtfulness with which she guided her actions, the high interest in its pursuit, and a formal imagination that is strikingly original.

With practice, Varda acquired a more differentiated repertoire of forms, and her drawings evidenced a visual intelligence that allowed her to create a meaningful pictorial universe. This visual intelligence, while at first playful, became increasingly able to express her deepest feelings. Over the next few years, Varda developed a highly decorative, ornamental style that, while typical of child art, is strikingly original in its conception and execution (see Figures 3.2, 3.3, 3.4). We see the full development of this style between the ages of 6 and 9, during which she experimented with color, design, and such new techniques as the overlay of different colors and the painterly potential of oil pastels to replace her former emphasis on linear contours. She also employed deliberate distortions of the human body that highlighted the symbolic meaning of her theme. Thus, at the height of the child art style, marked by figures drawn without regard for anatomical fidelity; colors used expressively, rather than naturalistically; and the overall flatness of her composition emphasized, Varda integrated familiar, well-practiced patterns with new techniques (see Figures 3.5, 3.6, 3.7).

It is quite striking that her work evolved according to the same principles that characterize all child art. Her figures are two-dimensional, drawn without regard for the realistic proportions of the model, and most objects are presented in full frontal view, each one occupying its own space in a grid defined by horizontal and vertical directions. Her themes mostly reflect an internal drama that, in its expression, overrides naturalism.

In the late childhood years, there was a growing interest in portraying her subjects more naturalistically. Nevertheless, Varda's art continued to express internal events concerned with thoughts and feelings, and the setting remained flat and demonstrated her lack of interest in creating the illusion of a three-dimensional world (see Figures 3.8 and 3.9). During her adolescent years, which coincided with the Yom Kippur war, she portrayed themes of larger social significance, of bereavement, fear, loss, and consolation (see Figure 3.10a and b). Once again, the treatment of the background was most commonly flat and two-dimensional. Broad strokes and color patches evoked the theme and its principal characters. These adolescent paintings represent Varda's continued search for symbolic forms of expression, and they demonstrate her reliance on color to convey deeply felt emotions (see Figure 3.11).

Varda's entering an art school became a turning point in her artistic development. She turned to sculpture as her primary medium of expression, and she preferred to work with multimedia, especially plaster, clay, and metals. Her work from this period is highly abstract and symbolic but also ornamental and reminiscent of some of her childhood work (see Figures 3.12a and b) and was featured in several group exhibitions of talented young artists.

The extensive record of her childhood art and the artistic choices she made as a young adult clearly indicate that Varda's artistic inclinations did not predispose her toward realism as a means for articulating her vision. There is consistency in her adoption of art forms that tend to recast the world in her own image.

Eitan

Eitan, born in Jerusalem, is the oldest of four children. Both parents are interested in the visual arts and have some talent in this domain. The collection begins with his second birthday and comprises a continuous record of drawings made daily that spans the period from ages 2 to 19.

Eitan started drawing recognizable figures at the age of 2-0, with his first drawings being of people, tractors, bicycles, trains, and compressors (see Figures 3.13a, b, c, d). Very soon thereafter, he modified the frontal orientation of his vehicles by adding "sides," and we can follow how he discovered, on his own, without any instruction, three major drawing projection systems: horizontal and vertical oblique projection, isometric projection, and divergent perspective (see Figures 3.14a, b, c). He controlled the orientation of his vehicles, turning them facing to the right or the left and with lines that are fluid and vibrant. He quite masterly depicted such details as rotors, propellers, cockpit, landing gears, wheels, and pneumatic brake boxes. The order in which he acquired these drawing systems, although spectacular in this preschooler's precocity and his autonomous development, is evidence that even the artistic child prodigy does not skip stages, but masters them more fully and

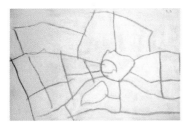
a. Varda, age 2-10

b. Varda, age 3-2

Figure 3.1. Experimentation with line and shape:
An early strategy of centering and symmetry

Figure 3.2. Dead bird
(Varda, age 5)

Figure 3.3.
Symmetrical
composition
of a girl against
a background of two
colors (Varda, age 6)

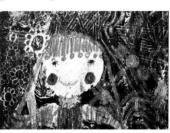

Figure 3.4.
Representational drawings
embedded in decorative
designs (Varda, age 6)

Figure 3.5. The
centrally placed figure
of a girl placed within
a decorative frame
(Varda, age 7)

Figure 3.7. Biafara's
starving children
(Varda, age 9)

Figure 3.6. A princess
against a background
of two colors
(Varda, age 8)

Figure 3.8. A woman dressed for
the carnival (Varda, age 10)

Figure 3.9. Portrait of a
young girl (Varda, age 11)

a. Grief (Varda, age 13)

b. My sister the communication
officer (Varda, age 13)

Figure 3.10. Themes from the Yom Kippur War

Figure 3.11.
Sadness and uncertainty
(Varda, age 16)

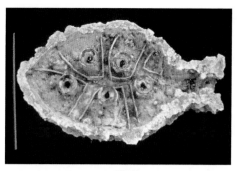

a. Fish

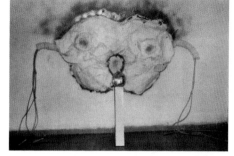

b. Toy elephants (part of a series)

Figure 3.12. Sculptures made
in art school

a. Kitten (age 3)

b. Let me smell
the flower (age 4)

Figure 3.18. Yani: A Chinese painting prodigy[3]

c. Monkey fishing (age 5)

d. Inoculation: I am not scared (age 5)

Figure 3.18 continued. Yani: A Chinese painting prodigy[3]

a. Guilin's autumn (age 7)

b. Last night I dreamt I saw the egrets racing (age 11)

Figure 3.19. Increasing maturity in themes and painting style[4]

a. Family (age 2-2)

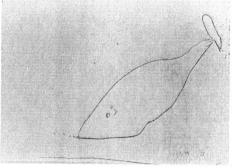

b. Fish (age 2-1)

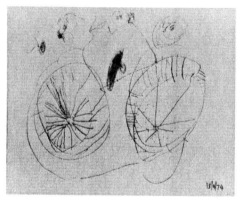

c. Bicycle (age 2-3)

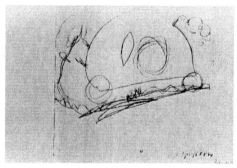

d. Compressor (age 2-3)

Figure 3.13. First drawings of Eitan

at a more rapid pace than his agemates (see Figures 3.15a, b, c).

Between the ages of 4 and 7, the isometric drawing system became the dominant one, with vehicles frequently drawn in three-quarter view, foreshortened, and with a marked diminution in the size of the receding parts. His drawings exhibit an expressiveness of lines that capture the essence of his vehicles (see Figures 3.16a and b). Thereafter, he expanded his themes to include airfields, cityscapes, and wild animals in the jungle. During adolescence, his interest turned to performers, first to the Beatles and then to athletes and rock stars. He grappled with the dynamics of motion, the flexing of muscles, and the way shading enhances the realistic appearance of the human body in action (see Figures 3.17a, b, c).

In many ways, Eitan and Varda are studies in contrast. Eitan's curiosity was focused on the outer world, its appearance and mechanics, and he set out to study it, understand it, and master it via his drawings. He was fascinated by the outer

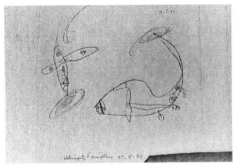

**a. Helicopter and airplane
(age 2-5)**

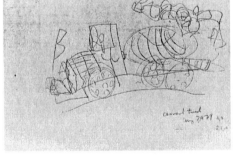

c. Moving truck (age 2-11)

b. Cement truck (age 2-7)

Figure 3.14. Eitan discovers new drawing systems

a. Police car (age 3-7)   **b. Volkswagen (age 3-7)**

Figure 3.15. Car models

a. Cement truck (age 4-4)

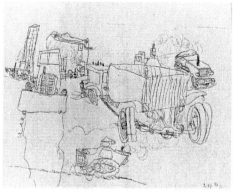

b. Construction scene (age 5-2)

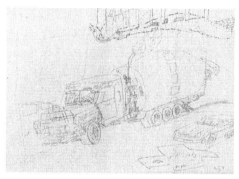

c. Cement of oil truck (age 6-7)

d. New York City (age 7-10)

Figure 3.16. The work of a young prodigy

world and eager to capture the essence of what intrigued him with as much fidelity to their looks as he could invent on paper. In this process, he taught himself the major projective drawing systems, and we can see "visual thinking in progress." In contrast, Varda developed a highly decorative-ornamental style that, though typical of child art, is strikingly original in its conception and execution, able to express deeply felt emotions and private concerns.

From the extensive collections of their drawings, it is clear that these children did not skip stages, and both demonstrate the lawfulness of a progression that is intrinsically motivated, displays universal features of development, and is also highly idiosyncratic in reflecting the personality of the individual artist. (For a more detailed account of these child artists, see Golomb, 2003.) Gifted children seem driven to explore their chosen medium, and the different styles they adopt exemplify the special, sometimes unique, manner in which they employ the medium to convey their personal view.

a. Cityscape (age 10)

b. The Beatles (age 11)

c. Athletes (age 16)

Figure 3.17. Expanding themes and interests

Yani

Yani was born in Goncheng County, in the Guanxi province of southern China. She was her parents' first-born child and seemed to have been destined for the arts. From the beginning, her relationship with her father, a painter, was a very close one, and she was given free access to his studio, which was located in the family's home. According to her father, she started painting at age 2, and, by the time she was 6, she had completed approximately 4,000 paintings and held her first exhibit.

Only a small sampling of her work has been published, and, on the basis of this material, painted with brush, ink, and pigments, authors who have studied Yani's artistic development have identified two or three major stages, beginning with age 3 and extending through the middle adolescent years (Andrews, 1989; Goldsmith, 1992; Goldsmith & Feldman, 1989; Ho, 1989; Tan, 1993; Wang, 1987; Zsensun & Low, 1991). The periods can be identified in terms of the dominant themes and the technical and compositional attributes that characterize the paintings of each period. Following Tan, the first period extends from 3 to 6 years and represents Yani's world of monkeys—their play, wishes, fears, and mischief.

The second period, from ages 7 to 11, is devoted to landscape paintings. The third period extends from ages 11 to 15, with the subject matter of her paintings revolving on flowers and birds.

The media with which Yani worked—brushes, ink, pigments, and rice paper—are the traditional tools of Chinese painters. Throughout the history of Chinese paintings, the brushstroke has been the central focus and the use of washes a fundamental element (Arnheim, 1997; Delbanco, 1989; Hejzlar, 1987; Siren, 1963). By the time Yani was 4 or 5 years old, she had mastered a number of basic brush strokes and was able to differentiate between lighter and darker strokes and the effects of the different sides of the brush, and she could handle light and dark ink washes. Within this relatively short period of intensive practice, she had mastered such difficult techniques as mixing ink and color, the flying-white brush stroke, the wet-ink technique, and control of the amount of ink. By manipulating various tones of ink and color, she created the texture of the monkey's body and its furry coat.

In the eyes of an observer familiar with children's artwork, Yani's paintings of monkeys playing, quarreling, waiting for food, swinging from trees, being drunk, and sniffing wine are a mixture of childish imagination, exuberance, and unusually skillful handling of the elements of composition. Some of Yani's early paintings from ages 3 and 4 portray single figures, for example, a furry kitten, tadpolish in its structure, but already notable for its expressive posture and charm (Figure 3.18a). She passed very quickly beyond the early global and undifferentiated forms, varied the monkeys posture, increased their number, and depicted them in a variety of actions and poses, clearly the work of a precociously gifted child (see Figures 3.18b, c, d). Along with increasingly more complex compositions, Yani at age 5 began to paint on larger sheets of paper and also explored the format of the handscroll.

Even at this early age, Yani's artwork is clearly defined in terms of the newly revived traditions of her environment and its long artistic history. Thematically, the choice of monkeys continues an old Chinese tradition in the visual arts and in narrative form. In painting, artists have developed formulae that involve the order and form in which parts of the monkey are drawn. While her compositions teem with the lively antics of her monkey friends, the figures are mostly flat and two-dimensional, and this young artist shows no inclination to create the illusion of three-dimensional space.

What sets Yani's work apart is more than the technical competence she achieved under the guidance of her father. The students of her paintings who are familiar with Chinese aesthetics praise the spirit of her painting, which endowed her art with "the breath of life" or a "lifelike spirit."

Around the age of 7, a major shift occurred in Yani's paintings as she began to focus her attention on the natural world of rivers, ponds, and mountains and the seasonal changes in their appearance. Her style became more fluid and painterly, and she imbued her compositions with a sense of expanding space with her skillful use of dark-white contrasts, tonal values, and a variety of textures in monochrome. Her work began to show the influence of contemporary Chinese painters, a trend that continued during her adolescent years (Figures 3.19a and b).

In terms of conventional criteria, the later work of flowers and birds represent Yani's most successful brushwork. However, according to several Chinese artists interviewed by Tan (1993), her most remarkable work was accomplished during the first period, which depicted in a highly individualistic manner her childhood world and its wishes, concerns, and fantasies. The intensity of feelings and the expressive powers of her brushwork created a magical world of great sincerity and beauty. Her later work became more conventional and more in line with highly trained art students.

Yani, the child prodigy, achieved a lifelike representation with artistic means that are not based on linear perspective, and her artwork remained relatively flat, though imbued with vitality and dynamic tension, aligned with the painterly traditions of her culture. Thus, Yani joins the two child artists described earlier in demonstrating the diverse paths artistically gifted children pursue in their artwork.

Drawings of Savant Artists

The notion that intelligence is positively correlated with drawing ability has found, in the past, wide acceptance among psychologists. This thesis underlies the early tests of drawings as measures of mental development (Burt, 1921; Sully, 1910; Thorndike, 1913), it motivated Florence Goodenough to develop her widely used Draw-A-Man test (1926), and some assessment of drawing ability continues to be part of most current tests of intelligence.

In line with the presumed linkage between intelligence and drawing ability, it is held that the mentally retarded draw like their normal counterparts of similar mental age (Cox & Bragal, 1985; Golomb & Barr-Grossman, 1977). These studies address cognitive aspects that are defined in terms of linguistic and mathematical competence and examine their relationship to representational development in children. This simple relationship has been questioned in the studies conducted by Henry Schaefer-Simmern (1948) and Max Kläger (1987, 1992, 1993, 1996, 2002), who documented that mentally retarded adults can generate drawings, paintings, and tapestries of exquisite beauty, an indication that the aesthetic dimensions of art making are not necessarily related to the artist's IQ or mental age.

The most serious challenge to the linkage of IQ and artistic achievement has come from the publications on autistic savants, mentally retarded autistic children whose drawings by far exceed the standards reached by ordinary children (Becker, 1980, Buck, 1991; Buck, Kardeman, & Goldstein, 1985; Morishima & Brown, 1977; Sacks, 1993; Selfe, 1977, 1995; Treffert, 1989; Wiltshire, 1987, 1989, 1991; Winner, 1996). The term savant refers to people with serious mental handicaps who have a spectacular island of ability that stands in marked contrast to their handicap of mental retardation, autism, or both. Savant skills are far in advance of those displayed by normally developing individuals.

The most informed studies on the savant phenomenon have been conducted by Hermelin and O'Connor and their colleagues at the University of London. From their extensive research, they concluded that artistic talent (above a certain

IQ range, usually 40–70) was independent of intelligence and independent of the autistic syndrome (Hermelin, 2001; Hermelin & O'Connor, 1990; Hermelin, Pring, Buhler, Wolff, & Heaton, 1999; O'Connor & Hermelin, 1987a, 1987b, 1990). Contrary to notions of the savants' "autistic art," Hermelin et. al (1999) have stated that

> [T]here is no stereotyped "autistic art." Individual differences in style and subject matter range from near abstract, through sensitive subtle portraiture and Dali-like surrealistic pictures, to precise and detailed line drawings. These latter often demonstrate a superb sense of perspective and frequently have an astonishingly personal and dynamic quality of line. (p. 1138)

Such findings highlight the specificity of artistic thinking and creating, and they provide some support for a modular view of the mind (Gardner, 1983).

Summary and Conclusions

The data on the precociously gifted normal children such as Eitan and Yani, as well as the findings on the mentally retarded autistic savants, highlight the discrepancy between their cognitive development and drawing achievement. This is especially striking in the case of such autistic savants as Nadia Chomyn (Selfe, 1977, 1995), Richard Wawro (Becker, 1980; Hermelin, 2001), and Stephen Wiltshire (1991), whose mental and chronological ages are highly discrepant.

Thus, talent emerges as a significant variable, and the hypothesized relationship between artistic achievement and IQ becomes more tenuous. The data from our diverse sources, the normally developing gifted, as well as ordinary children, and the findings on the autistic savants support a developmental analysis in terms of an orderly sequence in the acquisition of graphic skills, especially in the early years. We also note the powerful impact of the culture on the young artist's style and infer that these children acquired the pictorial skills valued in their culture by consistently exploring the possibilities and constraints of their medium and by discovering the major rules that underlie their chosen art form. As my review has indicated, the rate of acquisition of mature representational skills was greatly enhanced in the talented children; but, beyond their precocity, their artistic achievements also differed qualitatively from that of their ordinary agemates.

The three case studies of Varda, Eitan, and Yani clearly indicate that we are not merely dealing with accelerated development. Each one of these children created works that were vibrant, evocative, engaging, and original in conception and execution. Varda's painterly style, choice of themes, and daring color combinations appeal to us in the directness of the expression, the sincerity of the feelings, and the full development of the child-art style. Eitan's virtuosity in the use of fluid lines captures the dynamics of motion and the tension of bodies in action. He is quite masterful in recreating the visual world and endowing his compositions with a poetic touch. Yani's work does indeed exude the "breath of life" identified by the Chinese artists: It is lively and engaging in its themes, their often humorous composition, and technical sophistication. These children created pictorial worlds in forms that tell and sing, to paraphrase Arnheim (1995), and their work is more imaginative, original, and expressive than that of less talented children.

Finally, to what extent does prodigy status or childhood giftedness in the visual arts predict the pursuit of a career in the arts? We might reformulate the question and ask to what extent does our social environment encourage the pursuit of such a career?

In the case of Varda, after graduating with distinction from a well-known art school, she pursued her commitment to sculpture for several years and continued to exhibit some of her work. Serious economic constraints and the need to provide for her family redirected her concerns, and she eventually pursued training in art therapy. As an art therapist, she now fosters other people's personal growth, which she finds fulfilling.

Eitan never expressed a desire to become an artist, not as a young adolescent nor later after graduation from high school. He always stressed that he would either study architecture (his father's profession) or industrial design. He chose the latter, graduated with honors from his art school with a specialization in industrial design, and that is the profession in which he is currently engaged.

Yani's further course of development and her career choices are unknown. To the best of my knowledge, she enrolled in an art school after graduating from high school, but not much is known about her current status, and she might have given up painting.

From this limited set of data, one dare not lightly generalize to all children talented in the visual arts. However, from published data on gifted child artists, it appears that only very few have persisted in an artistic career. Eric, whose development was chronicled by Enid Zimmerman (1995), has geared his talents to computer and board games. Joel, whose artistic development was documented by Constance Milbrath (1995), had to relegate art to a sideline in order to support himself. Amnon, a highly gifted young artist described in my book *The Child's Creation of a Pictorial World* (1992, 2003), teaches industrial design with a focus on the design of furniture. For some time, he pursued sculpture in wood, but the economic necessities of providing for a family have redirected his efforts, and he is currently teaching in an art school.

These findings are quite congruent with a longitudinal study on male fine arts students enrolled in the Art Institute of Chicago conducted first by Getzels and Csikszentmihalyi (1976) and subsequently continued in follow-up studies of former students (Csikszentmihalyi & Getzels, 1988).

To pursue a career in the arts requires cultural supports and at least some financial rewards. Talent and an urge to create in the pictorial medium are necessary, but not sufficient conditions, and personality factors play a significant role. It appears that predictions based on the childhood work of child artists have little power and that the same applies to talented art students full of promise. To succeed as an artist in the Western world calls upon many propitious circumstances, both internal to the artist and external in terms of the gatekeepers of the art world: the curators, gallery owners, and critics who determine to a large extent the style and the subject matter that is valued and marketed.

The finding that childhood giftedness is not a good predictor of adult career choices need not detract from our appreciation of artistically gifted children's talents and the roles they can play in their lives. The ability to devote energy and passion to a domain, in this case the visual arts, provides a major avenue for giving form to thoughts and feelings and for construing and confirming one's identity. It opens avenues for relating beyond family and school to one's cultural heritage and for feeling connected to an ongoing creative enterprise. Child art—including the art of the gifted, prodigies, and savants—ought to be valued and enjoyed for what it is and might become and, of course, nurtured to the best of our ability.

End Notes

1. In this essay I do not distinguish the terms *talent* and *giftedness*; I use them interchangeably.
2. The first numeral indicates age in years, the second in months.
3. Illustrations courtesy of Wang Chiqiang.
4. Illustrations courtesy of Wang Chiqiang.

Children of the Starry Cope:
Gifted and Talented Native American Students

by Beverly J. Klug

I was trying to explain a concept in my government class, and the students were not getting it. One of the Indian students in the class then decided to explain it. Not only did he understand the concept and explain it well, but the other students finally understood, also. I thanked him and praised his abilities. That was the last time he ever spoke up in class. From then on, he got 60% on all of his tests. Do you know how hard it is to always get 60%? I wish I had known more about his culture so that this would not have happened to him.
—S. Jackson (personal communication, 2002)

Unfortunately, the story related above is not an isolated incident. Many times, American Indian students who are bicultural or traditional are placed in situations where they are forced by cultural standards to hide their talents and abilities. In this instance, the problem represented a cultural communication mismatch: When his teacher publicly praised him, he was made to look better than his classmates.

Why should this be a problem? As teachers, we have been taught to reinforce students for their responses. Ms. Jackson did this: She reinforced the student for his participation and abilities. However, in Native traditional and more traditional bicultural families, one is taught not to stand out from others in order to maintain harmony in communities. How, then, can we encourage Native students to continue to be successful in our classrooms?

We need to know where our American Indian students fall on the continuum from traditional to culturally assimilated to know the values and community norms to which they adhere. We can know this only by knowing our students and their communities.

Before proceeding, it is necessary to understand that I am not an American Indian, and I cannot speak for all Native Americans. I have taught children and adults of many different ethnicities for more than 30 years in many settings and in a variety of programs and situations. As with any other ethnically diverse group of people, generalizations are not always accurate. The information given here is a beginning point enabling you to proceed to discover the norms operating in the community where you are teaching.

Names used to signify Indigenous peoples include Indian, Native American, American Indian, First Nations (in Canada), Indigenous peoples, or Aboriginals. For this reason, I use the terms interchangeably. When speaking of specific groups of Native peoples, most prefer to be known by their tribal Nation affiliations, such as Shoshone, Paiute, Chippewa, Mohawk, Diné (Navajo), or Lakota. At this time, there are more than 510 federally recognized tribal Nations in this country (St. Germaine, 1995). Indian Nations are sovereign and maintain their own governments. Native peoples hold dual citizenship in their own Nations and as citizens of the United States, as awarded in 1928. During the period of termination from 1945 to 1965, tribal Nation status was removed from many Nations that the federal government considered too small or assimilated to continue to be listed on the federal register. Some Nations have been successful in petitioning Congress to have their status restored; others are preparing to do so (Sheffield, 1997). The cost is prohibitive for many tribal Nations, taking years to complete. In Alabama, Connecticut, Delaware, Georgia, Louisiana, Massachusetts, North Carolina, New York, Tennessee, and Virginia, a number of tribal entities have not been able to afford these costs, although they continue to enjoy state recognition of their tribal Nation status.

Who Qualifies to Be Considered an American Indian?

Many American Indians do not fit the typical stereotype of having dark skin, brown eyes, and straight black hair. They represent all ranges of color, from light to dark; have straight or curly hair; have dark eyes or blue eyes; have blonde, red, brown, or black hair; and are of all heights and body builds. Many have European, Hispanic, African, or Asian heritage(s) along with their Native heritages (Nagel, 1997).

To be considered an American Indian, individuals must be enrolled in their tribal Nations. In many instances, an individual must have at least one-fourth Indian blood quantum to enroll. However, this requirement varies by tribal Nations: Cherokees have the most liberal enrollment qualifications, whereas others require evidence of having been descended through the mother's or father's tribal affiliation (Sheffield, 1997; Tsosie, 2002). There are many instances of children who are genetically 100% American Indian, but who do not meet requirements for enrollment established by either their mother's or father's tribal Nations, or their tribal Nations have not been restored by either state or federal governments (Sheffield).

Complicating the issue is the migration to urban areas following World War II. This move was promoted to assimilate Native Americans more quickly into the dominant culture. Because of prejudices and the resulting verbal, physical, and mental abuse experienced on the job in urban settings, many parents declined to declare their Native heritages or enroll their children. Therefore, identification as an American Indian in urban areas has become a complicated process now being addressed across the country (Gonzales, 2001).

In the 2000 census, 4.1 million people claimed Native American lineage (Mohawk, 2002). Of these, 40% checked more than one category of ethnicity. The majority reported living in urban areas of New York City and Los Angeles, with large numbers also living in Chicago, Houston, Philadelphia, Phoenix, San Diego, Dallas, San Antonio, and Detroit. As teachers, we need to realize there are many American Indian children whom we may not recognize as such in our classrooms. Consequently, when searching for candidates who fit the criteria necessary for gifted and talented programs, we may overlook qualified students because we are unaware of their American Indian identities.

Contemporary Native American Communities and Gifted and Talented Students

How we relate to the rest of the world is learned mostly through interactions with our families and communities. Members of different tribal Nations do the same (Mohawk, 2002). There is no pan-Indian way of knowing, thinking, or acting, though there are some generalizable characteristics and similar beliefs common to many tribal Nations. Furthermore, American Indians vary from assimilated into the dominant culture, to retaining and actively practicing their traditional lifestyles. Many are bicultural, adjusting their behaviors, ways of interacting, use of language(s), and modes of sharing information with others according to the settings in which they find themselves. Urban American Indians may practice their traditional ways only when visiting relatives and friends on reservations, during pan-Indian powwows or other celebrations, or when involved in urban Indian centers (Gonzales, 2001). Individuals placed in foster care or adopted by non-Indian families may have no knowledge of their cultural heritages. As a result, there is not one "model" of a gifted and talented American Indian student. Not knowing this may lead us into thinking that the number of gifted and talented American Indians is far less than that of other populations. The following stories of Dr. Wilfred Denetclaw, Jr., Dr. Marian Schmidt, and Dr. Meda Spring illustrate these differences (the latter two names are pseudonyms).

Dr. Wilfred Denetclaw, Jr., a member of the Diné (Navajo) Nation, grew up traditionally on a Navajo reservation. He participated in community gatherings and rituals and worked in his family's sheep ranching operation. His teachers did not recognize that he possessed any special gifts, and it wasn't until his senior year in high school that he decided to pursue a college degree in biology with the idea of working with animals. His high school counselor told him that he did not have the grades for college and that he shouldn't set such high goals for himself because he couldn't achieve them.

Wilfred persisted and attended Navajo Community College, where he took the courses necessary to enter a 4-year degree program. Because the area of biology involved working with dead animals, which was forbidden by Navajo tradition, he consulted a Navajo medicine man about what he desired to do. The medicine man reassured him that he was taking his Nation into new territory. Wilfred is now a distinguished researcher in the area of genetics. While he considers himself now to be bicultural, he still tries to participate as much as possible in the life of his Native community (Denetclaw, 2002).

Dr. Marian Schmidt grew up in an urban area and attended a university demonstration school. While her mother was Euro-American and her father Choctaw, there was a "seamless quality" to her childhood as she participated in both cultures. Her parents were accepted and remained close to all of their relatives. As a young girl, Marian interacted a great deal with her Choctaw family as they gathered at the home of one of the aunties to work on quilts and other projects together. During these visits, the family spoke in both Choctaw and English. Her grandmother would not teach her Choctaw because she didn't want her to "speak broken English."

Marian was successful academically, and she began writing poetry and journals when she was 10 or 11. At this same time, she began giving piano lessons to neighborhood children. She had many opportunities for enrichment that were part of the school she attended. Teachers would make arrangements for students to study with colleagues at the university. Whenever there were special guest-artist appearances in the music department, Marian was sure to be provided the opportunity to attend.

According to Marian, school was easier for her than for some of the other Native students because she was lighter skinned, although she still had some physical features associated with American Indians, such as dark eyes and hair. She flourished, taking on leadership roles and being involved in the state chorus, and she continued through college to become a teacher. She was encouraged to go to college by her family, especially by her father, who was unable to attend more than 1 year of college due to inadequate finances. Influenced by her mother and her mother's sisters, who were all involved in education, Marian entered the field of special education. Later, she became a school counselor and then director of special education services for a local school district.

Marian now states that she is "definitely assimilated." She has entered a new phase of her life where she is exploring her Choctaw heritage and reconnecting with elder relatives. She wants to pass this heritage on to her children and grand-children, and she is actively pursuing this area. Her children and grandchildren are enrolled members of the Choctaw Nation and are becoming involved with their cultural traditions. Her sons, in particular, are finding connections with Native peoples they did not have while they were growing up, and this has been particularly satisfying for her family as a whole. In many ways, they are experiencing the feelings of new community connections.

Dr. Meda Spring is a college professor whose American Indian father's family moved to a rural area in northeastern Oklahoma after the Cherokee removal. When she was young, she lived on acreage that had cattle and horses, a woodland area, and hay meadows. The largest town was about 5 miles away. Her father raised her to be an independent thinker and to continue with traditional practices by telling her traditional stories. Meda attended a local elementary school, where she was one of a few culturally identifiable Native Americans in her grade level. Her brother had difficulty in school even though he was quite bright because he "acted like an Indian," according to one of his teachers.

As a child, Meda didn't know that she had any special abilities; they were just part of her world. Her father noticed from the time she was little that she had a way with animals and they always gathered around her. When Meda tried to bring this talent into the school setting, she was told, "This is what we're doing, period." Of her teachers, only two Native American teachers recognized her talents in high school and had her present information about her tribal heritage during the lessons.

No one at school spoke to Meda about going to college. Her mother was a traditional Euro-American homemaker concerned with status and what other people thought. Her ideal future for Meda was to grow up, get married, and have children. Meda's father, however, encouraged her to go to college because, as he said, "No one can take your education away from you. Education is power, especially for a Cherokee woman with a doctorate." He debated Native issues with her, allowing her to be vocal about her thoughts and insights. Consequently, she sees herself as more traditional in how she perceives the world, especially in terms of spirituality and the work she does. Meda's auntie provided a positive influence for her, as well, since she was involved in social justice activities in the 1960s and '70s, especially Native American issues. Meda continues to learn about her Native heritage and practices her language. As an educator, she tells her students that they need to bring their special abilities into the classroom.

Identification of Gifted and Talented American Indian Students

You have just read about three individuals who represent the many different faces of American Indian gifted and talented students. You can see that there is not one stereotype describing what it means to be Indigenous and gifted and talented. The dilemma for teachers is to identify gifted and talented Native students and provide the educational atmosphere that will nurture their talents without forcing them to choose between their roots and the dominant culture to be successful.

In this country, the primary emphasis has been on identifying academically talented students, rather than examining other talents. Howley and Howley (1995) made the distinction between intellect, or "thoughtful understandings," and intelligence, or the practical performances that are quantifiable products of mental activity. In the general public, there has been an anti-intellectual attitude. In institutions where mass education is the focus, lack of respect for the intellectual capacities of all students may be clearly evident (Howley & Howley), and this problem extends to schools serving American Indian students.

Use of Intelligence Tests and Academic Achievement Tests to Identify Gifted and Talented Students

The statistical bell curve gives testimony to the existence of as many gifted and talented individuals as those on the opposite end of the spectrum, the mentally challenged (McCluskey & Walker, 1986). Both populations have special needs. Regrettably, it is easier to provide for the needs of those who are mentally challenged than for those who are gifted and talented (Fetterman, 1988).

For impoverished children, there are fewer opportunities to acquire the preparatory skills needed to enter school, primarily those identified with the dominant Western, middle-class culture (Pulliam, 1987). Our public schools are not places of equal opportunity for all learners. They reinforce the values and norms of a society far different from Native Nations and those in the lower socioeconomic levels. At the same time, many girls, especially those from underrepresented populations, are socialized to accept subservient positions despite their intellectual prowess (Freedman, 2002).

School districts still rely heavily on tests of intelligence and measures of achievement to determine student eligibility for gifted and talented programs despite changes in the definition of giftedness in recent years (Stephens & Karnes, 2000). Tests of intelligence, whether group or individual, contain biases favoring identification of a disproportionate number of Euro-Americans for gifted programs. While the causal aspects are continually debated, we do know the language used for these tests is that of White, middle-class Americans and incorporates concepts with which these children are usually familiar (Bernol, 2002). Since language assists our development of understanding the world through interactions with others, children whose cultural symbols and ways of knowing are not reflected in assessments are disenfranchised. Moreover, values and ways of knowing of traditional American Indians are disaffirmed in the identification processes used.

We fail to acknowledge other factors that may blind us to the real talents of children. The politics of race and culture can inhibit attempts to identify ethnically diverse students for advanced educational services (Morris, 2002). It is imperative to include additional alternative instruments to nominate American Indian children for gifted and talented programs. These may include self, teacher, peer, and parent surveys; student work samples; and measures of creativity. Bernol (2002) suggested a greater need for involvement of ethnically diverse teachers in programs for gifted and talented students to provide more accurate recognition of students' eligibility.

Dynamic Assessment Procedure (DAP)

An alternative to measuring acquired, or static, knowledge and to counteract test biases is to utilize a process measuring the dynamic abilities of students to learn (Stanley, 1996), which is built on the work of Lev Vygotsky. According to Vygotsky (1978), students have a level at which they have attained knowledge, referred to as "static knowledge," and levels at which they can attain additional knowledge, referred to as "potential knowledge." The area between these two levels is referred to as the Zone of Proximal Development (ZPD), wherein teachers provide guidance to students during the process of acquiring new knowledge and adding to what they already know. Vygotsky advocated that we work with students at the higher levels of this zone so that we constantly challenge students to reach the next levels. This makes learning dynamic and ongoing.

Vygotsky's Dynamic Assessment Procedure measures students' static levels of knowledge on assessments by having them work alone in order to provide baseline data. The person conducting the assessment then structures opportunities for students to develop concepts at increasingly higher levels until the highest level of knowledge attainment with assistance is reached. The students are retested with an alternate form of the assessment measure. Students' upper level ZPDs are determined by comparing the two results. This provides both quantitative and qualitative data used to determine the kind of assistance teachers need to provide to students to continue making progress (Stanley, 1996). This type of assessment offers a more accurate view of ethnically diverse students' actual and potential developmental levels.

Checklists

Checklists for nominating gifted and talented students by teachers, peers, family members, and the students themselves have proven to be a valuable means for recommendations for gifted and talented programs. Checklists for identifying Native students must reflect the local Native community's culture; commercially prepared checklists primarily reflect the dominant culture (Brescia & Fortune, 1988). The following areas are appropriate for consideration on checklists developed at the school-district level:

Teacher observation checklists. Look at/for the student's:

- ability to handle responsibilities in and out of school;
- leadership capability;

- ability to assist others in learning;
- quick grasp of concepts that other students may be struggling to learn;
- use of vocabulary reflecting higher levels of knowledge attainment than typical of others of the same age and grade level;
- ability to focus on tasks and synthesize information from many different sources;
- ability to initiate new ways to solve problem situations; and
- response to situations when bored: Does the student request alternatives, begin to act out, or act in ways considered inappropriate?

Student work samples. Examine the products and the processes the student uses to complete them. The student:

- completes tasks assigned;
- is able to take a leadership role when working in cooperative groups to complete projects;
- undertakes assignments that are more challenging;
- uses technology to create new products or represent research in creative ways; and
- when older, is able to consider multiple viewpoints when examining problems.

Parent/Grandparent or guardian observations. Examine what the student does outside of school. This includes information garnered from community organizations/clubs to which the student may belong. The student demonstrates:

- outstanding abilities in completing traditional arts and crafts;
- efforts to be as perfect as possible in performance arts, such as dancing, singing, and drumming;
- acceptance of responsibilities at younger ages than other siblings/children in the household;
- the ability to read material at home that is more advanced than usual for his or her age;
- understandings of Native oral traditions that are more advanced for his or her age; and
- ability to find solutions to problems that make life better for the community.

Factors Impeding Identification of Gifted and Talented Native American Students

Due to cultural differences, values, and ways of knowing, the gifts and talents of Indigenous students may not be recognized in our schools. The following information shows how students may be overlooked because of factors outside of our control.

Language Differences as Barriers to Identification

Intelligence is defined as the ability to manipulate symbols and to remember and organize information as represented in linguistic and other symbol systems. Many American Indian students speak English as their second language or an American Indian English (AIE) dialect (Leap, 1993). The English language used in school is different than survival English heard on playgrounds (Cummins, 1981). Academic language related to our disciplines plays a necessary role as we convey information about complex concepts that may pose a challenge for all students, especially second language learners, to comprehend.

If verbal manifestations comprise a great deal of daily student assessment in schools, those who do not speak Standard English will be overlooked for consideration in special programs. Students who fail to grasp concepts as a result of language interference may develop lower academic self-concepts as a result. To prevent this from occurring, alternative ways of learning and demonstrating knowledge should be provided along with instruction in manipulating a second language. Attention should be focused on the positive aspects of speaking more than one language, for example, the increased flexibility in thinking processes many bilingual students demonstrate.

Prejudices and Stereotypes

Prejudices and stereotypes play effective roles in blocking our recognition of the endowments possessed by students from underrepresented populations. With respect to Indigenous peoples, stereotypes used by Europeans for the last 500 years influence our collective consciousness. The media employed pejorative terms from the very beginning to describe Indigenous peoples, from primitive, naïve, and childlike on the one hand, to savages, bloodthirsty, and warlike, on the other. Indigenous women who held political offices within their communities were regarded with horror by colonial powers encountering this "uncivilized" governmental structure (Freedman, 2002). The phrase "noble savage" did little to portray realistically male and female Native Americans during earlier periods of history, obliterating altogether the important roles played by Native women in their communities.

Anthropology in the 19th century solidified the concept of the "other" in modern history. Through making comparisons and contrasts between Europeans and the peoples of colonized nations, the process produced dichotomous ways of thinking that reinforced the supremacy of Europeans and European cultural knowledge (Smith, 1981). Claims made by colonizers concerning the inferior status of colonized peoples made justification of taking tribal Nation lands in America appear to be inevitable. This legacy of "truths" created about American

Indians obscured many positive characteristics of human capital that had been acquired over centuries of continuous practice and retention of traditional systems. As cultures are deconstructed during the current period of ethnic revival, the long-standing misinterpretations and denials of Indigenous peoples' cultural legitimacies are finally being recognized and rectified.

Family Reluctance to Involve Students in Special Programs

Native families may be reticent to enroll their children in any special programs for enrichment in schools. The boarding schools created for American Indian students in the late 1800s became venues for creating loyalties to the United States government by forcing Native students to speak only English, sing patriotic songs, read and recite patriotic rhetoric, and celebrate all national holidays. In 1891, education became mandatory at Indian schools to ensure the creation of loyalties to colonizing forces in the name of progress. Schools forcibly removed Native students from their cultural roots, languages, and families, while promoting the idea of a superior Western European culture (Meriam, 1928). The boarding school experiment has contributed to the dysfunctionality operating within many Native communities today since boarding school students did not have the opportunity to become connected with their natal cultures.

These events are evidence of the control the federal government strove to exercise over Native peoples and of the resistance of many toward cultural assimilation. These experiences are legacies that influence family decisions about whether or not to be involved in schools. In many families, there is not an option to place Native children in programs that have no cultural affiliations.

In families where children were sent to boarding schools voluntarily, this sentiment against formal education may not be echoed. This is due to the perceived advantages of Western education, such as developing the tools necessary to survive in a changing world (Adams, 1995). Even though the schools were still considered to be venues for acculturation, families alleged their children would have economic advantages if they acquired skills needed to survive in a changed society (Klug & Whitfield, 2003).

Political Influences in Schools

A phenomenon of inter- and intratribal Nation suboppression developed as a result of the general oppression of American Indian peoples (Adams, 1999). Tribal Nations were used against others by having people within and without enforce the wishes of the colonial governments. In some cases, tribal members were then elevated to positions of power. This created many jealousies and hatreds that continue to affect communities today as biases have been handed down from generation to generation. Who is teaching or working at a school may be just as important as the curriculum being taught. Parallels in European, Asian, African, and American societies can be found in the prejudices and hatreds constructed during the two world wars within and without the nations involved. Many of these prejudices still exist as strongly today as in yesteryears.

These realities make it imperative to understand that there may be multiple reasons that parents and grandparents may not want their children to be identified as gifted or talented in order to protect them from criticisms within their tribal Nations. We must respect the rights of the significant adults in Native students' lives to make choices they feel are best for their children.

Cultural Differences Impacting Schools

Institutional racism is a factor in American educational systems that affects everything from the way student assessments are constructed, to definitions of leadership and family. Teachers are predominantly Euro-American, female, and middle-class (Zimpher & Ashburn, 1993), influenced by Western European values, mores, and ways of knowing. These ways are reflected in classrooms across the United States today. When teaching strategies fail or elicit little response from our Native American students, we tend to place the blame on them and their communities, not knowing that the source of the misunderstanding is contained in our own teaching and cultural practices.

The notion that there is only one right way of doing things is prevalent throughout our country's school systems. European and Euro-American males primarily developed our educational systems by duplicating those of Western Europe (Pulliam, 1987). Because of this, Western European cultural values and belief systems have been privileged over all others from the beginning of formal education in this nation. An example of this is the way curricula are developed for study (Posner, 1992). Creating objectives for student learning is a common and highly recommended practice. However, the use of objectives that sanction curricula implicitly may blind us to the hegemonic thinking embedded in the objectives themselves. This leads to the disenfranchisement of students from underrepresented populations, especially when objectives are linked to assessment. In order to be aware of these influences upon our thinking as teachers, we need to explore the epistemologies, or knowledge systems, of ethnically diverse groups of students attending our schools.

Tribal Nations vary in their particular beliefs and practices. However, there are some generalities that, if heeded, make a difference in classrooms. These mainly concern the human relations aspects of teaching and learning and are found in areas of respect for others, especially elders; caring for others, including their mental, physical, emotional, and spiritual needs; community building and interaction patterns; appropriate ways of interacting with others to ensure harmony in communities; and making connections with the natural and spiritual worlds (American Indian Education Handbook Committee, 1991). We must recognize that not all tribal Nations exemplify the same beliefs, values, mores, and understandings, which is the case for any other ethnic group in the United

States and around the world. By having some knowledge of global Native values, we can see where our students may be on the cultural continuum from assimilated (acculturated to the dominate society), to bicultural (able to code-switch between the dominant cultural and Native traditional cultural expectations), to very traditional (working only from an American Indian tribal Nation cultural orientation).

Cultural values are socializing agents; they affect the ways in which students act and feel when in the classroom. Interestingly, while American Indian teachers cite the areas of spirituality, indifference to ownership, careful listening, caution, and careful observation as the most important cultural values influencing Native student classroom performance, non-Indian teachers perceive such negative, success-impairing cultural values as lack of the discipline, indifference to the work ethic, group harmony, and holistic approaches (Swisher, 1994). Clearly, we need to understand both cultural systems before attempting to ascribe motives to student classroom behaviors.

Family Patterns and Respect for Elders

In traditional families, elders are revered and grandparents play active roles in raising their grandchildren. In some Nations, children will live for extended periods of time with grandparents who teach them tribal songs, legends, and their tribal traditions. In many Nations, children are raised by the extended family, rather than in a nuclear family setting. In this way, children are always cared for and have a place in the family unit. They are taught not to look adults directly in the eye as a sign of respect.

Teachers who view these behaviors from a dominant-cultural viewpoint may misinterpret the importance of grandparents' involvement in schools. When grandparents attend parent-teacher conferences or visit schools, this demonstrates the importance of education to the family. The work of the child is considered the accomplishment of the entire family, not just the individual child. When students refuse to give teachers direct eye contact, they are transferring their cultural understandings to other significant adults in their lives.

The Importance of Harmony in Schools

Teachers working on or near reservations can be heard to complain that they are constantly reteaching information that their Native students seem unable to master. They cite as evidence that students never have the right answers when called upon, a situation presenting a double bind for learners. In keeping with the value of harmony, working together and in cooperation is valued over competitiveness. If teachers can acknowledge a response as correct simply by moving on, this nonverbal signal is enough to reinforce the students' responses and allows them to continue to participate. By understanding this cultural difference, teachers allow students to control their own learning and demonstrate their knowledge.

Perceptions of Language Use

Low teacher expectations for Native students based on observations of behaviors resulting from cultural misunderstandings are easily transformed into concrete generalizations extended to all Indigenous students. This problem is a major contributing factor to the lack of identification of gifted and talented American Indian students. Likewise, there is still a persistent belief that all Native American students work well only with their hands, are not talented academically, and should be steered toward vocational education (Rehyner, 1992). This perception arises from the differing views concerning the use of oral and written language in traditional societies.

Traditional and bicultural American Indian students are taught that words are sacred and should be used sparingly. In the dominant culture, the more words used, the better, with an emphasis on increasing students' vocabularies and abilities to communicate precisely. When asking students questions, in typical classrooms we wait less than half a second for them to respond. Native students are taught to consider questions thoroughly before answering them, and it is not uncommon for students or community members to answer questions many days or weeks after they are posed. These situations provide evidence of the deep thinking that may be required for students to formulate their responses.

Cross-cultural miscommunications often lead educators to develop false impressions of Native American students in their classrooms. Complicating matters, Indian students from all points on the traditional to assimilated continuum are represented in many of the same schools. Therefore, we must have contact with families to understand how they are raising their children and what the cultural expectations are for them in schools so that we will not be misled concerning their true abilities.

Culturally Relevant Pedagogy

The Indian Education Act passed in 1972 began a series of legislative efforts designed to incorporate Native ways, traditions, and languages within schools following the Civil Rights Movement of the 1960s. Despite the fact that there had been previous calls for incorporation of language and culture in schooling for Native children, most notably following the release of the Meriam Report in 1928, rarely were these measures carried out. In 1975, Congress passed the Indian Self-Determination and Education Assistance Act. This legislation resulted from the desires of Native communities to have more ownership of education for American Indian students, in particular to capitalize on the unique cultural heritages and abilities fostered in their communities.

The passage of the 1975 legislation marked a new phase in the relationships between Native American communities and educational institutions, signaling an end to silence concerning the way schools were used for assimilation purposes. Recommendations were made by Native American educators to incorporate Native arts and traditions in teaching concepts for content areas. By adhering to these recommendations, gifted and talented traditional and bicultural students are able to involve themselves legitimately in the educational process.

Concerns for Development of the Whole Child

At one time, educating children meant including in the curriculum the values, ethics, and morals that were thought to be part of what it meant to be a good person and teaching them directly to children in public schools, along with the use of prayer (Pulliam, 1987). Today, development of these areas are typically left to students' families and churches. For American Indian students, spirituality is defined as a way of life. Offering prayers of thanksgiving to the Creator is part of the routine from the time people awake in the morning and continues throughout the day. As teachers, we can work with parents and communities to determine the moral and ethical teachings the community desires of all its members and strive to reinforce these by how we handle situations that arise in our classrooms. This might entail letting go of absolute power by those who are "in charge" of students when they are in school and sharing responsibilities for student behaviors with extended family members. In many instances, this may be Grandma. Regardless, we need to reach out to families of our Indigenous students. By showing our respect of community norms, we are building trust and partnerships that benefit all students and schools.

The dominant culture influences all youth tremendously. Our country may be described as displaying cultural narcissism, or the moral disregard of others in our society (Ryan, Sweeder, & Bednar, 2002). Obsessions with money, immediate gratification, manipulating others, and self-absorption are all found in school environments. These influences present cultural disconnects for traditional and bicultural students. As a society, we are seeing the need to refocus all of our students and assist them in developing prosocial behaviors.

We know through research from around the globe that the more students' emotional needs are considered in schools, the more resilient they will be in the face of school truancy, drug and alcohol addiction, and dropping out. Schools that care for all of their students are supportive, offer opportunities for students to be involved and achieve, and work to ensure there is racial harmony (Brown, D'Emidio-Caston, & Bernard, 2001). Caring teachers counteract many of the negative elements Native students encounter in schools and provide positive reinforcement for their cultural values (Rehyner, 1992).

Glasser (1998) has examined areas that are necessary for quality schools and identified five basic needs that all children must have satisfied in order to enjoy quality school experiences: "love, power, freedom, fun, and survival" (p. 15). The first condition of quality schools is that "there must be a warm, supportive classroom environment" (p. 18). By paying attention to the needs of Native students in a fashion that considers the whole child, we are providing the type of atmosphere in our schools in which Native American students may thrive, a necessary condition for gifted and talented students to reach their full potentials.

Alternate Pathways to Learning

Whatever formal or informal approaches are available for providing opportunities for gifted and talented students in educational settings, it is essential that attention be paid to areas of Native students' learning styles and ways of knowing. Native American students tend to be more field-dependent, prefer visual learning, and respond to activities that require learning by doing (Swisher, 1994). These learning styles are reflected in Gardner's (1983, 1993, 1999) theory of multiple intelligences. He has identified eight types of intelligences: (1) linguistic, (2) logical-mathematical, (3) musical, (4) bodily-kinesthetic, (5) spatial, (6) interpersonal, (7) intrapersonal, and (8) naturalist. One way of assisting parents and peers with nominating students for gifted and talented programs is to provide models of American Indians who exemplify accomplishments in each of these areas. For instance, Billy Mills, Jim Thorpe, and Maria Tall Chief provide noteworthy examples of Native people who excel in the bodily-kinesthetic area. In the linguistic area, Chief Seattle and Chief Joseph are both known for their oratory skills; Simon Ortiz, Wendy Rose, and others are well known for their writings. There are many great Indian leaders such as King Philip (Metacomet), Crazy Horse, and Geronimo who exemplify the interpersonal skills necessary to lead their peoples. Accomplished Native American musicians such as Carlos Naki and Buffy St. Marie and artists such as Lloyd Kiva New and Margaret Tafoya, who led the Tafoya clan of Santa Clara Pueblo potters, provide role models in the arts and use of mathematical concepts. Medicine men and women, or shamans, exemplify intrapersonal skills. Native peoples as a whole exemplify the naturalist area, as the care for Mother Earth has always been a priority for their communities.

The people named above represent a small fraction of the talent of American Indians past and present. There are Indigenous peoples who are engaged in all of the multiple intelligences throughout the continent who could provide role models for children of their tribal Nations. The value of sharing models of outstanding Native peoples with our students is so that they, too, can recognize abilities they may possess. A discussion of multiple intelligences should follow, enabling them to identify areas in which they do well and matching these to multiple intelligence areas. Teacher observations, along with parental and peer nominations, make this task more reliable. For young children, teacher and family observations of the children's areas of strengths are important so that we can utilize these intelligences in the classroom.

Mediation of Instruction

Another area of consideration for teachers has to do with how knowledge is learned and demonstrated in the classroom. Hollins (1996) used the phrase "culturally mediated instruction" to describe a process of teaching and learning wherein the students' home cultures are central to the learning process. By making use of techniques that reinforce American Indian core values of cooperation and sharing, such as peer tutoring, cross-age tutoring, and cooperative learning, along with relating new knowledge to that stressed in the community, teachers are incorporating culturally congruent methodologies in their class activities (Klug & Whitfield, 2003).

The retention of many traditional practices is guaranteed in treaties with tribal Nations and the federal government. Some of these practices, such as hunting, fishing, and whaling, are being challenged in the media and courts as struggles evolve between different parties over resources necessary for the retention of these traditions. In the West, there is the ongoing struggle over water: Who has first priority when there is a drought, farmers who need the water for irrigation or tribal members who are concerned about the survival of salmon and other native fish? As teachers, we may never know the feelings of Indigenous peoples associated with colonization and treaty rights. However, we need to be knowledgeable of the debate and willing to address current issues that affect tribal members in our schools. We do not have to take sides in presenting issues; we only need to present balanced views and allow students to research and discuss the issues in order to draw their own conclusions.

Brown (2000) incorporated this approach when working with Native students to explore the development of large wilderness areas in Alaska. Students were able to participate in discussions concerning the pros and cons of development as they completed research about the effects on the environment and the impacts of expected changes resulting from this development. Students were challenged to think ahead about what was best for the long-term survival of their communities and cultures.

Meyer (2002) has written materials for American Indians and non-Indians to explore political issues contained in treaties and contemporary rights of citizenship from both Native and non-Native perceptions. This material would be more than appropriate for discussion in secondary education history classes to provide a legitimate venue for Native students to be involved in the dialogue.

If we truly believe in the concept of an educated populace that can make good decisions benefiting the democracy as a whole, we need to work with our students to develop the critical thinking skills necessary to become informed about issues that affect them now and in the future. We can find the necessary resources to present Indigenous viewpoints through journals such as *Native Peoples Magazine, Winds of Change,* and *Native Americas,* which are devoted to exploring these issues. By inviting tribal members to present their views on issues to our classes, we are providing both culturally and socially mediated instruction for our students. In addition, there are many Native writers, like Simon Ortiz, whose work explores political issues through the use of poetry. Poetry is reflected in the creation of lyrics for songs; hence, it is not a stretch to see the value of encouraging Native students to use the poetic art in their written expressions.

There are several ways that learning may be structured to maximize students' talents, including constructivist approaches and special-emphasis whole-school approaches that change the dynamics within faculty and school populations. Both of these are explored below, and some schools have successfully combined elements of each as a way of meeting the needs of their diverse student bodies.

Constructivist Approaches

When we speak of constructivist approaches to teaching and learning, we mean those approaches that require active participation on the part of students to develop their cognitive skills (Marlow & Page, 1998). The Progressive Education Movement as defined by John Dewey (1902) is an excellent example of this type of learning, which is also called discovery or experiential learning. A key feature of this type of learning is emphasis on the inclusion of as many firsthand or simulated experiences as possible, using a holistic approach that integrates knowledge across content areas. This type of learning is culturally congruent for Native American students of all ages. Experiential learning in Native traditions allows children to develop at their own pace; involves the community; provides instruction through listening, observing, and doing; offers opportunities for children to learn in peer groups; and utilizes games and other activities to develop new concepts and skills (Cajete, 1994; Hall, 1996).

Examples of constructivist models of teaching and learning. The "Alaska Standards for Culturally Responsive Schools" document was released in 1998. This document is seen as a model for successful educational programming for schools serving Native students (Fox, 2000). The document cites the critical roles that culture, language, parents, grandparents, and community members play in the educational lives of Indigenous students and provides guidance for incorporation of language and culture in educational settings.

Brown (2000) incorporated these standards in developing his curriculum for teaching Athabascan students in Alaska. Brown teamed with the bilingual teacher, who was an Athabascan elder, the shop teacher, and the home economics teacher to transform the English/language arts curriculum into an active learning experience for his students. In the process, students learned how to make miniature dog sleds and set up brush camps. They were involved in reading traditional stories, recording information, and writing about their experiences. Students who previously had experienced difficulty with traditional passive curricula blossomed through this type of curriculum. This approach requires that teachers view students as having ownership of their learning. Teachers who choose to be learning guides, rather than taking the position of directing all learning experiences, may be more readily able to adopt this type of learning (Squires, 2001), which is practiced in many traditional Native communities.

The Ga-GEMS (Georgia's Project for Gifted Education in Math and Science) program provides a model that offers integrated, hands-on experiences that promote higher level thinking skills and real-life laboratory experiences with math and science curricula for students (Tyler-Wood, Mortenson, Putney, & Cass, 2000). Achievement scores of students who participated in this program showed greater results than those of gifted students in a control group. Development of a similar program involving regional resources located close to many Native communities, such as universities and national energy laboratories, might offer potentials for American Indian students in both rural and urban settings. The use of technology to connect schools and resources may prove beneficial for communities located in isolated regions of the country.

A comparable type of program for challenging gifted and talented students while not singling them out is the Schoolwide Enrichment Model (SEM; Gibson & Effinger, 2001; Renzulli & Reis, 1997). This program consists of using strategies to integrate higher order thinking skills, processing, and advanced experiences into the curricula. Included are hands-on learning, firsthand investigations, and the application of knowledge to solve problems. One of the advantages of this approach is that it can be integrated into all content areas.

Community-based service learning projects are being promoted in schools for all grade levels across the country (Claus & Ogden, 1999). Through this approach, students are taught responsibilities regarding their communities by identifying problem areas that need attention and finding solutions. Throughout this process, students are taught such values as caring for the environment, caring for people in their communities, and positive ways of contributing to the overall good—again, all characteristics of culturally responsive teaching for Indigenous students.

Service-learning projects are a good way to integrate science, mathematics, social science, and literacy skills across the curriculum as they are mobilized for real-world purposes, such as exploring problems, developing goals, and creating action-plans to achieve goals. It is exciting to see that schools promoting service-learning projects are having real impacts in the lives of students and communities; examples include Native secondary students actively involved with replenishing salmon runs (Galindo & Reinhart, 1999) and reestablishing beaver habitats (Nez Perce Tribe, 2002). These activities can lead directly to students' choosing career paths to pursue following graduation from school.

Special Emphasis Whole-School Approaches

Magnet school concept. Following the Civil Rights Movement in the 1960s and '70s, many urban school districts began to develop magnet schools as a way to desegregate schools, as well as to attract students from suburban areas into core city areas and vice versa. Magnet schools are developed with emphases on particular types of knowledge, such as languages or the arts. Within these schools, students are given special opportunities they would not otherwise have to develop their abilities. Pewewardy and Bushey (1992) described how this concept was developed for an urban American Indian magnet school located in St. Paul, MN. A public school that is open to all students who apply, this school focuses on connecting students with Native cultural roots, traditions, practices, mores, ways of knowing, and histories while providing a school "family" within which to succeed.

Corwin (2000) found that gifted urban students were able to excel in magnet schools created especially for their needs. In this way, they were exposed to many areas relating to curricula in ways their peers attending regular public school were not. They had more opportunities to interact with experts in fields of study, visit museums, and be exposed to advanced study materials. In this type of situation, students are interacting with other bright students; therefore, they may not be as reluctant to share ideas or participate in activities where the expectation levels are high for all.

Technologically based programs. It is pedagogically sound for teachers to incorporate computer technology and other forms of technology in gifted and talented education programs for Native students. "Four Directions: An Indigenous Model" resulted from a grant awarded by the U.S. Department of Education's Technology Innovation Challenge Grants Program (Valdez & Waseta, 2000). It began in 1995 with nine Bureau of Indian Affairs (BIA) schools. By the end of the program, it had expanded to 19 schools in 10 states and provided excellent teaching and learning opportunities for all involved. Many products related to Indigenous education were created and put on a Web site. Students involved learned technology skills and made use of them for research and educating others about their cultures.

Mentorship programs. Various types of mentorship programs have met with success for gifted students. The idea of setting up mentoring relationships with other American Indians who are operating in various fields or who are teaching at colleges and universities is appealing. The American Indian Students in Science (AISIS) Association is one example of bringing Native students and those in the sciences together. Caution must be taken, though, in any program where the assigning of mentors for Indigenous students is done on a random basis. There are many differences within and between tribal Nations that could potentially lead to failure of any such program if considerations are not made for these factors. While pairing a mentor and mentee from two different tribal Nations who were traditional enemies may not be a difficulty for assimilated American Indians, for those who are bicultural and traditional, especially those who are living on or near reservations, this may prove to be a tremendous obstacle. Therefore, input from students' families concerning their children's involvement in such programs is an absolute priority.

School Retention Rates

While we are concerned with humanistic goals of developing students as whole persons who can take their places in the world following their educational experiences, we often overlook the results of the "sorting systems" in schools that force many to opt out of the educational process. Congress passed the School Dropout Prevention and Basic Skills Act in 1990 to address this problem. While dropout rates vary from tribal Nation to Nation, the overall rates for American Indian reservation communities range from 40 to 60%, while the overall percentage of Aboriginals, including urban Indians, failing to complete high school graduation in 1992 was 25.4% (St. Germaine, 1995). We can only assume that some of the Native students who are leaving schools before high school graduation are also gifted and talented individuals.

Materialism and Native Cultures

The tensions created between Native traditional expectations and those of the dominant culture were particularly evident in the 1960s and '70s, when materialism was an indication that one had succeeded in the larger community. According to Alfred (2002), in Northwest coastal communities the emphasis on getting jobs, making money, and buying large houses overwhelmed the need to continue many cultural practices. The mythology of American Indian students as not being equal to their Euro-American peers contributed to the lack of recognition of the rich cultural traditions Native students brought with them into educational settings. Consequently, many students arrived in school devoid of cultural knowledge.

Alfred (2002) proposed a system of education that encourages the coexistence of cultural frameworks. Embedded in native wisdom are many of the solutions to problems that plague our world today, and tapping into these resources through pedagogy that encourages contributions from Native cultural teachings provides a way for students to thrive in their home and school environments. These students, then, have the potential to bring into their places of employment and leadership roles greater insights into how to "reconstruct a just and harmonious world" (p. 19).

Keeping Students in Schools

Being identified gifted and talented and being provided programming does not guarantee that gifted Indigenous students will be highly productive in their future lives outside of schools. In fact, for every positive characteristic of giftedness, there is a negative correlation: Students who are goal-directed and task-committed may be very stubborn and recalcitrant, refusing to change directions when asked to do so; having a good memory and being able to analyze and synthesize information quickly may lead to boredom in the classroom and an unwillingness to participate in routine classroom assignments; having a questioning attitude may lead to problems in peer relationships as students are viewed as being different from others

(McCluskey & Walker, 1986). Gifted and talented students may also use their gifts for pursuits that would be considered antisocial in schools and communities.

It is important that teachers of gifted and talented Native American students enrich their students' learning by moving them from teacher-directed to student-directed learning (McCluskey & Walker, 1986). In doing so, we are also following culturally relevant pedagogy, guiding students in their pursuits of knowledge, rather than parceling out knowledge through the transmission model. By working with tribal members, we can develop programs that require active participation in more meaningful cultural pursuits that will be beneficial for all our students.

Conclusions and Recommendations

Nurturing the intellect takes place over a prolonged period of time and is not necessarily fulfilled with a simple focus on more academic rigor. During the modern period, focus on uniformity of schools and the use of the factory model for sorting students into different tracks was considered acceptable, as education was the way toward adult productivity in the marketplace. In our present postmodern period, we are more aware of diversity not only in languages and cultures, but in the talents our students bring with them into the classroom, whether they are recognizable through standardized assessment measures or not. We are also able to admit that we don't have all the answers and that we need partnerships with parents, extended family members, and communities in order to meet the needs of all students attending our schools (Fetterman, 1988). For gifted and talented American Indian students who are bicultural or traditional in their orientations, this need is especially significant.

Schools that embrace this ideal respect the students and communities with which they are associated. They also try to make education an experience that is not just beneficial to individual students, but also for the future growth and development of Native communities. Such communities are well aware of the needs they have, and the promised expectations of meeting those needs from within are real on many reservations. Because schools have been seen as taking away from, rather than adding enrichment to, community life, there may be initial resistance to any efforts on the part of the school to reach out to communities. However, once community members understand that there is a place for them in schools and that their voices are wanted and respected, changes in relationships between the two may take place.

Fetterman (1988) cautioned us against trying to find one program that will meet the needs of all gifted and talented individuals. As he stated, "The idea of a single program belies the fundamental tenet of gifted education—to serve the individual needs of the student" (pp. 29–30). As we explore different types of programs, we must also bear in mind that gifted education is education that is good for all students, not just those who demonstrate specific talents (McCluskey & Walker, 1986).

The use of constructivist teaching and learning approaches emphasizing active participation on the part of students is greatly needed in schools (Glasser, 1998), especially for American Indian students. Incorporating the arts within these programs involves multiple intelligences in learning and reinforces cultural values. Most of all, Native American students who are traditional and bicultural must feel supported in their efforts by families, extended families, and communities, especially in light of inter- and intratribal oppressions. Those who are assimilated (or "progressives") are not immune to criticisms emanating from their communities, and we must be sensitive to these issues.

Where From Here?

There have been tremendous injustices perpetrated on American Indian tribal Nations and their peoples in the many attempts to assimilate them into Western European ways of knowing, thinking, and living. There is a need for healing between those who represent the government's acculturation efforts through schools and the students and communities they serve. It is only in this way that recognition of Native students as bright, capable, and holding the potential for making our world a better one will be acknowledged.

In my speaking with members of tribal Nations, they stated repeatedly that education was important for their children and the economic success of their tribal Nations (Klug & Whitfield, 2003). They believed the type of education needed should be built upon tribal knowledge, teachings, and methods of teaching and learning for Native children. By incorporating this advice and offering programs for students that will allow their academic and other talents to emerge, we can have alternatives for traditional and bicultural American Indian students that allow them to grow, develop, and use their gifts for the benefit of their tribal Nations. Assimilated students and those attending public schools off reservations face the challenges of overcoming negative stereotypes and prejudices concerning the connotations of "Indianness."

Education for Gifted and Talented Indigenous Students in the 21st Century

It is imperative that American Indian students perceive reasons for staying in school and completing their education. These reasons may be for economic advancement, opening doors to opportunities for assimilated students, or enhancement of the tribal Nation as a whole in traditional communities. However approached, the decision to obtain an education is crucial. In order to complete this aspiration, students need the support of their families and communities. By creating caring communities and providing culturally relevant pedagogy, schools become part of the process enabling American Indian students to realize their potential.

As educators, we are automatically embroiled in the political forces that exert their power over public schooling. Antagonisms between politically conservative groups and progressive groups promoting more local control over education to reflect the diversity of languages, cultures, and ethnic groups are seen in most areas of the country today. These struggles have extended into schools and center on issues of teaching, learning, curriculum development, approval of textbooks and other materials utilized in teaching, and arguments for centralization or decentralization of power. As teachers, we need to be able to fight for what we know are best practices that help all of our students to succeed.

For too long, the talents of Native students have been neglected, and, as a result, they have suffered the resulting effects of discrimination and lack of economic opportunities. We hope to rectify this situation, knowing that our respect for all translates into opportunities for all. In turn, we are creating a healthier and more just society in which we work together to solve the problems we face. Only then may we enjoy the liberties promised to all of us as citizens of this country.

5

The Affective Dimension of Second Culture/Second Language Acquisition in Gifted Adolescents

by Judith A. Rance-Roney

At the age of 8, coming to the United States felt like falling into an enormous river without any swimming skills. After struggling, dog paddling, and consuming large amounts of water on the way, I learned to keep myself buoyant and steadily gained experience. Cultural and language adjustment was not a choice; it was a survival need.

—A gifted student from Vietnam

While hundreds of thousands of adolescents cross the boundaries of language and culture each year as they enroll for the first time in American schools, little attention has been given to the special needs and affective issues surrounding the translingual and trans-cultural experience of the gifted as they acculturate into their new communities.

The issues most often explored in the area of gifted education for the culturally and linguistically diverse (CLD) have focused on (1) the challenges faced in the identification of CLD students who are gifted, (2) federal and state policies addressing CLD gifted students, (3) effective curricular models and staffing for such programs, and (4) the unique cognitive and creative development of these students. Little research, however, has emerged on the affective needs and affective changes that occur with gifted adolescents during the acquisition of a second language and second culture, especially during the months and years following initiation of education in a culture different from that of childhood.

According to Kloosterman (1997), there is insufficient information to describe the socio-emotional and cognitive characteristics of this target group.

Who are these students? The majority of secondary English language learners (ELLs) are "foreign-born immigrants with a variety of educational experiences ranging from no formal schooling to grade-level equivalence" (Faltis, 1993, p. 93). The study of English may be as a second language, but it may also be the third or even fourth language acquired since acquisition of the mother tongue. While many of these new immigrants arrive with some knowledge of the English language, most are unable to compete on an equal footing with their English-speaking peers in the secondary or postsecondary educational environment because of a lack of academic literacy.

There is no unitary description that may address their cultural backgrounds. An ELL may have arrived after a childhood wholly lived in one foreign country or, instead, may be a member of an increasingly significant group of global nomads, children who have lived in multiple countries. An ELL, too, may be a member of an indigenous culture whose life has been lived within U.S. borders, but who shares many characteristics with the foreign-born.

Within this group of culturally and linguistically different adolescents, it is expected that the occurrence of giftedness in the population should parallel the membership of giftedness in the majority native-speaking culture. Yet, Castellano and Diaz (2002) have asserted that "these students are still dramatically underidentified and underserved in gifted and talented programs" (p. xviii), with perhaps only 5% of those eligible ELLs receiving special services for the gifted (Cohen, 1990, p. 1).

One of the areas of significant neglect is the discussion of the psycho-social changes that the CLD gifted adolescent faces in the acquisition of a second (or additional) language and in the process of acculturation. The focus of this chapter, then, is to explore the affective states and needs of these multiply exceptional adolescents.

Profiles of Gifted Second Language Students

For the gifted young adolescent arriving in the United States for the first time, we see America as a land in which opportunities are expansive and in which individual voices are recognized and honored. Yet, little has been written about the loneliness and frustration that occurs from being thousands of miles from homeland and countrymates, suddenly deprived of the basic knowledge of language and culture.

In their home cultures, these learners may have been enrolled in "key" or top high schools, and their value within their family structure may have been disproportionately linked to academic or creative prowess acquired in their first language and first culture. In choosing to come to the U.S., families may have sought out the educational opportunities for their gifted children in the American school system.

Yet, for many, those first interactions may lead to frustration and resistance as they encounter the American educational philosophy of egalitarianism, in which education of the majority is a priority above the education of the exceptionally gifted.

For the parent of the adolescent first encountering the typical American school system, perhaps hampered by difficulties communicating in English and with a limited knowledge of the structure of the system, the registration of an adolescent into a middle or high school can be especially frustrating. As one parent reported, "We weren't taken seriously, but we know our son."

Decisions on course placement and entry into gifted and talented programs may be based more on stereotyped attitudes than on actual potential or achievement. Students may be judged on English ability alone, not on academic potential. They may be labeled LEP (Limited English Proficient), categorized according to perceived disabilities, rather than abilities. "School personnel frequently view language differences as deficits that disable students rather than as strengths that empower them" (Robisheaux, 2002, p. 135). One father lamented that the district wanted to start his intellectually precocious son one grade behind in a suburban high school even though the young man had been doing college-level work in his European key high school. "Too often these students are slated automatically for low tracks or general courses because their limited English language skills fuel a perception that they are less intelligent or able (U.S. Department of Education, 1998, Talents, Schooling, and English Language Learners section, para. 9).

To exacerbate the problem, ways of learning or the learning styles of these adolescents may differ radically from the styles fostered within the U.S. culture. According to Robisheaux (2002), "Different learning styles, which are influenced by the home culture, may contribute to the underrepresentation of minority-language students with high potential" (p. 164). For example, the role of memorization has been deemphasized in the U.S. educational context in past decades and greater emphasis has been placed on individual creativity and analysis. In other countries, giftedness is often synonymous with the ability to remember large amounts of "expert-produced" information, with individual analysis in the lesser role. This means that gifted CLD students from some cultures may be fully competent in the subject matter, but may seem reticent in collaborative group work, may have difficulty producing individually creative work such as personal writing, and may not engage in classroom discussions without first having a complete grasp of the facts of the discussion.

The CLD adolescent, of course, will also be facing limitations in communicative competence, both in interpersonal contexts and in academic tasks. While general language competence for basic everyday functions may develop quite rapidly, full competence in academic linguistic interactions may require 6 to 8 years of academic experience in the new language (Collier, 1987, p. 617). For adolescents whose self-esteem revolves around self-worth estimations in the academic domain, the temporary inability to excel in school may be emotionally damaging. Yet, for many gifted adolescents, it is the difficulty of language in peer interaction that may be most damaging emotionally. As one student remarked,

I felt left out because of my inability to communicate. I remembered some kids assumed that I did not understand them, so they made rude remarks about my cultural background. I comprehended them, maybe not from tip to toe, but I knew the purpose of their message. I wanted to go back to Vietnam and do things freely, speak clearly, and be accepted.

As time passes, an individual who joins a culture different from his or her home culture will undergo a process of *acculturation* far different from the *enculturation* that took place in the first language and first culture (Saville-Troike, 1996). Second language and culture learning will always entail adaptation, and "few of these second language learners are likely to become full-fledged members of the second language speech community, at least if all of the shared language use and interpretation criteria determining speech community membership are applied" (p. 359). Acculturation increases over time, but an individual does not necessarily forfeit home language or culture, but instead enters a space of permanent interstitiality. In fact, it will be that acceptance of interstitiality that may mark the final step out of culture shock.

Initial Stages of Acculturation: Culture Shock

"Emotional sensitivity and emotional intensity are often cited as distinguishing most gifted children, and especially the highly gifted" (Piechowski, 1997, p. 366). Imagine, then, a gifted adolescent leaving behind the culture, language, and familiar patterns of life for an unfamiliar life in a country far different from his or her home, facing challenges of language, to be sure, but also having to adapt to and later adopt new ways of seeing and doing. The resulting syndrome, labeled "culture shock,"

> is thought to be a form of anxiety that results from the loss of commonly perceived and understood signs and symbols of social intercourse . . . in behavioral terms, of a basic underlying insecurity which may encompass loneliness, anger, frustration, and self-questioning of competence. (Peter Adler, as cited in Brown, 1994, p. 171)

For the highly sensitive gifted CLD adolescent, the effect of culture shock may be especially severe. And, while culture shock is most often thought of as a transitory phenomenon, something that the adolescent will eventually "get over," most agree that the effects of the culture shift, or more likely the straddling of cultures, will have long-term consequences.

Four stages of culture shock are generally recognized: first, the novelty stage, which is filled with awe and excitement; second, the shock stage, when the individual is assaulted with the divide between the first and second cultures; third, the recovery stage, as the individual begins to sort out and face the issues; and fourth, the assimilation or adaptation stage, with an "acceptance of the new culture and self-confidence in the 'new' person that has developed" (Brown, 1986, p. 36).

In the first stage, some individuals experience a sense of enchantment and excitement when meeting the second culture, but "see" it through the lenses of the first. For others, especially for the perceptive gifted adolescent who has little tolerance for ambiguity and a need for familiar patterns, anger and depression from the culture shock may be almost immediate. Brown (1994) has likened culture shock to

> phenomena ranging from mild irritability to deep psychological panic and crisis . . . associated with feelings of estrangement, anger, hostility, indecision, frustration, unhappiness, sadness, loneliness, homesickness, and even physical illness. (p. 170)

As one young émigré from South America lamented,

> I realized what a mess I was in. I was alone in a different country and culture where my parents and their reputation no longer protected me. . . . All of a sudden, my body lost all its strength; I could not breathe. . . . There I cried, desperately searching for a way to convince my parents to let me go home.

For the gifted adolescent, the effect of the keen intensity of emotion associated with the dislocation from the familiar may lead to a shutting down.

In addition to the immediate culture shock, Piechowski (1997) noted that children of high intellectual potential may experience overstimulation and overexcitability as a result of greater sensitivity to differences, comparisons, novel experiences, and feelings (p. 367). For the CDL adolescent, the first exposure to the new culture may, indeed, turn into excitability and may result in "cultural fatigue." The adolescent may self-isolate or sleep more in an effort to escape the newness of the smells, sights, and feelings of the novel culture and may seek to suspend, at least for a time, the energy demands required to attend to those stimuli that do not fit into the familiar patterns of existence.

In the second stage, the individual begins to recognize cultural dissonance and question his or her own cultural values and patterns in relation to the new culture. The gifted are more apt to notice the similarities and differences in the patterns of environmental stimuli (Daniels, 1997, p. 297) and may also have "difficulty adjusting to new environments" (Piechowski, 1997, p. 369). In this second stage, the gifted adolescent may "feel the intrusion of more and more cultural differences into his or her own image of self and security" (Brown, 1986, p. 36). As one young man from Mexico stated,

> The first month flew by like the wind, for the excitement of change blinded my eyes with awe and wonderful expectations. Yet, the second

month was torture. I had not met the friends I expected, I had no family to return to every night, no magic places to run away to on weekends, and no enchiladas nor *tacos al pastor* to remind me of a traditional Mexican meal.

Thus, in this stage, it is typical that the sensitive individual seeks the security of the first culture and of countrymen, perhaps even labeling the second culture as stupid, inefficient, cold, or crazy. This transitory backsliding into the familiar culture is not a failure to acculturate, but a normal and predicable stage of the process.

The third stage signals the truce in the conflict. Individuals begin to accept the contrasts in culture, losing the judgmental demeanor of the previous stage. For the gifted CLD adolescent, this period may mark intense and satisfying personal growth as he or she begins to form empathic relationships with members of the second culture and reassesses the formerly hidden patterns, values, and assumptions of the home/first culture. In looking back, one young woman from China related,

Being a student with a cross-cultural experience has enriched my vision. I felt like I had spent time out of my comfort zone. I experienced the forces that shape any society—religious, economic, social, artistic, geographic, historic—and reflected on similarities and differences with my own culture.

The fourth and final stage represents the lifelong process of acculturation and formation of a new interstitial identity. While many may view the outcome of acculturation as positive, for the CLD gifted adolescent, the awareness of the straddling of cultures is, at times, fraught with insecurity and questioning. According to Brown (1986), acculturation may entail "a feeling of homelessness, where one feels neither bound firmly to his native culture nor fully adapted to the second culture" (p. 37). Acculturation, too, may entail guilt and loss in that the culture of family, home, and memories will be, to some extent, left behind as the new language and new culture take up increasing space in life and identity. Yet, as McCaig (2002) noted, "This place in between, then, can be anywhere from confusion, chaotic, and paralyzing (encapsulated) to powerfully and positively dynamic" (p. 16).

Acculturation: Second Language Acquisition and First Language Loss

Most young gifted adolescent second language learners move through the process of acquiring a second language fairly rapidly relative to their peers. But, with some gifted adolescents, several factors may either accelerate or inhibit the rate of language acquisition.

One of the issues in the forefront of adolescent second language/second culture acquisition is the theoretical assumption that there exists a critical period in human development during which the learning of a new language is optimized. It is generally assumed that children learn languages more rapidly and completely than adults, with adolescents falling somewhere in the middle of the continuum. Yet, according to Marinova-Todd, Marshall, and Snow (2000), the neurobiological evidence of an age effect in second language learning is not as compelling as is generally believed. Factors such as environment and motivation play an equally significant role in achieving proficiency in the second language.

The desire of CLD adolescents to join peer groups and to become accepted members of the new culture leads to a focus on the acquisition of language for social interaction. The gaining of communicative competence in social settings, or the acquisition of what Cummins (2000) labeled BICS (basic interpersonal communicative skills), takes the forefront in most adolescent language learning. Proficiency in BICS means that the gifted ELL can manipulate the immediate environment to gain some control in the new setting, but also to gain membership in peer groups. According to Brown (1994),

> language learning and teaching are recognized as personal encounters. The affective domain has taken on primary importance as we recognize in human communication the building of interpersonal relationships through social interchange . . . intrinsically driven by their own personal need to gain competence. (p. 291)

As one gifted young man remarked, "I just wanted to fit in. Classes took a back seat to learning the language and what was happening around me."

Teachers and others who observe the gifted ELL may assume that, because of obvious proficiency in interpersonal communication, he or she will also be fully competent in the use of English in academic tasks. But, as Cummins (2000) has emphasized, while competence in BICS may be achieved within a 2-year span, competence in the decontextualized and abstract language of academic study may be far more difficult to acquire, taking from 3 to 5 years to reach sufficient proficiency. Cummins labeled this type of language CALP (cognitive academic language proficiency). For the perfectionistic gifted adolescent, this discrepancy between proficiency in more easily acquired social language stands in contrast to a greater difficulty in reading or producing academic written text, which may lead to a great sense of frustration. The motivation to acquire the new language is explored in two theoretical perspectives in the field of second language acquisition: Krashen's (1982) model of the affective filter and Brown's (1986) model of a critical period for language learning.

In Krashen's (1982) affective filter hypothesis, two conditions must be met in order for effective language learning to take place: (1) the language the individual hears or reads must be comprehensible, level-appropriate, and organized; and (2) the learner must be motivated to learn, must believe that he or she can learn, and must learn in an environment of low or moderate anxiety. One would expect that the emotional filter of the gifted adolescent attempting to fit into a peer group and coping with the frustration of academics in a new language might cause the student to exhibit high anxiety in both social and academic settings. However, there is evidence from interviews that taking on a new "disguising identity" may help the adolescent through this period. One methodology of language teaching, Lozanov's Suggestopedia, actually capitalizes on this concept in addition to using relaxation strategies. In Suggestopedia, learners assume a new identity, personality, and personal history so that they are "unencumbered" in learning a new language (Hadley, 2001, p. 127). However, this disguise may not always lead to an unencumbered identity; as one young woman from Taiwan mused, "I was gregarious and thrill-seeking in Chinese, but I am law-abiding and demure in English."

Brown (1986) theorized that there is a critical period for second language acquisition that exists independent of the age of the learner, an optimum period in the acculturation process for language learning to occur. According to Brown, a language learner can be neither too emotionally distant nor too closely comfortable with his or her new culture in order to engage in maximum language learning. In terms of culture shock, this would occur in the third stage, when the individual acknowledges cultural conflict, but has not yet become a member of that culture. This denotes a state of emotional disequilibrium, but without the intense trauma of the second stage. For the CLD gifted adolescent, this period can represent a period of rapid language growth, far in excess of the nongifted. The gifted adolescent's effective problem solving, ability to abstract hidden linguistic rules, and quest to learn the culture will drive intense language acquisition.

The gifted adolescent may, in fact, extend the time spent in optimal language learning because of a proclivity to perceive and question the socio-cultural and linguistic differences between first and second cultures. In the process of second language learning, he or she is faced squarely with conflicts in cultural values. For example, an awareness of cultural difference may emerge from the discovery of differing linguistic categories. In Czech, the personal pronoun *ty* is used for a young child before the age of puberty, a longstanding social acquaintance, or a closely related individual. In contrast, the pronoun *vy* is used for a stranger, a casual acquaintance, or a person deserving of respect (Salzmann, 1993). As one Czech student observed, the Czech language operates with nuances and "little twists in words," while English is focused, simplistic, and direct, a metaphor, in his opinion, for each culture, as well.

Even the idiomatic expressions Americans use in friendly conversation may signal the distance between cultures. A young student from Mexico questioned "the cold and meaningless 'What's up?'" used by American peers: "'What's up?' they would tell me without even looking me in the eye, as if it was just some automatic greeting programmed in an ATM machine or an arcade video game." Althen (1988) explained this apparent "superficial friendliness" as the difference Americans perceive between friendliness and friendship: "While most Americans seem relatively warm and approachable upon first encounter, they later come to seem to many foreign visitors as remote and unreachable" (p. 78).

Finally, learning and living a second language may mean erosion and loss of the first. While children who enter the second culture and school system as young children may exhibit significant loss, some adolescents also report erosion very soon after leaving their first-language environment (Wong-Fillmore, 1991). As one Bolivian teenager lamented, "I looked up at the sky one clear night. My friend asked me how you say *star* in Spanish. At that moment I couldn't remember. The word wasn't there. I became very sad for what I had lost." The slippery slope of language loss remains a significant issue until adult-like interpersonal language and secondary academic language proficiencies have been firmly established in the first language and culture.

The effects on the family must be considered, as well. Pressure to assimilate quickly into the new dominant culture can "lead to a profound disconnect between home and life in the outside world for LEP students" (U.S. Department of Education, 1998, Talents, Schooling, and English Language Learners section, para. 6). When an adolescent becomes proficient in the second language, but the parents do not, the adolescent frequently takes on the role of family caretaker and spokesperson, changing (and, in many cases, damaging) traditional family dynamics. Adolescents may use their superior ability to speak the second language not just as a tool, but as a weapon against the parents. But further, as Wong-Fillmore (1991) has asserted,

> What is lost is not less than the means by which parents socialize their children. When parents are unable to talk to their children, they cannot easily convey to them their values, beliefs, understandings, or wisdom . . . rifts develop, and families lose the intimacy that comes from shared beliefs and understandings. (343)

Acculturation and Identity

Developmentally, adolescence is a period in which the search for identity is at the forefront. The response to "Who am I?" may be problematic for gifted adolescents as they search for ways to slip quietly into peer groups, cloaking their exceptionality. During this time, the adolescent may experiment with different identities, observing significant others and the surrounding culture for affirmation of the desired effect. Gross (1998) believed that camouflaging one's real identity to conform to peer group norms can push a gifted adolescent to create a public image of mediocrity and to deny giftedness: "Highly gifted adolescents or adults who spend much of their lives concealing their true abilities and interests behind a protective mask risk losing touch with their innermost feelings and beliefs" (p. 6) and, at some point, will likely question who they really are underneath.

For the CLD adolescent, the achievement of a cohesive identity may be delayed because of the transcultural and translingual experience and the multiplicity of identity facets that must merge (Harris, 1993, p. 2). Indeed, a second camouflage may need to be donned as he or she aspires to look and talk like an American and, at least for a time, deny cultural heritage. Banks and Banks (1996, p. 68) labeled this transcultural identity formation stage "ethnic psychological captivity," a stage in which an individual strives to integrate into the dominant culture. Gifted adolescents are often successful at disguise, quickly assuming a second culture identity, but not without cost: "This inner conflict takes up a tremendous amount of emotional energy" (Vandrick, 1997, p. 154). As one young man from South America wrote,

> My cross-cultural experience was all about finding my identity. Thousands of questions started flying through my mind about who and what I was. I began to evaluate every small detail in my life. Was I really a good person? Was I really as tough as I thought I was? To be able to assimilate into this foreign culture, I had to reestablish my identity.

The acquisition of the language of the new culture is closely intertwined with the changing identity of the adolescent, for it is through the language of social interchange and the language of the classroom that an individual is led to continued renegotiation of the self.

Brown (1994, p. 62) explored the role of ego as a factor in the success of second language acquisition. For the child, the ego is flexible and able to tolerate risks in attempting to communicate in the second language. But, for the adolescent or adult who has grown secure in his or her identity within the first culture, the risk situation in the new culture may give way to inhibition and defensiveness. Further, for the adolescent or adult to risk the censure of native speakers if a message is misunderstood or miscommunicated, there must be a sense of value or payoff in order for the learner to invest him- or herself in a risky situation. As Peirce (1995) has contended,

> [W]hen language learners speak, they are not only exchanging information with target language speakers, but they are constantly organizing and reorganizing a sense of who they are and how they relate to the social world. Thus, an investment in the target language is also an investment in a learner's own social identity, an identity which is constantly changing across time and space. (p. 18)

Reforming an identity in the American cultural context may also necessitate the examination of the basic assumptions and values underlying the first culture in contrast to the second. By logical extension, in the reformation of identity, the individual must judge the "rightness" of a value before deciding whether or not to inculcate that value into the changed identity. Those basic assumptions and values may include the role and importance of family, male-female relationships, individualism vs. community action, religious beliefs, and even ways of reasoning (Althen, 1988). The external image one portrays, however, may be a function of the social and cultural setting and may be very different from what the individual feels is his or her true self.

For the CLD adolescent, the process of reforming an identity to better conform to the second culture may be a double-edged sword. As the individual meets success in integrating into the second culture, there is an increasing danger of losing affirmation from peers of the first culture who have not yet integrated or have chosen not to integrate. As a young woman from Pakistan commented,

> I encountered prejudice from my own race. I was surprised when I was called a "coconut" (a slang term used for people who are hypocrites in that they are dark on the outside, but white on the inside, just like a coconut) by the Asians. . . . Just because I developed close friendships with American students and did not limit the circle of my close friends to the people of my own culture, I have been criticized heavily. Very often, I have been accused of discarding my heritage and my moral values.

Other issues of identity are salient to the gifted. In first interactions with American peers, many gifted CLD adolescents experience stereotyping based on first-culture stereotypical attributes. For Asians, stereotyping may categorize the individual based on the "myth of the model minority . . . model citizens who perform exceptionally well without any need for academic or socio-emotional guidance" (Plucker, 1996, p. 89). However, there is little evidence that these adolescents need any more or less guidance than others. Negative stereotyping can inflict even more damage. According to Castellano and Diaz (2002), many more culturally and linguistically diverse learners experience institutional racism, discrimination, and lack of interest from the educational system and are perceived by teachers as underachievers (pp. xviii–xix).

Further, well-meaning professionals in the field of second language education may also unknowingly damage the academic self-esteem of gifted CLD adolescents by lowering expectations for achievement because of the difficult challenge of learning within a second language.

> Rather than establishing a demanding, yet nurturant, environment for Limited English Proficient students, they may find themselves so sympathetic with the economic plight or English language difficulties their students experience that they soften their expectations. (U.S. Department of Education, 1998, Talents, Schooling, and English Language Learners section, para. 10)

Yet, teachers of these adolescents can have a positive impact. When a gifted CLD learner is provided a safe space in the classroom to explore his or her transcultural and translingual self, there will emerge profound insight that could not have been achieved by remaining safely in one culture alone.

Late in the process of the CLD adolescent's second culture acquisition, Acton and Walker de Felix (1986) hypothesized that he or she may experience a second culture shock with the realization that the majority of individuals never reach full native competence in a second culture because of the inability to comprehend all cultural, social, and linguistic nuances of the new culture (p. 21). In effect, the learner will stay in a "permanent immigrant state." As one young woman from Taiwan stated, "I have become American in the sense I speak the language and wear the clothes, but I realize I will never truly be American because of my Asian ideas."

Although much of the literature on identity formation discusses the choice between one identity and another, this binarization can be critically damaging to individuals who either live between the boundaries of culture or who yearn to retain their mother culture and language while they acculturate to the second. Whether new immigrants "go native" by adopting the clothing, behaviors, and attitudes of the new culture in order to gain short-term peer acceptance or retreat to the safety of their first culture, each stance entails a judgment of the value of a culture. It is when the individual learns to suspend that biased judgment that eyes open to a range of possibilities. As one gifted young woman from Asia noted,

> The hardest thing for me [when first coming to the U.S.] was judging people. However, I soon figured that judging people the instant you meet them is not essential. As a result, I accepted people for who they were and what they believed in. And soon I discovered that all human beings are made of feelings and emotions and that race and culture have no bearing on the sentiments that one has. Our talents and our qualities exist regardless of ethnicity and race.

This increasing tolerance for ambiguity and the suspension of rigid judgments lead to the final stage of acculturation, the formation of an interstitial identity in which all of the cultures and languages acquired in a lifetime combine to form a unique individual identity. As O'Hearn (1998) wrote,

> Skin color and birth aren't accurate signifiers of identity. One and one don't necessarily add up to two. Cultural and racial amalgams create a third, wholly indistinguishable category where origin and home are indeterminate. (p. xiv)

Living in the interstitial state can lead to a sense of rootlessness and confusion. But, the gifted individual can capitalize on the in-betweenness and can "make a commitment to a value system honed from many contexts and an identity actively affirmed and based solidly on self as choice maker" (McCaig, 2002, p. 16). In this end stage, gifted adolescents grow in respect for all cultural difference, accept that values and choices are situated in cultural contexts, and celebrate the uniqueness of self. "If our understanding of race and culture can ripen and evolve, then new and immeasurable measurements about the uniqueness of our identities becomes possible" (O'Hearn, 1998, p. xiii).

In the view of one Asian adolescent, "I am the excellence of the two cultures combined into one. That's how I define myself."

Author Note

The student voices were collected by the author through interviews and public journal entries from 2001 through 2002.

6

Curriculum Compacting:
A Research-Based Differentiation Strategy for Culturally Diverse Talented Students

by Joseph S. Renzulli and Sally M. Reis

Tom Bernard, a fifth-grade teacher in an urban school, walked into the teachers' room, sank into the worn sofa in exhaustion and frustration, and started to speak without really caring who was listening: "I just don't know what to do with Miguel. He's so bright, and he finishes his math before everyone else, but he's started getting restless, and now he doesn't even want to do the assignments at all. He says he already knows this stuff and it's boring to have to do all of the problems. I know how he feels, and I've tried to have him help the other kids, but he's not really interested in doing that. It's the same in reading, but the others need so much help, and the state tests are coming up. I feel guilty because I know I'm not challenging Miguel, but I just don't know what to do."

Felice Castellano, another fifth-grade teacher, listened intently and replied, "I know exactly how you feel. Brandy, in my class, is the same way. She was zipping through her math so quickly that I decided to let her take the next few chapter tests. She sailed through them even though we haven't covered the material in class yet. I've accelerated her in math and she has some additional challenge now, but she's still able to do the accelerated work in less time than her peers. I've been talking with her about her interests, and I've found that she absolutely loves to read and her greatest passion is literature. I've been letting her read while my other students have been working on math, and she's really gotten into a book with excerpts from Shakespearean plays. So, I suggested to Brandy that she should try acting out a scene from one of the plays. She really likes *The Taming of the Shrew* and wants to do one of the scenes, but needs a Petruchio. Miguel is very dramatic. Maybe he'd like to work with her during the times that the others are working on things that he already knows and they can dramatize the scene."

*   *   *   *   *

These teachers face a common problem that can be addressed through the use of curriculum compacting, a strategy to differentiate for high-achieving and high-potential students (Renzulli & Smith, 1979; Reis, Burns, & Renzulli, 1992). Curriculum compacting can be used in all classrooms to help students who have proven mastery of material that must be covered by other students. "What do I do now?" is a refrain that causes frustration in many teachers and students, and it has been demonstrated that curriculum compacting is a successful intervention to keep high-potential students engaged.

The pressure to raise test scores permeates a teacher's day, especially in urban areas where many students underachieve due to repetition of content and the attention that must be given to students who are scoring below grade level or are unmotivated. In some urban schools, the most able academic students are at risk for becoming underachievers because of the lack of challenge they experience. Since the 1940s and 1950s, textbooks have been "dumbed down" by as much as two or three grades (Kirst, 1982), leaving material basic and predominantly on a factual level. This dumbing down can create problems for talented students, especially when a district adopts one textbook for all (Bernstein, 1985). Urban teachers are often told to use specific direct instruction programs or to depend on textbook instruction. To complicate the issue even further, budgetary restraints may result in outdated versions of these instructional materials that must be used longer than they should be.

Over the past decade, urban areas have been plagued with controversies over the nature of gifted programming because a disproportionately low number of culturally diverse children have been identified to participate in these programs; equity issues have been being raised by parents, journalists, and the Office of Civil Rights. Some parents of culturally diverse children are frustrated by the traditional identification strategies that often overlook their children, while others fight any attempt to change instruments or procedures, stating firmly that they do not want "watered down" identification or programming for their children.

Barriers for the participation of talented urban youth in gifted and enrichment programs and the rise of underachievement have been attributed to several factors, such as the use of definitions of giftedness that reflect middle-class majority culture, values, and perceptions (Frasier & Passow, 1994); standardized tests that do not reflect the exceptional abilities of minority children (Ford, 1994; Ford & Harris, 1990; Kitano & Kirby, 1986); and the effects of low socioeconomic status and differences in environmental opportunities that enhance intellectual achievement (Ford, 1996, Ford & Harris). Crocker (1987) has also found that social factors have been underestimated and that discrimination and low socioeconomic status have profound effects on the achievement of urban youths. High-ability students are frequently affected more severely, as their intellectual strength often goes hand in hand with emotional sensitivity and a sense of social justice (Neihart, Reis, Robinson, & Moon, 2001; Silverman, 1993), causing psychological impediments that Ford (1992) believes have a negative impact. In contrast to immigrant populations, many U.S.-born minorities consider obstacles to their achievement insurmountable. Thus, the key to change must be within the educational system (Ogbu, 1987).

A number of factors have been found that relate to success in talented urban students. These factors are true for all children, but even more imperative for the child who faces the societal obstacles posed by minority and low socioeconomic status. A study of talented students who either achieved or underachieved in an urban high school identified several factors that characterize high levels of achievement and success in school (Reis, Hébert, Diaz, Maxfield, & Ratley, 1995). Students who achieved (a) developed a belief in self and a vision of a hopeful future, (b) had relationships with supportive adults (e.g., teachers or parents) in their lives, (c) interacted regularly with high-achieving peers, (d) encountered intellectual challenge in honors or advanced classes, and (e) participated in extracurricular activities and opportunities to develop their talents. A study of 20 successful programs identified five strategies that can be used successfully with urban students: (a) high expectations for students, program, and staff; (b) personalized attention; (c) innovative structure and organization; (d) experiential learning opportunities; and (e) long-term support (James, Jurich, & Estes, 1999; Keith & Cool, 1992).

In the current climate of urban schools, teachers are expected to meet the needs of an increasingly diverse group of students in their classrooms. If advanced programs exist in urban areas, they are usually not available until middle school or high school, which may be too late for talented students who need, but do not receive, differentiated instruction. If their needs have not been previously met, they may already feel as if they have turned off to school and learning. Preventive intervention proves more effective than remedial, as the drop-out rate for urban teenagers includes many gifted students who have given up (James, Jurich, & Estes, 1999; Reis, Hébert, Diaz, Maxfield, & Ratley, 1995).

Strategies for Curricular and Instructional Differentiation

In order to accommodate for the simultaneous inclusion of diverse students and the increasing elimination of gifted programs in economically strapped urban areas, many school districts have adopted a variety of within-classroom strategies collectively referred to as "differentiated instruction." Differentiation is an attempt to address the variation of learners in the classroom through multiple approaches that modify instruction and curricula to match the individual needs of students (Tomlinson, 2000). Tomlinson (1995) emphasized that, when teachers differentiate the curriculum, they stop acting as dispensers of knowledge and instead serve as organizers of learning opportunities. Differentiation of instruction and curricula suggests that students can be provided with materials and work of varied levels of difficulty with scaffolding, diverse kinds of grouping, and different time schedules (Tomlinson, 2000).

Renzulli (1977, 1988; Renzulli & Reis, 1997) defined differentiation as encompassing five dimensions: content, process, products, classroom organization and management, and the teacher's own commitment to change themselves into a learner, as well as a teacher. The differentiation of *content* involves adding more depth to the curriculum by focusing on structures of knowledge, basic principles, functional concepts, and methods of inquiry in particular disciplines. The differentiation of *process* incorporates the use of various instructional strategies and materials to enhance and motivate different students learning styles. The differentiation of *products* enhances students' communication skills by encouraging them to express themselves in a variety of ways. To differentiate *classroom management*, teachers can change the physical environment and grouping patterns they use in class and vary the allocation of time and resources for both groups and individuals. Classroom differentiation strategies can also be greatly enhanced by using the Internet in a variety of creative ways. Lastly, teachers can differentiate *themselves* by modeling the roles of athletic or drama coaches, stage or production managers, promotional agents, and academic advisers. All these roles differ qualitatively from the role of teacher-as-instructor. Teachers can also "inject" themselves into the material through a process called "artistic modification," which guides teachers in the sharing of direct, indirect, and vicarious experiences related to personal interests, travel experiences, collections, hobbies, and extracurricular involvements that can enhance and make real the subject matter (Renzulli, 1988).

Curriculum compacting is a differentiation strategy that incorporates content, process, products, classroom management, and teachers' personal commitment to accommodating individual and small-group differences. The scenario at the opening of this chapter described the need for this strategy and how two teachers who wanted to improve instruction and provide more challenge for talented youth used a similar strategy that emanated from their common experiences. This approach can benefit teachers of all grades in many subject areas, and it also addresses the demand for the kinds of challenging learning experiences that will help urban youth achieve at high levels and realize their potential.

Curriculum Compacting: Definitions and Steps for Implementation

Curriculum compacting streamlines the grade-level curriculum for high-potential students to provide time for more challenging and interesting work. This differentiation strategy was specifically designed to make appropriate curricular adjustments for students in any curricular area and at any grade level. The procedure involves (1) defining the goals and outcomes of a particular unit or block of instruction, (2) determining and documenting the students who have already mastered most or all of a specified set of learning outcomes, and (3) providing replacement strategies for material already mastered through the use of instructional options that enable a more challenging, interesting, and productive use of the student's time.

Most teachers indicate that they are committed to meeting students' individual needs. Yet, many teachers do not have the requisite background information to put this commitment into practice. Related research demonstrates that many talented students receive little differentiation of curriculum and instruction and spend a great deal of time in school doing work they have already mastered (Archambault, Westberg, Brown, Hallmark, Emmons, & Zhang, 1993; Reis, Westberg, Kulikowich, Caillard, Hébert, Purcell, Rogers, Smist, & Plucker, 1993; Westberg, Archambault, Dobyns, & Salvin, 1993). Too often, for example, some of the brightest students spend time relearning material they already know, which can lead to frustration, boredom, and, ultimately, underachievement. Curriculum compacting has been effective in addressing underachievement when the compacted regular curriculum is replaced with self-selected work in a high interest area, making schoolwork much more enjoyable (Baum, Renzulli, & Hébert, 1995; Reis et al.).

Most teachers who use compacting learn to streamline or "compact" the curriculum through a practical, step-by-step approach to the skills required to modify the curriculum and the techniques for pretesting students and preparing options for enrichment, acceleration, or both based on individual areas of interest. Practical issues such as record keeping and how to use the compacting form are also necessary to help guide teachers toward implementing this strategy. Once they have tried to compact for students, these guidelines can save valuable classroom time for both teachers and students.

Curriculum compacting, as presented in this chapter, has been field tested since 1975. It has been used with individuals and groups of students with above-average ability in any academic, artistic, or vocational area. Most important, research has demonstrated that compacting can dramatically reduce redundancy and challenge gifted students to new heights of excellence (Reis et al., 1993). It can be particularly meaningful for high-ability students who are underachieving because it provides one clear way to streamline work that may be too easy and replace it with more challenging work and self-selected opportunities in that area or in another area of interest.

An overview of the curriculum compacting process is best provided by the use of the management form "The Compactor," as presented in Figure 6.1. It serves as both an organizational and a record-keeping tool. Teachers usually complete one form per student or one form for a group of students with similar curricular strengths. Completed Compactors should be kept in students' academic files and updated regularly. The form can also be used for small groups of students who are

INDIVIDUAL EDUCATIONAL PROGRAMMING GUIDE
The Compactor

Prepared by   Joseph S. Renzulli
Linda M. Smith

| NAME_____ | AGE_____ | TEACHER(S)_____ | Individual Conference Dates And Persons Participating in Planning Of IEP |
| SCHOOL_____ | GRADE_____ | PARENT(S)_____ | ___ ___ ___ ___ |

CURRICULUM AREAS TO BE CONSIDERED FOR COMPACTING Provide a brief description of basic material to be covered during this marking period and the assessment information or evidence that suggests the need for compacting.	PROCEDURES FOR COMPACTING BASIC MATERIAL Describe activities that will be used to guarantee proficiency in basic curricular areas.	ACCELERATION AND/OR ENRICHMENT ACTIVITIES Describe activities that will be used to provide advanced level learning experiences in each area of the regular curriculum.

☐ Check here if additional information is recorded on the reverse side.

Copyright © 1978 by Creative Learning Press, Inc. P.O. Box 320 Mansfield Center, CT 06250. All rights reserved.

Figure 6.1. The Compactor

Note. From *The Compactor* (pp. 77–78), by J. S. Renzulli and L. H. Smith, 1978, Mansfield Center, CT: Creative Learning Press. Copyright ©1978 by Creative Learning Press. Reprinted with permission.

working at approximately the same level (e.g., a reading or math group) and as an addendum to an Individualized Education Plan (IEP) in states in which services for gifted students fall under special education laws.

The Compactor is divided into three columns:

- The first column includes information on learning objectives and student strengths in those areas. Teachers should list the objectives for a particular unit of study, followed by data on students' proficiency in those objectives, including test scores, behavioral profiles, and past academic records.
- In the second column, teachers should list the ways in which they will preassess whether students already know the skills that will be taught in class. The pretest or preassessment strategies they select, along with the results of those assessments, should be listed in this column. The assessment instruments can be formal measures such as tests or informal measures such as performance assessments based on observations of class participation and written assignments. Specificity of knowledge and objectives is important; recording an overall score of 85% on 10

objectives, for example, sheds little light on what portion of the material can be compacted since students might show limited mastery of some objectives and high levels of mastery of others.

- The third column is used to record information about acceleration or enrichment options. To determine these options, teachers must consider students' individual interests and learning styles. They should not uniformly replace compacted regular curricular work with harder, more advanced material that is solely determined by the teacher. Many years of research and field testing have shown that, when teachers do this, students learn a major lesson: If they do their best work, they are rewarded with more and harder work. Instead, we recommend that students' interests be considered. If, for example, a student loves working on science fair projects, time to work on these projects can replace material already mastered in a different content area. Teachers should be careful in monitoring the challenge level of the material being substituted. Too often, talented students do not understand the nature of effort and challenge because everything they encounter in school is too easy for them. Teachers must attempt to replace the compacted material with work that is engaging and challenging.

How to Use the Compacting Process

Defining Goals and Outcomes

The first of three phases of the compacting process consists of defining the goals and outcomes of a given unit or segment of instruction. This information is readily available in most subjects because specific goals and outcomes are included in teachers' manuals, curriculum guides, scope-and-sequence charts, and some of the new curricular frameworks that are emerging in connection with outcome-based education models. Teachers should examine these objectives to determine which represent the acquisition of new content or thinking skills, as opposed to reviews or practice of material that has previously been taught. The scope-and-sequence charts prepared by publishers or a simple comparison of the table of contents of a basal series will provide a quick overview of new versus repeated material. A major goal of this phase of the compacting process is to help teachers make individual programming decisions; a larger professional development goal is to help teachers be better analysts of the material they are teaching and better consumers of textbooks and prescribed curricular materials.

Identifying Students for Compacting

The second phase of curriculum compacting is identifying students who have already mastered the objectives or outcomes of a unit or segment of instruction that is about to be taught. Knowing one's students well, is, of course, the best way to begin the assessment process, and teachers will find that many have the potential to master new material at a faster-than-normal pace. Standardized achievement tests can serve as a good general screen for this step because they allow teachers to list the names of all students who are scoring 1 or more years above grade level in particular subject areas.

Being a candidate for compacting does not necessarily mean that a student knows all of the material under consideration. Therefore, the second step in identifying candidates involves the use of assessment techniques to evaluate specific learning outcomes. Unit pretests or end-of-unit tests that can be given as pretests are appropriate for this task, especially when it comes to the assessment of basic skills. An analysis of pretest results enables the teacher to document proficiency in specific skills and select instructional activities or practice material necessary to bring the student up to a high level on any skill that may need some additional reinforcement.

The process is slightly modified for compacting content areas that are not as easily assessed as basic skills and for students who have not mastered the material, but are candidates for more rapid coverage. First, students should understand the goals and procedures of compacting, including the nature of the replacement process. Underachieving students often regard compacting as a bargain because they may able to compact out of a segment of material they already know (e.g., a unit that includes a series of chapters in a social studies text), so the procedures for verifying mastery at a high level should be specified. These procedures might consist of answering questions based on the chapters, writing an essay, or taking the standard end-of-unit test. The amount of time for completion of the unit should be specified, and procedures such as periodic progress reports or log entries for teacher review should be discussed and selected.

Providing Acceleration and Enrichment Options

The final phase of the compacting process can be one of the most exciting aspects of teaching because it is based on cooperative decision making and creativity on the parts of both teachers and students. Time saved through curriculum compacting can be used to provide a variety of enrichment and acceleration opportunities for students.

Enrichment strategies might include those found in the Enrichment Triad Model (Renzulli, 1977), which provide opportunities for exposure to new topics and ideas, creative and critical thinking activities, and opportunities to pursue advanced independent or small-group creative projects. This aspect of the compacting process should also be viewed as a creative opportunity for a teacher to serve as a mentor to one or two students who are not working up to their potential. Another interesting occurrence that has resulted from the availability of curriculum compacting is that, when some previously bright, but underachieving students realize that they can both economize on regularly assigned material and "earn time" to pursue self-selected interests, their motivation to complete regular assignments increases; as one student put it, "Everyone understands a good deal!"

Several strategies have been suggested for differentiating instruction and curricula for talented or high-potential students. They range from substitution of regular material for more advanced material, to options such as independent-program or specific-content strategies (e.g., Great Books or Literature Circles). Many of these strategies can be used in combination with compacting or as replacement ideas after the students' curriculum has been compacted, as can acceleration, which enables students to engage in content that is appropriately challenging (Southern & Jones, 1992; Stanley, 1989a) by joining students in a higher grade-level class or by doing advanced curricular materials while in the same class, a form of content acceleration.

Case Study of Rosa and the Use of Compacting in Language Arts

Rosa was a fifth grader in a self-contained heterogeneous classroom in a lower socioeconomic urban school district. While Rosa's reading and language scores ranged between 4 and 5 years above grade level, most of her 29 classmates were reading 1 to 2 years below grade level. This presented her teacher with a common problem: What was the best way to provide differentiated services to Rosa? He agreed to compact her curriculum. Taking the easiest approach possible, he administered all of the appropriate unit tests for the grade level in the Basal Language Arts program. He subsequently excused Rosa from completing the activities and worksheets in the units where she showed proficiency (80% and above). When Rosa missed one or two questions, the teacher checked for trends in those items and provided instruction and practice materials to ensure concept mastery.

Rosa usually took part in language arts lessons with the rest of her classmates for 1 or 2 days a week; she spent the balance of the time with alternative projects, some of which she selected. This strategy spared Rosa up to 8 hours a week of instruction and work in language arts skills that were simply beneath her level. She joined the class instruction only when her pretests indicated that she had not fully acquired the skills or when there was a discussion that her teacher thought she would enjoy.

In the time saved using compacting, Rosa participated in a number of enrichment activities. First, she spent as many as 5 hours a week with an enrichment specialist in a resource room for high-ability students. This time was usually scheduled during her language arts class, which benefited both Rosa and her teacher since he didn't have to search for all of the enrichment options himself. The best part of the process for Rosa was that she didn't have to make up regular classroom assignments because she was not missing essential work.

Because science was also one of her strengths, Rosa visited a regional science center with other students who had expressed a high interest and aptitude for the subject. Rosa was administered the Interest-A-Lyzer, an interest assessment tool (Renzulli, 1997), and, based on the results, a decision was made for her to proceed with a science fair project on growing plants under various conditions. Rosa's

Compactor, which covered an entire semester, was updated in January. Her teacher remarked that compacting her curriculum had actually saved him time—time he would have spent correcting papers needlessly assigned! The value of compacting for Rosa convinced him that he should continue the process. The Compactor was also used as a vehicle for explaining to Rosa's parents how specific modifications were being made to accommodate her advanced language-arts achievement level and her interest in science. A copy of her Compactor form was included in her permanent-record folder and provided for Rosa's sixth-grade teacher, and a conference between the fifth- and sixth-grade teachers and the resource teacher helped to ensure continuity in dealing with her advanced curricular needs.

Research on Curriculum Compacting

A national study completed at the University of Connecticut's National Research Center on the Gifted and Talented (NRC/GT; Reis et al., 1993) examined the use of curriculum compacting for students from a wide diversity of school districts. The study included 465 second- through sixth-grade classroom teachers from 27 school districts throughout the country. Several urban schools took part in the study, including a magnet school for Hispanic students in California.

Classroom teachers were randomly assigned to participate in either the treatment (implemented compacting) or the control group (continued with normal teaching practices). Treatment and control group teachers were asked to target one or two candidates in their classrooms for curriculum compacting, and all participating students in treatment and control groups were tested before and after treatment with above-level Iowa Tests of Basic Skills (ITBS). Next-grade-level tests were used to compensate for the "topping out" ceiling effect that is frequently encountered when measuring the achievement of high-ability students.

The most important finding from this research might be described as "the more-for-less phenomenon." Approximately 40–50% of traditional classroom material was compacted for targeted students in one or more content areas. When teachers eliminated as much as 50% of regular curricular activities and materials for targeted students, no differences were observed in posttest achievement scores between treatment and control groups in math concepts, math computation, social studies, and spelling. In science, the students who had 40–50% of their curriculum eliminated actually scored significantly higher on science achievement posttests than their peers in the control group. And students whose curriculum was specifically compacted in mathematics scored significantly higher than their peers in the control group on the math concepts posttest. These findings point out the benefits of compacting for increases on standard achievement assessments. Analyses of data related to replacement activities also indicated that students viewed these activities as much more challenging than standard material.

In a recent study (Reis et al., 1993), teachers were asked to use both curriculum compacting and self-selected Type III enrichment projects based on students' interests as a systematic intervention for a diverse group of underachieving talented students. In this study, underachievement was reversed in the majority of students.

Use of Compacting in the Future

In research on compacting (Reis et al., 1993), participating teachers were asked whether they would continue to use curriculum compacting in the future and why they would make this decision. Responses to this question from almost 400 teachers were coded into three categories: positive, negative, and uncertain. More than two thirds of all teachers indicated that they would continue to use curriculum compacting in the future, and most who responded positively explained why, including the following representative comments from urban teachers:

> Yes. I feel that the time talented students are in my classroom is better spent doing more challenging work than it is doing assignments on material they already know. When they share projects and reports with the class, it also enriches [the other students'] learning experiences.

> Yes, I will continue this method of differentiation because it has shown me a very meaningful strategy to use with students who already know grade-level material. In turn, this enables students to become interested in independent learning they would like to pursue. The capable students are less likely to be turned off by this approach. This was a strategy that kept all students challenged in my class. I will use this next year in math and hopefully other areas, as well.

> Definitely! This is such an exciting way to teach. The students involved in the compacting program had the opportunity to become such active, independent learners. They had a taste of learning through their own actions, not just the material spooned out through limited textbooks. It was amazing to watch this learning process in action. Sparks flew in my classroom this year! Now that I'm familiar with compacting, I can't wait for next year to begin.

Teachers who responded that they were uncertain about continuing with compacting discussed their concerns about available planning time, a need to learn more about compacting, and students' lack of independent skills. The reasons cited by the small number of teachers who gave negative responses about the future use of compacting included comments about large class sizes and a preference for their own method of meeting students' needs.

The vast majority of teachers were able to implement curriculum compacting for the student(s) they selected, although many experienced some frustration over a lack of expertise in knowing what to substitute for high-ability students, limited time for planning how to meet individual differences, and the logistics of teaching different topics to different groups of students. Some also indicated the lack of support staff needed to implement replacement activities (e.g., reading and math specialists, gifted and talented program staff) and other concerns relating to classroom management. While curriculum compacting is a viable process for meeting the needs of high-ability students in the regular classroom, it does takes time, effort, and planning on the part of classroom teachers. With urban teachers, especially those who work with students placed at risk because of poverty, compacting requires different types of efforts, particularly in finding different materials to substitute in environments that often rely primarily on addressing deficits and remedial instruction.

Many factors contribute to the creation of a supportive school environment for the use of curriculum compacting, including administrative support and encouragement, availability of materials and resources to substitute for the regular curriculum, availability of guided practice and coaching, and teachers' increased ease with how to fit compacting into their professional practices. Logs and interviews have helped us to understand the reasons why some teachers experience insecurity about the work involved with the compacting process. As teachers learned more about it and worked with each other to learn how to compact the curriculum, some began to doubt their ability to implement compacting successfully or their motivation to do the work required. The high percentage of teachers who used compacting in their classroom for one academic year who then expressed positive reactions about their future use of compacting is encouraging, as it suggests that this process may be useful in addressing the needs of able students in the classroom.

Our follow-up research study has also indicated that a substantial number of teachers involved in the study indicated that they were able to extend curriculum compacting to other students, many of whom were not identified and involved in the gifted program (Reis et al., 1993). This finding may indicate the usefulness of extending the types of gifted education pedagogy often reserved for high-ability students to a larger segment of the population, as has been previously suggested (Renzulli & Reis, 1991), and the need to extend differentiation services to a broader segment of the school population (Renzulli & Reis, 1997).

Why Teachers Can Successfully Implement Curriculum Compacting

Ninety-five percent of all teachers who participated in a national study on compacting completed the compacting form and identified students who were eligible for curriculum compacting (Reis, et al, 1993). This finding suggests that the majority of teachers were able to select accurately those high-achieving students whose curriculum needed to be adjusted.

One of the primary reasons for this high percentage of success can be traced to the fact that superintendents and principals supported the idea and committed time to the initial professional development opportunities. Indeed, before beginning the study, both superintendents and principals had to read and agree to a long series of commitments about this study and the implementation of curriculum compacting. Administrative support is important because curricular differentiation for capable students remains an area of concern in most districts. Principals are often the first people who know when parents are unhappy with the lack of challenge faced by some students. Therefore, some principals may have supported this because they saw it as a legitimate problem for students and a way to address valid parental concerns. Other contributing factors may have also been the excitement of participating in a national study and the opportunity for press releases about implementing an innovation like curriculum compacting in the school district. No doubt exists, however, that administrative support was a prime motivator in encouraging teachers to try the innovation.

Finding appropriate replacement activities was most difficult for classroom teachers, and urban teachers often did not know what to assign, had few materials or supplies for this task, and had neither the time nor the knowledge to design these activities. The analysis of Compactors indicated that teachers often replaced previously mastered work with any material or activity they could find, and, unfortunately, that work was often not appropriately challenging, such as extra problems, reading assignments, more difficult math activities, or alternative assignments suggested in the textbook. Research liaisons indicated that teachers needed time for reflection about appropriate work and additional guided practice. It is clear that more time and help would have addressed this issue. What remains to study is how much time and effort teachers will expend in implementing compacting if they encounter considerable obstacles such as larger class sizes, fewer materials to use for replacement of compacted work, and the inclusion of more students with a wide range of abilities and special needs in the classroom. The positive response of teachers and their ability to eliminate content and replace it with various activities and more advanced content provide an optimistic view of the use of this differentiation strategy.

Advice From Successful Teachers Who Implement Compacting

Research (Reis et al., 1992) has shown that the most successful teachers to use compacting, many of whom taught in urban areas with culturally diverse talented students, implemented the following strategies to successfully implement compacting.

1. They worked with a colleague or colleagues with whom they shared a common bond. They wanted to improve their teaching practices and were not afraid to ask each other for help or support.
2. They started with a small group of students and not their entire class. The successful teachers understood that this process would take some time and organization and became committed to working first with a group who

really needed the process. By not trying this with all students, they reduced the stress and challenges they would have encountered had they tried to do too much in the beginning of the process.

3. They asked for help from their liaisons, the district content consultants, and each other. In each successful district, teachers asked each other how they were handling pretesting and assessment. They shared strategies for management and replacement, and they visited each other's classrooms at their own suggestions or because a liaison suggested it. Modeling and sharing success stories made a difference.

4. They also understood that, like a novice practicing piano scales, they would continue to improve by trying and reflecting on their work in this area. The teachers who did the best work consistently asked their colleagues and liaisons what had worked best and how current practices could extend and improve this strategy. By reflecting on what had worked, they were able to modify and change their own attempts, which led to consistent improvement. In the most successful schools, teachers were provided with time to work with liaisons, small amounts of material funds for curricular replacement costs, and substitutes to enable them to visit and observe direct modeling in each other's classrooms.

Conclusion

The many changes that are taking place in schools require all educators to examine a broad range of techniques for providing equitably for *all* students. Curriculum compacting is one such process. It is not tied to a specific content area or grade level, nor is it aligned with a particular approach to school or curricular reform. Rather, the process is adaptable to any school organizational plan or curricular framework, and it is flexible enough to be used within the context of rapidly changing approaches to general education. The research described in this chapter and the practical experiences gained through several years of field testing and refining the compacting process, particularly in urban areas and in schools that serve culturally diverse students, have demonstrated that many positive benefits can result from this process for both teachers and students, particularly talented students who may be at risk for underachieving in school.

Like any innovation, curriculum compacting requires time, energy, and acceptance from teachers. Yet, educators we have studied who compact effectively indicate that it takes no longer than normal teaching practices. More importantly, they have reported that the benefits to all students certainly make the effort worthwhile. One teacher's comment about the compacting process reflects the attitude of most teachers who have participated in research about compacting: "As soon as I saw how enthusiastic and receptive my students were about the compacting process, I became more committed to implementing this method in all my classes."

7

An Unconventional View of Gifted Children of Indian Descent in the United States

by Beheruz N. Sethna

M any years ago, in a small town in upstate New York, Rick Meyer, a second-grade teacher, issued a challenge to his students: He would have optional assignments for which he would award points for doing well. Students who accumulated 100 points at the end of the year would be invited, along with their parents, to his home for a cookout. At the end of the year, he was true to his word, and he invited the students who had scored at least 100 points and their parents to his home.

As this celebration of student accomplishment was winding down, he remarked to the parents that, as he was sending out the invitations, he had noted that the vast majority of invited students lived on the same street. "It must be something in the water," he joked.

At that, one of the mothers present—she was an American, not of Indian origin—shook her head in disagreement. "Pushy parents," she said laconically.

That two-word explanation was accepted as sufficient by all the adults. The students, fortunately, were off having fun at more enjoyable activities at the time the remark was made.

While the preceding vignette was not about Indian children or Indian parents (in fact, only one of the students present was of Indian origin), this wisdom imparted by the mother of one of the students, in two words, is one of the main reasons behind the stereotype of giftedness of children of Indian origin.

The main reason is, of course, the talents and hard work of the students themselves. Nothing in this chapter should be interpreted as taking away from the accomplishments of the students. However, the essence of the belief systems of the parents of Indian origin is that their children can and will succeed and that no sacrifice on the part of the parents or the children is too great. These parents impart to their children a culture of hard work, clear focus, building strong credentials, and a single-minded pursuit of careers that lead to prestige and material rewards and recognition.

When I was in California recently, one of the teachers asked me why students from India are so smart. My husband's son is a dentist, and several of their neighbors are affluent physicians from India. The consensus seems to be that Indian/Indian American children study all of the time, are afraid of disappointing their parents and earning a grade that is less than perfect or an A, and see monetary links to good grades at an early age. (D. Boothe, personal e-mail communication, June 15, 2002)

Certainly there are other reasons—a cynic might say—such as pushy families, pushy friends of parents, perhaps pushy teachers who are encouraged by pushy parents, and others who will be mentioned later in this chapter. However, no discussion of the "giftedness" of Indian children and the pressures on them can be complete without recognition of the role of their parents (and their "pushy" inclinations). To obtain a more complete understanding of the pressures on children of Indian origin in U.S. schools today, we must go back in time to understand their parents and the culture in which they grew up. (Figure 7.1 illustrates hypothesized spheres of influence on the gifted child. In this article, of the spheres described in the figure, the main focus will be on the influence of the parents.)

This article includes text boxes with quotes from parents and children of Indian origin. These are included because they will prove useful to counselors and teachers of children of Indian descent who are trying to understand the background and philosophy of both children and parents. Many of these quotes originated in two articles (Chhibber, 2002a, 2002b) published in *Khabar*, a publication for Indian audiences in the United States.

A Look at the Parents of Indian Origin

In order to understand the pressures and opportunities for children of Indian origin living in the United States, one must understand the family structure and background of their parents. These parents, often first-generation immigrants to the U.S., have grown up with their own set of pressures and opportunities provided by their parents. While most of them recognize that their upbringing pertained to a different time and place, they have not escaped the significance of those pressures and opportunities in their own lives. Insofar as they believe those pressures

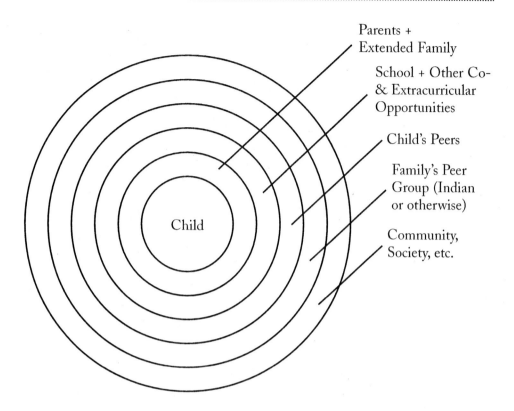

Parents +
Extended Family

School + Other Co-
& Extracurricular
Opportunities

Child's Peers

Family's Peer
Group (Indian
or otherwise)

Community,
Society, etc.

Child

Figure 7.1. Spheres of influence on the gifted child

and opportunities were beneficial to them, they are likely to behave in ways that are similar to those of the past.

Education for these parents was competitive—*extremely* competitive. Even today, the acceptance ratios for the most prestigious Indian institutions (e.g., the most prestigious medical schools, the Indian Institutes of Technology for Engineering, and the Indian Institutes of Management) are among the most competitive in the world. It is almost every parent's dream that his or her son or daughter goes to one of these institutions, regardless of the child's desire. "Go to IIT first and ask questions about your career path later," they seem to be saying. About 3 to 5 years prior to the time a student is even eligible to apply to the IITs, their parents let them know that that is what their aspirations are. And, given the Indian culture, the parents' aspirations become internalized as the student's aspirations.

It needs to be emphasized that there is no parallel to the IITs in the U.S. Every potential (even possibly potential) engineer does not wish to go to MIT or Stanford. On the other hand, almost every potential engineering student in India aspires to go to the Indian Institutes of Technology (IIT). There are five such IITs throughout India. In the "Special Report of *AsiaWeek* on Asia's Best Universities

2000," IIT Bombay was ranked third among the technology and science institutes in all of Asia (AsiaWeek.com, 2000). The other IITs (Delhi, Madras, Kanpur, and Kharagpur) also featured among the top 10 technology and science institutes.

Admission to these institutions is dependent exclusively on how a student performs on the IIT entrance examinations. There are now two sets of examinations. One is in December, at which only about 28,000 of a total of 178,000 applicants make it

> When I was a kid, I enjoyed tinkering with radios—this was not at the level that could be considered a hobby, nor was the tinkering at a high level of expertise. Yet, that was sufficient reason for my dad to expect me to go to the Indian Institute of Technology (IIT). About 4 years before I was even eligible to apply, he clipped the ad for the IIT application and carried it around with him. That was his dream, and it became a "must" for me as well. (B. N. Sethna, unpublished speech to Rotary Club, May, 1999)

through just to earn the right to compete for the final entrance examination. Then there is an arduous series of examinations in May in the content areas: physics, chemistry, and math. Only about 4,700 applicants are finally accepted of the 178,000 who applied initially, which yields a final acceptance rate of 2.7% (*Indian Institute of Technology Bombay*, n.d.; personal e-mail communication, October 10, 2002). In contrast, even Harvard accepts about 10% of its applicants.

On January 12, 2003, Leslie Stahl of *60 Minutes* did a story on the IITs. In that story, she said, "IIT may be the most important university you've never heard of. . . . This is IIT Bombay. Put Harvard, MIT, and Princeton together, and you begin to get an idea of the status of this school in India." In *Leslie Stahl's Notebook* (Jan. 9, 2003), she said,

> I remember telling you in November that I had just returned from Bombay, India. So, this story has taken 2 months. It's about a university that may be the hardest school in the world to get into. It's called IIT— Indian Institute of Technology. A stunning percentage of CEOs and innovators in the American high tech industry were graduated from IIT. (Stahl, 2003, para. 7)

In some fields, such as medicine and business, there are graduate parallels, as well. In medicine, the best graduate programs are extremely competitive, as they are in the U.S. In business, there is a close parallel to the Indian Institutes of Technology (IITs) called the Indian Institutes of Management (IIMs). The first of these, the Indian Institute of Management in Ahmedabad (IIMA), was started in close collaboration with the Harvard Business School; in the initial years, IIMA utilized Harvard cases and tests and U.S. faculty. It was rated, at least in one international survey (AsiaWeek.com, 2000), as being "World Class–Best in Reputation" among all business schools in Asia. In another article (Anderson,

2002), it was ranked second in all of Asia. The other IIMs have significant claims to fame, as well. Acceptance into the IIMs is very competitive, involving a multi-stage process that includes a thorough evaluation of the student's complete credentials, a set of examinations, interviews, and group discussions.

There are first-class educational opportunities available at the IIMs. Even for the skeptics, however, there is no question that it provides an exit benefit difficult to rival anywhere in the world. The placement "season" is a case study by itself. For example, the Indian Institute of Management in Ahmedabad (IIMA) allocates the last month of the second year for placement activities. There are no institution-sponsored placement activities before that, for reasons that will become clear in a moment. In actuality, the placement season lasts a little over a week, with the most highly rated students getting jobs in the most prestigious multinational companies by 9 p.m. of the first day and the least highly rated students receiving job offers from good companies about 10 days later. Students decide which companies may arrive on the first day, based on the most desirable multinational companies available. Shortlisted candidates at each stage are interviewed by senior managers in the morning, by divisional heads in the afternoon, and by the CEO in the late afternoon. Job offers are made by early evening, and the students have until later that night (a few hours) to accept or reject the offer. By the end of the first day, there has been a match between the best companies and the best students. This continues each day until, about a week to 10 days later, the students who are the least highly rated have at least one good job offer. Everyone is placed within a few days. This is the case in a country where unemployment is high and life is difficult for a middle-class person. The distance between those who obtain the great jobs and those who have few opportunities is extreme.

The message to those who grew up in India was clear: Great opportunities await the great students. However, there is rarely, if ever, a connotation of being "gifted." Without the benefit of empirical research, one can hypothesize that a negligibly small percentage (if that) of successful doctors, lawyers, engineers, or professors who grew up in India and live in the U.S. today would label themselves as being gifted. There is some implication of talent, but it is largely a matter of hard work, developed abilities, and a supportive environment.

In such an environment, there is no question of a high school graduate's taking time off to "find him- or herself." There is rarely, if ever, a decision to make whether to go to college. There is no question of taking time off from school to pay for a new car. When you are a student, you live like a student. A culture of postponed gratification is pervasive: Work hard and struggle now, and the good things will follow later.

The career decisions in India for the parents were relatively straightforward because the set of possible options was limited: Of those careers that provide good income and a prestigious career, what field do you like? Overlay this thinking with a strong "Father knows best" culture, and you will have a reasonable idea of the Indian culture the parents experienced when they were young(er). Because college is not considered to be the prerogative of the brilliant or the very rich, there is a presumption that "My kid will go to college and will attend the best college to which he or she can gain admission."

What about intelligence and giftedness?

The concept of giftedness is rarely mentioned in India. The presumption is that, given the right encouragement and plenty of hard work, every child can succeed. So, parents provide the encouragement (perceived as being pushy by some), and encourage a culture that reveres hard work, clear focus, building strong credentials, and dogged pursuit of careers that lead to prestige and material rewards and recognition.

> The immigrants who came here [the U.S.] in the late 1960s and the 1970s were essentially academics and professionals. Their profile was the same: conservative, middle-class upbringing, traditional views and focus primarily on education. As these immigrants struggled to carve a niche for themselves in an alien country and culture facing both subtle and blatant bias and racism, they stayed afloat because they remained a step ahead of the mainstream. By the time they had their children, their status had changed from middle class to privileged class *though they seldom forgot how they reached that zenith* [italics added]. (Chhibber, 2002b, p. 26)

In this discussion, it is important to point out that the term *giftedness* refers to the academic arena. People of Indian origin fully recognize that giftedness exists in music and other performing arts that *do* assume a tremendous amount of inborn talent. There is no implication that parents of Indian origin believe that any child, regardless of talent, can, with hard work, become a renowned artist, musician, or dancer. However, there is a general assumption that a child of Indian descent can, with hard work, achieve significant academic (and career) success.

This is the culture in which the parents grew up. This is the world they knew best. It is no surprise that these assumptions pervade their thinking, much to the consternation of some of their children who were raised in the U.S., are used to the good life, and never had to struggle. If one thing doesn't work out here, another will be along soon, they seem to say.

Giftedness in Other Cultures

Is this way of thinking an Indian aberration? Do other Eastern cultures reason in similar ways? Is there any support of alternative concepts of giftedness in mainstream American culture?

Stevenson (1998) has provided a body of evidence from China and Japan indicating that there are significant similarities between the Indian way of thinking and that of the Chinese and Japanese:

> Performance, therefore, is considered by Chinese and Japanese to be strongly dependent on the kinds of experience that teachers provide and is

not seriously limited by differences in children's innate levels of ability. All children, with appropriate teaching and guidance, are expected to be able to learn mathematics and other subjects in the school curriculum. The teachers' skills and the student's diligence—not innate intelligence—are considered to be the most important influences on children's performance. (p. 63)

Human beings are considered to be malleable and, like clay, are shaped by their experiences. According to Munro (1969),

The Chinese theory of learning assumes that people are innately capable of learning from models. This learning can occur unintentionally, through the unconscious imitation of those around one; thus it is important to choose one's neighbors well. Or it can occur intentionally, through the purposive attempt to supplicate the attitude and conduct of a teacher, scholar-official, or ancestor. . . . For the Confucians, model emulation was not just one way of learning; it was by far the most efficient way, and one could inculcate any virtuous behavior in people by presenting the right model. (p. 96)

(The reader should note the similarity of this reasoning and the description of the Indian system in the previous section and with Figure 7.1.)
  Stevenson (1998) has further noted,

Those who gathered in the capitol each year for the final stages of the examination were picked on the basis of what they knew. The tests did not attempt to assess cleverness, or intellectual potential but tapped what the individuals had learned—and, in parts of the examination, what they had memorized. (p. 64)

Again, there is considerable similarity between these findings and the entrance examination systems still used in India today.
  Stevenson (1998) also described the Japanese experience in the following manner:

During the years of compulsory education in Japan, every effort is given to making the educational system as egalitarian as possible. Tracking is not practiced. This means that from the time children enter elementary school until the time they graduate from junior high school, they attend school with students of all levels of ability. Regardless of what the students already know or the rapidity with which they can acquire new information, all must enroll in the same classes, use the same textbooks, and take the same tests. . . .

  Moreover, students are members of classes in which there are approximately 40 students on the average and a single teacher. . . . Special treatment, such as allowing a student to skip a grade, is nearly unheard of in Japan. (pp. 64–65)

So, we find that the culture of hard work and the respect for hard work is found in Japan, as well. According to Stevenson (1998),

> Teachers often indicate that they do not especially appreciate having gifted children in their classrooms. The children they find more impressive are those who work hard. . . .
>
> Students cannot automatically attend a high school of their choice but are admitted to high schools on the basis of their scores on a high school entrance examination. High schools are organized hierarchically, so that the most rigorous curriculum and the greatest competition are encountered at the Number 1 high school in each city. . . .
>
> Teachers and parents explain that the differences among children are not that great and that children differ mainly in the rate, not in the level, of development that can be attained. Quoting a well-known proverb, they point out that "The slow bird must start out early." (p. 65–75)

Note that there is no implication that the "slow bird" cannot succeed. He or she simply has to work harder.

Again, the implication is the same, and goes something like this: "My child can succeed; he or she can do anything if he or she works sufficiently hard and if I (the parent) can provide the correct family encouragement." The Indian formula for success and for the good life is relatively straightforward: Success is a function of the encouragement and environment provided by the parent/family and the amount of work done by the child. And, even the second variable is significantly influenced by parental pressure. In this culture, it is true that the child's talent is important, but that just makes ultimate success easier or more difficult. It does not mean that success is assured or is impossible. This way of thinking is not unheard-of in American culture either. Silverman (1986) found that fathers tend to perceive giftedness as achievement (though mothers perceive it as developmental precocity).

The gifted label may be important to parents of children of Indian origin more for the sake of the opportunities made available to them in the U.S. (and perhaps marginally for bragging rights) than for an implication that the child will be able to accomplish a level of achievement beyond the reach of a nongifted student.

In 1993, the U.S. Department of Education published a report, *National Excellence: A Case for Developing America's Talent*. That report (as quoted by Feldhusen, 1998) stated, "The term gifted connotes a mature power rather than a developing ability and, therefore, is antithetic to recent research findings about children" (p. 193). The report used the terms *talent, talented,* and *talent development* throughout and stressed the role of growth and development, as opposed to the concept of genetically transmitted ability.

Consistent with the Indian family way of thinking, Feldhusen (1998) suggested that the notion of pure giftedness is false, demotivating, and socially undesirable. Anecdotal evidence tells us that some teachers even dismiss youths as not really "gifted" because they see their achievements seeming to result from hard work. . . . The term *gifted* is a nontechnical referent for inherited or genetically determined abilities supposedly possessed by some and not by others. As such it is a fallacious conception because all known human abilities exist on a continuum from low to high and are not dichotomously present or absent. Instead we need a conception that connotes and communicates the true nature of how human abilities originate and grow. For the present the terms *talent* and *talent development* afford the better connotation and communication, especially for those who are concerned with the practicalities of talent recognition and nurturance. (p. 195)

Therefore, when Indian parents in the U.S. believe that their children can achieve success regardless of the gifted label, it is not without basis. So, we cannot, in understanding the Indian approach to success and gifted behavior, escape the "pushy parent"/"pushy family" syndrome. Moon, Jurich, and Feldhusen (1998) have supported this way of thinking, even in American culture:

Families are often one of the most important influences on the development of gifted children (Bloom, 1985; Csikszentmihalyi, Rathunde, & Whalen, 1993; Olszewski, Kulieke, & Buesher, 1987). The family environment also influences the development of talent (Bloom, 1985; Kulieke & Olszewski-Kubilius, 1989; Olszewski et al., 1987; VanTassel-Baska, 1989b). . . .

[W]hen gifted children in a summer school program were asked who was the most influential person in their lives, most of the children (70%) selected their mother or father (Roberts, Carter, & Mosley, 1982). This way of thinking is consistent with family systems theory (Boss, Doherty, LaRossa, Schumm, & Steinmetz, 1993). (p. 81)

Moon et al. (1998) also found that "individuals in a family are viewed within the context of their relationships and interactions with others rather than purely on the basis of their individual characteristics" (p. 82) and that

families with high-achieving and high IQ children tend to be child-centered and to have supportive, close family relationships (Bloom, 1985; Cornell, 1983; Cornell & Grossberg, 1987; Friedman, 1994). "These families set high standards for education and achievement, are vigilant about checking homework, and pursue intellectual and cultural activities" (Bloom, 1985; Cornell, 1983; Cornell & Grossberg, 1987; Olszewski et al., 1987; Prom-Jackson, Johnson, & Wallace, 1987). (p. 83)

Moon et al. (1998) hypothesized a correspondence between high-achieving and high-IQ children and child-centered, supportive, close family relationships.

The Indian approach would probably hypothesize more than a correspondence. There is at least an implication that child-centered, supportive, close family relationships lead to high-achieving (if not high-IQ) children.

Another intervening variable that typically applies to first-generation Indian immigrant families is the relative resilience of marriages. There is no implication here that a marriage between two people who grew up in India and now live in the U.S. is better or worse than any other. However, they do tend to be more resilient, since divorce is less accepted in the more traditional cultures. Moon et al. (1998) also postulated that

> Gifted children, especially those who are succeeding academically, tend to be the product of stable marriages (Barbe, 1981; Bloom, 1985; VanTassel-Baska, 1983, 1989a) and well-adjusted families (Beach, 1988; Matthews, West, & Hosie, 1986). . . . These families exhibit the high levels of bonding and flexibility that are characteristics of resilient families (Abelman, 1991; Bland, Sowa, & Callahan, 1994) and the high levels of hardiness and coherence that are characteristics of regenerative families (McCubbin, Thompson, Pirner, & McCubbin, 1988). (p. 83)

Another relevant finding cited by Moon et al. (1998) in American culture is that "Talented, low-income students are less likely to be the product of stable marriages than talented middle-class students" (Friedman, 1994, as cited by Moon et. al). For example, in a study of 767 bright, low-income, minority students, only 59% of the students lived with both parents (Prom-Jackson et al., 1987, as cited Moon et. al, p. 84).

Moon et al. (1998) also provided some support for other influences on the child as shown in Figure 7.1, such as the school system, family-school interactions, the neighborhood (these influences include the obvious correlation with the school system, but go beyond that to include other talent development opportunities and positive interactions with other adults), peer networks, and support networks.

Conclusions From the Parents' Perspective

To conclude the discussion from the perspective of the parents of Indian origin, we see that their way of thinking, in large part, has emerged from their own background and upbringing, but is not without support in other cultures, Eastern or American.

- They revere a culture of hard work, clear focus, building strong credentials, and dogged pursuit of careers that lead to prestige and material rewards and recognition.

- Desirable or acceptable career choices for their children are typically limited to the subset of those careers that typically provide good income and a prestigious career.
- They strongly believe that their child can succeed and that he or she can do anything if he or she works sufficiently hard and if the parents provide the appropriate family encouragement. No sacrifice is too great, whether it be money or material possessions for the parents, or instant gratification or peer-recognition acquisitions (sometimes labeled as "cool stuff") for the children. The Indian culture believes in postponed gratification, rather than instant gratification.
- The Indian formula for success and for the good life is relatively straightforward: Success is a function of the encouragement and environment provided by the parent/family and the amount of work done by the child. While it is true that the child's talent is important, this is not a dichotomous variable (i.e., gifted/not gifted), but a continuum that impacts only the amount of work necessary for ultimate success.

> Indira Sarma: Just because they don't seem to conform to the parents' way of looking at things does not mean they don't have values. Parents need to ask themselves this question. Are they being fair to their kids when the kids are being brought up exposed to so many different cultures? Their expectations are unrealistic. (Chhibber, 2002a, p. 72)

Opposing Points of View

Should this chapter end here, with the revelation of the "secret formula" for success of children of Indian origin? Are there opposing points of view? Yes, certainly there are, and some of them, grouped into three broad areas, are discussed below.

1. The philosophy and belief systems of the parents of Indian origin do not reflect the realities of the dual (or multiple) cultures that the children face in American schools and society.
2. Not only does the thinking of the parents fail to reflect the reality of American society, but it may also fail to reflect the reality of Indian society as it exists today. For example, many parents of Indian origin have traditional ideas against dating. Those ideas may have been prevalent in the 1960s when they were in India, but, at least in the big cities, they are not the norm today.
3. The parents, by their philosophy, place unrealistic burdens and pressures on their children in terms of both the level of accomplishment expected and the fields of accomplishment.

Since life was so hard in India, the important factor was to choose a profes-

It seems the south Asian community since the 1960s is frozen in time, each generation passing the baton to the next, stacking up honors as the "model minority," shoving mainstream issues and concerns under the carpet. It is only now that these very issues have come back to haunt them as their children struggle from turbulent teens to an anguished adulthood trying to bridge the gap between bearing the back-breaking burden of the "rich cultural heritage and our values" unceremoniously dumped on them without a gradual initiation, and living in mainstream America that engulfs and often overwhelms them in a flood of mind-boggling ethnic diversity. (Chhibber, 2002a, p. 64)

sion that, to the greatest extent possible, ensured that the family would survive and do well financially. The culture of "work till you drop" was crucially important; other interests were fine, but only as hobbies or side interests. That is why, even in the U.S., parents of Indian origin have great difficulty accepting career choices from their children that do not have a high probability of fiscal security for the family and the ability to educate their children well in turn. And, correspondingly, they have less difficulty accepting a lower mark than a lower level of effort. Education and hard work are regarded as the keys to the good life. So, even when the child does vary from the beaten career path, education is still a must.

Another adjustment for parents and children is the way in which influence is exerted in the home. When the first-generation immigrants were children in India, there was one way: The parents knew best and the children did as they were told, not necessarily out of fear, but because that was the only way they knew. Today, in the U.S., there is still more parental involvement and influence in Indian families than in the typical American family, but the ways of exerting that influence include more (although the children might say, not much more) two-way conversation.

In response to a request from the author, Sharma (personal e-mail communication, March 11, 2002), now an attorney, and one who had been designated as a gifted child when she was in school, wrote the following account. Reported almost verbatim, it enforces the findings of this article.

My response entails just my personal views based on my personal experience as a gifted student. I started in the gifted program in elementary school

Reshma Shah: You see these [Indian kids] struggling with what they want to major in. My mom and dad insist that I study engineering or accounting or something that is very much in vogue for the Indian community or prestigious or reputable. If they move to liberal arts or areas that don't lend themselves readily to these prestigious careers, I see my students really struggling. The parents came here in late '60s and '70s and their assumption of what is right and proper is based in that time period. (Chhibber, 2002a, p. 72) at an age too young to know the difference between the "special" class and the regular class. After having taken an IQ test, I was placed in the "special" class filled with about 10 Caucasian children. My memory tells me that the class was a challenge in that I was pushed harder to do more challenging work, particularly in literature. This pressure complemented the pressure from home, which was to be an A student and no less. Such requirement in and outside the home shaped my type-A personality.

I think there is a great emphasis put on Indian children, regardless of being in the gifted program or not, to make the best grade available, rather than possible. American children seem to not be pressured to get the best, but instead are encouraged to be the best that they can be. For parents of American children in gifted programs, it generally is enough that their child is gifted, whereas Indian parents generally require their child to be in the gifted program and make As while in it. Such high expectations make it tough for the child to bear any "failure," which may mean making less than the expected.

Vasanthi Ramchandran, mother of a 16-year-old, admits, "Every South Asian parent is frozen in time, talking about how things were tough for them, how good their kids have it today, and education, education, and education is all that matters."

Her son, Hemant, adds, "I appreciate and understand the struggles they went through, but I can't accept that as a basis for their saying that I can't have something. Nor does it mean we have to continue to live in the 1960s as our parents did."

Hemant's father, Kishore Ramchandran, a professor at Georgia Tech, agrees that although kids can try to understand their parents' struggles, it is still all an abstract concept for them. Kishore remembers the fire and motivation he had within him to excel after seeing how hard his parents worked to get him to where he is today. "We try to pass on the same fire and drive to our kids and perhaps seem a bit more unreasonable from the parents of their peers, but the fact remains that South Asian parents have a hard time accepting their kids opting for alternative careers. We have not seen too many success stories for someone who has not taken the beaten path of education." (Chhibber, 2002b, pp. 26–28)

The probability of an Indian child enrolling in the gifted program if given the option must be extremely high, possibly 100%. This is due to the fact that Indian parents encourage such attainment and will not accept their child turning down such an opportunity. American parents, on the other hand, solicit opinions and feelings from the child and are more likely to put those needs ahead of their own expectations and desires. They accept the child's individuality and generally do not try to mold the child to conform to societal expectations. Indian parents, on the other hand, hope that all of their children grow up to be doctors. Individualism and creativity is less encouraged, if at all. These are cultural issues, and it is my understanding that parents in our culture value the successes of their

> You are the only parent I know who asked why I chose not to do an extra-credit assignment, when I had a 100% average in a math course! (S. Sethna, personal communication, August 11, 2002)

children greatly, which to a great extent are measured with numerical values (i.e. best grade possible, class rank, highest salary, etc.).

With this in mind, I would encourage counselors and teachers to learn of the Indian culture or, in a broader sense, the Asian culture and understand the extent to which it is imbedded in Indian students and their parents. Have them understand why expectations from parents are so high, why children try to meet those high expectations at any cost, and how this shapes the child's personality. These answers help to explain the differences between Indian and American students, whether gifted or not.

There is an additional complication as it relates to the pressures on children of Indian origin, with particular implications for their counselors and schools. In a report on the Spelling Bee, a national spelling competition, Venugopal (2003) pointed out that four out the past five Spelling Bee winners have been of Indian descent (and there were two prior to these four). Certainly, the question might be raised as to what factors might lead to success that is so disproportionate to the number of Indian Americans in the U.S. population. One school of thought is that these skills are indicative of intellectual development and training. Another school of thought, suggested in the article by Lea Rangel-Ribeiro, past principal of the U.N. International School's primary division (1969–2001), is that these successes are a result of a belief in rote learning, which is "looked down upon" by American schools, but is "a carry-over from the Indian system in which their parents were raised, a system where rote learning and a competitive spirit were considered crucial to academic success." Either of these hypotheses are consistent with earlier findings of this chapter.

> Dr. Yogesh Joshi says it was hard balancing two cultures, and when Khyati chose to study religion instead of one of the traditional disciplines such as medicine, engineering, or law, there was a major struggle in the house. "We had no idea how her area of specialization would fare in the future, and although she stuck to her guns, I had a very hard time accepting her decision." Khyati is now a Professor at the Center for the Study of Ethnicity and Race at Columbia University. (Chhibber, 2002b, p. 32)

In the same article, Dr. Reeba George, a child psychiatrist in Houston, TX, raised an interesting point: She suggested that there is a double standard in the way Americans look at intellectually successful kids, which is much more critical than their view of athletes. Americans ask questions of the former such as "Is he normal?" or "Does he know how to socialize?" that they do not ask of the latter. If this is true, and there are indications to suggest that it might be, then there are implications for schools and for this chapter, which are mentioned in the following paragraphs.

Teachers and counselors need to be sensitive to this double standard of success. If adults consistently reinforce that athletic prowess is good, a sign of well-rounded youth, and that academic success is somehow an indication of less-than-normal or "geeky" behavior, then we are reinforcing only one model of prowess and success—that of the athlete—with all of its positive and negative implications. Furthermore, we are disenfranchising youth (whether of Indian descent or not) who do not fit this mode.

> Dr. Khalid Siddiq moved to the U.S. 25 years ago. With four sons, he says their household is very traditional, and the boys—especially the oldest—were raised the way he was: in a conservative household where the focus was on academics. He says the media, the influence of society, and the school system is so powerful that they felt from time to time that the values they wanted to inculcate and the objectives they had would be hard to implement. "These days if we tell a child you must do something, they will ask why instead of doing it because the authority and respect that parents or elders used to command earlier is no longer there. It was a difficult transition, and we had to learn to give and take and make compromises." (Chhibber, 2002b, pp. 32–34)

In Figure 7.1, the role of the parents and the extended family were hypothesized. If there are, in general, pressures on American youth (of any ethnic heritage) to be nonintellectual, the reason why youth of Indian descent still pursue more academic and intellectual activities with passion and vigor may be that Indian (extended) families in the U.S. still provide an atmosphere of support and encouragement for academic activities that is perhaps above the norm for American families in general.

The next wider concentric circle of Figure 7.1 indicates the important role of schools and school officials. There is an open question as to whether that circle or the concentric circle wider than that one—that which refers to the child's peers—is the more salient. It is likely that, in some situations, the child's peers do exert more pressure, while in others, the influence of a particular teacher or counselor may play the more influential role. The implications are clear: The teacher or counselor can play a salient role, influence the way the child reacts to external stimuli, and reinforce behavior that she or he believes is more important to the child's long-term development.

The Search for Middle Ground

Many American children of Indian descent feel that the Indian philosophies (e.g., hard work, delayed gratification, intense pursuit of a successful career) are not anchored in the realities of place and time and that the pressures on them are enormous. Is there middle ground? In my opinion, there is. However, being a parent in the U.S., rather than a child who grew up in the U.S., my inclination is to make adjustments to the parental philosophy to reflect the realities of time and place and the realities of pressure.

First, in areas outside the field of academics and career choices, only touched upon in this chapter (e.g., dating), the parents of Indian origin need to make significant adjustments. I do not recommend compromises in the area of a strong sense of responsibility and high ethical tone, but I do so in the area of normal, responsible relationships with the opposite sex.

In areas of career choice, parents and children of Indian origin need to educate themselves on the fiscal realities of different careers. Parents need to be aware that, in the U.S., one can make a good living in careers other than medicine, law, business, and engineering. Children need to be aware of the realities of tough economies and that there are few and low-paying jobs in some fields. They have, in the main, grown up living well, though typically not in luxury (because parents of Indian origin do believe in saving money for education). Some career choices will entail a considerable drop in their standard of living.

Good, workable solutions are possible with some understanding on the part of all parties—parents, children, teachers, counselors, extended family, and peers.

> Dr. Ramanna Dhara, who has raised two sons in this country, says, "...These kids are facing a lot of pressures not only that they have to fit in, but also they have to live up to the high expectations of their parents. Having to come to this country, we had to work extra hard being immigrants and we had to make it. Having done that, to think we should impose that culture on our children, we are sort of trying to transpose this concept. We cannot expect our children to be perfect. The children have to learn from their own mistakes. The younger generation is caught between a rock and a hard place. They have to conform to a peer group and then conform to their parents' expectation—then suicide comes in. They must be told, look, you are allowed to fail as long as you learn from your mistakes. This gives you hope that maybe I can make it after all. Give them unconditional support. Set examples and bring up children the way you want, but once they are old enough set them free. Experience is a great teacher. In the end those who learn from mistakes grow up stronger." (Chhibber, 2002a, p. 74)

Conclusions and a Look at the Future

This chapter has explored the connection between giftedness of children of Indian origin and the environment in the home, which, in turn, has been strongly influenced by parents' past experiences growing up in India. Will compromise

Rahul Dhara says, on the whole, his parents have been very liberal and nonconfrontational. He says, ". . . every one is a parent for the first time, and when they are trying to figure out things in their life and don't have the answers to everything, then the best thing to do is to be conservative." (Chhibber, 2002a, p. 74)

solutions dilute the successes of future generations of those of Indian descent? That answer is not clear.

Ultimately, the child gets the credit for his or her success. However, if you accept that the values of strong parental involvement and influence, hard work, dogged pursuit of academic and career goals, and a strong belief that great sacrifices for the cause of education are simply the "price of admission for success" are largely responsible for providing the atmosphere for the child's success, then it is reasonable to believe that, if these variables are diluted, it is possible that the percentage of successes might erode, too.

On the other hand, many first-generation Indian immigrants lack the infrastructure of connections—business, political, professional, and even those that come from childhood friendships. The second generation and future generations will gradually acquire those connections and contacts, which they can use as a springboard to even greater successes.

Meanwhile, Asian American parents search for special, often supplemental, educational opportunities for their children. They work hard and sacrifice financially to create the "cumulative educational advantage" that will put their children at the head of the Caucasian educational and professional "race to success."

8

Education of Supernormal Children in a Primary School

by Jiannong Shi and Jinghua Zhai

I n 1978, a special class for gifted young adolescents ages 11–16 was set up at the University of Science and Technology of China (USTC). Several dozen highly gifted adolescents were selected from all over the country and formed into a special class (Liu & Zhu, 2001; Xin, 1990; Zha, 1993). Meanwhile, a national cooperative research group for supernormal children was set up under the leadership of Professor Zha, a psychologist at the Institute of Psychology, Chinese Academy of Sciences. A new Chinese conception of gifted children called "supernormal children" was created.[1] The special class for gifted young adolescents and the Cooperative Research Group for Supernormal Children in China (CRGSCC) were evaluated as two milestones in the history of modern gifted study in Mainland China (Shi & Xu, 1999; Shi & Zha, 2000). After several years of empirical research, Zha and her colleagues set up principles of identification of gifted children (Zha, 1983, 1986).

In 1985, after the seventh gifted class for adolescents at USTC, the Institute of Psychology of the Chinese Academy of Sciences collaborated with the Beijing No. 8 Middle School to set up a special class for 10-year-old gifted children at that school in order to put the results of psychological research into practice in

---

[1] In this chapter, the phrases "supernormal children" and "gifted or talented children" are used interchangeably.

foundational education in China. This was a typical acceleration program, and it turned out that acceleration worked very well. Consequently, people wanted to spread the range of gifted education to elementary schools. So, in 1995, the Institute of Psychology of the Chinese Academy of Sciences collaborated with the Beijing Yumin Primary School to set up a special class for 6-year-old gifted children. All of the students who have taken part in this special class have developed very well academically. For example, six students from the second class (enrolled in 1997) took part in the Xicheng District Competition in Mathematics in 2000 and won 6 medals out of 10, which is particularly impressive given that there were several hundred participants involved in this competition.

In this chapter, we discuss some issues about gifted education and summarize our 6 years of experience in gifted acceleration in primary school.

Conception of Giftedness

Instead of the term *giftedness*, which is widely used in Western world, Chinese psychologists developed the term *supernormalness* to indicate the phenomena of human excellence (Shi, 2002). Chinese psychologists also use the phrase "supernormal children," rather than "gifted and talented children," in their work (Liu, 1980; Zha, 1983, 1986, 1990, 1993; Shi & Xu, 1998, 1999; Shi & Zha, 2000). There are two reasons for this: (1) *gifted* in Chinese, *tian cai*, means the God's bestowal upon humankind, and Chinese psychologists do not think that the very high ability of some children is totally inborn; (2) *supernormal* means some children are relatively superior to most normal children. In other words, supernormal children are only one group within the whole of "children." Hence, *supernormal* is a term with statistical meaning (Liu). In general, the performances of children on any psychological aspect follow the rule of normal distribution and can be mathematically expressed as

$$f(x) = \frac{1}{\sigma \sqrt{2\pi}} e^{-\frac{(x - u)^2}{2\sigma^2}}$$

where x represents the real performance of an individual; μ represents the expected performance or mean performance of the population tested; and σ represents the standard deviation. If $x \geq \mu + 2\sigma$, then the individual can be treated as supernormal (Shi & Xu, 1998).

For example, if there is a normal distribution in mathematics performance with a mean of 100 and a standard deviation of 15 and an individual's performance is 130 or higher, then this individual can be considered supernormal in mathematics. With this formula, one can identify many different kinds of supernormal children in different psychological aspects or domain-specific fields. Practically, we often use the cutoff of "2 or more years above" to identify a child as supernormal, that is, if a child's performance in a field or aspect is equal to or better than the average performance of a 2-years-older group, then the child is supernormal in that specific aspect (Shi & Xu, 1998; Zha, 1993). Ideally, we can find supernormal individuals either in general (i.e., general intelligence) or in any aspect or domain, such as mathematics, natural sciences, visual arts, music, language, spatial ability, leadership, social work, and so forth, even in daily life, such as cooking, sewing, and parenting. In other words, supernormal individuals exist in any field people can define. However, what we discuss here pertains mostly to children who are supernormal in academic fields.

Identification

The first challenge for psychologists in studying supernormal children is how to identify them. In order to find a way to identify supernormal children from the pool of all children, Zha and her colleagues started a series of psychological studies on supernormal children that pertained to cognitive abilities, such as perception (Chen & Shu, 1990; Zhang, 1987), memory (Huang, 1990; Shi, 1990a, 1990b), analogical reasoning (Wang, 1990; Zha, 1984), and creative thinking (Li, 1984), as well as nonintellectual aspects, such as curiosity and motivation, persistence (Hong, Zhou, Wang,, & Xu, 1989), and some aspects about children's personalities (Chen, 1990; Wang & Lu, 1990). After many years of study, they developed the Cognitive Ability Test for Identifying Supernormal Children (CAT-ISC; Zha, 1986) and a set of nonintellectual questionnaires.

Principles of Identification

Meanwhile, Zha and her colleagues developed some principles of identification, which are as follows:

1. Academically supernormal children should be identified in a dynamic comparative investigation because the intelligence of human individuals is developing, rather than fixed, and the development of an individual is influenced by some cultural, environmental, and educational factors. Meanwhile, the identification of supernormal children ought to be carried out in a dynamic comparison with normal children of the same age under similar social conditions (Zha, 1983, 1986).
2. Academically supernormal children should be identified with multiple criteria and multiple methods because the manifestations of giftedness are different (Zha, 1983, 1986).
3. Personality traits, as well as intelligence, should be considered in the identification of academically supernormal children because the application of one's intellectual potential may be directed and controlled by one's personality traits, consciously, unconsciously, or both (Zha, 1983, 1986).

4. Quantitative and qualitative responses should be recorded and analyzed (Zha, 1986, 1993).

5. In the identification, different aspects of abilities should be considered at several levels. For example, at the university level, besides intelligence and personality traits, knowledge in mathematics, Chinese, English, physics, chemistry, and biology are considered. Only three subjects—mathematics, Chinese, and English—are considered at the middle school level, while no subject knowledge is focused on at the primary school level (Zha, 1983, 1986; Shi & Xu, 1999).

6. The physical condition of an individual should also be considered because that can affect educability (Shi & Xu, 1999).

Procedure of Identification

With these identification principles in mind, psychologists from the Institute of Psychology of the Chinese Academy of Sciences and teachers from the Beijing Yumin Primary School started to set up a special class for supernormal children, especially for those academically supernormal. In identifying children for this class, they followed a set of procedures:

1. *Parents' nomination.* An announcement was posted in local newspapers and on local television stations to let people know about this kind of special class. The purpose, meaning, and special characteristics of the class were included in the notice. Parents of any 6-year-old child were encouraged to nominate him or her.

2. *Prescreening.* The children nominated by their parents were prescreened by professionals in order to exclude those obviously not suitable for this kind of class. For example, some children were too old to be enrolled, some lived too far from the school, or some had obvious characteristics of Attention-Deficit/Hyperactivity Disorder. After the prescreening, there were 826 candidates for the first year in 1995.

3. *Primary screening.* The group completed a set of standardized intellectual tests pertaining to general intelligence, memory, attention, observation, imagination, reasoning, and creative thinking. Of the 826 candidates, 120 passed the primary screening step.

4. *Second screening.* After the primary screening, children were tested individually with the CAT-ISC (Cognitive Ability Test for Identifying Supernormal Children). Forty-four children were selected after the second screening.

5. *Real Class Test.* After the second screening, these 44 children were placed in a special class to take part in several lessons such as Chinese, math, fine art, natural sciences, and physical activities. The children's behavior in the classroom and their daily life activities were considered. Finally, 33 children were enrolled after 2 weeks of the Real Class Test.

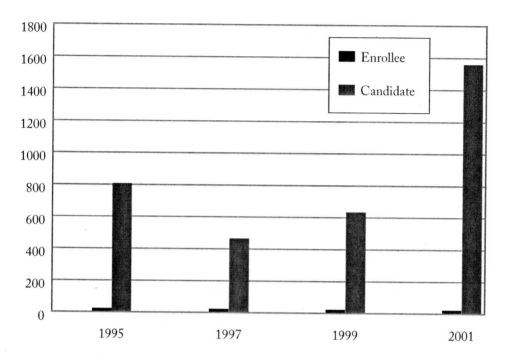

Figure 8.1 Number of candidates and enrollees

Using these specific screening steps, a special class is now set up every other year, thus far in 1995, 1997, 1999, and 2001. So far, 124 supernormal children have been selected and enrolled in the four special classes. The number of candidates and enrollees is displayed in Figure 8.1.

Education

After the supernormal children were identified, they were placed in a special experimental class for acceleration. Generally, they are expected to finish their primary education within 4 years, while most children have to spend 6 years in a regular elementary program. According to the theory of a natural perspective of giftedness (Shi & Xu, 1998, 1999), education for supernormal children has to pay a great deal of attention to children's socialization and physical development, as well as their mental development. Therefore, besides the intensive teaching programs in subjects such as mathematics, Chinese, and English, the special program has focused on children's physical development, social abilities, and divergent thinking ability, as well as building good relations between students and teachers and close cooperation between school and family.

Natural Physical Education

"Natural physical education" means, of course, doing physical education in a natural way. First used in the Beijing No. 8 Middle School (Gong & Cheng, 1998), it turned out that the notion is extremely beneficial for gifted children's physical maturity. Traditionally, the contents of physical education are arranged according to competition needs. For example, racing, basketball, table tennis, high jumping, and track and field are included in the Olympic games and other world-wide competitions, so these are assigned as the contents of school physical education. However, the question is, "Are these activities necessary for children's physical development or physical maturity?" The answer is, "Yes, but not primarily." While these sports are central to the Olympics, what children need most for their physical maturity are not competitive sports, but those physical exercises essential for their growth. Most important are those in which the children are interested. It has been said that physical education should be "in the sun, in nature."

In our practice, we arrange some physical activities in the open world, in natural surroundings. For example, we would like for students to climb mountains, rather than run races, to visit historical sites on foot, rather than by bus, and to pick fruit in orchards, rather than doing physical exercises on the playground. There are many more hours of physical education in our 4-year acceleration program than in the regular 6-year program.

Social Activities

In the last two decades, Chinese children have been frequently criticized as being "Little Emperors." To avoid this, students are frequently required to take part in social activities during the 4-year primary acceleration. For example, students are encouraged to investigate city pollution, visit farmlands, visit big companies such as the Legend Company (one of the largest information technology companies in China), interview different people about the problems of unemployment, and visit rest homes.

Divergent Thinking Skills

We believe that every student can be and wants to be creative, but at different levels. Students are encouraged to think divergently when they are learning or doing their schoolwork. For example, before we started a new lesson, *chi bi zhi zhan* (the war at Chibi in ancient China), we pointed out that the text was a story about an ancient war that was a typical example of "the less win the more." Before the lesson, a picture of this war was presented to the students, and they were asked to imagine the situation and then make make comments about the war. Who won the war? Why? Who lost the war? Why? What we can learn from the story?

The students were highly stimulated and excited during the lesson. Finally, they wrote some poems to summarize the story.

Good Relations Between Students and Teachers

There is a Chinese proverb "*qing qi shi, xin qi dao*" (here *dao* is *Tao*). It means that a chummy relationship between a student and a teacher can make the student follow the teacher's belief and learn better from the teacher. Therefore, good relationships between students and teachers are considered desirable in our program. Good relationships here mean that the relationships are developed with democracy, equality, harmony, and collaboration between students and between students and teachers. Teachers and students respect each other.

In the classroom, students are encouraged to listen, help each other, bring up questions, and express themselves. They are also encouraged to make comments or suggestions about the teaching activities. For example, a teacher might ask, "What do you think I should teach according to the text?" or "What should we learn from the text?," which is far different from the typical classroom, where teachers make their lessons according to the guidelines of the textbooks and no students' opinions are requested. Meanwhile, teachers are expected to be concerned not only with the students' academic progress, but also with their daily lives and their lives outside school.

School and Family Cooperation

Schooling is not an isolated matter for either the school or the student. It is a systematic procedure in a complex network among students, teachers, school, family, and social environments. As an essential factor for a child's schooling, parents are encouraged to make comments about the teaching arrangements and educational programs for their supernormal children. Teachers are asked to communicate with the parents. Parents are invited to the school to attend the parents' meeting. Normally, people may think that parents are invited to (in fact, called to) school to attend the parents' meeting because of their children's bad school performance or problem behaviors. But, in our program, the parents' meeting is a regular arrangement for establishing a good relationship between family and school. At the parents' meeting, the parents are informed of what has been going on in school recently, and what is going to be arranged.

Author Note

Studies on supernormal children have been supported by NSFC (39700045), Ministry of Education (GBB010921).

Part II

The View From the Core Education Community

9

Meeting the Diverse Needs of Gifted Students Through Individualized Educational Plans

by Linda E. Brody

C oncerns about equity and a lack of cultural diversity among many of the students identified for gifted programming have fueled criticism of identification strategies, standardized tests, ability grouping, and special programs for gifted students. These issues, as well as budgetary considerations, have led to the elimination in recent years of many programs designed to serve advanced learners (Benbow & Stanley, 1996; Gallagher, 2003). Consequently, there is currently great variability in the services offered by school systems. Some provide a wide variety of magnet school options, Advanced Placement classes, and special honors programs, while others expect their advanced students to remain with age peers in regular classrooms with little opportunity for a differentiated curriculum. For those concerned about equity issues, the disparity of opportunities across school systems can be alarming, with some segments of the population of gifted students clearly having far more access to special school-based opportunities than others.

Unfortunately, many of the school-based gifted programs that are still available fail to recognize the diverse needs of individuals within the gifted student population. For example, programs that use global measures to select participants may not address the needs of students with specific talents in mathematics. Even classes for mathematically talented students may provide instruction for those who are 1 or 2 years above grade level in achievement, but not those who are more advanced than this. Consequently, many gifted and talented students do not find a match between their academic needs and the instructional programs available in their schools.

As the number of special programs for gifted students in schools has decreased, there has been a dramatic growth in educational opportunities for academically talented students offered outside of school by public and private universities and a variety of for-profit and nonprofit organizations. These opportunities have enhanced the educational experiences of many thousands of students, but they are often more accessible to those whose parents have the knowledge and resources to seek supplemental opportunities for their children. Putting the full burden on families of identifying and gaining access to appropriate educational opportunities for their children raises additional equity issues, as some families are more prepared than others to assume this role. Clearly, schools need to evaluate and expand the opportunities they provide for their gifted students so that access to special programs is less dependent on where a student lives or on parental resources.

However, even students who attend schools with few formal programs for the gifted can obtain a challenging educational program if they utilize existing in- and out-of-school opportunities in a flexible way. By adjusting the level and pace of instruction and taking advantage of supplemental opportunities, there is much evidence that effective programs can be developed for even the most precocious students (Brody & Benbow, 1987; Brody & Blackburn, 1996; Stanley, 1979, 1989b, 1991a).

To facilitate the needed accommodations, individualized educational plans (IEPs) serve to outline the specific programmatic modifications needed to create an optimal program for a student with advanced academic needs (Brody, 2001; Durden & Tangherlini, 1993; Lupkowski-Shoplik, Benbow, Assouline, & Brody, 2003; Robinson & Robinson, 1982; Rogers, 2001). Routinely used in special education, some states (e.g., Pennsylvania) have broadened their requirements to include IEPs for gifted students. Whether legally mandated or not, IEPs can be helpful tools in counseling and serving gifted learners.

This chapter provides an overview of the process involved in designing an appropriate plan for an individual student. The programmatic options described are not intended to be a complete list; rather, they demonstrate the importance of considering a wide variety of opportunities and strategies to address an individual student's needs.

Assessment

Gifted students are a diverse group of individuals whose unique attributes need to be considered when designing an educational program to meet their needs. Thus, it is important to assess a variety of cognitive and affective characteristics, including a student's strengths, weaknesses, interests, and personality traits. The information gleaned from this assessment will inform the nature of the program recommended.

It is useful to assess both general and specific abilities to discern a student's cognitive profile. While some students have abilities that allow them to excel in most areas of achievement, others have strengths in specific content areas. To assess general ability, an IQ test is useful. Specific abilities can be assessed through aptitude tests. In Chapter 19 of this volume, Olszewski-Kubilius summarizes the talent search approach to identifying specific mathematical and verbal reasoning abilities (see also Lupkowski-Shoplik, Benbow, Assouline, & Brody, 2003; VanTassel-Baska, 1996). In addition to assessing these abilities, exceptional abilities in such areas as scientific reasoning, leadership, and the arts should also be evaluated and considered when determining an appropriate educational program for individual students. In her chapter, Olszewski-Kubilius describes the differential educational needs of talent search participants who score at different levels, even within a group of students who are all highly able. In general, the more exceptional the student, the less likely it is that a typical school curriculum designed for age peers will meet his or her needs.

If a student has any specific cognitive weaknesses, understanding the underlying cause will be important to making recommendations. The recommendations would be different, for example, for a gifted child who fails to achieve because he or she is bored from lack of challenge as opposed to a student who has a learning disability. A full psycho-educational assessment is important for gifted students with suspected learning disabilities (Brody & Mills, 1997) or young gifted students considering grade acceleration (Assouline, 2003).

In addition to evaluating a student's general and specific abilities, it is important to determine actual achievement levels and content knowledge for placement purposes. For example, you would make different programmatic decisions for a seventh grader who has not yet learned algebra from one who has mastered pre-calculus, even if both of them earned the same SAT-I scores in a talent search. Similarly, two students with exceptional verbal reasoning abilities may be quite different in their proficiency in writing creatively. A student's performance on standardized achievement tests can show the extent to which he or she has mastered a content area compared to other students, and this can guide placement decisions. Criterion-reference tests developed by textbook companies and others, as well as informal assessments by teachers, can also contribute to evaluating students' content knowledge in particular areas.

Gifted students also vary in their interests, personality attributes, and preferences, which are related to talent development (Lubinski & Benbow, 1995). For example, one student may have a passion for history, while another likes science. Interest, along with motivation and energy level, will influence a student's willingness to seek additional opportunities and work hard to master more advanced content. Finally, social and emotional adjustment and maturity are additional factors that should be considered in making educational decisions, particularly if placement with older students is being considered.

The student's educational history may help determine which specific tests and inventories are needed. Some comparison to age peers is valuable, however, in order to identify a student's special needs and the extent to which the typical school program must be modified to provide an appropriate level of challenge.

Programmatic Options

Since opportunities and resources vary considerably among schools and communities, it is necessary to survey and evaluate those that that are available in a particular area before choosing the ones that will best serve the needs of individual students. Then, programs can be chosen that best serve the students' needs as determined by their assessments. In general, students who live in urban areas are likely to have more opportunities available locally than rural students, but the presence of a local college may increase options. Flexible placement and pacing within the school, however, should be an option wherever students live. A family's financial circumstances will be a consideration in accessing programs that charge fees, although many programs do provide assistance to students with definite financial needs.

Selecting the Best School Environment

The first consideration is the school the student will attend. While most students attend their local public school, many have some choice and may be able to identify schools that are more likely to meet their needs. For those looking beyond their local public school, private or parochial day or boarding schools are possibilities, although, within the public system, there may be charter or magnet schools. Early college entrance or homeschooling are options some students turn to when school programs fail to meet their needs.

When choosing an elementary school, small-group instruction, flexible pacing and placement, and a critical mass of other advanced students are desirable attributes to look for. For secondary students, flexible placement and access to advanced courses (e.g., Advanced Placement or International Baccalaureate programs, cooperation with a local college) are important for students with advanced educational needs. The option of obtaining credit or placement for coursework completed outside of school, access to a variety of extracurricular activities, and the possibility of doing independent research with a mentor are also desirable.

While public magnet schools that serve gifted students are not available in all communities, they have a long history in the United States. For example, the Bronx High School of Science was founded in New York in 1938; a more recent addition to the scene is the highly respected Thomas Jefferson School for Science and Technology in Fairfax County, VA. Although modification of the curriculum may still be needed for individual students even within magnet schools, these schools typically offer a higher level of instruction and more opportunities for students to interact with intellectual peers than might be found in a neighborhood school. Magnet schools often focus on a specialty area such as math and science, the humanities, or the arts. Obviously, a student's specific interests and talents should determine whether a magnet school with a particular area of specialization is appropriate for him or her.

Rural areas typically do not have enough advanced students in their communities to justify developing local magnet schools. Consequently, a number of states have established publicly funded residential high schools to address the needs of advanced students who live throughout their state. Students who attend these schools must be willing to live away from home, but they benefit from the special resources provided and the continual, extensive interaction with intellectual peers provided by the residential environment (Kolloff, 2003; Stanley, 1991b).

Some students who lack adequate challenge in their high schools turn to full-time college entrance at younger-than-typical ages as an alternative, and many have successfully matriculated at colleges around the country (Brody & Stanley, 1991). Concern about meeting the academic and social needs of young college students, however, has led some universities to establish special early-college-entrance programs. These accept young college entrants as a cohort and offer more social and emotional support and counseling than is usually provided to regular-age college students. Research supports the efficacy of these programs as a viable alternative to meeting the learning needs of advanced students (Olszewski-Kubilius, 1995; Sethna, Wickstrom, Boothe, & Stanley, 2001).

Homeschooling has also grown in popularity as an alternative to the regular school enrollment (Kearney, 1998). It is important to note that homeschoolers today are unlikely to do all their learning alone in the home. Many take classes through distance education or in summer programs, organize small classes with other homeschoolers, or enroll in local colleges. The greater availability of these options has enhanced the educational experiences of many homeschooled students.

Some students do not have the option of choosing a school, or they may prefer to attend their neighborhood school even if course offerings are less rigorous than they might be elsewhere. These students can still develop an appropriately challenging program by adjusting the curriculum to meet their individual needs and filling in the missing pieces from elsewhere. Even at elite private or magnet schools, each student's program should be examined to determine whether it needs to be modified to provide a greater level of challenge.

Choosing Courses Within the School

For students who are advanced in cognitive abilities and achievement, age-in-grade instruction is often not appropriate, and some acceleration in grade placement, subject matter, or both may be needed. In general, more highly talented students are likely to need more differentiation, but this depends on the school they attend. Given two students with similar academic needs, one may be well served by his or her school while the other is not. At the same time, a particular school program may serve one gifted learner well, but not include the curricular components another student needs. The student's individual cognitive and personality profile and the level of the curriculum provided by the school will determine how much, if any, differentiation is needed.

In developing an educational plan for an advanced student, grade placement warrants consideration. While skipping a grade may not fully address a gifted student's needs, those with exceptional abilities who are advanced across content areas may find it helpful to be placed ahead with older students on a full-time basis. For example, talent search students who score high on the SAT-I in seventh grade and find the middle school curriculum repetitious may want to skip the eighth grade and gain access to the broader variety of available course offerings at a high school. Of course, a student's content knowledge and social and emotional maturity are important factors to consider when electing to place him or her with older students on a full-time basis. Many educators find that having a student skip the grade before entering a new school setting (e.g., early entrance to kindergarten, middle school, high school, or college) is advantageous from the point of view of social adjustment because the student can enter the new learning environment with other new students.

Often students have academic needs that require moving ahead in one or more subject areas without having to leave their age peers for other subjects. While many educators only associate acceleration with grade skipping, there are *at least* 17 identified ways to accelerate one's educational program (Southern, Jones, & Stanley, 1993). Students who are advanced in content knowledge need to be evaluated in each subject and given the opportunity to advance appropriately. For example, a second-grade student who is an advanced reader may need to take reading with fourth-grade students, although the second-grade placement accommodates his other learning needs. Or a sixth-grade student who is otherwise well served by the sixth-grade curriculum may need an accelerated math program. This student might either take algebra with eighth-grade students or work on algebra independently or through distance education.

While appropriate placement will satisfy the needs of many students, some need further differentiation within the classroom. Even that sixth-grade student in the eighth-grade algebra class may need to move at a faster pace than the other students, or diagnostic testing might reveal that he already knows a great deal of algebra at the beginning of the course. For students like this, Stanley (2000) described a diagnostic–prescriptive model for assessing what a student already knows and adjusting the student's academic program to eliminate repetition of those topics. Other techniques have also been developed to differentiate effectively for gifted learners within regular classrooms (Tomlinson, 1999), including compacting the curriculum, which is described by Renzulli and Reis in Chapter 6 of this volume. Flexible grouping within the classroom based on academic need can facilitate offering an advanced curriculum to a group of gifted learners (Kulik & Kulik, 1992).

Typically, more choices are available for secondary students who want to take advantage of any rigorous course offerings appropriate for them such as honors,

Advanced Placement (AP), or International Baccalaureate courses. The proliferation of AP courses in high schools has done much to bring advanced secondary students together and make college-level work accessible to them. For students who attend schools with few AP options, they should be made aware that they can prepare to take AP tests without having taken an AP course (possibly with the help of a mentor or tutor). With these and other opportunities available to accelerate in specific content areas, acceleration in grade placement may be less necessary for many students than in the past.

Accessing Courses Outside of the School

Students who move quickly through the regular curriculum may run out of courses within the school. While many school officials are concerned about this outcome, there is much available for students to fill the gap if they are not ready to go to college early.

One place to look is within the school system itself. If logistics permit, elementary students can spend part of their day at a middle school, and middle school students at a high school. These students can take advanced courses with older students, while remaining with chronological age peers for the rest of the day.

Outside of the school system, classes offered on weekends or in the summer provide students with access to accelerated learning or to subjects not offered in school. The number of academic summer programs available for talented students has grown dramatically since 1972, when the Study of Mathematically Precocious Youth was established at Johns Hopkins (Benbow & Stanley, 1983; Stanley, Keating, & Fox, 1974). The impact on students of participating in rigorous programs with intellectual peers cannot be overstated, with students demonstrating mastery of advanced content, improved study skills, stronger motivation, and better social skills as a result of these experiences (Olszewski-Kubilius, 2003).

Another major area of growth has been distance education. While traditional correspondence study courses are still available, computerized programs now play a large role in bringing the curriculum to participating students. Gifted students can take advanced courses independently (with or without a tutor) via distance education programs. Sometimes, schools contract to use distance education for a group of students whose needs go beyond the regular curriculum, rather than employ a special teacher to provide the instruction. Advanced Placement courses are available online for students whose schools don't offer them, and full virtual high schools are now making their debut.

Students who live near a college or university may take courses there on a part-time basis. In recognition of this, some states have passed dual-enrollment legislation enabling students who exhaust offerings at their high school to take college courses for both high school and college credit, often at no cost to the students (McCarthy, 1999). Whether the universities at which students eventually enroll will also grant credit for prior part-time college courses depends on the policies of those institutions, but appropriate course placement is usually provided. In addition, the experience of taking advanced courses while in high school helps talented students prepare for more rigorous college coursework (Kolitch & Brody, 1992).

Other challenging programs for students include study-abroad programs, working with a mentor, or doing an internship. To delay enrolling in college, students who graduate early from high school may choose one of these options to pursue. Clearly, there are more opportunities available for older students, who can be more mobile and independent than younger students. However, younger gifted students can progress at an appropriate but fast pace through the regular curriculum, and educators can be confident that there will be many options available for them later, as long as schools remain flexible.

Developing Special Talents

While this chapter focuses primarily on students with academic abilities, many also have exceptional talents and interests in the performing or visual arts or athletics. Society is often more accepting of students advancing in athletics or the arts than in academic subjects. The challenge, however, when working with students who have abilities in many areas is to balance their time—to develop their special talents while also providing an appropriate level of academic challenge.

Time needs to be set aside for lessons, summer programs, and extracurricular activities that promote talent development in the student's area of interest. Specialized high schools may be appropriate for students with musical or artistic talent. Individualized educational plans should incorporate programs to develop special talents, as well as to serve the student's intellectual needs.

Taking Advantage of Extracurricular Activities

Extracurricular activities are not just a way to fill up a student's free time or expand a résumé; many are true learning opportunities that contribute to talent development, encourage leadership skills, and help students gain recognition for high achievement. They also provide a mechanism for students to meet and interact with peers who share their abilities and interests. An educational plan for a gifted student should include appropriate learning opportunities both inside and outside of the classroom.

Participation in competitions and contests, in particular, can provide a high level of challenge. These are available in a variety of areas, including spelling, geography, mathematics, the sciences, computer science, and languages. Achievement at a high level can even bring national or international recognition. For example, the International Mathematics, Physics, or Chemistry Olympiads bring top young scholars from around the world together to compete each year and reward the winners with prestigious prizes. Top contestants in the Intel Science Talent Search demonstrate extraordinary levels of knowledge and research skills in scientific areas and earn much recognition and large scholarships ($100,000 for the top winner). Many highly able high school students find their senior year especially challenging because of their involvement in independent research and competitions.

In addition to competitions, numerous other challenges exist for students eager to develop their talents. Writing for a school or community newspaper or literary magazine can hone the skills of talented writers, and debating can develop critical thinking and oratory skills. Accepting a leadership role in school clubs, student government, and community organizations helps build leadership abilities and self-confidence.

Structured activities can provide important venues for learning, as well as interaction with peers. Students should not program all of their free time, however. Leisure time to pursue solitary interests is also important. Reading, writing, traveling, visiting museums, or conducting research on a topic of interest all serve to enrich a student's background and stimulate learning. Time spent with family and friends also enhances one's general self-concept and helps develop social skills.

Addressing Social/Emotional or Learning Difficulties

Although research provides strong evidence that, as a group, gifted students are well adjusted socially and emotionally, individual gifted students may exhibit social difficulties (Neihart, Reis, Robinson, & Moon, 2002; Terman, 1925). This can be particularly true for students who have had difficulty finding intellectual peers with whom they can relate.

For many gifted students, the implementation of an appropriate educational program with access to intellectual peers can enhance adjustment and eliminate social difficulties (Robinson, Reis, Neihart, & Moon, 2002). In particular, attending special high schools or academic summer programs or taking part in challenging extracurricular activities with others who share their abilities and interests have been found to impact positively on social and emotional development (Olszewski-Kubilius, 2003).

However, for students whose social and emotional issues are not resolved by appropriate educational placement, counseling may be needed to help them understand how their advanced abilities make them different from many of their age peers and how to cope with being different (Silverman, 1993). They may need help dealing with perfectionism or other issues related to their high abilities; or, if social skills are weak, special social skills training may be helpful.

Finally, while the greatest need for gifted students is to challenge them in their areas of strength and keep them moving ahead academically, some gifted students can have areas of weakness significant enough to require some remediation or tutoring in a particular content area. This is often overlooked even though it could ultimately impede learning. Sometimes, accommodations to compensate for a learning disability are needed, (e.g., using a computer for writing or a calculator for math computation; Brody & Mills, 1997). Highly gifted students may also lack appropriate study and organizational skills, especially if school has never been particularly challenging. As the demands increase with more advanced work, support may be needed.

Conclusion

With increasing concerns about equity in education, it is particularly important that programs be defensible and appropriate. If a special program for gifted students consists of extra field trips or the chance to work on any topic of interest in lieu of the regular curriculum, it may lead to envy among those who aren't given these privileges. But, when a sixth-grade student who is clearly ready to learn algebra is permitted to go to the eighth-grade class in which algebra is taught, it's unlikely that students less advanced in math will be clamoring to do the same. Meanwhile, the true learning needs of the advanced student are addressed through appropriate placement.

Gifted learners represent a very diverse group of individuals with differing cultural and economic backgrounds, educational experiences, abilities and talents, content knowledge, interests, and personalities. As a result, they differ in their educational needs and are best served through individualized programs that provide for flexible placement and pacing of instruction, effective articulation of out-of-school learning with in-school learning, and access to supplemental opportunities. A wide variety of programs and pedagogical strategies have been developed to serve gifted learners, and those students who need a differentiated education should gain access to these opportunities.

An individualized educational plan carefully designed for an individual student and reevaluated on a regular basis can ensure that the student's needs are not taken for granted and overlooked. When programs are designed to meet the current learning needs of individual students across the school population, equity issues are resolved and access to advanced work is provided for those who truly need it.

10

Realities in Desegregating Gifted Education

by Linda S. Gottfredson

E ducators of gifted children may always disagree, and probably wisely so, on how to define giftedness and best serve their students. But, they are likely united in imagining themselves Sisyphus, doomed forever to push a huge stone up a high hill only to have it roll back again. They struggle to gain even a small fraction of the support available for other exceptionalities, with that small fraction being treated as a dispensable luxury during the next budget squeeze. They must continually justify why children who "can take care of themselves" need special opportunities and defend against the charge that it is undemocratic and elitist even to identify some children as intellectually superior (Benbow & Stanley, 1996; Gottfredson, 2003c).

Critics suggest that gifted education is most self-evidently undemocratic when they demand to know, "Why are diverse students underrepresented—consistently and grossly underrepresented—in gifted education programs?" (Ford, 2003, p. 506). The underrepresentation of certain non-Asian racial-ethnic minorities is, indeed, "[o]ne of the most pervasive concerns in the field" of gifted education (Robinson & Clinkenbeard, 1998, p. 122). Its "palpable importance" stems, we are told, from "the loss of talent it incurs and the message of exclusion it sends" (Rizza & McIntosh, 2001, p. 402). Not surprisingly, the persistent underrepresentation of Blacks and Hispanics has generated calls for fundamentally reconceptualizing and restructuring gifted education so that it will "closely represent [a] community's demographics" (Ford, p. 518).

Unequal Representation in Gifted Education: Why?

One possible explanation for the racial imbalance in gifted education is that the ways we define and identify giftedness are biased in favor of Whites and Asians. A second possible explanation is that giftedness is not, in fact, distributed equally across all demographic groups. The first, Discrimination Theory, is usually offered as the *only* possible explanation; the latter, Distribution Theory, is offered as the *predominant* cause of racial imbalance in programs for the gifted.

Discrimination Theory: Unequal Recognition of Gifts and Talents

The two most commonly voiced reasons for unequal representation follow the first line of thinking: specifically, that traditional methods of identifying gifted children are culturally biased and, more importantly, that traditional conceptions of giftedness are narrow and skewed toward certain cultures.

Culturally biased and insensitive methods for identifying gifted children and their needs. Schools generally use some indicator of intellectual ability or academic achievement to identify gifted children. Richert (2003) exemplifies a cadre of critics who condemn this practice in her assertion that such "[m]easures of academic achievement . . ., including teacher recommendations, grades, and especially standardized tests, have been amply demonstrated to have cultural biases" (pp. 150–151). Some of these critics suggest switching to nonverbal tests of intelligence, such as the Raven Progressive Matrices, which require no language or background knowledge (e.g., Ford, 1995a, p. 59). Some (Stormont, Stebbins, & Holliday, 2001, p. 419) also recommend rescoring standardized tests or supplementing them with more qualitative measures of giftedness in order to equalize the rate at which students of different racial-ethnic groups are classified as gifted.

Richert (2003), for instance, incorporated both strategies in her four-part APOGEE procedure for guaranteeing racial balance in a school's gifted program: (1) use a wide variety of indicators, including tests of achievement, but also recommendations by teachers, parents, and the students themselves (e.g, using checklists of interests, social skills, emotional strengths, and the like); (2) classify all students into subgroups by race, gender, and economic advantage; (3) rank students within their own race-gender-economic group on each indicator (i.e., create separate norming tables for each subgroup); and (4) then pick those students "scoring among the top 25 percent of their demographic group on any test score or by teacher, parent, or self-nomination" (p. 151).

Students need not be performing well academically to be selected because, as Richert (2003) has argued, many poor and culturally diverse students are "underachieving students who particularly need a gifted program to develop their unmanifested potential" (p. 149). Low achievement levels among Blacks and Hispanics would rise, she suggested, if we conceptualized poor academic achievement as educators' failure to recognize and nourish giftedness, rather than as students failing to possess it. Equity, therefore, requires more diverse, more sensitive means of finding those unrecognized "potentially gifted" students who "have yet to reveal their true capabilities" (Ford, 1995a, pp. 59–60). Moreover, to identify only a few percent of students as gifted—and, worse yet, as "highly gifted"—is, in Richert's view, "elitist," "polariz[ing]," and puts in jeopardy the entire enterprise of gifted education (p. 149). In short, if our tools for identifying giftedness do not produce racial balance, we should modify them until they do.

Racial balance that is attained by changing selection tools will soon be undone, however, unless steps are taken to prevent higher failure rates among the lower achieving minority students identified as gifted. Gifted educators are therefore urged to better accommodate the needs of the minority children in their programs. For instance, Ford (2003, pp. 514–515; see also Stormont et al., 2001, pp. 419–421) has stated that gifted education programs must help underachieving gifted minority students by (1) providing more supportive learning environments (e.g., cooperative, rather than competitive), enhancing academic engagement and self-efficacy, and providing remediation as needed (e.g., study skills, time management); (2) improving instruction (e.g., smaller classes, higher teacher expectations) to close the achievement gaps; (3) enhancing the multicultural competence of teachers so that they better recognize the talents and needs of minority children; (4) providing multicultural education to reaffirm personal and cultural worth; and (5) developing home-school partnerships. In other words, sensitivity to culture-specific strengths must be followed by equal sensitivity to culture-specific needs.

Culturally biased or insensitive definitions of giftedness. Giftedness has traditionally been conceived as *intellectual* giftedness, as an ability to learn and perform remarkably well in any of a variety of intellectual domains, especially the academic and artistic; hence, the longstanding reliance on standardized tests and teacher referrals to identify unusually high levels of intellectual aptitude or achievement. In view of the "persistent gap in the intelligence, aptitude, and achievement test scores of [different racial-ethnic groups]," however, Ford (2003, p. 511) has argued that we must, in the name of equity, cease relying so exclusively on such tests and on the unidimensional notion of giftedness they seem to reflect. "[O]ne type of test cannot possibly measure the many types of intelligences that exist" (Ford, p. 514). In fact, Richter (2003) believes that "[a]chievement and IQ tests tend to *screen out* the most creative students, and teachers often have biases against nonconforming students" (p. 152, emphasis added). Reflecting a broader trend in gifted education (Robinson & Clinkenbeard, 1998), both Ford and Richert advocate a multidimensional view of giftedness and correspondingly multimodal ways of identifying it.

Popular multidimensionalist conceptions include Sternberg's (1997) set of three "triarchic" intelligences (analytical, creative, and practical) and Gardner's (1983) set of seven "multiple intelligences" (linguistic, visuospatial, logical-mathematical, musical, intrapersonal, interpersonal, and bodily-kinesthetic). Emotional intelligence, emotional expressiveness, wisdom, oral fluency, civic mindedness, spirituality, commitment to social connectedness, and much else have also been put forward as distinct forms of giftedness. In some discussions, just about any admirable trait or behavior, broad or narrow, whether exhibited inside or outside school, qualifies as giftedness as long as a relevant observer (teacher, parent, peer, self) considers it a personal strength.

Multidimensionalists present their broader conceptions as more democratic because they are more "inclusive" than the traditional intellectual one. "[P]rograms for exceptional students [must be] inclusive rather than exclusive" because

> [r]ecognizing the potentials and talents of all children requires a broad-
> ened vision of giftedness that reflects the understanding that talent and
> creativity vary markedly among individuals of varying cultural, ethnic,
> socioeconomic, and linguistic backgrounds. (Ford, 1995a, p. 60; cf.
> Richert, 2003, pp. 149–150)

The multidimensionalists' "egalitarian and pluralistic" conceptions of giftedness reinforce their admonition to use culture- and context-sensitive means for iden-tifying diverse forms of talent, as well as their reluctance to set many (if any) *a priori* boundaries on what constitutes giftedness. Because giftedness, like beauty, is often in the eye of the beholder, they would increase the number and variety of beholders. For instance, laypeople sharing the child's everyday world (e.g., parents) might identify strengths that professionals typically would not recog-nize as potential gifts. Whereas some multidimensionalists are willing to specify a delimited set of gifts and talents, others are more radical in preferring not to set any boundaries.

Distribution Theory: Unequal Distribution of Gifts and Talents

Proponents of Discrimination Theory either assert or take for granted that giftedness is evenly distributed across all demographic groups. Groups may exhibit different forms of giftedness, but all in equal quantity. There would be no demographic imbalances in programs for the gifted, they believe, but for discrim-ination and inept identification of talent. Any suggestion to the contrary—that giftedness may not exist in equal measure in all race-gender-economic groups— is labeled "deficit thinking" and rejected as destructive or racist. For example, speaking of the "persistent and pervasive underrepresentation of diverse students in gifted education," which "is likely to have devastating, long-lasting effects," Ford (2003) stated that "We can attribute much of this difficulty to deficit think-ing, which limits access and opportunity" (p. 518). The premise that groups dif-fer on the average in general mental ability (intelligence) "is harmful and unsound, and has no place in educational settings" (Ford, p. 511). Thus, to ques-tion the assumption that groups exhibit giftedness in equal proportion is itself said to create or magnify underrepresentation.

But, is it true that giftedness is equally distributed across all demographic groups? And is it true that, but for the ill will, ineptitude, and cultural myopia of school personnel, there would be racial parity in gifted education?

IQ/achievement gaps are real and important. An essential claim of Discrimination Theory is that standardized tests of IQ and academic achievement are culturally biased. However, that claim was disproved decades ago, with ever more refined investigations only reconfirming the conclusion that the major norm-referenced tests measure cognitive ability without bias (i.e., equally well) among native-born, English-speaking Americans, including Blacks (Neisser et al., 1996). (In fact, professional testing standards prohibit the publication and use of biased tests.) One must always be careful to use appropriate, culture-reduced tests when assessing the cognitive abilities of recent immigrants and language minorities, but test bias is not a frequent problem when proper precautions are observed. The "persistent gap in intelligence, aptitude, and achievement tests scores" about which Ford has written (2003, p. 511) therefore reflects real differences in important cognitive skills and achievements (Neisser et al.).

Criterion-referenced achievement tests show the same real differences in academic capability as do norm-referenced ability tests. The "Nation's Report Card" provides the clearest example. Proficiency levels of 9-, 13-, and 17-year-olds in reading, math, science, and other subjects are assessed by the U.S. Department of Education's National Assessment of Educational Progress (NAEP), which has been administered to large national samples of elementary and secondary students for the last three decades. Far from accusing the NAEP of cultural bias, educational policymakers (including those enacting the No Child Left Behind Act in 2002) take the NAEP results quite seriously, especially because they *do* reveal large racial gaps in demonstrably important academic skills, ranging from the most basic to the most advanced, at all three ages in all academic subjects in all 30 years that the NAEP has been conducted. These achievement gaps are comparable in magnitude to the IQ gaps between Blacks, Hispanics, and Whites, and by grade 12 they translate into Blacks' being an average of four grade levels below Whites and Asians in achievement in core subjects, with Hispanics averaging about three grade equivalents behind (Gottfredson, 2003b). Because standardized tests are honest measures of intellectual and academic competence, we must conclude that racial-ethnic groups do, in fact, differ—and sometimes markedly so—in their distributions of intellectual talent.

Predictions from Distribution Theory. Standardized intelligence tests predict school achievement, job performance, and socioeconomic advancement moderately well in all American racial-ethnic groups, meaning that the skills deficits they reveal portend socially significant gaps in achievement, as well. What levels of racial-ethnic imbalance would Distribution Theory predict if gifted programs relied on (unbiased) intelligence tests to identify eligible students? If IQ 130 were set as the minimum threshold for giftedness, as many programs have done, about

2 to 3% of the general population would be found to exceed the threshold, but Blacks and Hispanics would only rarely be identified as gifted.

Figure 10.1 illustrates the degree of underrepresentation that would be expected across the nation were the entry threshold set at various different points along the IQ continuum. The ratios (or, more precisely, the odds) in the bottom rows of the figure are derived from the proportions of Blacks, Hispanics, and Asians, relative to the proportion of Whites, who score above given IQ levels in national samples. (Results for Native Americans would be much like those for Hispanics; Gottfredson, 2003b.) The ratios show that Blacks and Hispanics are relatively sparse at the highest levels of IQ. Severity of underrepresentation falls steadily at successively lower IQ thresholds, but is still meaningful as far down the IQ continuum as IQ 75. More specifically, if the threshold for entry into gifted education were set at IQ 125, the ratio of Blacks to Whites in representative samples would hover around 1:30, and for Hispanics 1:5. Asians would tend to be *over*represented above this IQ level by 2:1. Were the threshold lowered to the 50th percentile (IQ 100), racial imbalance would still be large: 1:3 for Blacks, 1:2 for Hispanics, and 6:5 for Asians.

Were standardized tests of achievement in core subjects used to identify gifted students, the same pattern of racial imbalance would emerge as for IQ tests. Table 10.1 shows the percentage of students in four racial-ethnic groups in grades 4, 8, and 12 who achieved at or above the "basic" level of proficiency in NAEP reading, math, and science from 1996 to 2000. (*Basic* is defined as "partial mastery of prerequisite knowledge and skills that are fundamental for proficient work at each grade"; Donahue, Voelkl, Campbell, & Mazzeo, 1999, p. 9). The table also shows the percentages who achieved at or above the "proficient" level in those subjects. If students were selected randomly from among those achieving at or above the "proficient" level, we would predict the proportion of minority students relative to the proportion of White students selected to be about 1:4 for Blacks, 1:3 for Hispanics, and 1:1 for Asians (these predictions are based on averaging the percentages across the three subjects and two grade levels). Once again, the ratios would be better for lower thresholds, but still far from "racial equity." For instance, were students selected randomly from among those performing merely at or above the "basic" level, the gaps would be, respectively, 1:2, 3:5, and 14:15 for the three groups. These latter ratios are similar to those for the relative percentages of each group scoring above the 25th percentile in IQ (IQ 90): 1:2 (Blacks), 2:3 (Hispanics), and 10:9 (Asians).

Equity-excellence tradeoff. Ford (2003, p. 507) reported the levels of under- or overrepresentation actually observed in gifted education programs from 1978 to 1992. In 1992, the proportions of Blacks, Hispanics, Native Americans, Asians, and Whites in gifted education relative to their proportions in the general population were, respectively, .57, .58, .50, 1.75, and 1.21. Representation of the three underrepresented groups relative to Whites (about 1:2) is therefore far better than one would achieve even with random selection from among students in the top

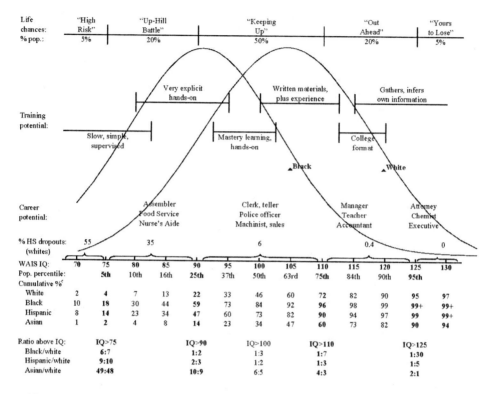

Life chances:	"High Risk"	"Up-Hill Battle"	"Keeping Up"	"Out Ahead"	"Yours to Lose"
% pop.:	5%	20%	50%	20%	5%

Figure 10.1. Relative representation of American Whites, Blacks, Hispanics, and Asians at different points along the IQ continuum

Note. Cumulative percentages are based on mean Wechsler Adult Intelligence Scale (WAIS) IQs of 101.4 for Whites and 86.9 for Blacks and SDs of 14.7 and 13.0, respectively. Means for Hispanics and Asians are set, respectively, at 91 and 106, and SDs at 15 (based on data in Gottfredson, 2003b). Percentiles for IQ scores were estimated by use of cumulative normal probability tables. Minority/White ratios were calculated before percentiles were rounded.

Adapted from "Why *g* Matters: The Complexity of Everyday Life," by L. S. Gottfredson, 1997, *Intelligence, 24*, p. 117. Copyright ©1997 by Elsevier Science. Adapted with permission.

half of the distribution for either IQ or standardized achievement. These degrees of actual representation are similar to the racial imbalances found in Table 10.1 among students performing merely at or above the "basic" level in NAEP reading, math, and science. The underrepresentation observed is far smaller than what would be expected on the basis of group differences in cognitive ability and academic achievement. It therefore appears that standardized tests—and the real intellectual capabilities they measure—have played a far *smaller* role in identifying gifted children than usually claimed. From the perspective of the traditional definition of giftedness, there has been a sizeable tradeoff between racial balance and intellectual rigor in the identification of the gifted.

Ford (2003) has stated that discussion of any equity-excellence tradeoff is harmful and nonproductive. However, the tradeoff clearly does exist and warrants atten-

Table 10.1

Percentages of Students Exceeding Particular NAEP Proficiency Levels in Reading, Math, and Science, by Race in Grades 4 and 12 During 1996–2000

	% at or Above NAEP "Basic" Level of Proficiency[a]					
	Grade 4			Grade 12		
	Reading[a] 1998	Math[b] 1996	Science[c] 2000	Reading 1998	Math 1996	Science 2000
White	73	76	79	83	79	62
Black	36	32	34	57	38	22
Hispanic	40	41	42	64	50	30
Asian	69	73	66[d]	75	81	59

	% at or Above NAEP "Proficient" Level					
	Grade 4			Grade 12		
	Reading 1998	Math 1996	Science 2000	Reading 1998	Math 1996	Science 2000
White	39	28	38	47	20	23
Black	10	5	7	18	4	3
Hispanic	13	8	11	26	6	7
Asian	37	26	29[d]	38	33	26

Note.
[a]Source of reading scores: Donahue, Voelkl, Campbell, & Mazzeo (1999).
[b]Source of math scores: Reese, Miller, Mazzeo, & Dossey (1997).
[c]Source of science scores: O'Sullivan, Lauko, Grigg, Qian, & Zhang (2003).
[d]Data for Asians is for 1996, not 2000.

tion. The tradeoff between (non-Asian) minority representation and the rigor of selection standards is a problem not only in gifted education, but anywhere that intellectual competence matters. Personnel psychologists have written extensively about exactly how large the tradeoff will be under different selection scenarios in both education and employment (Sackett, Schmitt, Ellingson, & Kabin, 2001). They have also documented that achieving racial parity in selection requires either that race itself be a major factor in selection or that selection be effectively stripped of intellectual demands (for a concrete example in police selection, see Gottfredson, 1996).

Can Democratization Produce Racial Parity in Gifted Education?

The tradeoff between racial balance and rigor in intellectual standards has led educators of the gifted, like personnel psychologists, to consider evaluating participants' strengths against other, less cognitive standards. The aim is to "desegregate" gifted education by "democratizing" it, in particular, by expanding the range of skills, abilities, and achievements counted as gifts and the variety of people enlisted to identify them. The merits of such democratization rest on answers to three questions: (1) How evenly is the suggested panoply of gifts distributed across demographic groups? (2) How independent of IQ/academic achievement are these other gifts? (3) Which ones should qualify as giftedness for instructional purposes?

Major Domains of Human Gifts and Accomplishments

The upper half of Figure 10.2 schematizes the growing consensus among differential psychologists on the structure and relatedness of human traits in the realms of cognitive ability and personality. These are, respectively, the major "can do" and "will do" traits known to affect performance. These two structures are used to organize the cacophony of specific gifts and talents that multidimensionalists have proposed. The entry in Figure 10.2 for "have done" factors (experience and practice) reminds us that no gift results in accomplishment without the opportunity and desire to exercise it.

The "can do" (ability) traits. The most important fact about cognitive abilities for our purposes is that, while there are many of them, they all correlate moderately to highly with each other. They can, however, be distinguished by their breadth of application, from highly general to very specific, which is referred to as the "hierarchical structure of mental abilities." Usually, three levels of generality-specificity are distinguished: general (Stratum III), broad (II), and specific (I). The most compelling evidence for this structure is provided by Carroll's (1993) Herculean reanalysis of a century of factor-analytic studies on the issue. Carroll reconfirmed that there is only one highly general ability, called g (short for the general mental ability factor). It is the major component and essential backbone of all other cognitive abilities. He could find no second general factor at the Stratum III level, and no one has ever been able to create a useful cognitive test that is not moderately to highly "g loaded." IQ tests measure g well.

At the next level of generality are the broad Stratum II abilities, often known as "group factors." Carroll (1993) referred to them as flavors of g because they are so highly correlated with it. He has identified eight (p. 626). For simplicity, Figure 10.2 includes only four and relabels them: verbal, mathematical, spatial, and auditory. These four appear to correspond to the four most intellectual of Gardner's hypothesized (but yet-unmeasured) "multiple intelligences" (linguistic, logical-mathematical, visuospatial, and musical; Carroll, p. 641). We may or may not wish

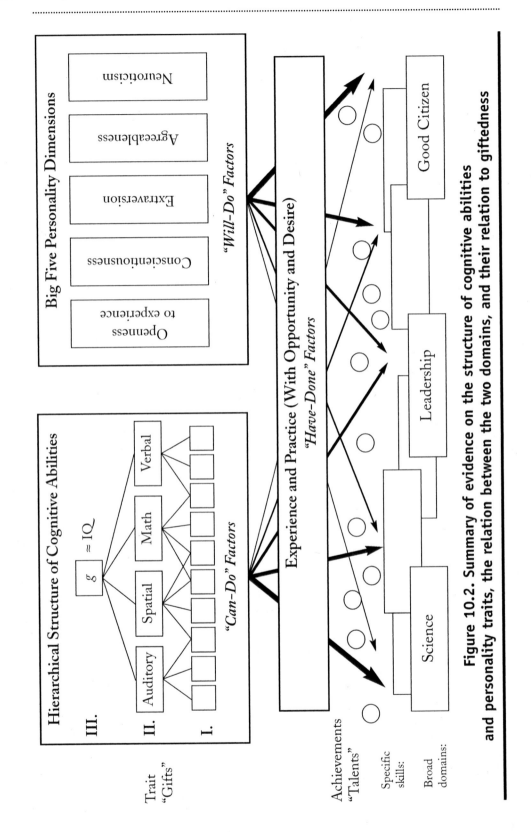

Figure 10.2. Summary of evidence on the structure of cognitive abilities and personality traits, the relation between the two domains, and their relation to giftedness

to label Gardner's constructs as intelligences, but Carroll's work now requires us to presume them all to be highly correlated manifestations of g. At the lowest level of the hierarchical structure are the dozens of Stratum I specific abilities, such as reading decoding, visual memory, flexibility of closure, and sound-frequency discrimination. They generally are not considered forms of giftedness for purposes of instruction in the public schools because they are so narrow in application.

Sternberg has suggested that his creative and practical intelligences sit astride analytical intelligence (g) as independent intelligences atop the hierarchy of mental abilities. However, his attempts to demonstrate their independence have not withstood scientific scrutiny by independent investigators, who have used his data to show that the three postulated intelligences are actually highly correlated (Brody, 2003) and that his often strong claims for the practical value of "practical intelligence" are unfounded (Gottfredson, 2003a). In other words, no one has ever demonstrated the existence of "many types of intelligences," if by "intelligence" we mean independent, empirically verified, highly general abilities in the cognitive realm. Gifted programs cannot take the measure of what does not exist.

Gifted programs generally target either the most general level of ability (g) or the next most general (the broad group factors). When targeting the latter, talent searches and gifted education programs often focus on one rather than another. For example, there are summer programs in mathematics and others in writing or music. The important point with regard to racial representation, however, is that, if a program selects students based on one of these broad Stratum II abilities, it will also be *implicitly selecting on g at the same time*, albeit somewhat less effectively than if it did so directly. Remarkable gifts in all these more specific, but still broad realms of ability rest on the same foundation of high g. No one possesses them in rare measure without also being considerably above average in g. Gardner himself has estimated that the famous exemplars of his seven intelligences all exceeded IQ 120 (the 90th percentile of the general population; Jensen, 1998, p. 128). More garden-variety gifts in these realms are likely to require at least an above-average level of g (IQ > 100; cf. Simonton, 1994, ch. 8). As can be calculated from Figure 10.1, racial imbalance relative to Whites is severe above IQ 120 (1:10 for Blacks, 1:3 for Hispanics, and 9:5 for Asians) and is still high above IQ 100 (1:3, 1:2, and 6:5, respectively, for the three groups).

To summarize, selecting on any cognitive ability will mean selecting on g, and the broader the ability is, the stronger the selection on g will be. The broader the cognitive ability targeted, the bigger the racial imbalances in gifted enrollments will be, all else equal.

The "will do" (personality) traits. We see a quite different picture in the realm of personality traits. There is no highly general "personality" factor comparable to g, but probably three to seven independent dimensions. The "Big Five" scheme is most often used, so that is what Figure 10.2 portrays: openness to experience, conscientiousness, extraversion, agreeableness, and neuroticism. Whereas the major group factors of ability are highly correlated, the major personality dimensions are independent of each other. In addition, with the exception of a small correlation between facets of openness and conscientiousness, on the one hand, and crystallized *g* (i.e., verbal ability) on the other, none of the personality dimensions correlates meaningfully with *g* (see overview in Jensen, 1998, pp. 573–574). In other words, selecting on personality traits will *not* simultaneously select implicitly on *g*.

Although less is known about average racial differences along the "Big Five" dimensions of personality, evidence to date suggests that they range from small to nonexistent; but, when present, they often favor minorities (Russell, Reynolds, & Campbell, 1994). (Perhaps for this reason personality inventories are not accused of racial bias.) Identifying giftedness *solely* on the basis of personality traits would therefore produce near racial balance or a slight overrepresentation of minority groups. Neither the traditional definition of giftedness, nor the federal Javits Gifted and Talented Education Act, includes personality traits per se as gifts or talents; for instance, being extraverted (or its opposite, introverted), neurotic (or emotionally well-adjusted), or open to experience (or intellectually rigid). The radical multidimensionalist perspective makes room for them, however. Ford's (2003, p. 508) list of Black cultural strengths would appear to include some such strictly noncognitive personal characteristics, for example, "verve" (energetic and lively) and "expressive individualism" (risk taker, independent, and impulsive). Stormont et al. (2001) also seemed to suggest extraversion as a gift when they included "expressiveness" as a form of giftedness (p. 419). It nonetheless seems unlikely that many educators of the gifted would, if explicitly asked, endorse attributes like extraversion and agreeableness (or their opposites) as gifts requiring special academic instruction.

Certain personality traits are important, however, in facilitating (or inhibiting) the translation of any gift into actual accomplishment. Renzulli's (2003) conception of giftedness explicitly includes such factors—task commitment and creativity (conscientiousness and openness to experience?)—in addition to above-average ability. High ability, when not exploited, remains potential undeveloped—little more than an empty promise. This, of course, is the point of all discussions of greatness or genius that stress high intelligence as essential, but hardly sufficient, for culturally notable levels of achievement. Remarkable accomplishment in adulthood seems to be the multiplicative product of high intelligence, determination, and energy exercised in a chosen field (Simonton, 1994)—likewise in children, high intelligence (quick learner), the rage to master, and marching to one's own drummer (Winner, 1996). That is, high levels of actual achievement—Gagné's (2003) "talents" or Gardner's (1983) "intelligences"—require the *combination* of favorable "can do" and "will do" traits, not just one or the other. Favorable personality traits may therefore supplement, but cannot replace, cognitive abilities when identifying children who do, or could, achieve academically or artistically at very high levels with suitable opportunity and support.

Actual accomplishments. Whereas the top half of Figure 10.2 highlights the major human traits that we might want to identify and students to exercise, the bottom half samples the valued forms of cultural accomplishment that such exercise can produce. Some systems for identifying gifted children look to such signs of achievement in addition to, or instead of, indicators of mere promise of such. Figure 10.2 arrays sample achievements from left to right according to how dependent they are on cognitive ability relative to personality traits. This ordering is based on research examining the correlations of different personal traits (abilities, interests, temperaments) with different dimensions of job performance (core technical performance, leadership, self-discipline, etc.) when both the predictor and outcome domains are measured multidimensionally (see Gottfredson, 2002, for a review of relevant research).

Science appears to the left because academic and artistic achievements are highly *g* loaded. Leadership is displayed toward the center, as a moderately *g*-dependent achievement, because effective leadership depends at least moderately on favorable levels of both *g* and certain traits of personality and temperament. We might therefore expect selection for gifted leadership to be somewhat more racially balanced than selection on the more strictly intellectual achievements, but it would still be far from parity (at least in racially mixed groups). Among the least cognitive of the indisputably worthy social contributions is good citizenship—not necessarily being a leader of others, but contributing more than one's share to the common good and otherwise being a worthy role model. Being a person of high moral character who contributes to his or her community is within the reach of people of virtually all ability levels.

Because the dependence of achievements on *g* decreases from high to low as one moves left to right across the figure, we would also expect racial imbalance in selecting for specific achievements to drop from severe to mild (or nonexistent).

Prospects for Racial Balance Using Multidimensional Definitions and Multimodal Methods

Figure 10.2 arrays the full range of gifts and talents that both the traditional and multidimensionalist conceptions of giftedness encompass. The most traditional, most intelligence-based conception limits its focus to Stratum II and III cognitive gifts and their related, highly intellectual accomplishments to the lower left of the figure. The most radical multidimensionalists would include the entire spectrum of human strengths and accomplishments, befitting their effort to be maximally inclusive. This figure allows us to gain perspective on the claim that democratizing giftedness will desegregate it.

Multidimensional definitions. Among the traits in Figure 10.2, racial-ethnic groups differ most on the average on precisely those traits that are most intensely targeted by traditional conceptions of giftedness, that is, the most *g*-loaded abilities (general intelligence, verbal ability, spatial or mathematical reasoning, etc.) and accomplishments (in science, math, writing, or academics overall). As described earlier, racial imbalance among students enrolled in gifted programs will typically be severe when these abilities and accomplishments are identified in a reliable, valid, race-blind manner.

Three strategies for defining giftedness more inclusively have been promoted as means of gaining racial balance in gifted enrollments. The first is simply to lower the threshold for classifying an intellectual strength as a gift: IQ or academic achievement need not be remarkable, but just above some moderately high level (Stormont et al., 2001). Recall Richert's (2003) APOGEE procedure, which classifies 25% of students in all schools, even low-performing ones, as gifted. Another example is the effort to make Advanced Placement (AP) courses more inclusive by enrolling students of more diverse ability levels. As the College Board now advertises, "AP isn't just for top students or those heading to college. AP offers something for everyone" (Bleske-Rechek, Lubinski, & Benbow, in press).

The second is to incorporate a greater variety of cognitive abilities, or "intelligences," in the definition of giftedness. However, any conception that emphasizes intellectual strengths will yield big racial imbalances because all cognitive abilities are moderately to highly correlated with g. Multidimensionalist conceptions of this moderate sort will produce racial imbalances almost as severe as the traditional conception when both are implemented in an equally reliable, valid, and race-blind manner. So, too, will full, faithful (and race-blind) implementation of the Javits Gifted and Talented Education Act, which defines giftedness as the potential for remarkably high performance in intellectual/creative/artistic areas, leadership, or specific academic fields. Adding somewhat less cognitive traits such as leadership and "interpersonal intelligence" to the basket of intellectual gifts and talents does virtually nothing to decrease racial imbalance because those additions are themselves moderately g-loaded. The democracy promised by the more inclusive, but still primarily cognitive, definitions is chimerical because it rests on the mistaken notion that the new abilities are independent of the old.

The third way of democratizing giftedness is to extend it beyond the cognitive realm. Successively more expansive conceptions will produce smaller racial imbalances to the extent that they incorporate and weight heavily the primarily noncognitive traits and accomplishments to the right in Figure 10.2. But, even the most inclusive definition will not yield anything near racial parity as long as cognitive abilities and accomplishments remain in the basket. The addition of noncognitive traits can dilute, but never erase, the influence of g, as personnel research has shown (Sackett et al., 2001). To erase the racial imbalances that are created by average differences in g, there would have to be (but are not) group differences in noncognitive gifts that are equal in size, but opposite in direction, to those in the cognitive sphere.

Impact of multimodal measurement. Multimodal techniques cannot identify gifts that do not exist. Human competence is not unexplored terrain, with major continents of ability yet to be discovered. Anyone who claims to glimpse them must provide solid proof of their existence. Multidimensionalists, however, tend to reject, rather than embrace, sound psychometric techniques for certifying talent.

Their multimodal approach to assessment seems to attain more even demographic representation mostly by degrading the measurement of competence, even if unwittingly so. No one, of course, would openly espouse such degradation, but it is actually a well-trod path in the pursuit of racial balance. There are periodic claims in personnel psychology, for instance, to have dramatically reduced disparate impact (racial imbalance) in hiring by inventing more "sophisticated" selection techniques. When unraveled, these "modern," "nontraditional" assessments are always shown to work by systematically *reducing* the validity and reliability of selection batteries (Gottfredson, 1996).

The same Faustian advances are now being advocated in gifted education to solve the same sociopolitical problem: When the distributions of g for different groups in a setting differ substantially, the only way to achieve racial balance while still claiming to look for exceptional cognitive abilities is to *avoid* using valid, unbiased (psychometrically sound) measures of g-loaded abilities and accomplishments while appearing to do otherwise. One method is, in the name of racial justice, to score tests differently by race (e.g., race-norming) in order to compensate for average differences in g, a practice that is now illegal in hiring. A second is to use highly subjective or otherwise unreliable identification procedures (ratings of unclear constructs by diverse, untrained raters) in order to greatly degrade or randomize selection on g. A third is to look for any of a wide variety of *narrow* (and hence highly experience-sensitive) cognitive skills, a practice that will give greater weight to any adventitious context-specific experience than to enduring cross-context general abilities. Richert's (2003) APOGEE program employs all three methods.

What Should the Aims of Gifted Education Be?

Critics of gifted education argue that it must be "desegregated"—that is, mirror the demographic composition of the community—to assure racial equity. The term *desegregation* connotes a moral or legal imperative. It falsely presumes that Discrimination Theory is correct when, in fact, Distribution Theory has far stronger empirical support. Racial discrimination may still occur, but the large racial disparities in school performance and eligibility for traditional gifted programs can be explained fully by group disparities in g.

Gifted education is in an especially difficult position among instructional programs because it has typically targeted individuals at the right tail of the IQ bell curve—just where racial disproportions happen to be most extreme. I know of no other distributional difference between the races that is as large as this one. The equity-excellence tradeoff is thus especially stark when giftedness is defined in traditional terms, but it can be expected to be substantial even under the most inclusive conceptions when intellectual giftedness is allowed to influence selection, as it should.

Because psychometrically sound methods of identifying giftedness yield the biggest racial imbalances, it was entirely predictable that pressure would mount, as it has, to compromise validity for racial parity in gifted placements (VanTassel-Baska, Johnson, & Avery, 2002). In the name of democratizing gifted education, we are now being urged to reject reliable, valid, unbiased measures of well-recognized broad cognitive abilities in favor of their opposite: unreliable, subjective, undocumented measures of unspecified narrow strengths. Advocates justify this call by labeling the psychometrically superior methods "biased," "narrow," and "exclusionary," while anointing the psychometrically unsound methods as more "democratic," "inclusive," "equitable," and "authentic."

Democratizing the selection of gifted children has also predictably led to efforts to democratize the instruction of students so identified. By enrolling students with many different and vaguely defined kinds of personal strengths, but often weaker academic ones, educators cannot differentiate the curriculum to suit the needs of remarkably talented students of any sort. In fact, multidimensionalists themselves speak of instructing their wide variety of potentially gifted students within the same classroom. This is akin to asking a single coach to develop, in the same training sessions, the talents of the school's top prospects in basketball, football, tennis, and swimming. When all types are served together, none is served well.

The multidimensionalists' relative lack of interest in instructional programs for truly exceptional students who languish unchallenged in the regular curricula that schools provide suggests that their first goal is to equalize educational outcomes across the races, rather than provide appropriate instruction to unusually gifted individuals of any race. They focus on inequality, not exceptionality (Benbow & Stanley, 1996). Consider Ford's (2003) five strategies for better meeting the needs of gifted minority students: They have nothing to do with giftedness per se, but represent typical recommendations for raising achievement levels in poor-performing minority populations. Multidimensionalist recommendations for instruction focus not on compacted curricula, acceleration, or early entrance, but on remediating academic deficiencies. They don't focus on providing intellectual challenge, but on emotional support. Block out the word *gifted* in such discussions, and it is hard to discern that giftedness is their ostensible focus. Likewise, the evidence that Richert (2003) provides for the success of her APOGEE program is that it increased average test scores in poor-performing schools. That is a worthy accomplishment, to be sure, but it suggests that the cachet and resources of gifted programs are being appropriated for the larger effort to close the achievement gaps between demographic groups.

Narrowing the current large racial gaps in academic achievement is an important social goal, one that often dominates American political discourse and drives social policy. But, these gaps are precisely the reason why we cannot attain "racial equity" in gifted education at this time, at least not without repudiating its *raison d'être* and emptying equity of meaning.

No one questions the need for special educational services for students in the lowest percentiles of the IQ distribution (IQ < 70). All students need appropriate developmental placement. Students who are equally atypical at the other extreme

(IQ > 130) also merit instruction that is more suitable to their cognitive capacity than what regular school curricula can provide. Gifted programs should continue to search out the extraordinarily talented in all social groups by using the soundest techniques at their disposal. They should likewise continue to do what they do best and what no other education program attempts to do: provide a menu of developmental opportunities for exceptionally able children so that they may realize their potential.

11

The Mental Chronometry of Giftedness

by Arthur R. Jensen

T he term *giftedness* has two aspects, both of which are deserving of scientific study: (1) Giftedness in the broad sense refers to human abilities and traits that are out of the ordinary—a rather unbounded assortment of not necessarily correlated categories generally comprising exceptional levels of intelligence; precocity; various specialized physical and mental abilities; and talents, idiot savants, creativity, charisma, leadership, and genius, to name a few. (2). Giftedness in the narrow sense refers to a high level of general mental ability, or psychometric g. The present article pertains only to giftedness in this narrow sense, i.e., high g.

As a theoretical construct or latent variable, g is not directly measurable in individuals, but an individual's position on this dimension relative to some defined population can be roughly estimated by mental tests (Jensen, 1998, 2002). Schools typically consider as gifted those pupils who score more than two standard deviations above the population mean of children their own age on certain mental tests. This is equivalent to an IQ of 130 or above, a cutoff score that includes approximately the top-scoring 2–3% of the population. Any particular IQ cutoff, however, is not essentially important for the following discussion. An arbitrary point on an age-standardized and normalized ordinal scale that roughly estimates psychometric g theoretically has the same statistical and predictive properties throughout its entire range. Empirical evidence, so far, has not contradicted this theoretical conjecture.

Individuals classified as gifted in the narrow sense are not uniquely different from the rest of the population.

The Biological Basis of the *g* Dimension

The *g* factor has a biological basis reflecting genotypic individual differences in certain physical properties of the brain. The high heritability of *g*-loaded tests, such as IQ, indicates that a substantial part of the population variance in *g* is attributable to genetic factors. Moreover, *g* is correlated with anatomical and phys- iological aspects of the brain, such as brain size; the brain's glucose metabolic rate during mental activity; the latency, amplitude, and habituation of brain-evoked potentials; nerve conduction velocity; and the brain's intracellular pH level (lower acidity = higher *g*; for specific citations of this research, see Jensen, 1997, 1998, 2000). Recent studies based on functional magnetic resonance imagining (*f*MRI) have discovered specific brain loci, mainly in the frontal-lateral cortex, that are most directly involved in performance on *g*-loaded tests (Duncan et al., 2000), and individual variation in these particular structures is largely genetic (Thompson et al., 2001). In view of these findings, our hypothesis predicts that individuals iden- tified as gifted (in the narrow sense) should differ from the average on these bio- logical correlates of *g*. However, I am not aware that any of these brain variables has figured specifically in studies of the gifted.

A closely related question concerns how far up we have to go in the hierarchy of complexity of information processing tasks for the differences between gifted and average individuals to become apparent. Do the academically gifted differ only in higher level and more sophisticated cognitive performance involving scholastic knowledge, specific problem-solving skills and strategies acquired through expo- sure to an enriched environment and motivated by intellectual interests? In other words, are gifted children just like average children in basic information process- ing capacity, but with something extra added on the top in the way of more com- plex cognitive skills, or is giftedness also manifested in the most basic and elementary forms of information processing?

Chronometry of Information Processing

This can best be investigated with elementary cognitive tasks (ECTs). These are tasks that are so low in the hierarchy of information processing complexity that all the individuals tested in the study can perform the tasks correctly and easily in less than 3 seconds and the only reliable measure of individual differences is response time (RT), that is, the interval between the onset of a stimulus and the subject's response. For any given ECT, the response stimulus (RS) consists of one or more lights going on or a simple problem appearing on a computer monitor. On every test trial, the subject is alerted to the imminent appearance of the RS by an auditory signal (a "beep") occurring 1 to 4 seconds before the RS. The subject's response has two measurable components: (1) RT is the time interval between the onset of the RS and the subject's lifting his or her index finger of the preferred hand from a "home" button on the subject's response console; (2) the movement time (MT) is the interval between leaving the home button and pressing another button a few inches above to select the correct choice, which ends the trial. Both RT and MT are measured in milliseconds (msec). Highly reliable measurement of an individual's performance is ensured by giving adequate practice trials followed by a large number of test trials, of which the median is registered as the subject's RT (or MT). Two studies have compared gifted with average school children on these chronometric measures.

Study 1

In the first study (Kranzler, Whang, & Jensen, 1994), the gifted (G) subjects were 55 participants in a summer academic talent program at the University of California, Berkeley. They were junior high school pupils 11 to 14 years of age selected for having Scholastic Aptitude Test scores on a par with the average of college freshmen. The nongifted (NG) group of 53 students, ages 11 to 14, were selected at random from a junior high school. The G group had nearly the same average score on the Raven Advanced Progressive Matrices (APM) as Berkeley undergraduates and averaged 1.74 standard deviations higher than the average APM matrices score of the NG group (equivalent to 26 points on an IQ scale).

Three ECTs were given—Simple RT (SRT), Choice RT (CRT), and Discrimination RT (DRT)—using the consoles shown in Figure 11.1. For SRT, the subject (S) pressed the home button, heard a beep, and in 1 to 4 seconds the single light went on, whereupon the subject left the home button as quickly as possible and touched the light, turning it off. CRT was exactly the same as SRT, except that on each trial one out of eight lights went on at random. DRT was an odd-man-out task: On each trial, a different set of three of the eight lights went on simultaneously such that one of the lights (the target odd-man-out) was always further away from the other two; only touching the odd button turned off all the lights. Thus, subjects had to discriminate the distances between the three lights.

Two kinds of measures were recorded for each subject: RT (i.e., releasing the home button) and RTSD (the standard deviation of the RTs over trials), a measure of trial-to-trial fluctuations (*intra*individual variability) of a subject's RT, which is also correlated with psychometric g (Jensen, 1992). Figure 11.2 shows the groups' means of RT (panel A) and of RTSD (panel B). Figure 11.3 shows the group differences in RT and RTSD on each of the tests in terms of effect size (ES = the group mean difference divided by the average standard deviation within groups). The overall differences between the G and NG groups were highly significant ($p < .001$) for both RT and RTSD. It is noteworthy that on DRT the

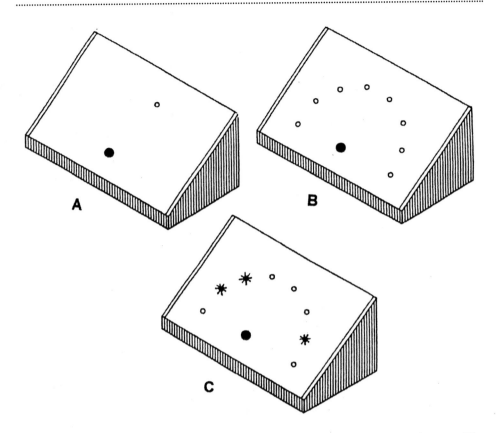

The black dot in the lower center of each panel represents the home button. The open circles, 6 inches from the home button, are green underlighted translucent pushbuttons. In the SRT and CRT conditions, only one button lights up on each trial; on the DRT task, three buttons light up simultaneously, with various unequal distances between them (as shown in C, the remotest one from the other two being the targeted odd-man-out). RT is the time interval between the light(s) going on and the subject's lifting his or her index finger off the home button.

**Figure 11.1. The subject's response console
for (A) SRT, (B) CRT, and (C) DRT (odd-man-out)**

GN-G difference was about three fourths as large as for the Raven APM despite the fact that the DRT task involved no knowledge base, higher order cognitive skills and strategies, or retrieval of special information from memory. A discriminant function based on both RT and RTSD classified 78.5% of all of the 118 subjects correctly; 92% of the G and 64.2% of the NG were correctly classified. The NG group, having been randomly selected from regular classes, likely included some gifted pupils.

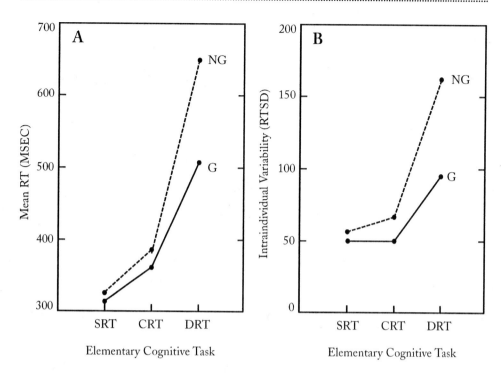

Figure 11.2. (A) Mean RT and (B) mean RTSD of the Gifted (G) and Nongifted (NG) groups on each of the cognitive tasks

Study 2

That the findings of Study 1 were not merely an accident of the particular samples or tests is shown by Study 2 (Cohn, Carlson & Jensen, 1985), which employed a considerable variety of ECTs, yielding 11 experimentally independent measurements of RT on each subject. The study compared three groups: 70 pupils 13.2 years of age selected at random from seventh-grade classes in an upper-middle-class neighborhood (NG); 60 exceptional students, age 13.5 years, who were enrolled in the university on three different campuses (G); and 100 university undergraduates (Un) averaging 21 years of age.

Again, RT is always the time taken to lift the index finger off the home button after the appearance of the response stimulus. The various ECTs include several classic paradigms. The Hick paradigm (see Jensen, 1987) consists of SRT and CRT (as in Study 1) and two additional degrees of CRT (two and four lights) using the apparatus shown in Figure 11.1. The Sternberg paradigm (here labeled "Digit") measures the time needed to scan a set of one to seven digits held in short-term memory to determine the presence or absence of a given probe digit; the subject responds on a binary console, releasing the home button and pressing one of two other buttons labeled respectively "yes" and "no." In the Words para-

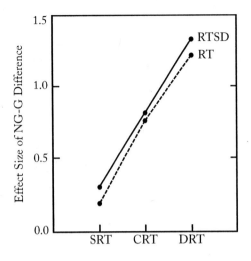

Figure 11.3. Differences in terms of effect size between the G and NG groups for RT and RTSD

digm, pairs of words are presented that are either physically the same (e.g., hat-hat) or different (e.g., bat-cat); the subject presses buttons labeled "same" or "different." In the Synonym-Antonym paradigm, pairs of simple words are presented that have either the same meaning (e.g., little-small) or opposite meaning (e.g., good-bad); the subject responds as in the previous task. In the Semantic Verification test (SVT), a brief statement about the order of two letters (always AB) appears on the monitor (A before B, or A not before B, or B before A, or B not before A) for 3 seconds followed by the appearance of either AB or BA; the subject responds on buttons labeled "true" or "false."

To increase the processing load on working memory, three of these paradigms (Digit, Words, Synonyms-Anonyms) are also used in combination as dual tasks, such as the following sequence of events when the dual task comprises the Digit and Words paradigms: A set of one to seven digits appears on the screen for 3 seconds, then the Words task is completed, then a probe digit appears, to which the subject responds "yes" or "no." (Detailed descriptions of the ECTs and procedures are given in Cohn et al., 1985.)

Figure 11.4 shows the mean RTs of the three groups on each of the ECTs (only the mean of the four RTs on the Hick paradigm is shown, as "RT mean"). Note that the G group was not statistically different from the Un group; the index of profile similarity (Pearson r) of their RTs on the eight tasks is +0.99. The NG group had a consistently and significantly ($p < .001$) longer RT than the Un and G groups, yet the profile similarity between G and NG is = .0.96. The virtual equality of the G and Un groups on these ECTs is perfectly consistent with their equality on the SAT and the Raven Matrices tests and their success in the university curriculum. At about 13 years of age, they had acquired the same levels of general scholastic knowledge and cognitive skills as the university students had acquired by age 21.

Figure 11.5 shows the NG-G differences on the various ECTs in terms of effect size (ES). A discriminant function based on a combination of all the ECTs correctly classified 87% of the 130 members of the G and NG groups, with 92% of the G group and 83% of the NG group correctly classified. Again, the larger percentage of misclassification in the NG group probably represents the presence

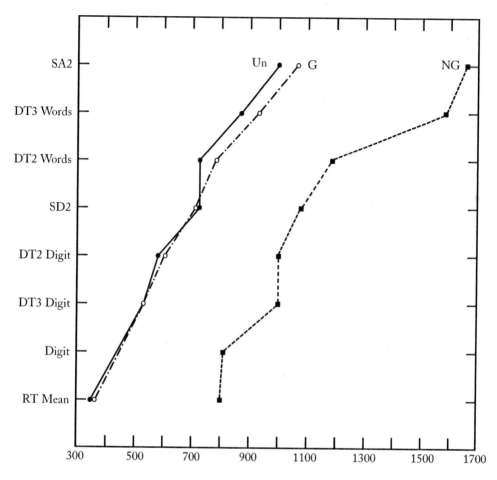

Figure 11.4. Mean RT on 8 ECTs for university students (Un) and gifted (G) and nongifted (NG) children

of some gifted pupils among the nominally NG group, as the school from which the NG were randomly obtained was at the 75th percentile in statewide scholastic achievement scores.

As yet, there is no satisfactory theory of why individual differences in RT in a wide variety of ECTs is correlated with IQ and particularly with psychometric g. Many psychological hypotheses have been suggested, but it seems that only an explanation in terms of neurophysiology, yet to be discovered, can provide a really scientific answer (Deary, 2000, ch. 6; Jensen, 1998, ch. 8). In the meantime, it seems a reasonable hypothesis that the speed of information processing limits the amount of information and its mental manipulation and storage in long-term memory, encountered in almost every waking moment in a person's life. Hence, individual differences in the rate of information processing, acting over considerable periods of time, can result in marked individual differences in the amount and

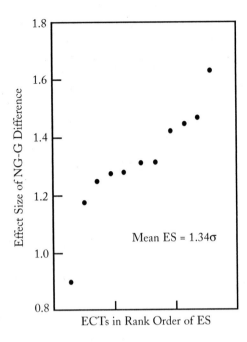

Figure 11.5. Differences on 11 ECTs between the NG and G groups expressed in terms of effect size (i.e., mean difference/SD).

complexity of cognitive skills and information about one's world acquired in the process of living. Thus, the gifted 13-year-old children, with a much faster speed of information processing than that of their average agemates, are on a par in general knowledge and developed cognitive skills with university students who are 6 to 7 years older.

Diversity in Processing Speed Among Population Groups

Because of the socially sensitive nature of the subject of diversity in processing speed among population groups, it has been little studied. Jensen (1998, pp. 389–402) provided an entry to the recent studies, most of which are based on comparisons of White and Black American school children. A few similar studies have been done in various parts of Africa.

The two most general findings in all these studies are: (1) On ECTs that are at a higher level of cognitive complexity than SRT, Blacks, on average, show a slower speed of information processing, or RT, and greater intraindividual variability, or RTSD, than Whites; and (2) both of these measures are correlated with psychometric g within each racial group. Consequently, if RT and RTSD on ECTs of the types described here and used for these racial comparisons are intrinsic attributes of giftedness in the narrow sense, one would expect unequal proportions of the Black and White populations to be selected as gifted if they are selected on any g-loaded measures from above a common cutoff score falling above the mean of the combined groups. Such outcomes are conspicuous in highly selective programs for gifted youths aimed at early college admission, such as the well-known Study of Mathematically Precocious Youth (SMPY) initiated by Julian Stanley at the Johns Hopkins University.

The only chronometric data related to mathematical aptitude for which there are different age-matched racial groups tested with the same ECTs and procedures are reported in two studies (Jensen, 1993b; Jensen & Whang, 1994). White, Black, and Chinese American elementary school children in grades 4 to 6 were given the Math Verification Test (MVT), which measures the speed of accessing

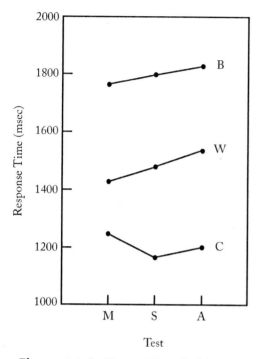

Figure 11.6. Mean RTs of Chinese (C), White (W), and Black (B) pupils in grades 4 to 6 on the Math Verification Test for multiplication, subtraction, and addition (consistently in that order from bottom to top in each group).

already learned elementary arithmetic facts in long-term memory. To ensure that the subjects were familiar with these number facts, only those subjects were selected who obtained a perfect score on a nonspeeded paper-and-pencil test that included all the problems contained in the chronometric form of the MVT. The MVT is constructed as a true-false test (with pushbuttons so labeled) with three parts: addition, subtraction, and multiplication, each using only single digits. Following instructions and 15 practice trials, a "beep" focuses the subject's attention on a small square on the monitor where, within 1 to 4 seconds, a single problem appears. In response, the subject lifts his or her index finger from the home button and touches either the true or the false button, after which immediate feedback ("correct" or "incorrect") appears on the screen. For example, 3 + 2 = 5, (or 6 - 3 = 4, or 7 x 4 = 21) , with equal frequencies of randomly ordered T and F answers. Again, RT is the time taken to leave the home button following the presentation of the problem. There were 20 test trials for each type of problem. No RTs by any subject were longer than 2 seconds, and error rates were negligible (mode = 0) and nonsignificant across groups. The results are shown in Figure 11.6.

The three group means all differed significantly from one another, with an average effect size between groups of about 0.50. The means of RT for multiplication, subtraction, and addition maintained the same order and nearly the same differences apart within each racial group, suggesting that whatever processes enter into solving these simple problems was the same for all groups. (One may speculate about why multiplication takes the least time, addition the most, and subtraction is intermediate, but that is another issue.) Overall, RT on the MVT test was found to predict much more complex levels of math achievement as measured by standardized tests, and it has significant incremental validity for predicting math performance in school over and above the predictive power of IQ alone.

Although the chronometric studies described here are of an exploratory nature and are confined to giftedness in the narrow sense, they do indicate that chronometric methods may prove to be a sensitive tool for research on the cognitive characteristics of children who are considered as gifted not only in the narrow sense, but also in other dimensions of giftedness, as well. It is a blessed certainty for humankind that giftedness in abilities, sensitivities, talents, and proclivities is multidimensional in its origins and expression in all populations.

12

Curricular Diversity and the Gifted

by Joyce VanTassel-Baska

I n order to design appropriate curricula for any target group, it is necessary to understand their nature and needs as they relate to curriculum design. This is especially true for gifted learners, whose major characteristics of advanced development immediately render them at risk in a school system committed to a rigid age-grade curricular model.

What is Intelligence?

Various views prevail in our thinking about what intelligence is. Perkins (1999) characterized it in three broad areas: Intelligence may be neural, experiential, and reflective.

By neural, he means that psychometric views of intelligence have continued to suggest that intelligence is related to one's genetic potential for problem solving, the so-called *g*-factor (Jensen, 1999). This review of intelligence suggests that one's intelligence is malleable, but only within limits. Like a rubber band, we can stretch ourselves to handle difficult problems; but, within areas where expertise is lacking, we will encounter very real limits in our effectiveness and efficiency.

By experiential, Perkins is referring to domain-specific intelligence within which individuals can develop expertise. This view of intelligence suggests that motivation, time, and practice are the most important variables that may separate gifted individuals from those not gifted. Expertise involves the development of highly specialized skills matched to the nature of particular endeavors, such as chess playing or writing an argument paper. The more we engage in these endeavors with expert instruction, the better we become. This domain-specific view of giftedness has a long history and has been popularized by Gardner's (1983) multiple intelligence model.

Perkins' third view of intelligence, that of reflection, mirrors well the work of Sternberg on the role of executive processing in intelligence. This view suggests that metacognition is central to understanding intelligent behavior. The capacity to plan, organize, monitor, and assess one's situation is crucial to behaving intelligently and adapting to various kinds of environments, from school to work. Sternberg and Williams (1998) have studied these processes under the domain of practical intelligence, our way of coping with the world and adapting to its demands, as well as shaping its contours.

All three views of intelligence are useful in thinking about curriculum development for the gifted. Many school districts still ascribe to an IQ model of giftedness for identifying students who can demonstrate high-level problem-solving abilities from early ages. Other school programs adhere more to the experiential or domain-specific view of giftedness, where students may be identified on aptitude and achievement measures for participation in specialized programs in discrete academic or arts areas. Currently, no school-based programs use the reflective orientation to intelligence as a central force in shaping identification procedures, but it is a facet included in most multiple-criteria approaches. Teacher recommendations frequently ask for work habits and motivational behaviors that signal whether students have developed these metacognitive tools sufficiently enough to be included in a gifted program.

What is Giftedness?

If intelligence involves the capacity to solve problems at higher levels; develop high-level expertise in a discrete area; and plan, monitor, and assess one's work in a reflective manner, then giftedness must be an appellation reserved for those students who perform these feats at very high levels in comparison to same-age peers. At a simplistic level, giftedness is evidence of advanced development across intellectual areas or within a specific academic or arts-related area, *or* unusual organizational power to bring about desired results. Functionally, schools look for such advanced development through the tools available to them, namely tests, inventories, checklists, and actual student performance.

In school-based settings, giftedness is most frequently identified by a combination of criteria numbering anywhere from three to five. Table 12.1 reflects an overview of the tools most commonly employed and characterizes them as being either traditional or nontraditional in orientation. Such a characterization provides the basis for demonstrating how dissatisfied the field of gifted education has

Table 12.1

Overview of Commonly Used Identification Tools

Traditional	Nontraditional
• Intelligence tests • Achievement tests • Aptitude tests (domain-specific) • Grades • Teacher recommendations	• Nonverbal ability tests • Creativity tests • Student portfolios/performance by audition • Performance-based assessment • Parent/peer/community recommendations

become in using only traditional tools that have not yielded enough students of color, students of poverty, or students with uneven profiles. In recent years, the use of both performance-based and portfolio approaches have gained favor and are included in several states' identification guidelines (Karnes, 2000).

The Optimal Match Between Characteristics and Curricular Intervention

The pathway for considering the concept of giftedness through a curricular lens is by analyzing the underlying characteristics of gifted children and organizing curricula that are responsive to them. At the same time, teachers must be cognizant of the identification data on each gifted child and tailor curricula to ensure that actual student profiles are housed in the classroom. Figure 12.1 illustrates the relationship between conceptions of giftedness and effective curricular planning. Inputs to curricular planning are derived from the conception of giftedness employed in a school district and its interplay with group and individual student characteristics and needs. Outputs from an appropriately tailored curriculum, instruction, and assessment system are gifted student creativity and productivity.

Assumptions of Specialized Curricula for the Gifted

Curricula for gifted learners are based on several assumptions not commonly adhered to in practice. These assumptions, nevertheless, are critical to ensuring that these students receive appropriate services.

1. *All children can learn, but in different ways at different times in different contexts.* Educators of the gifted support this fundamental principle of the standards-based reform movement and applaud it as a necessary belief to improving schooling. Yet, the implementation of common standards

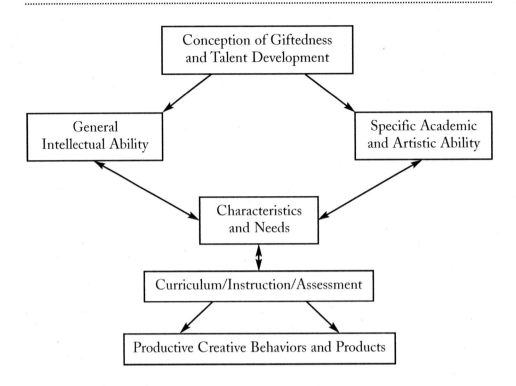

must recognize individual differences and accommodate them through flexible means.

2. *Some children learn more quickly than others.* This assumption has been demonstrated over and over again in research studies, yet the power of this difference in learning rate is obscured by age-grade notions of curricular readiness. Gifted students can learn new material at least twice as fast as typical learners. If the curriculum is reorganized in "larger chunks," learning rates can often increase exponentially.

3. *Gifted children differ from each other as to what curricular areas they find easy to learn and, therefore, the rate at which they can learn them.* Gifted learners vary as much from one another as they do from the normal population, both in rate of learning and areas in which they may be ready for advanced learning. Consequently, schools must provide curricular options across all areas to ensure equity in developing different academic talents.

4. *Gifted students also vary considerably amongst themselves in intrinsic motivation for cognitive learning.* The individual differences in motivation for learning may not be unrelated to cognitive capacity, but they do tend to show up in critical ways as students attempt schoolwork. These differences

should be addressed by tailoring the curriculum to the talents and needs of individual learners.

5. *Not every student (or gifted student) will attain a useful mastery of concepts and skills beyond a certain level of complexity and abstraction.* Many students, including some of the gifted, cannot handle advanced mathematics and science, both very abstract subject matters. Other gifted students encounter difficulty in interpreting complex passages of written text. What may be occurring is their encounter with the maximal degree of abstraction they can handle at a given point in time.

6. *Learning should provide "a basic diet, but also favorite foods."* One of the current assumptions about curricula for the gifted is that "specialization" is fundamental to strong growth in important areas, but that opportunities for other modes of learning are also important. Self-selected subjects, special project work, and mentorships all provide such broader opportunities.

7. *Intra- and interindividual variability is the rule in development.* Neither gifted students nor any other learners can be reviewed as a group phenomenon for purposes of learning. Rather, the individual differences of mind coupled with the subtle dynamics of group classroom interactions determine the nature and extent of understanding at any given moment. As Dimitriou and Valanides (1998) have observed, "classrooms are developmental mixers in which each student's developmental dynamics constrain and are constrained by the developmental dynamics of every other student and of the classroom as a whole" (p. 195).

Thus, the beginning point for all meaningful curricula for the gifted must be their individual and group characteristics and needs. Existing curricula found to be effective with them have evolved primarily from such understandings (Maker, Nielson, & Rogers, 1994; VanTassel-Baska, 1995, 2003). Although most effective approaches to curricula rely on the introduction of advanced skills and concepts at younger ages, thus tuning in to advanced cognitive development in specific domains, such an approach demands sensitivity to the level and learning capacity of students at a given stage of development. Research has also documented the effectiveness of this program. Sternberg, Ferrari, Clinkenbeard, and Grigorenko (1996) have studied the effects of teaching students a college-level psychology course based on the strongest cluster of learning characteristics. Results suggest that gifted students learn better when instruction is matched to learning characteristics.

While these characteristics and needs have been perceived as important for identification, they are also indispensable for curricular design. It may be useful to consider a few characteristics of the gifted and show their relationship to curricular interventions.

Manipulate Abstract Symbol Systems Readily, Learn New Material Rapidly

In the cognitive area, the ability to manipulate abstract symbol systems much better than their average age peers obviates against a lockstep, incremental part-to-whole teaching-learning process, which, in essence, is what often results in the regular classroom. The rate and pace of the gifted student's ability to learn material and the manner in which he or she can process large amounts of information point to the need for advanced work early. Many of the gifted are early readers who operationally are 2 to 6 years ahead of their age peers. The power of gifted students' intellectual thought enables them to master concepts and systems of thought holistically, rather than piecemeal, thus reducing the needed time to teach them any given topic. The general quickness and alertness of the gifted can cause boredom and frustration when they are held back in a regular classroom situation or when they are submitted to a start-and-stop method of reaching a particular point in a set of materials and are told to wait until the rest of the class is ready to go on. Such situations become extremely problematic for them based on this particular characteristic.

Affectively, there tends to be in many gifted learners a great impatience. When the disparity between appropriate pacing and what's actually happening in the classroom emerges, they reveal heightened frustration. A greater degree of sensitivity, even mild hyperactivity and central nervous system reaction, can cause an internal reaction against the "braking mechanism" that tends to occur in learning when they are not allowed to move ahead at their own rate. Moreover, the socio-emotional development of the gifted is impaired by lack of exposure to peers at their intellectual level. The only satisfactory balm for a gifted child who is ostracized in a typical classroom is to find "learning mates," even if they are imported from across a city or found two grades beyond his or her placement.

Symbol system manipulation is probably first noticed in young gifted children who read early. Since learning language is a powerful key to other forms of learning, it becomes a good example of a crucial symbol system. The gifted tend to access this symbol system earlier and more intensely, and they master it more rapidly than typical learners. They also tend to rate reading as a favorite leisure-time activity during the secondary years (VanTassel-Baska, 1983). A curricular design question regarding this characteristic is: Should we focus on this *one* symbol system primarily, thus allowing the gifted to advance and be enriched in all their reading and related language arts experiences? If the answer is "yes," then the following elements are important staples in a reading program for the gifted at all levels:

- diagnostic assessment in reading skill areas with instructional follow-up;
- a literature program based on appropriate children's adolescent and adult literature;
- a writing program that encourages ideas from literature to be elaborated on in building stories and essays;
- sustained foreign language opportunities; and
- an emphasis on logic and critical thinking behaviors.

Without this set of interwoven responses to the advanced reading level of a gifted child, there will be limited progress, with the child working out of basal worksheets provided as opposed to direct instructional intervention to produce sustained growth. Acceleration of content, then, is a key intervention for all gifted learners at each area where advancement is shown.

Mathematics represents another field of study where many young gifted learners typically excel and show advanced behavior. Beyond the diagnostic assessment and intervention with basal materials at appropriate levels, there is also a need to consider the following in their curriculum:

- a focus on developing spatial skills and concepts through geometry and other mathematical topics;
- a focus on problem-solving skills with appropriately challenging problems;
- an emphasis on the use of calculators, computers, and other instructional technology as tools in the problem-solving process;
- a focus on logic problems that require deductive thinking skills and inference;
- an emphasis on project-based applications of mathematics in the real world; and
- work with statistics and probability.

Again, the emphases of an appropriate mathematics curriculum need to be balanced between advanced content early and enrichment so that skills, concepts, and requisite materials are at a challenging level for the child, rather than being geared to grade-level considerations. The capacity of the child to manipulate symbol systems is recognized and responded to as a positive learning trait.

Power of Concentration, Diversity of Interests, Curiosity

This is another powerful characteristic of the gifted that needs an appropriate outlet. Educators can manipulate learning time in such a way as to promote or impede the gifted. For example, focusing on a topic for longer periods of time, but not every day, may respond well to this characteristic, as would doubling the amount of time spent on advanced topics with the gifted. In a secondary English program, for example, a stronger time emphasis on composition might be warranted; thus, the ideas of a double period twice a week for such efforts could be scheduled.

Manipulation of time, however, is only one variable of importance here. Additionally, it is important to consider how these characteristics might best be nurtured. One way to make such a curricular decision is to ask the student to make choices about tasks to be accomplished and topics to be studied. This can be accomplished by engaging students in independent and small-group investigations based on an area of interest. These investigations typically follow a model of organization that stresses the processes of problem-finding and problem-solving behaviors and also employ a project orientation negotiated between teacher and learner. A contract solidifies the learning agreement to be accomplished, and the resultant product is selected from a set of alternative options (written, oral, graphic, etc.). Higher level thinking processes are exploited to stimulate student thinking and work on project development. Often, research skills such as finding a problem, locating sources, and asking researchable questions are taught as a part of the background process for developing products. Such skill development is essential for gifted students to engage in effective research.

Affinity for Making Meaning and Connections

This characteristic of the gifted relates to their interest and capacity for constructing knowledge for themselves and their capacity to generate new ideas and engage in a creative synthesis of existing ideas. It is the characteristic that may be most powerful in any program where gifted students are given the opportunity to explore an idea and make meaning out of it through alternative teaching-learning approaches. Two learning outcomes based on these ideas might be:

1. given the theme of alienation in much of modern literature and art, create a personal statement about this theme in some mode of expression (e.g., poetry, painting, film); and
2. using art, music, dance, and literature, demonstrate the concept of "pattern" through creating a skit, performing a play, making a film or video, or creating an exhibit.

Research-Based Curricular Approaches

These examples provide a way of deriving appropriate curricula for the gifted from an understanding of their specific characteristics as learners. These same characteristics also form the basis for the major curricular approaches used in developing programs for such learners. Content-based instruction at advanced levels has been a staple of gifted curricula since the early years and has gained in popularity, particularly with middle school and secondary students through the national network of talent searches (Benbow & Stanley, 1983; Sawyer, 1982; VanTassel-Baska, 1985).

The use of process skills as a basis for curriculum making for the gifted has been popularized through model curricula developed around higher level thinking skills, creative thinking, and problem solving (Feldhusen & Treffinger, 1985; Maker, 1982). An emphasis on product development has emerged with curricular models that stress independent learning for the gifted, the gifted as practicing investigators of real-world problems, and an emphasis on generative learning practices resulting in creative products (Betts & Knapp, 1981; Kolloff & Feldhusen, 1981; Renzulli, 1977, 1986a; Treffinger, 1986).

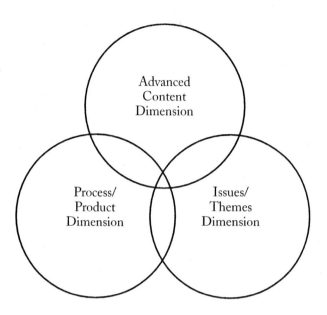

Figure 12.2. The Integrated Curriculum Model for Gifted Learners

Note. From "The Development of Talent Through Curriculum," by J. VanTassel-Baska, 1995, *Roeper Review, 18,* p. 99. Copyright © 1995 by The Board of Trustees of the Roeper School. Reprinted with permission.

Concept or theme-based curricula for the gifted are derived from early work on the importance of students' understanding of the disciplines (Phenix, 1964; Schwab, 1964) and the later translation of these ideas to the field of gifted education (Ward, 1980). Theme-based curricula for the gifted also receive support from general education, as well through the ideas engendered in Adler's (1984) *The Paideia Program.*

The Integrated Curriculum Model (ICM)

The Integrated Curriculum Model (ICM), first proposed in 1986 and further explicated in subsequent publications (VanTassel-Baska, 1992, 1994, 1998, 2003; VanTassel-Baska & Little, 2003), is comprised of three interrelated curricular dimensions that are responsive to different aspects of the gifted learner (see Figure 12.2).

1. *Emphasizing advanced content knowledge that frames disciplines of study.* Honoring the talent search concept, this facet of the model ensures that careful, diagnostic–prescriptive approaches are employed to produce new learning, rather than remedial instruction. Curricula based on the model represent appropriate advanced learning in that area. For example, teachers routinely determine what students already know about their yearly instructional plan by testing them on end-of-year or end-of-chapter

material before it is taught and then adjusting classroom instruction to their level of learning (Stanley, 2000).

2. *Providing higher order thinking and processing.* This facet of the model promotes student opportunities for manipulating information at complex levels through employing generic thinking models like Paul's (1992) Elements of Reasoning and more discipline-specific ones like Sher's (1993) Nature of the Scientific Process. This facet of the model also implies the utilization of information in some generative way, whether it be a project or a fruitful discussion. For example, students may use the reasoning element "point of view" to discuss and write about a short story by William Faulkner. Students may conduct a science experiment reflecting on whether or not their findings supported their research question and, if not, why.

3. *Focusing learning experiences around major issues, themes, and ideas that define both real-world applications and theoretical modeling within and across areas of study.* This facet of the ICM honors the ideas of scaffolding curricula for talented learners around the important aspects of a discipline and emphasizing these aspects in a systematic way (Ward, 1980). Thus, themes and ideas are selected based on careful research of the primary area of study to determine the most worthy and important issues and ideas for curriculum development, a theme consistent with new curricular specifications (American Association for the Advancement of Science, 1990; Perkins, 1992). These ideas become an important framework for curriculum development. The goal of such an approach is to ensure deep understanding of ideas, rather than superficial responding.

This model synthesizes the three best approaches to curriculum development and implementation documented in the literature for talented learners (Benbow & Stanley, 1983; Maker, 1982; Ward, 1980). Recent reviews of curricular models for the gifted have found the greatest effectiveness prevailing in the accelerative approach, guided by content modification (Johnsen, 2000; VanTassel-Baska & Brown, 2000). The fusion of approaches is central to the development of coherent curricula that are responsive to the diverse needs of talented students while also providing rich challenges for optimal learning for all.

The ICM model (VanTassel-Baska, 1998) also represents an inclusive curriculum in respect to approaches employed, models used, assessment techniques, and the blend of general reform principles with gifted education pedagogy. Table 12.2 displays this integration pattern.

Research has been conducted to support the effectiveness of this curricular model with gifted populations within a variety of educational settings. Specifically, significant growth gains in literary analysis and interpretation, persuasive writing, and linguistic competency in language arts have been demonstrated for experimental gifted classes using the developed curricular units in comparison to gifted

Table 12.2

The Integrated Curriculum for Gifted Learners

Dimensions of Connectivity

Organizational	Employs content, process, product, and concept opportunities.
Models	Uses concept development, reasoning skills, and research models that transcend curricular areas studied.
Assessments	Performance-based and portfolio assessment are integrated into regular use.
Reform elements and gifted education	Emphasis is on meaning-making through student-centered challenging activities.

groups not using them (VanTassel-Baska, Johnson, Hughes, & Boyce, 1996; VanTassel-Baska, Zuo, Avery, & Little, 2002). Other studies have shown that using the problem-based science units embedded in an exemplary science curriculum significantly enhances the capacity for integrating higher order process skills in science regardless of the grouping approach employed (Boyce, VanTassel-Baska, Burruss, Sher, & Johnson, 1997; Gallagher, Stepien, Sher, & Workman, 1995; VanTassel-Baska, Bass, Ries, Poland, & Avery, 1998). Further, research has documented positive change in teacher attitude, student motivational response, and school and district change (VanTassel-Baska, Avery, Little, & Hughes, 2000) as a result of using this curricular model over at least 3 years.

A key issue in the curriculum development process for the gifted is the relative heterogeneity of highly gifted learners and the degree of intellectual power they possess that is well beyond more mildly gifted students. Strengths, interests, and a predisposition toward learning among this population call for special attention on the part of educators. The general provisions for gifted learners are rarely sufficient in number or intensity for these students. They demand a more individualized approach to planning that may require a combination of the following interventions:

1. development of an individual learning plan that is mutually derived between school and home;
2. development of a mentor relationship with an older student or adult; and
3. development of a collaboration with universities that sponsor special programs, offer dual-enrollment opportunities, or both.

Thus, educators need to consider alternative contexts for meeting the needs of such learners effectively.

Conclusion

Curriculum design and development for the gifted must be sensitive to the nature and needs of the population for which they are planned, including young gifted children and the highly gifted. Not only must we have in mind the individual gifted student, but also the intervention approaches found to be most effective with groups of learners. The Integrated Curriculum Model has proven to be an effective tool in organizing curricula that work with these learners. Further research on its effectiveness continues to be conducted.

13

Gender Differences in Achievement and Aptitude Test Results:
Perspectives From the Recent Literature

by Diane Boothe

Gender has often been identified as a critical factor when identifying multidimensional perspectives of giftedness. The performance of highly gifted students has been documented and analyzed for several decades by numerous leaders of the gifted child movement throughout the United States and the world, and the results have proven to be of great interest to researchers. Often, mixed messages are received regarding expectations and academic achievements of male and female students. Are gender stereotypes directly related to student performance, or is it simply a fact that males and females display different aptitudes?

This chapter is designed to provide an overview of gender differences found among intellectually gifted students and examine the research addressing males and females in a variety of dimensions of cognitive giftedness, but most frequently those related to manifesting quantitative gifts. This is often a controversial topic. Gender-related differences, when clearly shown by researchers, are not always embraced with enthusiasm.

Men and women differ from each other in both fundamental and superficial ways. Physiological differences are well-known. Other differences are less obvious. Many of the cognitive ones are small and unimportant. A few are larger and influential, especially educationally. In this chapter, only differences on certain aptitude and achievement tests are considered, chiefly for above-average examinees. To obtain a comparative base, the scoring pattern of a representative sample of boys and girls in grades 8–12 on the

Differential Aptitude Tests (DAT; Stanley, Benbow, Brody, Dauber, & Lupkowski, 1992) are presented in Figure 13.1. The effect sizes shown are the output of a widely used standard analysis of variance calculation, comparing the difference between the mean scores of males and females divided by the average of their two standard deviations[1] on various DAT test segments.

Girls were a little ahead on the DAT Numerical Ability in all five grades. Actually, the boys were far ahead only on Mechanical Reasoning, whereas the girls excelled on three of the eight tests, their highest effect size being .50 on Spelling in the 12th grade. The boys' highest was .89 on Mechanical Reasoning in the 12th grade. This is the picture for typical middle and high school students on these tests. As shown below, however, the picture changes somewhat when abler groups of students and more difficult tests, especially of academic achievement, are given.

In the values and interest areas, the differences can be larger (Stanley, Stumpf, & Cohn, 1999). On the Allport-Vernon-Lindzey Study of Values (1970), administered during the 1970s, effect sizes favoring gifted seventh-grade boys were 1.01 for Theoretical, 0.95 for Economic, and 0.56 for Political, whereas those favoring seventh-grade girls were 1.13 for Aesthetic, 0.69 for Social, and 0.48 for Religious. These agree substantially with the standardization figures for college students.

Eighty-six nationally standardized aptitude and achievement tests were examined over several years for the purpose of considering gender differences on a wide variety of cognitive tests (Stanley et al., 1992). It was determined that, with few exceptions, the scores of the males exceeded those of females. The majority of comparisons included large groups of examinees, so questions of statistical significance are not relevant. Females excelled in Spelling (effect size .50) on the Differential Aptitude Test in the 12th grade. Males (effect size .89) were strongly favored for Mechanical Reasoning on the same battery of tests (Stanley et al.). On the advanced examination of the Graduate Record Examinations, males were furthest ahead on Political Science (effect size .76), followed by Mathematics (.71; Stanley et al.).

The researchers noted that there was a strong tendency for tests taken predominately by males to result in the largest effect sizes, while those taken predominately by females yielded smaller effect sizes. In this case, females scored higher on certain verbal measurements and on Clerical Speed and Accuracy. Males scored considerably higher than females on all six physics tests and on 11 of 16 quantitative tests. Stanley and his fellow (1992) researchers also pointed out that the results revealing male scores far ahead of female scores in History and Computer Science were among the most surprising of the study because it was expected that females would receive similar scores to males on those tests. They further commented on the perplexing nature of these results in light of research indicating that girls and young women tend to be better students in school. Stanley et al. suggested that, by examining these discrepancies, perhaps ameliorative procedures will be found

---

[1] For more detailed information on the calculation of effect size, and an explanation of its significance, see http://web.uccs.edu/lbecker/Psy590/es.htm.

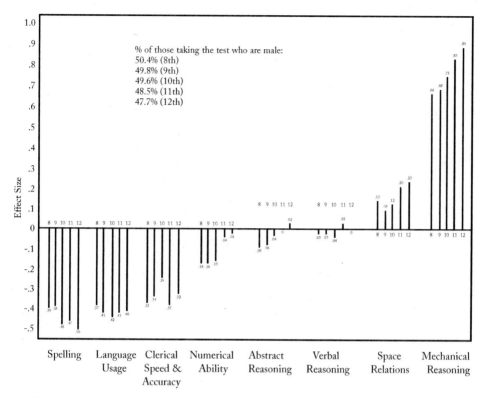

Figure 13.1. Effect sizes for the Differential Aptitude Test (DAT)

to assist more young women in preparing for careers in science, math, history, and political science. Another question that arises is whether differences in test-taking skills may be a partial explanation of these results.

Stumpf and Stanley (1997) examined gender differences on 50 College Board achievement tests as a follow-up on findings published in 1996. They examined gender-related differences on the SAT II (College Board high school achievement tests), as well as Advanced Placement (AP) tests. The findings revealed that the differences in scores for the SAT II tests were stable from 1982 and, for the AP examinations, from 1984, both through 1996. Twelve of the 21 SAT II tests favored males, while only 2 favored females; 18 of the AP examinations favored males, in contrast to 6 that favored females (Stumpf & Stanley, 1996).

It is interesting to note that, in these studies, the largest gender differences favoring males (one standard deviation each) occurred for the Theoretical Evaluative Attitude test and Mechanical Reasoning. Conversely, girls excelled on the Social Evaluative Attitude test. In addition, large differences were indicated in the area of spatial ability, particularly mental rotation.

Stumpf and Jackson (1994) and Stanley and Stumpf (1996) have pointed out that the largest gender differences favoring females are found in the areas of aesthetic and social-service evaluative attitudes. Other significant differences favoring females are also found in spelling, language usage, clerical speed and accuracy, and memory performance (Stanley et al., 1992; Stumpf & Elliot, 1995).

Halpern (1989) has conducted near-definitive research on cognitive gender differences and has argued that differences between males and females are not disappearing. Particularly large and reliable differences in the upper levels of mathematics are demonstrated by results on the PSAT and SAT examinations. Because Halpern is convinced that a decrease in cognitive gender difference depends on the type of test administered, who is being tested, and that the most important determinant is achievement, she believes that females' scores will increase as they take more advanced mathematics exams and courses.

Stumpf and Stanley (1996, 1997) concluded that males are advantaged with respect to their scores and the percentage who sign up for the more important tests. They noted that encouraging young women to take Physics and Mathematics Level II (precalculus) achievement tests has had positive effects. However, they expressed concern regarding the limited number of females who take the AP Computer Science A and AB tests.

Stumpf and Stanley (1997) conducted further studies to address the gender gap in Advanced Placement in the areas of computer science. The first two college semesters of the subject are covered by Advanced Placement Computer Science AB. Many colleges and universities will award two semesters of course credit for a score of 3 or higher on a scale ranging from 1 to 5. Apparently, in elementary school, male students demonstrate a stronger preference for computer-related activities, display more confidence than girls with respect to computers, and experience less computer anxiety. Following an examination of the distribution of grades for men and women on the AP computer science exams, gender-related differences in performance were assessed from 1984 to 1996. The results indicated decreasing differences in mean grades, highest grades, and lowest grades. It is interesting to note that far more males than females have taken the AP Computer Science examinations, yet the scores of males and females are becoming more similar over time. Stumpf and Stanley pointed out that a large gender difference continues to exist and even increase in the number of males and females who choose to take this exam. They admitted that the reasons for the low participation on behalf of the females are not known, yet they recognized the need to search systematically for causes and help close the gap because it may have serious implications in terms of losing a great deal of talent in an important subject area and fields dependent on it.

In her review of current research that reveals intricate gender differences, Halpern (2000) explained that women score higher on tests of memory, production, and comprehension of complex prose. Females also excel in fine motor tasks and speech articulation. On the other hand, Halpern indicated that men score higher on tests of fluid reasoning, tasks that involve moving objects, transformation of objects, and tasks that require aiming. It is interesting to note that Halpern and others have determined that females on average receive better grades in every subject in school, while males are in the majority in both gifted and mentally disabled populations.

Historical Perspectives

Does society hold two different sets of expectations for gifted males and females, or do complex social factors contribute to achievement levels that are not commensurate with females' abilities? Kerr (1997) has suggested that gifted behaviors for both genders are imbued with Western society's notion of appropriate gender identity. Our culture suggests early on that mechanical and analytical activities are inherently masculine, while social and relationship activities, including language, are inherently feminine. This would seem to be borne out in the test scores above. That which is emphasized and practiced becomes stronger and more dominant. On the other hand, do complicated biological factors influence gender differences? Even to conjecture this would be most unpopular to some, as Benbow and Stanley (1980, 1982) learned.

In her studies with a group of highly gifted students, Hollingworth (1926) recognized that the males experienced feelings of rejection and suffered from being different from other students. Unfortunately, as early as the 1920s, it became evident that the stereotypical small, studious "nerd" image of the highly gifted male was not a popular role to assume (Kerr, 1997). In order to be accepted as a gifted student, one is led to believe that males' academic skills have to be coupled with athletic prowess (Coleman, 1959).

Prior to this time, most studies of intelligence considered eminent males exclusively. Terman and Oden (1935) addressed the masculinity of gifted boys and portrayed them as healthy, well adjusted, and excelling in athleticism. They initially began their studies of gifted students in an attempt to validate questions on the Stanford-Binet Intelligence Scale. The subjects for this study (IQ at least 135) consisted predominately of middle-class White students from California schools. Although Terman and Oden included in their study as many girls as qualified, they were considered similar to gifted boys, with the incorporation of female interests. Kerr (1997) has pointed out that, although Terman and Oden suggested there was a possibility that these gifted girls (born, on the average, about 1910) were able to achieve academically and maintain their femininity, most of them possessed little power in society. By midlife, most yielded to traditional women's occupations, the most popular being teaching in elementary and secondary schools.

It is interesting to consider that, during the 21st century, teachers are being blamed for the low test scores and lack of achievement of their students. If highly gifted females tended to enter the teaching field 70 years ago, then it is reasonable to assume that they had a strong impact on the quality of education. So, now that many highly gifted females are selecting careers in math, business, public service, science, and engineering, does this have a profound impact on the intellectual quality of the pool of teaching candidates?

Identification During Childhood

It is worthwhile to note that more than 50% of gifted kindergarten students are girls, yet only 30% of female eighth graders are identified as gifted (Koppel, 1991). To what can we attribute this decline? Does the asynchronous development that challenges all exceptionally able students take a particularly devastating toll on gifted females? If a disproportionate number of identified gifted females are underachieving, what physiological, social, and psychological factors could be contributing to these outcomes? Also, how do the differences in the instruments employed to measure giftedness influence these outcomes? To what extent does the concept of multiple intelligences contribute to the differences, with the gifts of some females not being accurately measured because the instruments employed are not sensitive to them?

Giftedness is often evident at an early age in girls, who are likely to speak, read, and write sooner than males of the same age (Silverman, 1986). Girls often demonstrate precocious reading skills when quite young (Kerr, 1997), yet these skills do not necessarily translate into identification as exceptionally able learners. Often, public schools in the United States tailor literacy programs to the reading readiness levels of male students who may have been delayed entering kindergarten due to a parental decision based on social, emotional, and physical attributes. In the case of academically gifted youngsters, their intellectual abilities often exceed these other developments.

Once exceptionally able students embark on their educational careers, a variety of interesting patterns emerge. Teachers have been observed to interact differently with male and female gifted students, and their expectations also vary according to gender (Sadker & Sadker, 1985). There is evidence that boys often dominate classroom discussions and that this is accepted by teachers (Sadker & Sadker, 1985). On the other hand, when girls are required to raise their hand, they do not participate in class to the extent that their male counterparts do, and they may even avoid responding to questions (Kramer, 1985). It is reasonable to suspect that the perceptions of this favoritism toward gifted males and the suggestion of males' superior intellectual capability does not result in positive long-term effects for female students' self-concept or academic success. These perceptions certainly have the potential to impact their motivation and perception of classroom interaction negatively. These differences in classroom situations may also affect gifted girls' decisions to take mathematics and science classes and eventually their career success (Fox, 1977). Are these merely excuses to explain differences in achievement levels of males and females? Certainly, a multiplicity of variables contributes to each individual's degree of success in the classroom, university, and profession. Horner (1972) argued that girls fear success. Can that still be the case 30 years later? Does a competitive climate result in more anxiety for females than males?

According to Feldhusen and Willard-Holt (1993), evidence indicates that boys perceive inequalities in the classroom to a greater extent than girls. The subscale of their study addressing preferences in math or science-related tasks indicated that gifted male students scored higher than females. However, no differences were determined on the subscales measuring high aspirations or effort.

Robinson, Abbott, and Busse (1996) conducted research addressing the structure of abilities in math-precocious young children in regard to gender differences and found that, among intellectually bright students, there were significant differences favoring males in elementary school and even among preschoolers. It is worth noting that gender differences were manifested not only in the quantitative results, but also in the nomination of more boys than girls and qualification of more boys than girls. On the psychometric battery, boys' scores in the mathematical domain surpassed girls' scores on 8 of the 11 mathematical subtests administered.

In a study addressing gender differences for able students, Stanley (1992) found that sizeable gender differences on aptitude and achievement tests occur prior to high school. Stanley cited the first academic talent search conducted by the Study of Mathematically Precocious Youth (SMPY) at Johns Hopkins University in 1972. Seventh- and eighth-grade boys scored higher than girls on the mathematical section of the College Board Scholastic Aptitude Test (SAT-M) to the extent that 43 of the 223 boys tested scored higher than any of the 173 girls who took the test. Since then, this difference has diminished considerably.

In an additional study (Stanley, 1994), the Johns Hopkins University Center for Talented Youth administered the upper level of the Secondary School Admission Test (SSAT), which is designed for students in grades 8–10, to fifth and sixth graders during a regional talent search at the elementary school level. The results revealed that approximately seven times as large a percentage of boys scored in the top 1% of the distribution as did girls on the SSAT-Quantitative. The upper 1% ratios for SSAT-Verbal, which also favored boys, were 1.46 for sixth graders and 1.38 for fifth graders.

Additional tests (Stanley, 1994) such as the EXPLORE test, the Mathematical Olympiad for Elementary Schools, and MathCounts provide evidence suggesting that these gender differences on selection and achievement tests are present as early as the second grade. As noted earlier, Robinson, Abbott, and Busse (1996) found that gender differences are present in math-precocious youngsters even as early as preschool. Maccoby and Jacklin (1974) asserted that, even at a young age, parental and societal influences, as well as children's own play preferences, interact with existing biological propensities, and they recommended extensive further research to sort out the nature of these interactions. Stanley (1994) pointed out that, whereas much information is available regarding the "whats," little except speculation is available that addresses the "whys." This cries out for further research, particularly on instrumental effectiveness.

The Dilemma of Adolescence

Gender differences at the high school level become even more obvious, particularly early in the subject areas of mathematics and science. The ratio of males to females is significantly skewed in favor of males (Rose, 1999). The jury is still out regarding concrete evidence indicating that young males have a better capacity for understanding math and science, but it is clear that gifted females do not routinely embrace these disciplines.

During the high school years, social and psychological factors exert a tremendous influence on the achievement of gifted girls. Strong family ties, female mentors, appropriate guidance toward more demanding college preparatory courses, and acceptance at prestigious colleges or universities are defining factors that contribute to high levels of success. The social intelligence and leadership talents of females may be more developed, but they are not measured in the indexes or instruments typically used to define giftedness. Gifted females need to be encouraged to enroll and excel in higher level, rigorous math and science courses. Parents and teachers have the ability to contribute to the success of gifted females by encouraging their positive perceptions of their abilities.

Factors That Make a Difference

Kerr (1994) investigated the factors that set the eminent women in her study apart from other women who were not gifted or who were identified as gifted, but did not achieve to their level of capability. Experiences that strengthened self-esteem were key factors that led to feelings of being special or different, reading and falling in love with ideas, and being capable of establishing relationships without sacrificing personal identification or goals. This led to convictions that their values were worthy and guided by their own actions and beliefs. These gifted females were empowered, developed relationships aligned to their passion for their work, and assumed equality with men.

It is interesting to note that Kerr (1994) also found that many experienced an awkward or socially difficult adolescence and were often educated in a same-sex environment. They also tended to spend time alone and received individualized instruction as children. These factors indicate that these young women were unusual in that they were provided with opportunities that led to eminence and reinforced successes. Kerr pointed out that they had mentors to nurture their talents and provide access to professional involvement. As a result of the above factors, they were able to eschew mediocrity and integrate a variety of roles and responsibilities into their life. It would be interesting to compare lives and contrast these factors with those of bright males (Zuckerman, 1977). Were their success and achievement profiled by similar characteristics?

According to Kerr and Colangelo (1988), males outscored females at the very highest score levels on the 1988 American College Testing (ACT) exams taken during their senior year of high school. Males comprised 61% of students scoring above the 95th percentile on the composite score; 72% of students scoring in the top 1% were males. On the four subtests, males outperformed females in mathematics, natural sciences, and social sciences, but females scored higher than males on the English subtest. It is not surprising to note that lower scores for females are linked to course selection and enrollment. Unfortunately, choices made during adolescence and college have the potential for greatly jeopardizing female students' future career opportunities.

Extensive research has been conducted among the participants of the Study of Mathematically Precocious Youth (SMPY) at Johns Hopkins University, designed by Julian Stanley in 1971 to identify gifted youth who reason exceptionally well mathematically. Students were identified chiefly at the seventh-grade level by virtue of their scores on the College Board Scholastic Aptitude Test (SAT-M). Lubinski and Benbow (1992) have documented gender differences among these highly gifted students over the past 20 years. Normative samples revealed that, in cognitive functioning, highly able males and females are converging toward a common mean on a variety of abilities, including mathematical reasoning. Equal numbers of males and females participated in the testing. Lubinski and Benbow reported the proportion of males to females on the SAT-M as SAT-M > 500, 2/1; SAT-M > 600, 4/1; and SAT-M > 700, 13/1. They further pointed out that the effects of these disparate ratios will be that a greater number of males than females will meet the qualifications for advanced training in areas that require high levels of mathematical reasoning and expertise. Further findings in this study address educational and vocational decision making and suggest that males excel in mechanical and spatial abilities important for success in physical science and engineering. As a result, females are not entering math and physical science fields in numbers even close to their male counterparts. Less than 1% of females in the top 1% of mathematical ability are pursuing doctorates in mathematics, engineering, or physical science (Lubinski & Benbow).

Progress in Narrowing the Gender Gap

Leta Hollingworth, cofounder of the gifted child movement in the United States, began her studies in the 1920s and can be credited with making exemplary progress regarding opportunities for gifted females. As educational barriers diminish, further interest is dedicated to the achievements of gifted females. As Read (1991) pointed out, through history, significantly fewer women have been considered as eminent as their male colleagues. Because females are often underrepresented in mathematics, science, and industry (Rensburger, 1984), special intervention and investigation may be helpful.

Ford (1996) has been concerned that research on gender issues among gifted students focuses on White females and does not consider Black, Hispanic, or Native American females. She has pointed out that important cultural differences carrying crucial implications for their educational achievement exist among females from diverse ethnic backgrounds. These females may be at an even greater risk for underachievement due to lack of self-confidence and concern about peer acceptance and social issues. Ford has commented that some gifted females can attribute their underachievement to a variety of social, environmental, and cultural issues, including rejection by family, teachers, and peer groups for achieving at high levels, as well as less encouragement and fewer incentives than males. These are not limited to persons of color, though: The results may have more to do with socioeconomic position than anything else. While aspiring to higher education may be seen as a ticket out of the lower levels, there are pressures to begin to contribute to family financial needs as quickly as possible.

While Arnold (1995) found a direct link between exceptionally high school grades, postsecondary achievement, and degree attainments, it became clear that nonacademic factors such as gender, social class, and ethnicity overshadowed academic talent in determining career accomplishments by former valedictorians (Heller, Mönks, Sternberg, & Subotnik, 2002). Subotnik and Steiner's (1994) report on the Westinghouse Science Talent Search study revealed that women's conceptions of their role as parents continued to shape career aspirations. Females headed for science careers were concerned about balancing family and career responsibilities (Sadker & Sadker, 1994), and such concerns are certainly not limited to career aspirations in science.

Socialization and Gender Stereotypes

In a continual effort to explain the discrepancies between academic performance of males and females, Luscombe and Riley (2001) examined the self-concepts of a group of academically gifted adolescents in New Zealand. Their research revealed that males scored higher than females on most dimensions, with the exception of Self-Criticism, Inconsistent Responding, and Moral Self-Concept. Two suggestions have been made to address this result. Klein & Zehms (1996) pointed out that too many gifted girls—ebullient, confident, and filled with high aspiration—simply and quietly disappear. This perspective suggests that females encounter challenges that impede their success as they progress through the educational system. Silverman (1993) has attributed this to socialization practices that undermine gifted females' self-confidence and aspiration, which further influences academic success and career selection.

As gender roles and psychosocial challenges have rapidly changed throughout the past 50 years and are constantly evolving, males continue to outperform females on most standardized tests. A flood of questions continues to perplex researchers and educators regarding the myriad factors that contribute to these findings. Is mentoring for gifted females keeping pace and are efforts to reverse lower achievement appropriate? As the gender gaps close, are females continuing to compromise their educational and career goals? Do gifted females possess unique social and psychological needs that continue to remain unmet and adversely affect their academic achievement? Are researchers and educators unable to accept the fact that males and females excel in different areas, display strengths in diverse fields, and prefer to be in them? It is clear that males excel mathematically and outnumber females in the disciplines of mathematics and physical science. Should this be accepted as a fact of life or questioned? Because males or females can excel in a particular area, this should not mean that members of the opposite sex are summarily excluded from participating. It is unfortunate if educators, parents, or those in the work force discourage or fail to treat students of both sexes equally and value conflicts continue to impact female success negatively. It is also essential not to coerce males or females into academic or professional areas they don't prefer.

The gender gap in the United States has been closed in numerous ways (Campbell & Clewell, 1999). Positive strides have been made in the examination of standardized test questions, and a look at current textbooks reveals that gender bias in print and illustration has decreased significantly. As educators transform the curriculum and include materials that eliminate stereotypes and incorporate meaningful perspectives, gifted students of both sexes will be motivated to excel. Are teacher-training programs keeping pace with the needs of gifted students? Do school districts implement identification procedures in a timely manner and apply methodology appropriately designed to meet these unique needs?

Kerr and Niepon (2003, cited in Colangelo & Davis, 2003) pointed out that, where intellectually gifted eighth-grade girls are on a par with boys in math achievement, they are taking more challenging high school courses in the areas of math and science. Many efforts are underway to encourage girls to raise their career aspirations and select more rigorous coursework (Kerr & Niepon). The common goal is to provide challenging and quality programs that lead to maximum utilization of both males' and females' talent and inspire intellectually gifted students.

As Stanley (1994) has noted, "We have a sizable set of information that defines the fact of gender differences regarding quantitative excellence." What is missing is any clear explanation as to why this is manifested in standardized tests and tests for identifying giftedness. To what extent does the nurturing style of our Western culture influence test performance? Clearly, more research is needed to determine the extent to which esteem correlates with quantitative test performance, to identify the "other intelligences" not currently measured in standardized tests that may be the sites of stronger female presence, and to catalog more clearly the impacts of socioeconomic and peer pressures on gender differences in high cognitive intelligence. The time to begin that research is now.

14

Counseling Gifted Students and Their Families

by C. Marie Jackson and Brent M. Snow

ounseling for the gifted bears no mark of distinction in most typical school settings. Could this be due to the underlying misconceptions found in the often-stated and now tired and worn concept that "the gifted can make it on their own?"

According to Kerr (1990), "Youthful brilliance in one or more areas does not always translate into adult satisfaction and accomplishment in . . . life" (p. 1). Studies (e.g., Kerr, 1985; Watley, 1969) have shown that a gifted student's transition from school to career to a successful life is often hampered by the differing academic, social, and emotional needs found concomitantly with identified giftedness. The unique needs and concerns of gifted individuals and their role and relationships within families are critical areas of concern for parents, teachers, counselors, administrators, and all others who live and work with gifted students. In a report to the United States Congress by the Commissioner of Education in 1972, it was stated that this group is the most educationally deprived of all groups of students in the U.S. Yet, somehow in our equality-based society, the concept of equity is often overlooked (Benbow & Stanley, 1996). With 21st-century concepts such as those found in the U.S. Department of Education's "No Child Left Behind" Act (January 2002) and more specifically in Subpart 6 A of the Jacob K. Javits Gifted and Talented Students Education Act of 2001, which declares that schools nationwide need to meet the special educational needs of gifted and talented students, it behooves educators and counselors alike to focus upon the differential counseling needs of gifted students.

This chapter provides a historical background on counseling for the gifted, including defining giftedness and the identification of gifted students. Other areas addressed are differential needs, family issues, counseling for gifted students, and special concerns.

Historical Background

The identification of gifted children dates back as early as the beginning of the 20th century (Perrone & Pulvino, 1979). Leta Hollingworth began the movement toward guidance for the gifted in the 1920s and 1930s. Yet, large-scale efforts to guide (or counsel) the gifted came later in the early 1950s. The decade opened with publications such as Strang's (1952) article on guidance of the gifted followed by Barbe's 1954 publication on differentiated guidance for the gifted. With the impact of Sputnik came the launching of counseling for the gifted and talented through the now historic reactive legislation of 1958, the National Defense Education Act. This event has been both praised and criticized within the counseling profession, with accolades for the recognition of the need for better counseling services in schools and criticism for the emphasis upon only gifted and talented students. However, it is a historic marker for the real beginning of differentiated counseling for the gifted.

Gowan (1979) noted that "a good guidance program for the gifted is an outgrowth of a good general guidance program" (pp. 190–191), and he emphasized that guidance is not just for crisis removal or treatment of psychopathology. Gowan was ahead of his time in his recognition that school counseling programs should be concerned with the normal development of all students. He further suggested a need to differentiate guidance for gifted students in order to help them fully develop their multipotentiality. His advocacy for counseling the gifted is captured by the following:

> Making a life, as Thoreau has reminded us, is more important than making a living. And often the gifted student marches to the music of a distant drum. We may not be able to adjust him to society, for he may perceive much in society that should itself be adjusted. (p. 191)

In the 21st century, in an era of transforming school counseling to meet the needs of all students, the desire for uniformity in counselor program objectives, as well as in school counselor training, has led the American School Counselor Association (ASCA) to develop national standards and a national model program to address the differentiated needs of all students. The philosophical base of the ASCA national model (2002) reflects the work of the Transforming School Counseling Initiative administered by the Education Trust (1998) to redesign school counselor education training programs (Hanson & Stone, 2002; Hayes & Paisley, 2002; Hines, 2002; House & Sears, 2002; Jackson et al., 2002; Jackson et al., 1999; Martin, 2002; Musheno & Talbert, 2002) to help school counselors more effectively meet the needs of all students. The concepts of *advocacy, leadership, systemic change,* and *collaboration* form the border of the ASCA schematic (Hatch & Bowers, 2002). This philosophical base represents the intent of the developers of the model to provide a program that calls for advocacy for educational equity for all students.

A frequent comment in recent reform literature goes something like this: In order to assist students in meeting their academic potential and achieving at high levels, it may be necessary to provide support systems and safety nets. While many may not associate this statement with gifted students, it clearly applies to them, as well. In 1993, in the U.S. Department of Education's report, *National Excellence: A Case for Developing America's Talent,* reference was made to the education of gifted youth in the U.S. as being in a quiet crisis due to the lack of challenge for these students. The perception that they fare well on their own leads to a lack of appropriate counseling, tutoring, and mentoring for gifted and talented students. Often, the needs of these students are quietly ignored, never making it to the table when policies are being developed. Although efforts to identify gifted students have improved, educators and counselors continue to struggle with how best to meet their needs (Milgram, 1991).

Definition and Identification of Gifted Students

The definition presented on the National Association for Gifted Children's Web site (http://www.nagc.org) states that a gifted person is someone who shows, or has the potential for showing, an exceptional level of performance in one or more areas of expression. The most commonly used definition of gifted children is the one presented by a former U.S. Commissioner of Education (Sidney P. Marland, Jr.) in his report to Congress:

Gifted and talented children are those identified by professionally qualified persons who by virtue of outstanding abilities are capable of high performance. These are children who require differentiated educational programs and/or services beyond those normally provided by the regular school programs in order to realize their contribution to self and society (Marland, 1972, p. ix).

Marland's definition went even further to include a description of areas of giftedness for consideration singly or in combination. These were general intellectual ability, specific academic aptitude, creative or productive thinking, leadership ability, visual or performing arts, and psychomotor ability.

According to the National Association for Gifted Children's Web site, the majority of states continue to use the foregoing definition and are primarily serving those with general intellectual ability determined by a standardized intelligence test score, at least two standard deviations above the mean. Using this definition, approximately 3–5% of the population are likely to be identified as gifted. Other states are using multiple-criteria approaches, which allow for varying definitions and conceptions of giftedness. For example, Georgia's definition of a student eligible for gifted education services (Rule 160-4-2-.38; Georgia Department of Education, 1998) is as follows:

> Gifted Student—a student who demonstrates a high degree of intellectual and/or creative ability(ies), exhibits an exceptionally high degree of motivation, and/or excels in specific academic fields, and who needs special instruction and/or special ancillary services to achieve at levels commensurate with his or her abilities. (p. 1)

Obviously, Georgia is operating within a more broadly defined conceptualization of giftedness, one that includes those with creative or artistic talents in addition to the academically gifted. Students are assessed for mental ability, achievement, creativity, and motivation. Following the four assessments, Georgia uses two ways of determining eligibility for gifted programs: (1) the psychometric approach, wherein the student qualifies on the basis of mental ability and achievement assessment results only, or (2) the multiple-criteria approach, in which a student may qualify by meeting the standards in a variety of ways. Any three of the four qualifying areas (mental ability, achievement, creativity, and motivation) may be used for identification (Georgia Department of Education, 1998). By using this multiple-criteria approach, the representation of minority and ethnic groups in gifted programs has increased (Stephens, 1998).

A review of some of the conceptual definitions of giftedness (Gardner, 1983; Renzulli, 1986b; Sternberg, 1985; Tannenbaum, 1983) reveals many ways to describe a gifted child. A new definition of the term *giftedness*, referred to as the "Columbus group definition" (Silverman, 1993), included a focus on the asynchronous development of cognitive abilities and heightened intensity. This combination of high-level cognitive abilities and increased sensitivity is perceived as creating experiences and awarenesses in gifted individuals that are different from the norm. Even the observation of a young child by parents, teachers, and significant others can help to identify the unique qualities indicative of giftedness present from birth.

There is no universally accepted definition of giftedness; yet, since 1904, and especially today, Spearman's concept of "general intelligence" (g) has been widely accepted by psychologists (Jensen, 1998). Even so, counselors of gifted students need a working knowledge of the local definition in use and an understanding of the process for identification of these students (Meckstroth, 1991). Many school systems use a broadly defined conception of giftedness involving multiple criteria and thereby expect to identify 10–15% of students for their gifted and talented programs (*Giftedness and the Gifted*, 1990). The authors of the Jacob K. Javits Gifted and

Talented Students Education Act of 2001 (Subpart 6—Gifted and Talented of "No Child Left Behind" ESEA Legislation, 2002) defined the gifted and talented as

> students, children, or youth who give evidence of high achievement capability in areas such as intellectual, creative, artistic, or leadership capacity, or in specific academic fields, and who need services or activities not ordinarily provided by the school in order to fully develop those capabilities. (Title IX, Part A, Section 9101[22])

Differential Needs

Gifted students are "different" (diversity, perhaps) and should be provided appropriate differentiated counseling services. Cross (1998) wrote, "If a school truly embraces diversity, human differences such as giftedness will be acceptable and considered a meaningful difference" (p. 1). Gifted students face the same emotional issues as other children, yet their unique personality traits impact how they meet these issues. For example, gifted students may have an increased self-awareness, perfectionistic and self-critical tendencies, or low self-esteem. The following common characteristics of intellectually gifted students can be exhibited either positively or negatively:

- superior reasoning powers;
- persistent intellectual curiosity;
- wide range of interests;
- markedly superior in quality or quantity of written/spoken vocabulary;
- reads avidly and absorbs books well beyond his or her years;
- learns quickly and easily and retains what is learned;
- shows insight into arithmetical problems and grasps concepts readily;
- has a keen sense of humor;
- sets high standards for him- or herself; and
- gets excitement and pleasure from intellectual challenge (*Giftedness and the Gifted*, 1990).

While many children exhibit these traits, gifted students tend to possess these characteristics to a much greater degree than others of their same age.

Problems often evolve due to inconsistent development, both intra- and interpersonally. For example, being able to deal with problems at a higher cognitive level than one's peers may cause many misunderstandings. Silverman (1993) suggested a need for counselors to modify their techniques to adjust for both gifted students' cognitive complexity and their emotional sensitivity. Just simply seeing things from a different perspective through superior or unique reasoning powers may cause a conflict between a gifted student and the classroom teacher. Often, a gifted student sees humor in a situation and may express it in creative ways, perhaps even inappropriate ways, or at inappropriate times or places. The desire for intellectual challenge may ultimately lead to underachievement or boredom when a gifted student's desire to seek challenge is neither allowed nor encouraged. Frustration, boredom, or both can occur as a result of the ability to learn quickly and easily while possessing great insight and curiosity. The tendency of gifted students to set exceptionally high standards for themselves may lead to feelings of being inferior or not good enough when they are unable to meet them. A wide range of interests and absorption in books or even exploration of the World Wide Web can detract a student from assigned academics. Each of the common identifying characteristics can be an underlying factor when a gifted student appears in the counselor's office.

Mendaglio (2003) described how the tendency of gifted students to have heightened sensitivity might contribute to being emotionally volatile. His description of sensitivity included an increased awareness of self and of one's social environment. This heightened sense of self and others can be a positive attribute, but it is often a characteristic of concern, bringing emotional pain. Counselors should be aware of the emotional intensity of gifted students and be prepared to modify counseling techniques as necessary. Other affective differentiating characteristics of the gifted noted in the literature are intensity, self-criticism, and perfectionism, all potential problems (Mendaglio; Silverman, 1993).

Accepting oneself, including one's gifted abilities and shortcomings, is another potential area of difficulty. It is in this area that social interactions may become a problem. When gifted students are perceived as "strange" and are avoided or ridiculed by their peers, they may withdraw from further social interactions. Because of this avoidance of social interaction, they fail to learn much-needed social skills, which then sets the stage for more ostracism. According to Goleman (1997), social ineptitude can lead to isolation and loneliness. Sometimes, problems in peer relationships, as well as sibling relationships, develop through issues associated with the gifted identification process itself. Even the *label* of giftedness can create problems for the gifted student and his or her parents. Not wanting to be recognized as gifted, these students may attempt to hide their abilities. Some reasons for this denial of giftedness may be fear of being rejected by their peers, fear of the inability to live up to the expectations of others, and confusion about what giftedness means. This is so common that the phrase "closet giftedness" has been used to refer to those who deny their giftedness. Sometimes, parents have problems accepting a child's giftedness, not knowing what it actually means or whether something, if anything, should now be done differently. Feeling threatened or challenged intellectually by their gifted child, some parents have been known to rebel at the idea of their child's being identified as gifted. Others, of course, may perceive it as a status symbol.

Family Issues

The concerns of the parents of gifted students include social concerns, fears of insufficient educational stimulation, lack of challenge for their child, and feelings of parental inadequacy. The reaction of parents to their child's giftedness some-times motivates them to seek counseling assistance. Some parents may have been unaware of their child's giftedness prior to the identification process, while others may have ignored their child's special abilities, wanting him or her to remain "nor-mal." At these times, parents may need to be pointed to recommended readings about gifted children.

Meckstroth (1991) cautioned parents against valuing their child's accomplish-ments more than their child's feelings or personhood. Parental encouragement to achieve is a strong underlying factor in a student's success. However, there is a fine line between enough and too much parental pressure. It takes great parenting skill and know-how to give the right amount of needed attention to a gifted child (i.e., to discern where facilitation is most needed and how much).

Sibling relationships sometimes become difficult when one child in the fam-ily is identified as gifted and another is not. Parents need to be made aware of ways in which they can support their gifted child without seemingly neglecting a sib-ling not so identified. Sibling rivalries can create much family dysfunction. Parents should attend to the individual interests of all their children and validate each child's endeavors.

Other parental concerns often voiced are underachievement and, surprisingly, overachievement. Meckstroth (1991) addressed underachievement due to lack of motivation to learn. Many possible reasons for a gifted child's underachievement have been discussed in the literature, such as disadvantaged backgrounds, social-ization patterns, problematic interpersonal interactions, and family conflicts, among others. In general, to overcome underachievement, a gifted child needs a sense of confidence and competence.

While some parents encourage their children to do their very best at all times and believe that the rewards are worth the effort, there are others who have nega-tive reactions to what they perceive to be overachievement. Sometimes, these parental reactions to high academic involvement or focused achievement are based in the fear that their child will not be well rounded or balanced in his or her approach to life. However, these negative reactions may also be motivated by a par-ent's own inadequacies, real or imagined, or by misunderstandings of giftedness. The best encouragement a parent can provide is to be an active, positive role model.

A key factor for the success of gifted children is the development of a secure home with healthful relationships. The following are some suggestions for parents:

1. Listen for understanding, especially for what is *not* being said.
2. Help your child *recognize* feelings, rather than *intellectualizing* them.
3. Make time to talk and have private time.
4. Teach ways to express anger constructively.
5. As gifted children tend to be more sensitive and take things personally (Saunders & Remsberg, 1985), help your child remain grounded in reality.
6. Help your child avoid harmful self-imposed stress.

7. Teach your gifted child to be prepared for increasing amounts of stress as he or she progresses in school.
8. Model the behaviors you wish your gifted child to acquire.
9. Uphold diversity and teach your gifted child to recognize and accept differences within and outside the home.
10. Seek out counselors and mentors who are knowledgeable about gifted students.
11. Help your child develop leisure-time activities and take time to relax.
12. Teach your child social skills and the ability to see another person's point of view.
13. Help your child realize that other people cannot or will not always understand or agree.
14. Cheer your child on to success in all areas of development without undue pressure.
15. Do not focus exclusively on academic accomplishments.
16. Be positive about challenges and problems and find ways to compliment and affirm.

Parents occupy a major role in the development of their gifted children. Positive influences from parental figures is critical for the success of nearly all children, but the added dimension of giftedness creates an even greater need for parents to understand the nature of giftedness and their role in the development of their child's special abilities.

Counseling for Gifted Students

Gifted students need basic guidance on issues like developing study skills, effective time management, and dealing with stress (Walker, 1982). Mahoney (1995) suggested the following as common counseling issues for counselors to address with gifted students: (1) the meaning of giftedness and forming a gifted identity; (2) denial of giftedness; (3) struggling with deviance; (4) dealing with related family concerns; and (5) handling deficits (p. 1). Johnson (2001) proposed integrating into the curriculum for gifted and talented students an affective component, which school counselors are in a position to provide in the form of affective guidance.

Due to unique learning characteristics of gifted students, it is important to vary the presentation style when providing guidance for them. Variation in technique will maintain attention and challenge intellectual curiosity. For example, when working on social skills, it is helpful to use a range of techniques such as group interaction, role-play, perspective taking, communication skills, and demonstrating empathy. These are enjoyed by most students and are particularly beneficial to gifted children.

VanTassel-Baska (1990) identified guiding principles and recommended that counselors of the gifted should

1. be attuned to differences in the emotional and intellectual systems of gifted students;
2. help students understand their special characteristics to counter possible feelings of being different, alienated, and inferior;
3. focus on cognitive and affective needs through provision of academic, psychosocial, and career counseling;
4. advocate by helping negotiate and facilitate progress;
5. provide an information clearinghouse for outside resources;
6. aid students in decision-making skills and planning; value, encourage, and reward self-initiated learning;
7. assess tested strengths and weaknesses and help develop a plan of action around the results;
8. encourage the reading of books related to particular problems (bibliotherapy);
9. be sensitive to students coming from low socioeconomic backgrounds and provide support in clarifying and actualizing goals;
10. establish a network of female students to encourage course taking in mathematics and science;
11. act as chief communicators to other educational personnel regarding needs of gifted students;
12. serve as initiators in the identification process for inclusion in special programs or for individual attention; and
13. team with parents and others to conduct "staffings" on problems related to underachievement, social adjustment, or personal crises (pp. 3–5).

Janos and Robinson (1985) referred to counselors and psychologists as being among the most crucial resources for gifted children and their families. Gifted students need guidance for successful career planning and problem solving. However, in a technologically based world, it also is important to train gifted students in the discovery, retrieval, use, and even production of information on their own (Renzulli, 1977). Jackson (1987) developed a counseling model for gifted students based on Renzulli's enrichment curriculum model to develop awareness and skills sufficient for students to analyze and solve problems as they apply to real-world issues when they arise. A premise of this model is that gifted students need help in gaining self-direction, rather than always looking to well-meaning parents, teachers, and even counselors for step-by step directions. This model focuses on developing self-awareness, awareness of one's own social milieu, and valuable skills through training in such areas as problem solving, decision making, and goal setting in order to make later application to real-world concerns. Teaching gifted children to analyze a personal problem, especially when it is a criticism, can help them resolve such problems and handle the related stress and anxiety by using analysis and reasoning. In this regard, the use of Webb, Meckstroth, and Tolan's (1982) three-step questioning process—(1) Are the criticisms accurate? (2) Do I want to do anything about it? and (3) If so, what?—is suggested. This and similar processes allow gifted students to deal with their own special concerns in a self-directed and less stressful manner.

Another model to which school counselors should refer when planning counseling for the gifted is one presented by Silverman (1993). This is a developmental model focused on prevention, rather than remediation. Strategies for both individual and group counseling are included along with tips and techniques for prevention counseling, academic and career counseling, learning-disabled students, families, and at-risk gifted students. Her treatment of special issues includes discussion of multicultural counseling, social development, leadership, and gender issues specific to gifted students.

Special Concerns

Only a brief discussion of a few selected concerns is presented here. The reader is encouraged to explore related literature (e.g., Milgram, 1991; Silverman, 1993; VanTassel-Baska, 1990) for more in-depth coverage. Other gifted student counseling concerns too complex for an adequate review in this chapter are underachievement, learning disabilities, the disadvantaged, at-risk students, and gifted preschoolers.

Multipotentiality

Difficulty with decision making concerning topics, projects, hobbies, social and recreational activities, and academic and career choices is likely to occur among gifted students due to their multipotentiality. Frederickson and Rothney (1972) defined multipotentiality as the ability to select and develop any number of career options because of a wide variety of interests, aptitudes, and abilities. A variety of problems may result from this characteristic. Some common ones are over-scheduling oneself, assuming too many duties and responsibilities, or even having no real preferences.

To cope with multipotentiality, Kerr (1990) recommended intervention strategies at each educational level. Some examples drawn from her work include: (1) at the elementary level, encourage such things as achievement of Scout merit badges, for example, which require goal setting and follow-through; (2) at the middle school level, discourage overinvolvement in social and recreational activities for the sake of involvement; rather, prioritize and decide on a few extracurricular involvements; (3) at the high school level, discourage conformist, stereotypical career choices and explore paid internships.

Culturally Diverse Gifted

Colangelo and LaFrenz (1981) provided direction on counseling the culturally diverse gifted. One suggestion they gave is to focus on raising career aspirations for these students and build on their accomplishments for career directions. According to Kerr (1990), minorities are less likely to do well on standardized achievement tests, but often are exceptional leaders and succeed at various out-of-class accomplishments. Encouraging the use of multiple approaches to identifying gifted students and then establishing guidance programs and educational curricula to recognize and build strength areas is essential for culturally diverse gifted students.

Gifted Girls

Some gifted girls are much less likely than gifted boys to achieve at high levels. Acculturation, socialization, or both continue to impact many females' decision to forego some of their own achievement goals for those of their husband and the role of motherhood. The facts remain that salary, promotions, and achievement throughout their working lives lag behind their male counterparts (Kerr, 1990). Counselors should encourage gifted girls to maintain high career aspirations and pursue rigorous academic preparation (Schwartz, 1991), but not condemn them if they choose to do otherwise. Gifted females need assistance in recognizing cultural barriers to their achievement and encouragement to weigh carefully the barriers to and options for successful attainment of their goals.

Early Emergers

Those students who exhibit specific gifts and talents from a very early age are referred to as "early emergers." These students seem to have a passion for a particular talent or interest very early in life. Kerr (1990) cautioned against neglecting early emergers by failing to provide education and resources for the development of their demonstrated passion. Parents may extinguish the flame by insisting on well-roundedness. On the other hand, however, too much pressure can remove it as well. Tips for handling early emergers include the following:

- Consult with experts in the talent area regarding proper nurturing.
- Allow the child the freedom to change direction because early emergers may change to a closely related interest area.
- As the child gets older, seek a mentor in the chosen area of interest.
- Seek career guidance from someone familiar with the talent area.

Summer Camps, Day Camps, and Other Summer Programs

School counselors need to be aware of summer programs for the gifted. Quite a variety of such programs exist, such as university-based residential programs, summer camps of various length, and day camps. These programs offer opportunities for academic acceleration and enrichment, as well as for personal and social growth not provided during the academic year through regular public school programs (Piskurich, 2002).

Some of these summer programs are focused on a specific interest area, such as math or science, while others are designed more for enrichment in a variety of areas. Enersen (1993) interviewed program participants in the Gifted Education Resource Institute (GERI) summer camp at Purdue University. The results of her study indicated that participants thought the camps provided academic challenge, appropriate peer groups with the same interests and level of ability, improved self-concept, and increased confidence. Being in these programs after having been in their home school helped gifted students to recognize that, with a little hard work, they were capable of much more than they had previously acknowledged. The experience was a valuable one, as it provided an opportunity to gain independence and self-responsibility. Some high school gifted students who have previously attended such camps now have an opportunity to be leaders and peer counselors for the elementary-level day camps. Often, the high school camp counselors are gifted adults who have a desire to mentor gifted youth.

School counselors should become knowledgeable of these programs and the sources of information concerning them in order to provide assistance to gifted students and their families as they select the most appropriate experiences. Many Web sites provide an overview of the existing programs.

Conclusion

This chapter has provided a brief history of counseling for the gifted and included definitions and identification of gifted students, differential needs, family issues, counseling for gifted students, and special concerns.

Just as Campbell and Stanley (1966) reminded us that every experiment has imperfect internal and external validity, so it is with counseling gifted and talented students and their families. Programs and services can be developed, but none can or will address all the myriad aspects of the life and times of students with exceptional gifts. In the end, the *attitude* of significant others will bridge the gap in determining the quality and impact of any intervention with gifted students. Clayton A. Morgan, a counselor educator, when interviewed by Snow (1990), expressed it this way:

> [I]f you must stumble, don't stumble over a toothpick. With all the imper-
> fections we must deal with every day, it is essential we work at keeping
> things in perspective. Much time and energy can be squandered on things
> of little importance. (p. 675).

This chapter, indeed this book, is an attempt to help find those activities that are important in helping gifted students.

15

Urban Poverty and Homelessness as Hidden Demographic Variables Relevant to Academic Achievement

by Margarete Parrish

While various demographic factors have been considered in relation to the measurement of students' academic and intellectual abilities, the role played by poverty has remained underaddressed, an oversight that is particularly noteworthy given the great disparities between the academic performances of children in affluent settings and those in deprived settings. Far more complex than measurable intellect alone, the role of poverty on children's development pervades such factors as school readiness, expressive language skills, and familiarity with books, as well as requisite social skills that influence scholastic success. When children live in homes lacking electricity, they are subject to poorer health (resulting from lacking heat, etc.) and are unable to study when there are no lights. When a lack of basic health habits (such as hygiene and routine bed times and meal times) is superimposed on marginal nutrition, children living in poverty are unlikely to be prepared to focus on academic success, when survival itself is a primary issue.

Nearly one out of every five children under the age of 18 in the United States is living in poverty (U.S. Bureau of the Census, 2000). Rates of poverty and homelessness among children in the U.S. have risen during the last quarter-century and range between 1.5 and 4 times the rates found among children in Canada and Western Europe (Duncan, Brooks-Gunn, Yeung, & Smith, 1998). In recent decades, urban poverty has become increasingly concentrated in the Midwest in such cities as

Chicago, Detroit, and Milwaukee (National Research Council, 2000). While the majority of children living in poverty in the U.S. are of European ancestry, rates of childhood poverty among children of African American and Native American ancestry, as well as some Latino groups, are typically two to three times higher than the rates of poverty among non-Latino White children in the U.S. (McLoyd, 1998). African and Hispanic children are much more likely to live in high-poverty urban neighborhoods than their non-Latino White counterparts; 27% of poor African American children live in high-poverty urban settings, compared with 20% and 3% of their Hispanic and non-Latino White counterparts, respectively (National Research Council). Spending childhood in high-poverty urban neighborhoods brings with it increased risks of living in overcrowded public housing that may resemble a war zone thanks to crime, violence, and illicit drugs.

As a variable, poverty consistently appears to be even more strongly related to children's cognitive ability and achievement than to their mental health outcomes (Brooks-Gunn & Duncan, 1997). As such, it transcends such variables as ethnicity and gender (Battle & Lewis, 2002). Spending early childhood in poverty can strongly influence a child's preparedness to enter and succeed in school. Multiple factors may intervene to exacerbate or mitigate the effects of poverty on children's achievements, such as mother's age and academic achievement, the duration of poverty, and family norms (Brooks-Gunn & Duncan). The combination of family poverty and neighborhood poverty typically entails a particularly complex array of risk factors, including social and psychological conditions, lack of positive role models, institutional deficits, and exposure to violence (National Research Council, 2000).

Regardless of actual intelligence, children in poverty are less likely to complete high school than their more affluent counterparts. Not completing high school in and of itself serves as a powerful risk factor for lifelong difficulties including unemployment, chronic poverty, crime, substance abuse, and other counterproductive behaviors (Bee, 1997; National Research Council, 2000; Rutter, Giller, & Hagell, 1998). Even for those children living in poverty who complete high school, further educational attainment is often compromised. While children coming from the lowest economic quarter of the population are more likely to enter college than they have been in the past, they remain much less likely to complete college than their counterparts in the upper economic quarter. Those from the upper economic quarter are estimated to have a 19 times greater chance of completing college by age 24 than those from the lower quarter (Mantsios, 2001).

Several noteworthy physical factors demand consideration in the discussion of the role played by poverty in children's earliest development. For the purposes of this chapter, aspects of poverty will be addressed in relation to both biological and environmental risk factors; a bio-psychosocial framework will be applied to the consideration of poverty's influences on children's academic potential and achievements.

Biological Factors Related to Childhood Poverty

Because of the correlations between poverty, lack of prenatal care, and premature childbirth, the roles played by prematurity and low birthweight (LBW) are salient factors in the consideration of children's cognitive prospects (Bradley et al., 1994; Watson, Kirby, Kelleher, & Bradley, 1996). In recent decades, neonatal intensive care units' technological capacities have greatly improved the survival prospects for premature and very low-birthweight infants (Meisels & Wasik, 1990). While premature birth is an inconsistent factor in a child's development, the combination of prematurity and poverty has important implications for a child's cognitive development. Particularly when prematurity is linked with such factors as young maternal age, lack of prenatal medical attention, and fetal exposure to alcohol or other drugs, a premature child born into poverty is likely to experience considerably more academic difficulties than his or her more affluent premature counterpart (Bradley et al.).

More important than just gestational age, however, the role of low birthweight (LBW) can prove crucial. Long-term poverty has been linked to higher rates of LBW infants across ethnic groups (Gould & LeRoy, 1988; Korenman & Miller, 1997). Low birthweight is strongly associated with behavioral, cognitive, and academic difficulties throughout childhood (Aylward, 2003; Hack & Fanaroff, 1999; McCarton et al., 1997; McCormick, Gortmaker, & Sobol, 1990). The cognitive difficulties associated with low birthweight continue to influence cognitive and academic disadvantages in adolescence and young adulthood, resulting in lower measured IQs and lower rates of high school graduation (Hack et al., 2002; Saigal et al., 2000).

Important environmental variations in the predictable cognitive difficulties experienced by LBW infants are noteworthy. Improved longitudinal testing scores for LBW children are associated with increased maternal education, residing in a two-parent home, and access to special educational services (Ment et al., 2003). Particularly in cases in which maternal education is limited, the implications of the role played by supportive services in schools for LBW children living in poverty are potentially crucial. Even in cases in which children initially lag behind their peers in language and cognitive abilities, academic failure is not necessarily inevitable. Early interventions can and do make a difference in LBW children's academic prospects (National Research Council, 2000).

Beyond poverty alone, homelessness is specifically associated with poorer health and cognitive outcomes for children. Low birthweights are more common among homeless infants, and homeless children have higher levels of acute and chronic illness throughout childhood, including asthma, ear infections, and anemia (Better Homes Fund, 1999).

Aside from the risks associated with low birthweight, children living in poverty are also subject to various health problems that result in repeated school absences, subsequently leading to academic difficulties. For children living in poverty, asthma can be directly correlated to academic achievement as it relates to absenteeism. Older children and adolescents continue to be at risk for adverse asthma outcomes (Calmes, Leake, & Carlisle, 1999), typically entailing repeated hospital admissions and school absences. Asthma is more prevalent among children from urban, minority, and low-income environments (10–20% vs. 6%) for U.S. children in general (Mansour, Lanphear, & DeWitt, 2000). The incidence of asthma has been associated with various factors, including substandard living conditions, rodents, roaches, dust and other allergens, and stress (Bukstein, 1996).

While causes of asthma remain debated, the differences in consequences are noteworthy, as urban children have both higher morbidity and mortality rates from asthma (Calmes et al., 1998; Halfon & Newacheck, 1993; Mansour et al., 2000). Socioeconomic status has been documented as a primary contributor to asthma severity (Apter et al., 1999). Access to and utilization of health care resources appear to be primary variables in pediatric asthma outcomes and are directly related to insurance status and poverty.

Crowded and noisy living conditions are often associated with living in urban poverty. Children living in crowded conditions and noisy homes with limited privacy generally perform more poorly on cognitive measures than their counterparts living in more stable, structured settings (Aylward, 1992). Findings vary, however, in their implications for children's ideal test-taking settings. Hambrick-Dixon (1988) found that children attending daycare facilities near elevated subway trains appeared to perform best on a coding task in a noisy test-taking situation, while children unaccustomed to such noise levels performed best in quiet conditions. Conversely, chronic exposure to airport noise has been associated with significant reading difficulties and may also be associated with language acquisition problems for children (Evans & Maxwell, 1997).

Homeless children have six times the national average levels of speech and stammering problems (Better Homes Fund, 1999; Weinreb, Goldberg, Bassuk, & Perloff, 1998). Homelessness during childhood has been specifically linked with receptive language skills (Bassuk et al., 1997; Better Homes Fund). Factors such as unhealthy living conditions, close proximity to other infected children, and lack of access to medical care typically exacerbate such health problems among homeless children. Thus, school attendance is further compromised among those whose academic prospects are already complicated by various barriers to school enrollment, including those homeless children who lack stable home addresses.

Children in general appear to be at heightened risks of and susceptible to exposure to toxic chemicals (Bearer, 1995; Hambrick-Dixon, 2002). Children living in poverty are more likely than their more affluent counterparts to be exposed to various toxins in play areas (such as warehouses and urban parks built near industrial sites), pesticides (when living in insect- or rodent-infested settings), and asbestos (in substandard housing). Urban children living in poverty remain at the greatest risk for lead exposure (Hambrick-Dixon; Juberg, Kleiman, & Kwon, 1997; National Research Council, 2000). Consequences of high blood lead levels include well-documented decreases in IQ; neurobehavioral-cognitive difficulties are associated with considerably lower levels of exposure (Finkelstein, Markowitz, &

Rosen, 1998). Urban children living in high-rise buildings with trash incineration or near coal-burning power plants are also more likely to be exposed to mercury (Hambrick-Dixon).

While no single physical factor explains all the various cognitive and academic difficulties experienced by children living in poverty, the likelihood of multiple factors converging to influence their capacity to learn is a crucial consideration. Various environmental and exposure-related conditions appear to compound the complexities of such factors as low birthweight and other vulnerabilities. Thus, the compounded factors become increasingly relevant to both the assessment of actual cognitive capacity and the needed attention to suitable interventions on behalf of children living in poverty.

Psychological Factors Related to Childhood Poverty

Children in poverty are also subject to elevated rates of emotional and behavioral difficulties when compared with their more affluent counterparts (Brooks-Gunn & Duncan, 1997; Zito, Safer, DosReis, & Riddle, 1998). Those difficulties may reflect depression, trauma-related disorders, behavioral disorders, and learning disorders.

The role of depression among children and adolescents is complicated by an assortment of barriers to its diagnosis (McLeod & Nonnemaker, 2000). One social barrier to the recognition of depression among children is the premise that childhood is supposed to be a happy time, thus minimizing the expectation of depression occurring before adulthood. Other barriers include behavioral and developmental differences in the manifestation of depression among children. For example, children with depression are more likely to appear irritable than sad, and thus risk being misdiagnosed with Oppositional-Defiant Disorder or Attention Deficit-Hyperactivity Disorder than with depression. Children living in poverty, who may also be subject to genetic risk factors for depression, are unlikely to have a sufficient comparative frame of reference with which to recognize depression as being abnormal (Eamon, 2002; Siegel et al., 1998). Further compounding the risks associated with childhood poverty and asthma, asthmatic children who are prescribed steroids for treatment (such as inhalers, etc.) may also be subject to greater levels of depression due to the steroids' potentially exacerbating effects (Sapolsky, 1998).

The role of trauma among children living in poverty demands careful consideration, particularly when children are exposed to violence and crime on a regular basis. As many as one in four urban youths reported having witnessed a murder during childhood (Buka, Stichick, Birdthistle, & Earls, 2001; National Research Council, 2000). Among children living in poverty, the incidence of posttraumatic stress disorder (PTSD) is associated with exposure to violence, crime, and other factors that may be routine in urban settings. For children living in poverty, PTSD may also be associated with specific barriers to academic achievement such as diminished concentration, numbing of responsiveness, and the occurrence of flashbacks associated with various stimuli (Aisenberg & Mennen, 2000; Breslau et al., 1998; Goenjian et al., 1997; Pynoos & Eth, 1985). PTSD is also associated with externalizing behavioral disorders, which are more common among children who have witnessed violence (Singer, Anglin, Song, & Lunghofer, 1995).

Among homeless children, rates of anxiety, depression, and withdrawal are often combined with behavior problems such as severe aggression and hostility (Bassuk et al., 1997; Better Homes Fund, 1999). Whereas 18% of school children in general have documented problems with anxiety, depression, or withdrawal, 47% of homeless children have such problems. Among homeless children, 36% manifest delinquency or aggressive behaviors, compared with 17% of the general school-aged population (Buckner & Bassuk, 1997). Such emotional difficulties may be further compounded by the lack of treatment provided them, despite the known risks of mental health problems among homeless children.

Simultaneously, children living in poverty are at increased risk of being diagnosed with learning disorders and developmental delays, with persistent poverty appearing to have more damaging effects on children's cognitive abilities. Those living in poverty have scored lower on various standardized IQ measures for verbal ability and achievement (Brooks-Gunn & Duncan, 1997; Smith, Brooks-Gunn & Klebanov, 1997). It remains unclear whether such measurements reflect more strongly any inherent intellectual differences or, instead, deficits in the academic opportunities afforded to children living in poverty.

Children living in poverty also appear to be at increased risk of being diagnosed (labeled) with conduct disorders. Beyond various cultural biases and implications, risk factors for conduct disorders demand particular attention in relation to children living in poverty, as they include biological and social vulnerabilities that are also associated with living in poverty. Those vulnerabilities include neurological factors such as exposure to toxic agents or child abuse and neglect, as well as social factors such as lacking positive social schema, problem-solving deficits, and poor attachment patterns (Cicchetti, Ganihan, & Barnett, 1991; Price & Lento, 2001). Such vulnerabilities relate to various cognitive vulnerabilities, influencing the ways in which children approach social and academic tasks and what their expectations may be.

An important consideration in children's acquisition of skills and confidence is the role played by their reactions to failure. Children who exhibit levels of learned helplessness in response to failure also display challenge avoidance and low expectations for future success (Smiley & Dweck, 1994). Even as young as age 4, children who appear negatively affected by failure display diminished self-confidence in relation to academic tasks and problem solving (National Research Council, 2000).

Children living in poverty generally move through the cognitive developmental sequences described by Piaget more slowly than their more affluent counterparts (Bee, 1997). Language development represents a primary area of difficulty for children in poverty. Beginning prior to starting school, children in poverty have consistently demonstrated difficulties in the development of receptive language, which pertains to reading difficulties and all that reading entails to their academic prospects (Whitehurst & Fischel, 2000). These disparities may relate to such factors as parental access to suitably stimulating resources for their child, as well as parental levels of verbal and emotional responsiveness to their child. Encouraging exploration and active, diverse verbal interactions are examples of family patterns of interaction that are associated with children whose IQs show a rising pattern over time (Bee). Such patterns may not be realistic for single parents with limited education, time, and choices when raising children in high-poverty urban settings in which normal childhood curiosity and exploration could prove hazardous. In such settings, parental access to resources that promote learning (e.g., high standards of child care, educational materials, books, and visits to museums) is not necessarily available.

Social and Environmental Factors Related to Childhood Poverty

Urban poverty appears to function as a greater risk factor for children's mental health and academic prospects even than suburban or rural poverty (Bee, 1997; Bickel, Smith, & Eagle, 2002). Especially when cities lack the infrastructure to provide the educational and social services that children and families need, adverse long-term outcomes for children are predictable. Urban poverty is increasingly associated with multiple stressors, such as crowding, substandard housing, greater levels of unemployment, single-parent families, delinquency, exposure to substance abuse, and exposure to violence (Black & Krishnakumar, 1998).

Access to childcare is just the beginning of many stressors for families living in poverty. Women in the U.S. have the highest poverty rate of any developed nation, and single mothers in the U.S. are the most likely to earn poverty-level wages (Christopher, 2002). At least 23 states require mothers receiving benefits to be employed when their children reach the age of 1 year (State Policy Documentation Project, 2001). Most states require that those mothers work 30 or more hours weekly (National Research Council, 2000). For children of single mothers living in poverty, even their mother's employment rarely suffices to alleviate poverty, even if she manages to maintain employment, housing, and childcare. Nor does maternal employment necessarily entail sufficient income to provide adequate standards of childcare during her working hours (Bee, 1997; Mantsios, 2000).

The incidence of unmarried motherhood among teenagers living in poverty is almost triple that of their more affluent counterparts (Brooks-Gunn & Duncan, 1997). Children born to young, unmarried mothers (especially those under the age of 20) consistently perform more poorly in math and reading in their early school years than those children born to older, more socially supported mothers (Cooksey, 1997). Young motherhood has consistently been correlated with diminished maternal educational attainment, which, even after controlling for poverty, remains significantly and positively associated with the level of cognitive stimulation provided to children in the home (Miller & Davis, 1997). Children of young mothers are more likely to be required to repeat grades and are at risk of a variety of behavioral difficulties such as aggression, truancy, and the early onset of sexual activity (Levine, Pollack, & Comfort, 2001). Importantly, the combined factors of early motherhood and poverty have an impact on children's academic prospects that is effectively greater than the sum of the two parts.

Institutional resources that are taken for granted in more affluent neighborhoods may or may not be available as sources of enrichment and stimulation for children living in poverty. Parks, libraries, and extracurricular programs for arts and sports may not be accessible. Further, when neighborhood safety is an issue, mothers may understandably protect their children from going outside after dark at the expense of such potential opportunities for enrichment. Thus, parental safety concerns may limit the interactions children living in poverty have with positive role models, peers, and adults.

Access to positive role models is another critical aspect of children's development when living in poverty. Particularly for boys, lack of access to a positive frame of reference for male academic success may be a not-so-subtle factor in school performance, particularly when being raised in single-female-headed households and attending overwhelmingly matriarchal school systems. Issues such as teachers' expectations of children living in urban poverty are also pertinent (Battle, 1999; Battle & Lewis, 2002). Long before their more privileged counterparts, girls living in poverty are often juggling multiple caregiving roles such as providing supervision to younger siblings or caring for ailing relatives, sometimes at the expense of their own school attendance or study time (Hrabowski, Maton, Greene, & Greif, 2002). For girls living in poverty, access to role models who completed high school and achieved success in ways besides motherhood can prove crucial.

Conclusions

For children's cognitive capacities, poverty alone has clear disadvantages that transcend demographic variables of ethnicity and gender. The longer a child lives in poverty, the more devastating the effects are likely to be (Bee, 1997; National Research Council, 2000). The level of disruption caused by repeated moves and changes of schools may further compound children's academic performance (Mantsios, 2001). Such frequent changes have particularly dire implications for children who are homeless. Importantly, evidence indicates that relocation from high-poverty to low-poverty neighborhoods can enhance children's physical and mental health, with noteworthy reductions in violence committed by adolescents (National Research Council).

Despite the worrying implications of the great disparities between children growing up in poverty and their more privileged counterparts, disadvantages need not be mistaken for destiny. For example, standardized measures of intelligence are

not sufficient to assess other, sometimes equally critical, factors of a child's potential, such as aptitude to learn, creativity, social skills, spatial relationships, or survival skills ("street smarts") that will serve children living in dire poverty in ways
that math or verbal scores might not (Battle & Lewis, 2002; Bee, 1997; Smith et
al., 1997).

Interventions can and do make a difference in the cognitive outcome of children living in poverty. While the Head Start Program has a good history of
enhancing its participants' school readiness and health status (immunizations,
etc.), it may not be sufficient to remedy some of the deficits that have accrued
before the ages of 4 and 5. Early intervention is crucial; it is ideally begun during
infancy, rather than during the preschool years (Bee, 1997; National Research
Council, 2000).

Children living in poverty can beat the odds (and some do), although those
odds have increased in recent years. The disparity between privilege and deprivation for children in the U.S. has increased in the past decade. As there are growing numbers of children living in chronic poverty who are subjected to various
environmental deficits and increasingly disadvantaged schools, success stories are
becoming increasingly rare. Educators, physicians, clinicians, and policymakers are
called upon to advocate for children living in poverty in ways that recognize and
maximize their intellectual potential and that will serve those children and the
society to which they will contribute. Educators working with children living in
poverty are called upon to pay particular attention to the needs of those who are
at profound risk of academic failure because that failure can be avoided with sufficient attention and support. Encouragement, compassion, respect, and material
support such as providing a safe, quiet space in which homework can be supervised
after school can make a considerable difference in a child's academic outcome and
future prospects. As any educator knows, children are remarkably resilient and
have amazing capacities to overcome even the barriers created by poverty and deprivation during childhood, especially if they receive adequate support to do so.

Part III

Pertinent Perspectives on the Challenges of Giftedness

16

Using Multiple Intelligences to Overcome Cultural Barriers to Identification for Gifted Education

by Mindy L. Kornhaber

T he theory of multiple intelligences (MI) was advanced by Howard Gardner in his 1983 book, *Frames of Mind.* Since its initial publication, the theory has been applied in numerous educational settings and instituted in the hope of addressing many different educational needs. This chapter focuses on the application of MI to one such need: overcoming barriers to the identification of students from diverse cultural backgrounds for participation in gifted education programs.

This chapter briefly describes the theory of multiple intelligences. Then, it details the methods, results, promises, and pitfalls of three different identification methods that have drawn on MI. The conclusion considers how the identification methods were influenced not only by MI, but also by the particularities of the local context in which the method was developed.

The Theory of Multiple Intelligences

Gardner had several motivations for devising the theory of multiple intelligences. First, as a developmental psychologist with extensive clinical and research experience in neuropsychology, he had become persuaded that the then-traditional conception of human cognitive capacity as one overarching general intelligence, known as g, was inadequate. Second, he wanted to join into a defensible framework evidence about brain function and cognitive development. Conceptions of intelligence focused on analyses of mental tests had long made inferences about the structure or organization of human intellect, but were notably short on biologically based evidence. Third, Gardner had long been intrigued by the diversity of adult roles that exist across cultures. Therefore, he sought to produce a theory that would go beyond explaining mental test performances to show how people come to excel in endeavors as different as, for example, poetry and pole vaulting.

Gardner did not rely exclusively on psychometric data. Instead, he proposed that any potential or "candidate" mental ability should manifest the following criteria before it is deemed an "intelligence":

- potential isolation of the ability through brain damage (e.g., when a stroke victim loses motor functioning, but language use remains unimpaired);
- the existence of special populations, such as prodigies or autistic savants, who demonstrate one or two exceptional capacities against a background of capacities that are, respectively, normal or impaired;
- evolutionary plausibility for the current ability to have evolved from selection pressures (e.g., precursors to modern humans likely needed communication, social, and navigational abilities);
- distinct, core information-processing operations (e.g., in language, syntax, and phonology) are central, whereas, in music, rhythm, alongside pitch and timbre discriminations, are fundamental operations;
- encoding in a symbol system, such notations for language, mathematics, music, movement, and spatial information, which harnesses the intelligence to the transmission of important cultural information;
- a distinct developmental path from childhood expression to expert end-state (intelligences are expressed in cultural activities such as hunting, medicine, and poetry that have distinguishable developmental trajectories);
- experimental psychological tasks that explore how people simultaneously process two different activities (the extent that people can carry out two different activities indicates separate processing abilities are at work); and
- psychometric investigations, which have commonly yielded evidence for separate linguistic and spatial abilities and, more recently, provided evidence for a distinct social/emotional ability (Rosnow, Skedler, Jaeger, & Rind, 1994).

On the basis of these criteria, Gardner (1999a) has asserted that there are at least eight "relatively autonomous" intelligences: linguistic, logical-mathematical, musical, spatial, bodily-kinesthetic, intrapersonal, interpersonal, and naturalist. Barring brain damage, all individuals possess all eight intelligences, and what varies among individuals are the relative strengths and weaknesses of the intelligences. In addition, he has noted that real-world accomplishment requires using combinations of the various intelligences.

Gardner (1999a) formally defined an intelligence as "a psychobiological potential to process information that can be activated in a cultural setting to solve problems or create products that are of value in a culture" (pp. 33–34). According to Gardner, culturally valued products and problem solving occur within "domains." These are any activities "in which individuals participate on more than a casual basis, and in which degrees of expertise can be identified and nurtured" (Gardner, 1995, p. 202). For example, in mainstream U.S. culture, automobile engineering, movie making, journalism, football, and computing qualify as domains. In Navajo culture, native dancing and weaving qualify as domains.

On a conceptual front, Gardner's theory is quite compatible with efforts to identify gifted students from diverse cultural experiences. According to Gardner (1993), a gifted youngster is one who advances rapidly through a cultural domain due to strengths among his or her intelligences and environmental opportunities. Given that different cultures emphasize different domains, giftedness can be manifested in different ways. In line with this notion, it makes little sense, from an MI perspective, to rely on psychometric tests to identify gifted youngsters. First, such tests privilege a narrow range of mental abilities. Second, and relatedly, such tests are not "intelligence-fair." That is, they require individuals to demonstrate thinking and problem solving only through notations or language, rather than in actual demonstrations using materials of a domain. Finally, psychometric tests too often strip away domain-relevant contexts in which valued problem solving occurs (Gardner, 1991).

On a practical front, however, the theory provides little guidance on how it should be applied for any educational purpose, and, until relatively recently (e.g., Gardner, 1999b), Gardner has had little to say about how the theory might be used. In the 400-plus pages of *Frames of Mind*, the volume introducing the theory, Gardner offered perhaps six paragraphs of information about how to apply the theory to education, with no guidance offered at all for its use in identifying gifted youngsters.

Despite an absence of clear guidelines for applying MI, educators began implementing the theory for a great variety of student populations (Kornhaber, 1994; Kornhaber & Krechevsky, 1995). In the realm of education for the gifted, the theory was applied to identification and services beginning in the late 1980s. The explicit aim of several such efforts was to increase the opportunities for traditionally underrepresented minority students to be included in gifted programs (see U.S. Department of Education, 1994). Educators of the gifted who sought to use MI for this purpose—and all other educators who sought to apply the theory—had to rely primarily on their own interpretations, instincts, and experiences or those of consultants who had attempted to interpret and apply MI for use in identification. Three such efforts are described below.

Application of Multiple Intelligences
for the Identification of Gifted Youngsters

DISCOVER

DISCOVER (*Discovering Intellectual Skills and Capabilities While Providing Opportunities for Varied Ethnic Responses*) was developed by C. June Maker, a professor at the University of Arizona. The DISCOVER assessment has undergone many modifications over the course of its development. The version analyzed here was in effect for fourth and fifth graders at least into the late 1990s and was implemented across numerous schools and school districts.

DISCOVER relies on a set of five activities, most of which are organized from closed (or highly structured), to open-ended problem solving. The regular classroom teacher administers two of the activities: an open-ended storywriting task and a math worksheet containing arithmetic problems, magic squares, and fluency-type problems (e.g., create problems whose solution is a given number). Three other activities are administered over a 2.5- to 3-hour period on a separate day by a DISCOVER assessment team. The Pablo activity includes a set of construction tasks using geometric and free-form Pablo cardboard pieces. The tangram activity entails six pages of tangram puzzles to be solved using 21 tangram pieces. The storytelling activity involves three storytelling tasks that use small figurines and brief prompts, for example, choose a toy and "think of all the things you can say about it" (Maker, Rogers, & Nielson, 1995, p. 7). The stories are told one-on-one to the DISCOVER team observer. The observer tape-records and later transcribes all the students' storytelling tasks.

The DISCOVER assessment team members have complex roles. A team member sits with a table of four to six students to administer one activity and rotates at the end of that activity to a new table to administer the next one. At each table, the team member must establish rapport with the youngsters; deliver the instructions for that activity; respond to students' questions; offer clues from a prescribed list; observe, monitor, and record the children's interactions; and observe and record the children's problem-solving processes and their solutions on two different instruments that employ checklists and written notes (and, for Pablo, he or she must make a sketch of each child's constructions). Following the administration and documentation of students' performances in these activities, the observer team members complete a third checklist for each child, one that asks which of the multiple intelligences each child drew on in the course of performing each of the three activities. Then, the assessment team meets for several hours to score each student's work in the three activities. The scoring is on a four-point scale with regard to the likelihood of high ability: unknown, possibly, probably, or definitely strong in the activity. (Graduate students separately score the writing task and math worksheet.) A child who is scored as "definitely" on at least two of the five tasks is identified as gifted.

In the two schools on the Navajo Reservation in which I observed DISCOVER in action, identification for gifted education rose from effectively zero to

10% in one school and 30% in the other. Could they learn their school subjects faster and better than the ones labeled "nongifted"? Anyone can be labeled "gifted." If you call a dog's tail a leg, how many legs does the dog have? Still four, because *calling* a dog's tail a leg does not make it a leg. Perhaps the newly discovered "gifted" students do better schoolwork because they were identified on only three of Gardner's "intelligences." But, can't the three chosen be measured more reliably with standardized tests? And, of course, *far* more economically in time and effort? Long ago, Louis and Thelma Thurstone developed excellent tests for these purposes.

The Problem Solving Assessment (PSA)

The Problem Solving Assessment drew on, but simplified, DISCOVER's assessment. It was devised by educators of the gifted in North Carolina's Charlotte-Mecklenburg Schools (CMS). The version I observed was for second graders.

The PSA is divided into two phases. The first is a period of preassessment. During this time, educators of the gifted visit each classroom several times to provide activities that draw on spatial, linguistic, and logical-mathematical intelligences. During preassessment, the school's special educator and the classroom teacher take notes on each child's work on special checklists. These checklists include behaviors associated with each intelligence-related activity, (e.g., for linguistic, a behavior listed is "enjoys telling detailed and expressive stories"). Alongside checkmarks, observers can add a few lines to record their own observations of a child's work. Preassessment both familiarizes students with the assessment process and also provides additional information to be used in the actual identification process.

The second phase entails the PSA assessment. It uses nine activities to evaluate strengths in spatial, linguistic, and logical-mathematical intelligences. Two of these are administered and scored by the school's teacher of the gifted. These are a Matrix Analogies Test, a standardized test of figural reasoning (Naglieri, 1985), and a storywriting task, in which children are asked to write about the place in Charlotte that they would choose to spend a whole day. Then on a separate day, over the course of 4 to 4.5 hours, a PSA assessment team works within a given classroom to administer seven other activities. For spatial intelligence, these include DISCOVER's tangrams, a slightly modified Pablo activity, and a map activity. The latter asks students to navigate a simplified map using the shortest route possible according to directions that are read aloud in a brief story. The linguistic activities include storytelling to a structured prompt (explain how a given plastic animal the child chooses came to be the way it is), an activity in which children must replace a nonsense word in a sentence with one that has a correct meaning, and a third activity that calls upon children to provide a correct title for a column of related words (e.g., dogs, horses, cows, and fish need the title "animals"). The logical mathematical activities include two forms of sequencing problems, a fluency problem akin to DISCOVER's (i.e., "Write as many problems as you can that have 10 as the answer"), and a math story activity. In the latter, children are told to tally objects as these are added to or removed from a narrative that is read aloud to them.

The PSA observers, like those of DISCOVER, have a complex role. However, the PSA reduces the complexity of the DISCOVER's checklists. Observers use only one instrument, the Problem Solving Behavior Observation Card, to record their observations. The checklist for each task contains 15 to 34 items, fewer than half the items on the DISCOVER checklist. Directions are given by a lead member of the PSA team, rather than by each team member at a table. Finally, the PSA seeks to have no more than five students at a table.

Following the assessment, the PSA observers spend about 5 hours together to discuss and score the work of the students assessed in one class. The scoring considers the extent to which high ability was manifested on a four-point scale: not evident, possibly evident, evident, or highly evident. Students with scores of evident or highly evident in two or more of the areas (spatial, linguistic, logical-mathematical) qualify for gifted education. In the two schools in which I observed the PSA, there was not a marked increase in the number of African American students identified. However, in the district as a whole, the rate of minority student participation roughly doubled to 18% after the PSA was implemented. The district as a whole was 60% White and 40% minority, almost all of whom were African American.

The Gifted Model Program

The Gifted Model Program was developed by educators for the gifted in Montgomery County, Maryland, a large school district bordering Washington, DC. The Gifted Model Program does not rely on new assessment tasks. Rather, the county already had in place an identification protocol that used a variety of both objective measures (e.g., Raven's Progressive Matrices, the Test of Cognitive Skills) and subjective measures, including the Renzulli/Hartman teacher checklist, parent or community nominations, teacher recommendations, and "other performance data." Students who had high marks on three or more of these indicators were identified as gifted. Those who had high marks on one or two were considered for placement by school-based screening committees. In these committees, teachers, counselors, and the principal advocated for a given child based on information from the identification protocol and on their individual knowledge of the child. For this group of children, identification was partly driven by the philosophy of "identification through teaching." That is, some of the information used by the screening committee came from the child's classroom experiences.

Within the Gifted Model Program, which I investigated in two schools, it was in the screening committee that MI was influential: The theory had been used to enrich classroom curricula with such things as learning centers that drew on a variety of intelligences (e.g., a construction center, a movement center, and drama area) and interdisciplinary, thematic units. The theory thereby enriched the bases for identification. In addition, the Gifted Model Program developed an MI checklist, which included behaviors associated with each intelligence. For instance, for the bodily-kinesthetic intelligence, one behavior was "mirrors or repeats movements easily." The checklist was used in several ways, including to guide teachers' observations of students, to plan instruction, and to develop curricula.

Results from this Gifted Model Program did not show an increase in the proportion of traditionally underrepresented students relative to White students identified for gifted education. Instead, because of the prior adoption of multiple assessments and efforts to enrich the curriculum, a roughly proportional group of African American and Latino students were already being identified in the two schools in which I collected data. Instead, what happened was a substantial increase in the overall number of students who were identified, from fewer than one quarter to 34% of students.

Analysis of These MI-Influenced Efforts

Two key considerations are central to the discussion of these three MI-influenced efforts.

First, is it reasonable to associate increases in the identification of minority students with the assessments? Operationally, I argued that, for this to be the case, five "general conditions" need to be met: (1) students should understand the assessment tasks; (2) students should be encouraged to do their best work; (3) evaluators should be adequately trained to carry out the assessment method; (4) scoring procedures should be clear; and (5) evaluators' judgments should be reliable.

Second, is it reasonable to associate these assessments with MI? Operationally, to be associated with MI, I have established three additional "MI-specific" conditions: The assessments should (6) go beyond the traditionally assessed areas of language, mathematics, and spatial abilities; (7) draw on media beyond language and notations ("intelligence-fair"), and (8) take place in culturally valued domains.

To shed light on these eight conditions, I relied on observations of the assessment in process, which were audiotaped or videotaped semistructured individual interviews with assessment developers, audiotaped or videotaped semistructured individual interviews with assessment administrators, review of assessment manuals/guidelines, and reviews of research papers produced by the different assessment developers. Interviews and observations were transcribed verbatim. Interview and observational data were coded and sorted according to whether the data supported a given condition, undermined the condition, or was neither supportive nor contradictory. Each of the three assessments met a different set of conditions, as summarized in Table 16.1.

Table 16.1

General- and MI-Specific Conditions Met by Each of the Three Sites

	DISCOVER	PSA	Gifted Model Program
General Conditions			
1. Children understand tasks.	yes	yes	n/a*
2. Children are encouraged to do their best work.	yes	yes	yes
3. Evaluators are trained to carry out their work.	–	yes	yes
4. Scoring procedures are clear.	–	–	–
5. Observer agreement.	–	–	–
MI-Specific Conditions			
6. Assesses abilities beyond those traditionally assessed.	–	–	yes
7. Intelligence-fair.	yes	–	yes
8. Domain-based.	–	–	yes

Note. *No new tasks were developed in the Gifted Model Program.

Discussion of General Conditions

The general conditions constitute a fundamental groundwork for making inferences about students' ability and are consistent with general practice in test development and use and are synchronous with the ideas set forth in the *Standards for Educational and Psychological Testing* (American Educational Research Association, National Council on Measurement in Education, & American Psychological Association, 1999). Since none of the assessments had yet met all the general conditions, it was not yet reasonable to associate improved identification rates with the assessment's power to detect giftedness. Efforts to shore up some of these weaknesses have continued with the DISCOVER assessment, and it may be that, at some point, training, scoring procedures, and reliability will be sufficient to allow reasonable inferences to be made. In what follows, the emphasis is on those conditions that were problematic.

Regarding training (Condition 3), DISCOVER has run training sessions that are essential to enabling observers to carry out their complex and multifaceted roles. In practice, however, when the assessment team was sometimes short on staff, untrained or not yet fully trained individuals were drafted into service.

Regarding scoring (Condition 4), DISCOVER's procedures were exceedingly complex, using multiple checklists and up to 90 different student behaviors to consider over three different instruments. It was clear from observations and interviews that not all these behaviors were clearly understood, even by highly experienced DISCOVER team members. In addition, observers were supposed to apply the four-point scale relative only to the performance of other students in the classroom (i.e., "gifted" within only *that* classroom). This was considered the fairest approach, since children were being judged against others with similar experiences. At the same time, in practice, observers' actual scoring occasionally referenced performances in other classrooms. In addition, the choice of classroom reference meant that two particularly similar performances could be judged quite differently with regard to eligibility for programs for the gifted. A similar kind of referencing problem confronted the PSA assessment team. As one PSA designer put it, she was torn between referencing classroom and gifted program performance. She noted that youngsters "need to participate programmatically [in the county's programs for the gifted], no matter where they come from. And, on the other hand, you've got the context of their school and classroom." In the Gifted Model Program, scoring was problematic during the screening committee procedure. Sometimes, students' artifacts might be brought in and considered, but the criteria against which to consider such artifacts were never articulated. A screening committee member noted that "dogged persistence" on the part of a member might often tip the balance for a given student.

Observer agreement (Condition 5) was problematic across all three programs. DISCOVER has carried out its own investigations to show it had high agreement among observers with considerable experience (30 or more observations). However, as noted above, in actual field situations, observers were often not nearly this experienced. While DISCOVER might therefore achieve agreement under idealized conditions, in practice this was not demonstrated. The PSA had not yet undertaken efforts to demonstrate agreement. Given the simplified scoring sheets and in-depth, ongoing training of PSA observers, it is reasonable to speculate that a greater degree of agreement relative to DISCOVER would be possible. The Gifted Model Program was found to have achieved moderately high intrarater consistency on the MI checklist, which was administered formally by teachers twice a year. However, an instrument's reliability is associated with its purpose (American Educational Research Association, National Council on Measurement in Education, American Psychological Association, 1999; Shepard, 1993). The MI checklist was used by teachers for a variety of purposes, including curriculum development and instructional planning. Its interrater agreement for the purpose of identification was never established.

MI-Specific Conditions

Neither DISCOVER nor the PSA was found to be deeply associated with MI, as neither went beyond the three traditionally assessed areas of linguistic, mathematical, and spatial abilities (Condition 6). In addition, neither was truly domain-based. Few of the activities besides storytelling and perhaps the math computation worksheet were ones "in which individuals participate on more than a casual basis" (Gardner, 1995, p. 202). DISCOVER did prove to be intelligence-fair (Condition 7), as did the Gifted Model Program. That is, both allowed students to express their abilities without mostly having to translate them into notational or linguistic form. For example, in DISCOVER, students could demonstrate spatial problem-solving ability through manipulation of objects. In contrast, the PSA did not meet this condition because it added several tasks that placed high demands on linguistic and notational skills. The Gifted Model Program was much more domain-based (Condition 8) than either of the other two assessments. Screening session members considered how students performed on classroom-based activities that were often hands-on projects reflecting science, literature, drama, history, and art activities found beyond testing or school situations.

Conclusion

Each of these three assessment efforts were pioneering. They explored new ground in an endeavor to bolster identification rates among diverse students from groups that have often been marginalized in education generally and in gifted education in particular (Ford, 1995b). On the one hand, each did increase the number of such students who were identified. On the other hand, these results do not yet rest on grounds that are technically strong enough to withstand modest scrutiny, which is increasingly likely in times such as these, when school budgets are threatened and courts are reconsidering issues of educational access and affirmative action. In such a climate, it is especially important to have a defensible basis for selecting students for programs with limited access. For this to be so, at minimum, the five general conditions need to be met.

Several features of the settings in which these assessments were developed influenced their ability to meet the conditions outlined above. These included funding, the state policy environment, leadership, and the context in which the assessment was developed. On the funding front, none of the projects had enough funding to develop assessments that might adequately tap a broader array of intelligences in domain-relevant activities. Regarding context, because DISCOVER was developed by academics in a research university, it was less likely to be critiqued by teachers or administrators. The instruments, which encompassed some 90 items, many of which were rarely if ever used, were therefore insulated from a range of potentially useful feedback. In addition, validation of the instrument was a key aim of the research. Given that aim, revision of the instrument itself might disrupt longitudinal studies and make statistical analyses more complex. In contrast, the Charlotte-Mecklenburg's PSA had to be transparent to the district's 55 teachers of the gifted, each of whom participated at some level in its administration. These educators provided regular feedback to the designers, who worked to make sure that each item on the instrument was clear and useful.

To improve the likelihood that these and other assessment efforts are as defensible as possible, it is important that they be critically reviewed by both the developers and by external reviewers. This applies particularly to DISCOVER, which is the only one of the three assessments still in active use and which has relied heavily on validation efforts by graduate students whose analyses are central to their dissertations. While there is no doubt that giftedness is found across all cultures, for political, as well as technical reasons, the tests that are used in identification must pass through the eye of reasonable measurement principles (American Educational Research Association, National Council on Measurement in Education, & American Psychological Association, 1999). Given the problematic history of such instruments with regard to equity, another possibility would be eliminating testing from the process entirely. In an ideal world, students would not need to be selected. Rather, from the earliest point in their education, they would be supported, enriched, and challenged by highly able teachers so that their potential could be fully realized.

17

Getting Practical
About Gifted Education

by Jonna Kwiatkowski and Robert J. Sternberg

ow is it that a person becomes successful in life? Is there any one measure that can predict an answer to this question? Is there any one curricular plan that can be used to achieve such ends? Certainly not. However, there are some options that are more likely to succeed than others.

This chapter is focused on two such options: (a) using the model of successful intelligence to identify students for inclusion in gifted programming and then (b) using community partnership programs to serve students identified as gifted. This combination offers a unified plan for identifying and serving students with great potential for success in life.

Current Trends and Practices

Identification

Most school districts use standardized ability and achievement test scores as the primary identifiers for inclusion in gifted programming (Feldhusen & Jarwan, 2000; Perleth, Schatz, & Mönks, 2000) because such measures are relatively inexpensive, easy to administer, and usually well normed. Therefore, it can be argued that using these measures leads to realistic and objective identification practices for access to desirable programming opportunities.

Yet, a quick review of the literature on gifted education reveals that new theories of gifted identification comprise a potential goldmine of new procedures. Alternative models include everything from Caroll's (1996) Three Stratum Theory, according to which all factors contributing to giftedness derive from *g*, or general intelligence, to Gardner's (1993) multiple intelligences model, according to which there is no general-intelligence factor, but instead a set of multiple domains in which a person might excel.

What is common to many theories of gifted identification is the claim that current practices are not satisfactory. Anecdotally, specialists in gifted education complain that every year they are forced to include children who do not benefit from gifted programming, while at the same time excluding children who obviously would benefit. To meet state and local budgetary requirements, as well as conditions of objectivity, they must follow their gifted identification rules, even if it is to the detriment of the program, students, and, ultimately, the community.

Formal evaluations of gifted programming in the United States reveal more insidious problems with current practices. The recent Bush Administration report, *Minority Students in Special and Gifted Education* (Committee on Minority Representation in Special Education, 2002), offered the following summary:

> While "risk" may not be the appropriate term to use for being classified as gifted and talented, the pattern of data is almost the mirror image of what was found for mental retardation in the OCR (Office of Civil Rights) surveys. . . . large differences in the initial placement rates leave a distribution that is still very heavily weighted toward Asians and Whites. (pp. 2–11)

The report goes on further to describe Miller's (2000) report on minority academic achievement patterns. The conclusion in this report was that, although parental education level does predict increases in standardized test scores, even after controlling for this factor, large discrepancies between majority and minority student populations still remain.

Without attempting to interpret this result (a task acknowledged in the report to be nearly impossible with the currently available data), it can be concluded that (a) if minority students score lower on standardized tests and (b) standardized tests are the major determinant of inclusion for gifted programming, then (c) minority students will be underrepresented in gifted programming. In fact, this conclusion is the current reality. African American, Hispanic American, and American Indian students' chances of identification for and inclusion in gifted programming are well below the chances for the population as a whole (Committee on Minority Representation in Special Education, 2002).

In summary, while the most common gifted identification practices provide objectivity, they are not satisfactory. This unsatisfactory status is confirmed by the multiple attempts to define alternative gifted identification procedures, as well as by the anecdotal and quantified reports of inadequacy. Anecdotally, teachers report frustration with procedures that exclude students who could benefit from gifted services. Quantifiably, current practices result in drastic underrepresentation of minority students in gifted programs.

Programming

Gifted education is often organized to follow the model of special programs for students with learning disabilities, and it is justified as serving a similar need: that of children who cannot succeed in the regular classroom without special programming that addresses their cognitive and emotional needs. Instead of looking for low or discrepant IQ scores (as is typical of learning disability identification), gifted programs primarily identify participants based upon high IQ. Instead of working to raise children's performance in school to an average or near-average level, gifted programs work to maintain and surpass the students' current (usually outstanding) academic performance.

The irony of IQ-driven identification is that the model for programming often does not match the model for identification. The programming is often not designed to address the skills identified by IQ or achievement tests or it uses "simplistic approaches to programming and instruction [that] are too often implemented with the claim that they are specifically designed for the gifted" (Cohen, Ambrose, & Powell, 2000, p. 332). This approach leads to a dual problem, where (a) identified students might not benefit from the program and (b) unidentified students might benefit from the program, if only they were identified.

It is apparent that the current system does not satisfy the goals of educators: (a) to identify students who represent the diversity of a given school district or (b) to create programming that benefits identified children. Are there viable alternatives to the IQ-driven model of gifted education, ones that can surmount the current problems while maintaining the objectivity of current practices? How can educators move beyond a system in which identification is driven largely (although usually not exclusively) by IQ?

Moving Away From the IQ-Focused Model

The first question that must be answered is who, exactly, is supposed to be served by gifted education? Of course, there are many other choices, but this section will focus on one that holds particular promise: a model whereby strong real-life problem-solving skills are used to identify potential and then community partnership programs are used to challenge that potential. Instead of creating programs for the gifted that serve the abstract principle of successful test-taking ability, this model works to challenge and enlighten students through meaningful community interaction and to serve the community by selecting those students most likely to contribute effectively.

The Model of Successful Intelligence

The skills used to identify participants for this program would be those of Sternberg's model of successful intelligence (Sternberg, 1997, 2000, 2002). In this model, intelligence is the ability to achieve success in life by capitalizing on strengths and correcting or compensating for weaknesses through a balance of analytical, creative, and practical abilities (Sternberg, 1985). With this model, it is not possible to infer levels of intelligence from a single ability or achievement test, as any single score is too narrow an indicator. Conventional tests, moreover, focus almost exclusively on analytical abilities. Instead, intelligence must be determined through an evaluation of a combination of analytical, creative, and practical abilities.

The model of successful intelligence has been studied in a number of educational and cultural settings with promising results. In one study (Sternberg, Grigorenko, Ferrari, & Clinkenbeard, 1999), the Sternberg Triarchic Abilities Test (STAT; Sternberg, 1993) was used to investigate the internal validity of the theory. A group of 326 high school students identified as gifted by their schools took the test. The test comprised 12 subtests, including 9 multiple-choice sections (Analytical-Verbal, Analytical-Quantitative, Analytical-Figural, Practical-Verbal, Practical-Quantitative, Practical-Figural, Creative-Verbal, Creative-Quantitative, and Creative-Figural) and 3 essay sections (Analytical, Practical, and Creative). A confirmatory factor analysis of the data supported the model by yielding separate and uncorrelated analytical, practical, and creative factors. However, this result was dependent on the inclusion of the essay scores in the analysis, suggesting that, particularly for practical and creative skills, multiple-choice items should be combined with performance-based measures to work effectively.

In a separate study, Sternberg, Castejón, Prieto, Hautamäki, and Grigorenko (2001) tested 3,278 students of varying ages in the United States, Spain, and Finland using the multiple-choice sections of the STAT. In this study, the goal was to compare five alternative models of intelligence using confirmatory factor analysis. The poorest-fitting model was the single first-order factor, or the model of a general intelligence factor. The best-fitting model was the model of successful intelligence allowing for intercorrelations between the analytic, practical, and creative factors.

The Successful Intelligence Model in Identification

The previous two studies were done both to construct-validate the model and to test aspects of successful intelligence. There has also been research that shows the effectiveness of the model in identifying gifted students (Sternberg, Grigorenko, Ferrari, & Clinkenbeard, 1999). In a study conducted at Yale University, high school students identified as gifted by their schools were invited to complete a STAT pretest, which was then used as a selection tool for a summer college-level psychology course taught at Yale University. Students were invited to join the summer program if they scored in one of five categories: high analytical scores, high practical scores, high creative scores, high balanced profile (i.e., high in all three abilities), or low balanced profile (i.e., low in all abilities).

Initial observations of the adolescents selected for the program revealed that students in the high creative and high practical groups were more diverse in terms of racial, ethnic, socioeconomic, and educational background than were students in the high analytical group, suggesting that the measurement of creative and practical abilities in gifted identification methods holds the potential to create a more balanced group of students with respect to profiles of abilities. Furthermore, all three sections of the STAT (Analytical, Practical, and Creative) were significant predictors of course performance, suggesting that skills other than the analytical can contribute to successful classroom performance. In a recent study of more than 1,000 students at 15 different institutions, we also found that inclusion of creative and practical ability tests in addition to SAT scores, GPAs (grade-point averages), and sex and socioeconomic status information significantly and substantially increased prediction of freshman grades (Sternberg, 2002).

In summary, the successful intelligence model works for identifying those students who show great potential while also identifying a more balanced profile of students in terms of racial, ethnic, socioeconomic, and educational backgrounds. It is evaluated through objective measures while addressing the major problems of IQ-based identification.

The Successful Intelligence Model in Programming

There must be a match between the methods used to identify students for special programming and the methods used to deliver the special programming. If gifted-identification practices do not match gifted services, then the children who are supposed to benefit from the programming may not, in fact, benefit. This is the case with the successful intelligence model, as well as with more traditional models. For example, in the Sternberg, Grigorenko, Ferrari, and Clinkenbeard (1999) study described above, students who were placed in an instructional condition that better matched their pattern of (analytical, practical, or creative) abilities outperformed students who were mismatched with respect to instructional condition.

Although it is certainly possible to use the model of successful intelligence to create classroom-based instruction for identified students (e.g., Grigorenko, Jarvin, & Sternberg, 2002), we would instead like to suggest a plan for instruction that more fully capitalizes on the basic tenets of the model—that a balance of analytical, creative, and practical skills will lead to the greatest potential for success in life, whether inside or outside the classroom. This instruction plan takes students identified as gifted by the successful intelligence model out of the classroom and into their communities to participate in community-building exercises that double as exercises for building successful intelligence. It often is in community (i.e., real-world) interactions where analytical, practical, and creative skills are best challenged and strengthened.

Moving Toward a Model for Community Success

Whether specific to gifted education or organized for all students, community partnership programs have led to positive educational outcomes. By integrating learning into the community, people within the community become more aware of how they can support education (e.g., Bouillion & Gomez, 2001; Fatt, 1999; Lim & Renshaw, 2001; Linnemeyer & Shelton, 1991; Rahm, 2002). At the same time, students gain confidence in their ability to affect change within their communities using the tools provided through formal education (e.g., Bouillion & Gomez; Rahm).

Interestingly, the reported benefits of community partnership programs in education match many of the goals of teaching for successful intelligence. Many of the programs are designed to enhance critical thinking, creativity, and problem solving (e.g., Fatt, 1999; Linnemeyer & Shelton, 1991). The problems with which students are challenged often have no single answer, but rather require deeper thought and investigation to create solutions (e.g., Bouillion & Gomez, 2001). Finding solutions to these community problems gives students a sense of success within their specific sociocultural context (e.g., Lim & Renshaw, 2001).

Although there are many programs that could be described to elucidate and illustrate the fit between community partnerships and successful intelligence as a paired model for gifted identification practices, there are two that are particularly fitting to this discussion: One was used to expand access to gifted services in a school district with minority underrepresentation by calling upon community members for assistance, and another challenged students to identify and then solve a real-world problem in their community.

Minds in the Making

The first program, Minds in the Making, was organized to expand available services for students with gifts and talents (Linnemeyer & Shelton, 1991). The urban district where it was implemented had approximately 3% minority placement in gifted programming, but 33% minority representation across the district. It was evident that there was a need to find ways to support the gifts and talents of students who were not being captured through the standardized tests used for gifted programming identification.

The chosen means to recognize additional students was a community resource program whereby people within the community volunteered their time to work with individual children on specific projects within the children's areas of gifts and talents. Teachers reviewed files on the community volunteers to match students with appropriate opportunities. The main results of this program were: (a) increased inclusion of minority students (from 3% to 12%); (b) increased inclusion of students with learning disabilities who also had specific gifts or talents (e.g., local artists volunteered to work with two learning-disabled students with exceptional talent in the visual arts); (c) acquisition of new materials by teachers for their classroom lectures through their interactions with community members; (d) addition of new curricular areas within the participating schools (e.g., an exploratory program in a foreign language such as Chinese, French, German, Italian, or Spanish); (e) expansion of students' repertoires of potential careers; (f) acquisition by students of a sense of ownership and responsibility over their learning experiences; and (g) sparking of students' imaginations by hands-on experiences fostering creativity and motivation in ways that regular classroom experiences could not.

Linnemeyer and Shelton's (1991) report on the Minds in the Making program is certainly encouraging. Not only did it work as a model for gifted education, but, by calling upon the community for additional support, it also expanded services to students who would not have been included using the typical standardized testing model. Furthermore, the experiences that these students were offered included more creative and practical activities than would have been found in most traditional, in-school gifted programming experiences. Students were challenged to be successful in community-relevant situations, and they gained skills that will surely benefit both the students and community throughout their lives.

The Chicago River Community Partnership

The second program of note, The Chicago River Community Partnership, did not work specifically with gifted students, but instead with all children in a fifth-grade class at Whittier Elementary School in Chicago (Bouillion & Gomez, 2001). It challenged students to find a "mutual benefit" program in their community. Students first identified a problem in their area through a community walk with their teachers. They decided that a site on the riverbanks of the Chicago River called the Laflin River Site was in particular need of attention because of illegal dumping and lack of upkeep.

The teachers created a curriculum that linked the project's goals to classroom goals in science (e.g, understanding soil erosion), language arts (e.g., letter writing), social studies (e.g., history of the Chicago River), and math (e.g., data analysis). Then, the teachers sought community partnerships with outside organizations that also were interested in improving the Laflin site, as well as with the students' parents as lay representatives of the community. The teachers called upon their community partners to achieve specific curricular goals. For example, they partnered with the Chicago Academy of Sciences to learn how to test the water at the Laflin site, and they partnered with a group called Friends of the Chicago River to learn about conservancy strategies. Parents became the focus of a student-written survey to determine what should be done with the cleaned-up site. They used the information they collected in a letter-writing campaign in which they reported their research results to the organization that owned the Laflin site.

Within the school year, the students' work paid off. The organization that owned the site reversed its original position and cleaned away the trash, coincidentally while the students were actually visiting the site. The students worked with other community organizations to leave the riverbanks landscaped with grass and flowers. Finally, the students obtained a "community green space" designation for the site from the city.

There were a number of positive outcomes from this project. Students reported interest in specific topics in science, such as animal habitats and river ecology. They also reported an increased sense of efficacy in changing their community and using science effectively. For example, one child reported:

> It made me real glad that grown-ups would listen to us kids 'cause I thought they weren't going to listen to us 'cause we're little kids. It made me feel glad when we went again to Laflin River Site and we saw that the whole place was cleaned up. And now I think that I could do almost anything that I wanted to if I just set my mind to it. (p. 891)

Furthermore, the authors emphasized that students gained experience in dealing with real-world problems, which are often interdisciplinary and open-ended. This type of problem, the authors proposed, leads to a more collaborative classroom experience where students and teachers must work together to find solutions. The authors named this type of community-school interaction "connected science," as it linked practical problems from the community with a formal school curriculum, ultimately emboldening students to continue connecting community action with learning.

As with the Minds in the Making program, the Chicago River Community Partnership offered students analytical, creative, and practical opportunities that were difficult to match within the classroom. By leaving the classroom, students were able to see the link between learning and successfully affecting change in their community.

Successful Identification and Practice in Gifted Education

These community programs, Minds in the Making and the Chicago River Community Partnership, supported classroom learning in ways that necessitated the integration of analytical, practical, and creative problem solving. As such, they can also be used as a model for teaching successful intelligence. When combined with the use of successful intelligence assessments for identifying students for gifted programming, community partnership programs offer a unified plan for identifying and serving students with great potential for success in life.

There are many benefits to combining community partnerships with an explicit successful intelligence curriculum for gifted education. Assessing for successful intelligence has been shown to identify a more diverse group of students (e.g., Sternberg, Grigorenko, Ferrari, & Clinkenbeard, 1999). At the same time, creating programming that focuses on analytical, practical, and creative problem solving will ultimately better prepare students for success in the classroom and in life.

Author Note

Preparation of this chapter was supported by a grant under the Javits Act Program (Grant No. R206R000001) as administered by the Institute of Educational Sciences, formerly the Office of Educational Research and Improvement, U.S. Department of Education. Grantees undertaking such projects are encouraged to express freely their professional judgment. This article, therefore, does not necessarily represent the position or policies of the Institute of Educational Sciences or the U.S. Department of Education, and no official endorsement should be inferred.

18

Racial and Ethnic Preferences in Higher Education Admissions Policies:

An Empirical Overview

by Robert Lerner and Althea K. Nagai

For nearly 30 years, many colleges and universities have boosted the enrollment of students whose racial and ethnic backgrounds historically excluded them from higher education by granting them preferences during the admissions process. The degree and the extent of the operation of racial preferences in colleges and university admissions has been one of the nation's better kept secrets (Beer, 1987; Gottfredson, 2000, p. 20). There has been some grudging admission that such preferences have been used in admissions—or as Bowen and Bok (1998) put it, that admissions have been "racially sensitive" (469).[1]

Yet, the nearly total absence of information has made it practically impossible to assess the extent of racial and ethnic preference policies in undergraduate admissions and to evaluate conclusively various defenses of these policies, to which university administrators routinely resort. The first defense is that all who are accepted are qualified (e.g., Association of American Universities, 1997). The second defense is that race/ethnicity is

---

[1] Justice Lewis Powell, in his famous *Bakke* opinion, cited only the Harvard College *catalogue* to justify using diversity as a criterion in admissions decisions. At no time did he have access to the data describing the actual admissions process. Klitgaard (1985) described the actual process of admissions at Harvard. For an extensive statistical review, see Lerner (1998) and Thernstrom and Thernstrom (1999). When one of the authors of this paper asked to examine Bowen and Bok's database, he was turned down (Quandt, personal communication, December 14, 1999).

only "one of many factors" that are used in admission decisions. The third defense is that racial differences in admission rates and the like are actually the results of other factors, including preference for in-state residents. The fourth defense (without always saying so explicitly) is that we have the data and you don't, so you don't really understand what is going on.[2] The fifth defense of racial and ethnic preferences is one that has been raised by others who have presented quantitative data on admissions, the argument being that preferences are used at only a few of America's leading colleges and universities (Bowen & Bok, 1998; Kane, 1998).

These claims have been subject to virtually no empirical tests. Public colleges and universities have made their admissions data virtually impossible for outsiders to obtain. Studies by Klitgaard (1985), Herrnstein and Murray (1994), Lynch (1997), Sniderman and Piazza (1993), and, most notably, Thernstrom and Thernstrom (1997) focused on admissions preferences only as part of their larger projects as indicated by the title of their books. Similar observations could be made of the recently published *Color Lines* (Skrentny, 2001), an edited collection of journal articles dealing very broadly with the topic of affirmative action, but which has relatively little material on preferential admissions; the July 2000 "After Affirmative Action?" issue of *Society*, which was a series of essays in response to the College Board's 1999 National Taskforce on Minority High-Achievement; and *The New White Nationalism in America* (Swain, 2002), which is on the rise of White nationalist movements and their causes, including racial preferences in higher education admissions.

Additionally, few statistical analyses have been done on racial preferences beyond comparing Black and White applicants. This limitation is marked in light of both the diversity defense of preferential admissions used by major universities and the growing levels of immigration, which have for the first time raised the number of Hispanics in the United States higher than the number of Blacks (see Graham, 2002).

The major quantitative study of admissions has been Bowen and Bok's *The Shape of the River* (1998).[3] Despite its size, *The Shape of the River* includes largely cursory statistical analyses of applicant data for only Black and White applicants at five elite colleges. None of these institutions is named, so as to preserve secrecy. They provide information on the performance of Black and White enrollees at an additional 23 institutions, but ignore Hispanic and Asian students, despite their defense of "diversity" policies.[4]

The findings below summarize the statistical studies carried out by the authors since 1995 for the Center for Equal Opportunity (CEO).[5] They are based on results

---

[2] For example, this was Georgetown University Law School's response to an article reporting racial disparities in admission rates (McGuire, 1992; Presser, 1991).

[3] Two other analyses of preferential admissions focused upon law school admissions and produced findings similar to ours (see Larntz, 1998, and Klein, 2001–2002).

[4] For a fuller methodological and statistical critique, as well as a substantive review, see Lerner (1998) and Thernstrom and Thernstrom (1999).

from 47 four-year public colleges and universities from seven states and include the U.S. Military Academy at West Point and the U.S. Naval Academy at Annapolis.

Since no college or university voluntarily participated in this study (see below), a random sample of public colleges and universities was not obtainable. However, we believe that the admissions preferences exhibited by most of the institutions in our study exist nationwide. Moreover, since the use of race and ethnicity as "plus" factors in admissions are policies advocated by the Association of American Universities and other professional associations of higher education (Association of American Universities, 1997), we have no reason to doubt the general nature of our findings. As stated before, *if universities and colleges were more forthcoming with data, more statistical analyses could be done.*

Because of the extreme resistance of colleges and universities to providing raw admissions datasets, which would allow for outside scholars to analyze their operation, it becomes necessary to develop a novel strategy of data collection, not typical of social science research. Attorneys for the Center for Equal Opportunity (CEO) requested data from every public 4-year college and university in the continental United States where Freedom of Information Act (FOIA) filings were applicable to that state's public institutions of higher education. Our analyses are limited by both the states' willingness to comply with a request for data and the availability of those data in proper format for statistical analyses.[6]

The Academic Gap

The gap in average academic performance among different racial and ethnic groups is the most important boundary condition for preferential admissions policies and any debate over their merits. The performance gap itself has been well documented as far as test scores are concerned. For example, a recent College Board report (2002) indicated that SAT-M average scores range from 566 among Asians to 426 among Blacks, while SAT-V average scores range from 529 among Whites to 433 among Blacks.

The grade gap among members of different racial and ethnic groups is less known, but it is also important for college and university admissions. The College Board (2002) also found that the high school grade-point averages among all SAT test takers varied substantially, ranging from 3.42 for Asian test takers to 2.94 for

---

[5] The Center for Equal Opportunity is a conservative think-tank in the Washington, DC, area. Detailed reports on each of the institutions discussed here are available on the CEO Web site, http://www.ceousa.org.

[6] For example, some institutions would provide only summary statistics of applicants, while others retained data on enrollees only and others refused to provide any data at all. In Washington state and Wisconsin, CEO attorneys successfully sued in state courts to obtain the data. See Lerner and Nagai (2000, 2001a) for more detailed discussion of the data gathering and statistical methodology used.

Black test takers.[7] While the existence of these performance gaps is well known to specialists, there is no consensus as to the causes of the Black-White and other racial and ethnic test score and grade gaps.[8] Discussion of the fact that there is no White-Asian academic performance gap and the fact that Hispanic and American Indian students perform at levels intermediate between those of Blacks and Whites or Asians is just beginning to be recognized, much less studied.

Some authors argue that average differences among racial and ethnic groups reflect socioeconomic factors—differences in the quality of schooling available, parental socioeconomic status and education, or the residuals of past societal racial discrimination (e.g., College Board National Taskforce on Minority High-Achievement, 1999; Jencks & Phillips, 1998; see Zuriff, 2002a, for a critique of modern racism theory). One author has hypothesized that the differences were created by a self-fulfilling prophecy resulting from the actions of college admissions officers themselves (Loury, 2002, pp. 32–33). Others have stressed cultural differences in achievement orientation among the groups (D'Souza, 1995; McWhorter, 2000; Sowell, 1993; Thernstrom, 2000) or the incentive effects of preferential admissions policies as weakening student performance (McWhorter; Sowell; Steele, 1990; Swain, 2002). Still others more controversially point to genetic differences in intelligence, both among and between different racial and ethnic groups (Gottfredson, 2001; Herrnstein and Murray, 1994; Jensen, 1998; Rushton, 1997; but, see Nisbett, 1998).

For our purposes, it is unnecessary to choose between these competing views. All that matters is that there is a substantial Black-White gap in all measures of academic qualifications among the general population. That is, there is a substantial Black-White gap in academic qualifications; there is no White-Asian gap in practically any measure of academic qualifications for those applying to college; and, on all measures, Hispanics and American Indians score between Blacks and Whites. These differences are relatively large and persisting.

As a result, to paraphrase Thernstrom (2000), racial preferences have become "the quick fix that depends on fudging [this] inconvenient fact" (p. 45). Our statistical findings below support her point.

Test Score Gaps Among Admittees and Enrollees

Twenty-seven schools provided SAT data on Black and White admittees or enrollees (see Appendix 1, Tables 18.1 and 18.2). At all schools, the White

---

[7] The NAEP results are similar, showing that the gaps are not due to individual self-selection, which affects aggregate SAT score comparisons (National Center for Educational Statistics, 2001).

[8] The grade results do not take into account either how academically demanding high schools are or the relative difficulty of courses in which the grades were earned. A grade of B in AP physics indicates that more learning occurred than does a B in a regular physics class.

median was greater than the Black median on both the verbal and math SAT. Of the 26 schools with SAT data on Hispanic admittees or enrollees, the White median was greater than the Hispanic median on the verbal SAT at 19 schools and the Hispanic median was equal to or exceeded the White median at 7. At 25 schools, the median math score of Whites was greater than that of Hispanics, while in 1 case the median math score for Hispanics was equal to or exceeded that of Whites.

Regarding Asians and Whites, the pattern was split between the verbal and math portions of the SAT. At 24 schools, median verbal scores of White admittees/enrollees were greater than those for Asians, while Asian median verbal scores were equal or greater in 3 cases. The opposite was true for the math SAT: Median math scores were greater for Whites at 2 schools, while they were equal or greater for Asians at 25.

Gaps in test scores appear on the ACT, as well as on the SATs (see Appendix 1, Table 18.3). On the ACT, White medians exceeded those of all minorities in most cases. White medians were greater than Black medians at 22 schools, while there were no schools where the Black median was equal to or exceeded the White median. Similarly, White medians exceeded Hispanic medians at 22 schools, while Hispanic median ACTs were equal to or exceeded White medians in 1 case. Lastly, ACT medians of Whites were greater than Asian medians in 14 cases, while Asian medians were greater in 8.

The next section summarizes our findings on the differences that we found among Whites, Blacks, Hispanics, and Asians regarding high school grades.

Gap in High School Grades

Forty-five schools provided data for high-school grade point averages (GPAs), class ranks, or percentiles (see Appendix 1, Table 18.4).[9]

For 44 out of 45 schools, the median GPA or class percentile/rank for Whites was greater than that for Blacks. All of the White-Black differences in median GPAs were less than a full grade point; but, at 17 schools, they were more than one third of a grade point. At 7 of 8 schools providing percentiles or class rank, Whites finished higher in class standing than did their Black counterparts.

Forty-five schools provided data that allowed comparisons of White and Hispanic median GPAs, percentiles, or high school rank. Differences in high school grades were smaller on the whole compared to White-Black differences. White median GPAs were greater than those for Hispanics at 30 schools, while the Hispanic median GPA was equal to or slightly exceeded the White median at

---

[9] Eight schools provided the high school percentiles or the class rank of admittees/enrollees, while 37 schools reported GPAs. West Point and Annapolis provided an admittee's high school rank from the top of his or her high school class, whereby a rank of 1 meant finishing first in one's high-school class. The others are reported in top down percentile form.

7. For percentiles/class rankings, median high school standings were higher for White versus Hispanic admittees/enrollees in all 8 schools.

The Asian median was equal or greater than the White median in 30 out of 44 schools. In 24 of 36 schools with GPAs, the median GPAs of Asians were identical or the White median was lower, while Asians had equal or higher percentiles than Whites at 6 of 8 schools.

In short, the differences in academic credentials among those admitted or enrolled, whether measured by test scores or by grades, varied considerably among racial/ethnic groups. With the exception of grades at the University of Minnesota at Morris, for GPAs, percentiles, and class ranks and not just test scores, medians for White admittees/enrollees exceeded those of Black admittees/enrollees. Academic credentials of White admittees/enrollees were stronger than those of Hispanics in a majority of cases, but there were instances where Hispanic medians exceeded those of Whites, and the gaps were not as great as those between Blacks and Whites. Regarding Asians and Whites, medians for Whites were generally higher than those for Asians on the verbal SAT and the ACT, while Asian medians were almost always greater for the math SAT and at a majority of schools for high school performance.

Even defenders of racial preference policies acknowledge the gaps in academic credentials, but contend that race is constitutionally allowed as a factor in college admissions. In the next section, we explore statistically how much of a factor race/ethnicity plays in admission.

Minority Versus White Odds Ratios

Twenty-three undergraduate institutions (four state systems plus the two military academies) provided databases whereby individual applicant grades and test scores were linked to their admission status and their racial/ethnic group membership.

Multiple logistic regression equations predicting the likelihood of admissions were computed for these 23 schools, controlling for SAT scores and grades.[10] From these equations we were able to derive the odds of admission for each minority group relative to that of Whites, while simultaneously controlling for the effects of those other variables (see Appendix 2, Table 18.5).

The size of the odds ratio reflects the magnitude of race or ethnicity in predicting admissions status. Odds ratios can vary from 0 to positive infinity, where 1.0 means no effect is present. An odds ratio equal to or greater than 3.0 is commonly thought to reflect a strong effect; one of about 2.0, a moderate effect; while one of 1.5 or less is conventionally treated as weak. Finally, a *very* strong effect might be taken to be the rough equivalent of the relative odds of smokers as opposed to non-

---

[10] For UVA, applicant's alumni and residency status were also controlled. For a list of the 23 schools, see Table 18.1.

smokers dying from lung cancer, which in one well-known study is given as 14 to 1 (Agresti, 1996, p. 47; on logistic regression and odds ratios, see Lilienfeld & Stolley, 1994, pp. 200–202, 226–228, 316–317; Agresti, pp. 103–144).[11]

Fourteen undergraduate schools had extremely large odds ratios favoring Blacks over Whites, while 1 school had moderate odds favoring Blacks to Whites, controlling for test scores and class rank. The University of Michigan's relative odds of 173.1 to 1 resulted from the operation of its well-known point system of admissions, whereby underrepresented minorities are granted 20 additional points toward the 90 points necessary for admissions there.[12] Six other schools had relatively small, statistically nonsignificant odds ratios favoring Blacks over Whites, but 2 schools exhibited odds ratios suggesting racial preferences are granted to Whites over Blacks.

Regarding Hispanic applicants, the pattern was mixed. Ten schools exhibited statistically significant Hispanic-White odds ratios favoring Hispanics, but 3 schools had statistically significant odds ratios favoring Whites, while 10 had no statistically significant odds ratios. Six other schools exhibited large Hispanic-White odds ratios, but none to this extent. At 3 schools, there were statistically significant, but only modest odds ratios favoring Hispanic over White applicants. In contrast, 3 schools had statistically significant odds ratios that modestly favored Whites over Hispanics. Lastly, at 10 schools, the odds ratios were relatively small and not statistically significant.

Regarding Asian applicants, of the 23 schools subjected to logistic regression analyses, 14 showed no statistically significant odds of either Asians over Whites or Whites over Asians. Of the remaining 9 schools, 5 showed some signs of preference of Whites over Asians; while statistically significant, they were small in magnitude. Of the 4 schools where the odds ratios favored Asians over Whites, the 2 Minnesota schools exhibited relatively large odds ratios, although they were smaller in magnitude than the Black-White and Hispanic-White odds ratios found at other schools. The other two Asian-White odds ratio favoring Asians were weak, although statistically significant.

Discussion

College and university admissions officers are confronted by a continuing dilemma: the academic gap among various racial and ethnic groups. Under current

---

[11] The conversion of some of these odds ratios into probabilities is given in Lerner and Nagai (2001b, pp. 48–55).

[12] It is possible that moderate or small odds ratios are a function of the residency status of the applicant, but this is not likely with regard to the extraordinarily large odds ratios at institutions such as the University of Michigan at Ann Arbor. We have never seen odds ratios of this magnitude reported in any research literature.

conditions, no admissions policies exist that satisfy the following three objectives simultaneously:

1. being racially nondiscriminatory,
2. admitting a "critical" mass of Black students, and
3. admitting applicants based on high academic standards.

The academic achievement gaps among the ethnic groups—Black to White, Black to Asian, with Hispanics falling in the middle—make satisfying all three objectives simultaneously impossible. Racial preference policies such as those at the University of Michigan admit a "critical mass" of minority applicants, as administrators use race as a factor and resort to different academic standards when considering applicants by race to admit this critical mass of minorities. If admission committees rely on one set of standards for nonpreferred White and Asians students, but use different criteria for "underrepresented" minorities, they create the on-campus Black-White academic performance gaps discussed above, which represented the *status quo* everywhere until the enactment of Proposition 209 in California, the enactment of Proposition I-200 in Washington State, and the Hopwood Decision of the 5th U.S. Circuit Court of Appeals.

In contrast, a race-neutral admissions policy can satisfy objectives #1 and #3, but will fail in producing a critical mass of minorities, particularly at the most competitive schools. The cascading effect, however, indicates that Black and Hispanic applicants who do not attend the top schools will be admitted and attend the second- and third-tier schools in greater numbers than previously, precisely as White and Asian students have done throughout.

One popular alternative to either policy is the percentage plan. This approach, now used at the public universities of Texas and Florida, requires public colleges to admit the top 10 or 20% of all high school graduates in the state. These plans can satisfy objectives #1 and #2, but not objective #3. The cost of satisfying the nondiscrimination requirement and the critical mass requirement simultaneously is the lowering of academic admissions standards for all groups, given the existing academic performance gaps among groups.

In short, the more an institution strives to be an elite college or university, the greater its dilemma will be if ethnic proportional representation is as important an institutional objective as admitting the most qualified students. Unless the racial and ethnic performance gaps are eliminated or unless racial/ethnic proportional representation is no longer a policy objective, this will remain a permanent dilemma for colleges and universities.

Appendix 1: SATs, ACTs, and Grades Among Admittees/Enrollees.

Table 18.1

Median Verbal SAT Among Groups

School, State	White	Black	Wh-Bl Diff.	Hisp	Wh-H Diff	Asian	Wh-As Diff
GMU, VA	540	490	50	510	30	510	30
JMU, VA	600	520	80	600	0	570	30
Longwood, VA	520	480	40	500	20	500	20
MSU, MI	490	430	60	520	-30	460	30
MTU, MI	565	470	95	570	-5	535	30
Naval Academy	580	510	70	490	90	590	-10
NC State, NC	510	430	80	505	5	490	20
Norfolk State, VA	440	410	30	430	10	430	10
ODU, VA	520	490	30	520	0	510	10
UC Berkeley, CA	600	450	150	480	120	590	10
UC Irvine, CA	490	395	95	410	80	430	60
UC San Diego, CA	550	490	60	470	80	490	60
UM Dearborn, MI	490	400	90	Missing	Missing	440	50
UM Ann Arbor, MI	580	480	100	520	60	590	-10
UNC Asheville, NC	580	500	80	510	70	550	30
UNC Chapel Hill, NC	570	480	90	590	-20	560	10
UNC Charlotte, NC	460	400	60	450	10	430	30
UNC Greensboro, NC	450	400	50	440	10	395	55
UNC Wilmington, NC	460	390	70	490	-30	440	20
US Military Academy	550	510	40	530	20	575	-25
UVA, VA	690	600	90	670	20	680	10
UWashington, WA	500	420	80	470	30	440	60
VCU, VA	540	480	60	510	30	500	40
Virginia Tech, VA	580	520	60	560	20	560	20
VMI, VA	560	480	80	560	0	510	50
Washington State, WA	430	360	70	390	40	400	30
William & Mary, VA	680	580	100	640	40	660	20

Table 18.2

Median Math SAT Among Groups

School, State	White	Black	Wh-Bl Diff.	Hisp	Wh-H Diff.	Asian	Wh-As Diff.
GMU, VA	530	460	70	510	20	550	-20
JMU, VA	610	500	110	590	20	610	0
Longwood, VA	510	455	55	500	10	520	-10
MSU, MI	570	450	120	510	60	620	-50
MTU, MI	640	530	110	600	40	640	0
Naval Academy	670	590	80	625	45	690	-20
NC State, NC	590	480	110	570	20	630	-40
Norfolk State, VA	430	390	40	415	15	410	20
ODU, VA	520	470	50	500	20	540	-20
UC Berkeley, CA	690	510	180	560	130	710	-20
UC Irvine, CA	580	475	105	480	100	590	-10
UC San Diego, CA	640	540	100	550	90	640	0
UM Dearborn, MI	570	430	140	Missing	Missing	600	-30
UM Ann Arbor, MI	670	540	130	600	70	710	-40
UNC Asheville, NC	560	490	70	545	15	560	0
UNC Chapel Hill, NC	630	530	100	620	10	680	-50
UNC Charlotte, NC	520	420	100	520	0	520	0
UNC Greensboro, NC	490	410	80	480	10	510	-20
UNC Wilmington, NC	520	420	100	510	10	520	0
US Military Academy	650	590	60	640	10	675	-25
UVA, VA	690	600	90	660	30	710	-20
UWashington, WA	590	450	140	520	70	570	20
VCU, VA	510	450	60	490	20	540	-30
Virginia Tech, VA	600	520	80	580	20	610	-10
VMI, VA	570	505	65	560	10	590	-20
Washington State, WA	490	380	110	465	25	510	-20
William & Mary, VA	660	550	110	635	25	670	-10

Table 18.3

Median ACTs Among Groups

School, State	White	Black	Wh-Bl Diff.	Hisp	Wh-H Diff.	Asian	Wh-As Diff.
Adams State, CO	20.0	18.0	2.0	18.0	2.0	21.5	-1.5
CMU, MI	22.0	18.0	4.0	20.5	1.5	20.0	2.0
Colorado State, CO	24.0	21.0	3.0	23.0	1.0	24.0	0.0
CU Boulder, CO	25.0	21.0	4.0	22.0	3.0	22.0	3.0
CU Colo. Springs, CO	23.0	20.0	3.0	20.0	3.0	22.0	1.0
CU Denver, CO	24.0	20.0	4.0	21.0	3.0	20.0	4.0
Ferris State, MI	19.0	15.0	4.0	18.0	1.0	17.0	2.0
Fort Lewis, CO	21.0	Missing	Missing	20.0	1.0	21.0	0.0
Mesa State, CO	20.0	18.0	2.0	18.0	2.0	18.0	2.0
Metropolitan St., CO	20.0	17.0	3.0	18.0	2.0	17.0	3.0
MSU, MI	24.0	20.0	4.0	21.0	3.0	23.0	1.0
MTU, MI	26.0	20.0	6.0	24.5	1.5	27.0	-1.0
Northern Colo., CO	22.0	18.0	4.0	20.0	2.0	20.0	2.0
Saginaw Valley St., MI	20.0	18.0	2.0	19.0	1.0	Missing	Missing
School of Mines, CO	27.0	22.0	5.0	25.0	2.0	25.5	1.5
Southern Colo., CO	20.0	17.5	2.5	18.0	2.0	18.0	2.0
UM Dearborn, MI	24.0	19.0	5.0	21.0	3.0	24.0	0.0
UM Twin Cities, MN	25.0	20.0	5.0	23.0	2.0	22.0	3.0
UM Ann Arbor, MI	29.0	23.0	6.0	25.0	4.0	29.0	0.0
UM Crookston, MN	19.0	18.0	1.0	20.5	-1.5	19.0	0.0
UM Morris, MN	25.0	18.0	7.0	22.0	3.0	24.0	1.0
UMD, MN	23.0	19.0	4.0	21.0	2.0	21.0	2.0
Western State, CO	20.0	17.0	3.0	19.0	1.0	22.0	-2.0

Table 18.4

Median GPAs & Class Rank Among Groups

School, State	Type	White	Black	Wh-Bl Diff.	Hisp	Wh-H Diff.	Asian	Wh-As Diff.
Adams State, CO	GPA	3.10	2.55	0.55	2.80	0.30	2.70	0.40
CMU, MI	GPA	3.20	2.76	0.44	3.09	0.11	3.19	0.01
Colorado State, CO	GPA	3.40	3.00	0.40	3.40	0.00	3.56	-0.16
CU Boulder, CO	GPA	3.30	2.90	0.40	3.20	0.10	3.40	-0.10
CU Col. Sprs, CO	GPA	3.10	2.80	0.30	3.10	0.00	3.30	-0.20
CU Denver, CO	GPA	3.30	3.10	0.20	3.10	0.20	3.40	-0.10
Ferris State, MI	GPA	2.70	2.45	0.25	2.51	0.19	2.84	-0.14
Fort Lewis, CO	GPA	2.90	2.50	0.40	2.90	0.00	2.70	0.20
GMU, VA	GPA	3.08	2.93	0.15	3.07	0.01	3.25	-0.17
JMU, VA	Perc	85.00	80.00	5.00	80.00	5.00	86.00	-1.00
Longwood, VA	GPA	3.03	2.85	0.18	2.76	0.27	3.07	-0.04
Mesa State, CO	GPA	2.90	2.25	0.65	2.80	0.10	2.90	0.00
Metro State, CO	GPA	2.90	2.70	0.20	2.70	0.20	3.00	-0.10
MSU, MI	GPA	3.43	3.16	0.27	3.22	0.21	3.56	-0.13
MTU, MI	GPA	3.48	3.20	0.28	3.46	0.02	3.47	0.01
Naval Acad.	Rank	15.00	36.00	21.00	32.00	17.00	7.00	-8.00
NC State, NC	GPA	3.65	3.27	0.38	3.57	0.08	3.83	-0.18
NMU, MI	GPA	3.20	2.76	0.44	3.09	0.11	3.19	0.01
Norfolk St., VA	GPA	2.40	2.30	0.10	2.20	0.20	2.22	0.18
Nrthrn. CO, CO	GPA	3.10	2.90	0.20	2.90	0.20	3.10	0.00
ODU, VA	GPA	2.95	2.90	0.05	2.87	0.08	3.23	-0.28
Saginaw Valley, MI	GPA	2.84	2.39	0.45	2.67	0.17	Missing	Missing
School of Mines, CO	GPA	3.80	3.35	0.45	3.70	0.10	3.80	0.00
Sthrn. Colorado, CO	GPA	3.00	2.60	0.40	2.80	0.20	2.80	0.20
UC Berkeley, CA	GPA	4.00	3.42	0.58	3.75	0.25	4.00	0.00
UC Irvine, CA	GPA	3.64	3.39	0.25	3.50	0.14	3.61	0.03
UC San Diego, CA	GPA	3.92	3.88	0.04	3.76	0.16	3.86	0.06
UM Dearborn, MI	GPA	3.40	3.20	0.20	3.40	0.00	3.30	0.10
UM Twin Cities, MN	Perc.	82.00	73.00	9.00	77.50	4.50	81.00	1.00
UM Ann Arbor, MI	GPA	3.70	3.30	0.40	3.40	0.30	3.70	0.00
UM Crookston, MN	Perc.	50.00	29.00	21.00	32.50	17.50	25.00	25.00
UM Morris, MN	Perc.	88.00	91.00	-3.00	87.00	1.00	88.00	0.00
UM Duluth, MN	Perc.	74.00	71.50	2.50	66.50	7.50	78.00	-4.00
UNC Asheville, NC	GPA	3.54	3.36	0.18	3.25	0.29	3.60	-0.06
UNC Chapel Hill, NC	GPA	3.99	3.60	0.39	4.00	-0.01	4.00	-0.01
UNC Charlotte, NC	GPA	3.38	3.10	0.28	3.25	0.13	3.72	-0.34
UNC Greensboro, NC	GPA	3.14	3.10	0.04	2.99	0.15	3.18	-0.04
UNC Wilmington, NC	GPA	3.40	2.95	0.45	3.45	-0.05	3.42	-0.02
US Military Academy	Rank	14.00	18.00	4.00	16.50	2.50	11.00	-3.00
UVA, VA	Perc.	97.30	91.85	5.45	96.20	1.10	97.50	-0.20
UWashington, WA	GPA	3.68	3.21	0.47	3.50	0.18	3.66	0.02
VCU, VA	GPA	3.00	2.91	0.09	3.04	-0.04	3.27	-0.27
Virginia Tech, VA	GPA	3.44	3.30	0.14	3.33	0.11	3.50	-0.06
Wash. St., WA	GPA	3.32	2.95	0.37	3.20	0.12	3.24	0.08
Western State, CO	GPA	2.80	2.60	0.20	2.70	0.10	3.00	-0.20

Appendix 2: Results of Logistic Regression Analysis

Table 18.5

Odds Ratios

Schools	Black-White	Hisp.-White	Asian-White
NC State (*n* = 10,332)	177.10****	0.85	0.79
UM Ann Arbor (*n* = 16,292)	173.70****	131.23****	0.76****
UVA (*n* = 15,521)	111.10****	4.84****	1.21
UNC Wilmington (*n* = 6,865)	57.23****	0.47*	0.68
UM Dearborn (*n* = 1,399)	36.50****	3.73*	7.10
William & Mary, VA (*n* = 7,061)	27.98****	1.93****	1.52****
JMU, VA (*n* = 13,280)	25.65****	1.74*	1.24*
Longwood College, VA (*n* = 2,248)	18.52****	4.41****	0.58
UNC Asheville (*n* = 2,100)	10.00****	14.40****	0.97
UNC Charlotte (*n* = 5,890)	8.37****	0.72	0.61
Naval Academy (*n* = 9,843)	4.44****	3.32****	0.67*
UMINN Duluth (*n* = 7,691)	4.09*	2.40	4.52****
UNC Chapel Hill (*n* = 9,002)	3.40****	0.31****	0.62****
UMINN Twin Cities (*n* = 23,638)	3.04****	4.96****	6.56****
Military Academy (*n* = 11,954)	1.94****	1.20	0.68*
ODU, VA (*n* = 4,512)	0.64*	0.37*	1.14
VCU, VA (*n* = 4,728)	0.60**	0.73	1.36
Ferris State, MI (*n* = 4,440)	1.79	1.33	34.14
Norfolk State, VA (*n* = 3,152)	1.20	0.67	0.68
UMN, Morris (*n* = 1,921)	1.01	0.17	5.79
GMU, VA (*n* = 4,803)	0.99	1.43*	1.01
UNC Greensboro (*n* = 5,333)	0.97	1.21	0.43
Virginia Tech (*n* = 15,981)	0.89	0.80	0.47****

Note. * $p < 0.05$; ** $p < 0.01$; *** $p < 0.001$; **** $p < 0.0001$

19

Talent Search:
Purposes, Rationale, and Role in Gifted Education

by Paula Olszewski-Kubilius

T he first talent search was instituted by Julian Stanley at Johns Hopkins University with the support of the Spencer Foundation of Chicago in September of 1971. Stanley was interested in children who reasoned extremely well mathematically, and he founded the Study of Mathematically Precocious Youth (SMPY) in order to study them.

In an effort to measure and identify mathematical aptitude, Stanley began to use the Scholastic Aptitude Test (SAT) with students of pre-high school age who appeared to be precocious in mathematics. He found that the test had value in measuring mathematical reasoning ability. In fact, it was so valuable in this regard that Stanley and his colleagues extended their use of it from individual students to groups of students, thus beginning the talent search concept (Stanley, Keating, & Fox, 1974). The first talent searches, conducted almost annually during the 1970s, were a deliberate effort to find youths of middle-school age within circumscribed geographical areas who reasoned exceptionally well in the area of mathematics. Later, the talent search was broadened to include assessment of verbal, as well as math-

---

Portions of this chapter have been previously published in Olszewski-Kubilius, P. (1998). Talent search: Purposes, rationale, and role in gifted education. *Journal of Secondary Gifted Education, 9*, 106–114 and Olszewski-Kubilius, P. (1998). Research evidence regarding the validity and effects of talent search educational programs. *Journal of Secondary Gifted Education, 9*, 134–138.

ematical, talent and extended to the entire United States, Canada, Australia, New Zealand, The Peoples' Republic of China, and countries in Europe, especially Ireland and Spain.

These early talent searches identified so many academically advanced students whose highly specialized needs were not being met and provided such a successful method of identifying these students that the idea grew enormously over the next two and a half decades. Currently, talent searches exist nationwide to serve children in every state, and the services have been augmented to include educational programs, newsletters, analogous talent searches for younger students, and services for parents. There are currently four university-based centers that conduct annual talent searches: the Center for Talent Development (CTD) at Northwestern University, the Talent Identification Program (TIP) at Duke University, The Center for Talented Youth (CTY) at Johns Hopkins University, and the Rocky Mountain Talent Search (RMTS) at the University of Denver. In addition to these, other centers across the United States conduct identical or analogous talent searches and state-level talent searches.

The Rationale Behind Talent Search

The talent search is built upon the idea of "off-level" testing. A basic premise is that, because children develop at different rates, they should be allowed to take tests at the level of their abilities, not at the level that school officials or testing companies deem appropriate for their age. Students who are scoring very well on typically used standardized achievement tests (above the 95th or 97th percentile of their school grade) are eligible for the talent search. For these students, in-grade achievement tests indicate a high level of mastery of the in-grade curriculum. However, these tests cannot tell how far beyond the grade curriculum children are functioning because they do not have an adequate "ceiling," that is, enough difficult items. In-grade achievement tests are useful only as an initial screening device for gifted children, that is, as a means to find those children who need to be tested further.

Tests such as the Scholastic Aptitude Test (SAT)[1] or the American College Testing Program (ACT) have adequate ceilings to provide better measurement of gifted students' abilities because they are designed to be used with older students. Typically, these tests are taken by high school 11th and 12th graders who are preparing to go to college. Historically, the tests were developed to predict college performance (SAT) or to place students appropriately within the college curriculum (ACT).

---

[1] The SAT is now known as the SAT-I, Scholastic Assessment Test. The College Board high school achievement tests are now known as SAT-II.

The Components of Talent Search

Nowadays, when one uses the term "talent search," it means much more than the testing described above. It is more properly viewed with three different "lenses": as a tool for diagnosis/evaluation, as a guide for educational placement, and as a structure to provide talent development opportunities. Stanley (1983) described SMPY as a "vast, far-flung set of educationally facilitative special opportunities for young students who reason exceptionally well mathematically or verbally" (p. 1). This description applies to talent search, as well (see Figure 19.1).

Diagnosis/Evaluation

When first conceived, the talent search was viewed primarily as an identification and selection device. That is, the testing identified those students who were exceptionally talented in math and verbal areas and selected them for special programs. However, the talent search has slowly been reconceptualized as a diagnostic tool, one that discovers *areas* (math or verbal) and *levels* of ability within a population already considered academically gifted and matches students to programs that are appropriate in pace of learning and content.

Consider, for example, two seventh-grade students who both score at the 97th percentile on the mathematics composite of their in-grade achievement test. When they take the SAT-Math, however, one student scores a 650 and the other a 350 (see Figure 19.2). These students look extremely similar to one another on the basis of the in-grade achievement test and would be given similar educational treatment by schools and teachers. In reality, though, they are quite different and need different educational placements and programs. Despite those differences, one would be reluctant to conclude that one child is gifted and the other is not.

The child who scores 350 on the SAT-Math has achieved a high level of mastery of his or her grade-level mathematics and probably is functioning in this area like a child in an advanced grade. This child would benefit from enrichment in mathematics and might need to be moved to the next grade for mathematics instruction. The child who scores 650 on the SAT-Math is functioning mathematically like a child 4 to 5 years older—like an average 12th grader. A student who earns a 650 as a seventh grader is likely to know a great deal of precalculus without having taken a formal course (Bartkovich & Mezynski, 1981). For this student, an individualized mathematics program that allows him or her to move at a much more rapid pace is appropriate. For both of these children, however, the typical curriculum is probably insufficient—insufficient in scope, pace, or both.

The talent search provides assessment to students during the mid to late elementary school years. This time period is one in which differentiation of abilities across different areas—verbal, mathematical, scientific—begins to emerge. In addition to discerning areas and levels of ability within areas, the talent search gives educators a rough yet useful estimate of learning rate or the extent to which typical school instruction will be inappropriately slow paced or, conversely, the rate

Diagnosis/Evaluation

- Assesses areas of talent
- Measures level of talent
- Yields estimate of learning rate

Educational Placement and Guidance

- Recommendation in sequential sets of educational experiences that develop area of talent
- Grade acceleration
- Subject acceleration
- Curriculum modifications such as compacting and telescoping

Talent Development Opportunities

- Saturday programs
- Summer programs
- Contest/competitions
- Informational newsletters
- Clubs
- Magazines
- Career programs
- Weekend courses and programs
- Contact with gifted education experts
- Awards ceremonies
- Contact with other gifted children and their families
- Internships and mentorships
- Distance education courses

Figure 19.1. Components of talent search

at which instruction should proceed in order to be appropriately challenging for a particular student.

Educational Placement and Guidance

The information yielded from talent search testing can be extremely useful for educational placement and guidance. Northwestern University's Center for Talent Development has developed recommended course sequences within each of the content areas (see Figure 19.3 for an example) and program recommendations depending upon a student's talent search scores (see Figure 19.4). The basis for these recommendations are differences in students' reasoning capabilities and the

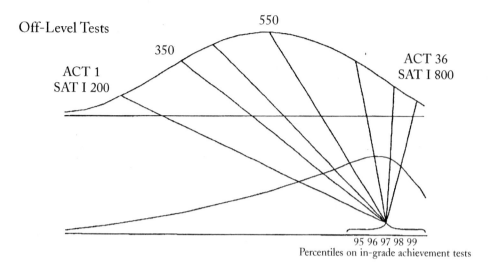

Figure 19.2. The relationship between performance on in-grade achievement tests and off-level tests

belief that these differences should be matched to educational programs that are appropriate in level, scope, and pace. The recommended course sequences are an attempt to provide a sequential set of educational experiences that utilize and further develop the student's talent and interest over time.

On the basis of their talent search scores (e.g., high and relatively equal in math and verbal), some students may be candidates for grade acceleration and others for subject area acceleration (e.g., high in math or verbal), as illustrated above. Other students may be able to be accommodated within the typical school organizations by being advanced one or more grades for instruction or by early access to high school or college classes. Schools may need to institute special kinds of classes, such as those that compress 2 years of mathematics instruction into 1 to accommodate certain students. A small group of students may need programs that depart radically from their school's typical array of opportunities (e.g., early college entrance).

Accelerating children through the curriculum or making accommodations that allow them to proceed at a more rapid pace of learning are not widely used or accepted by many schools (Southern & Jones, 1993). Within schools, age or grade is still the main determiner of placement and readiness for the study of certain subjects or courses, despite the fact that this is not true of other talent domains. Children talented in most sports or performing arts are allowed to proceed with advanced training once they have developed the appropriate skills or techniques. Further, it is widely accepted and not considered problematic that individual children will have their own rates of development within these talent domains. The most extreme example of this is children who are defined as prodigies and who are so advanced within a domain that they reach adult levels of performance while still chronologically children. Talent search is consistent with current understandings

	Sequence 1	Sequence 2
7th	Etymologies, Word Usage, Linguistics	1st year Level I Language (according to the American Council of Teachers of Foreign Languages)
8th	1st year Level I Language* (according to the American Council of Teachers of Foreign Languages)	2nd year Level I Language
9th	2nd year Level I Language	3rd year Level I Language and 1st year of Level II, III, or IV Language
10th	3rd year Level I Language* & 1st year of another Level I Language	4th year Level I Language and 2nd year of Level II, III, or IV Language or AP Language course or AP Literature
11th	4th year Level I Language & 2nd year of second Level I Language or AP Language course	3rd year of Level II, III, or IV Language
12th	3rd year of second Level I Language or AP Literature	4th year of Level II, III, or IV Language

*Level I or II languages refer to the American Council of Teachers of Foreign Language's guidelines for the difficult mastery of a given language. The commonly used romance languages are Level I. Higher level languages are those considered to be of a greater difficulty because they do not use the English alphabet. Japanese, Russian, and Chinese are examples of Level IV languages.

Extracurricular or Enrichment Activities

Travel to foreign countries; contemporary foreign magazines, comparable to *People*, are available in larger cities and university bookstores or by subscription; college language departments sponsor a variety of activities centering around languages; many popular computer programs and board games are available in common second languages; competitions sponsored by the Junior Classical League, a national organization that offers scholarships for students and hosts a summer convention for Latin students.

Figure 19.3. Recommendations for foreign language

A Range	B Range	C Range
230–470 on SAT-V 200–510 on SAT-M OR 0–21 on ACT-Eng or ACT-Read 0–17 on ACT-Math	480–580 on SAT-V 520–600 on SAT-M OR 22–27 on ACT-Eng or ACT-Read 18–23 on ACT-Math	580+ on SAT-V 600+ on SAT-M OR 28+ on ACT-Eng or ACT-Read 24+ on ACT-Math
Program options should include:	Program options should include:	Program options should include:

A Range

Program options should include:

1. Long-range academic planning, following Sequence 1 in area of academic strength
2. Early access to advanced school courses
3. Supplement course-work with enrich-ment-oriented school, Saturday, or summer programs
4. Early career counsel-ing
5. Sequence 1 of "Recommended Course Sequences"

B Range

Program options should include:

1. Long-range academic planning, following Sequence 2 of "Recommended Course Sequences" in area of academic strength
2. Fast-paced school, Saturday, or summer classes in area of strength, using cur-riculum compacting to compress courses into shorter time frames
3. Early access to col-lege-level coursework through Advanced Placement (AP), dis-tance learning, dual enrollment, or sum-mer courses
4. Early career counsel-ing, including access to mentorships, tuto-rials, and internships

C Range

Program options should include:

Options 1–4 from B Range, plus:

1. Individualized pro-gram of study, using "test-out" approach in areas of strength, helping advanced students avoid spend-ing time on material they already know
2. Consider grade accel-eration (grade-skip-ping) or early admission to college)
3. Individualized work with a mentor to pursue advanced study in an area, pos-sibly aimed at specific AP exam

Figure 19.4. Ranges of performance on SAT-I or ACT

of the process of talent development, especially given its emphasis on educational accommodation to individual trajectories of development within domains.

Talent Development Opportunities

When children participate in a talent search program, they are able to access a whole host of outside-of-school opportunities, including award ceremonies, summer programs, after-school or Saturday programs, distance education programs, weekend workshops and seminars, and chat groups and other online programs. In addition, they receive information in the form of newsletters and magazines on other opportunities such as contests and competitions, scholarships, study abroad programs, and research fellowships. Newsletters and magazines also include expert advice on issues such as acceleration, college programs for academically talented students, early college entrance, and social/emotional aspects of giftedness.

Talent search participants become part of a network of support that includes direct services from the talent search universities themselves: educational programs, advice and information from expert professionals, information about and access to programs from other universities or organizations, and contact with other families and students with similar interests and capabilities. Typically, students who participate in a talent search as seventh or eighth graders continue to be notified about opportunities and receive information from the talent search institution until the completion of high school. The effect on talent development for an individual talent search participant can be pervasive and long-lasting. Talent search is more properly viewed as the gateway to many other important, educationally advantageous opportunities.

Approximately 130,000 seventh- through ninth-grade students took the SAT with a talent search organization during 2001–2002 (J. Zumoff, personal communication, April 4, 2002). Another 40,000 students took the ACT, most of these with a talent search organization (P. Dana, personal communication, April 4, 2002). Another 21,000 third- through sixth-grade students took the EXPLORE test through ACT (P. Dana, personal communication, April 4, 2002), and more than 19,000 fifth and sixth graders took the PLUS test (D. Freeman, personal communication, September 23, 1996). While these figures represent a substantial number of children, many more are qualified to participate and are not aware of the opportunities that talent searches can bring them.

Research on the Talent Search Model

There is an ample research base to support the premises underlying the talent search model.

First, the validity of the two-tiered identification process has been established. Ebmeier and Schmulbach (1989) found that it is appropriate to use the 95th percentile on in-grade, standardized achievement tests as a criterion to choose students who need further assessment. Using this percentile does not eliminate many students who would score well on the test (false negatives), nor does it subject many students to the testing who would perform poorly (false positives).

Second, research has shown that the tests are not too difficult for most of the middle school students who take them. The percentages of students who score at the low end of these tests are about the same for the talent search and high school populations (*The 2002 Student Guide*, 2002), indicating that most of the younger students are not overwhelmed by the test. Additional evidence that the test is not too difficult is the fact that most talent search students score above chance level on the SAT, the score they would get from purely guessing (Burton, 1988).

Third, research has shown that the talent search has predictive validity, as well. Students who participate in a talent search continue to achieve at higher levels compared to other students (Burton, 1988). Specifically, talent search students score better than average college-bound seniors on the SAT when they take it in high school, take more accelerated and advanced courses, earn more awards and honors, and continue to have high educational aspirations (Burton). Benbow (1992) found that scores on the SAT are predictive of achievement 10 years after talent search participation and that differences in scoring levels relate to measurable and, in some cases, significant differences in academic achievement. Research done by Lubinski, Webb, Morelock, and Benbow (2001) showed that talent search participants identified before age 13 as having mathematical or verbal reasoning abilities at the level of the top 1 in 10,000 were more than 50 times as likely to pursue doctorates compared to the general population. Talent search students identified as scoring in the top 1% in mathematical or verbal reasoning ability were found to be 25 times more likely to earn doctorates compared to the general population. According to these authors,

> the capability of identifying at over 50 times base-rate expectations as observed in this study is even more profound and constitutes, according the great applied psychologist Donald G. Patterson, a *difference* (here in ability level) *that makes a difference.* (p. 725)

Finally, research has also shown that the recommendations for students based on their talent search scores have validity. The SAT scores used for entrance into fast-paced accelerative courses select students who succeed academically (Olszewski-Kubilius, Kulieke, Willis, & Krasney, 1989). Student achievement in classes that are matched in rate and pace with students learning capabilities as assessed by talent search scores is consistently high (Bartkovich & Mezynski, 1981; Lynch, 1992; Olszewski-Kubilius et al.). Students who participate in talent-search-sponsored summer programs tend to pursue more rigorous courses of study, participate in more extracurricular educational opportunities, and accelerate their education more than students who do not participate (Barnett & Durden, 1993; Olszewski-Kubilius & Grant, 1996). The effects of such programs can be especially beneficial for mathematically talented females, helping them to match the achievement levels of males, maintain high educational aspirations (Brody & Fox, 1980; Fox, Brody, & Tobin, 1985), and extend beyond mathematics by fostering advanced course taking in other content areas (Olszewski-Kubilius & Grant). Talent search and subsequent summer programs can increase motivation, create academic challenge, and provide social support that helps girls who, for complex social reasons, do not achieve at levels commensurate with their abilities.

The Effects of Talent Search on General Education

Talent searches have had a positive effect on general education in the following areas.

Timing and Pace of Instruction

Talent search and the educational programs that have developed from it challenge firmly held notions about the timing and pace of instruction. Most schools adhere to the model of 120 hours of minimum instruction for a single course. But, talent search programs have demonstrated that students with SAT-M scores above 600 can accomplish as much as two high school mathematics courses within only 50 hours of instruction (Bartkovich & Mezynski, 1981) and many can master an entire year's worth of material within 75 hours of instruction (Olszewski-Kubilius et al., 1989). Talent search summer programs have shown that some students can learn at a much faster rate and that instruction can proceed at a much faster pace than heretofore believed without sacrificing the level of subject mastery or preparation for future courses and with higher student satisfaction (Mills, Ablard, & Lynch, 1992). These findings, along with other gifted program models that compress learning into shorter time periods, challenge the current structure of schools (McCarthy, 1998). How much more could students learn if they were allowed to study at a more appropriate, challenging pace?

Mastery of Subject Material

Talent search programs challenge traditionally held ideas about subject mastery. In most high schools, mastery is determined by both a student's performance in a course or subject and by the amount of time spent on the subject. Students who attend talent search summer programs and successfully complete courses often have difficulty getting credit for those courses, despite high-level mastery, because they spent less than 120 hours of instruction (typically 75–90) in the subject area (Olszewski-Kubilius & Grant, 1996). The performance of students in talent search educational programs challenges traditionally held beliefs about the criteria for granting credit or determining mastery.

Readiness for Learning

Talent search educational programs allow students of middle school age to study subjects and take courses typically reserved for high school or college-aged students. Talent search programs have shown that chronological age is not a good indication of readiness, although it remains the primary criterion for students to study particular subjects in most schools. In fact, many younger students often possess the mastery of prerequisite subjects, maturity, and motivation needed to succeed in advanced courses.

Focused Intense Study

In most talent search educational programs, students study one subject at a time in a very focused, intense manner. They pursue this subject to mastery and then proceed on to another. Many students report a strong preference for this type of study, rather than the smorgasbord/sampling approach of a "bit of time on many subjects" typical of most high schools. School officials are very committed to this "small dose" approach to learning, believing that it allows students to digest new materials fully and gives ample opportunity for repeated exposure to it. Contrary to concerns that the reduced instructional time of most talent search summer programs results in superficial learning, the model of intense study of a single subject at a time promotes in-depth learning of subjects (Kolitch & Brody, 1992; Mills et al., 1992).

Grouping of Students

Talent search educational programs add to the already existing literature about the value of homogeneous grouping for academically talented learners (Rogers, 1991). The success of students in talent search programs attests to the validity and benefits of such grouping arrangements for both instruction and social development and interaction.

A Need for Greater Access

A major problem with talent search is access to the program, which is troublesome at several levels:

- Talent search is a program operated by universities, not by local schools. However, personnel within schools are invited to identify students who have the requisite in-grade achievement test scores to qualify for talent search and let them make the decision to be a part of the program. Only a small percentage of the schools that could send students to the talent search actually do so. Because the schools act as a gatekeeper, many students are not afforded the opportunity to be a part of a talent search program.

- Participation in the talent search involves a fee. While it is reasonable, typically around $50, it may prohibit some students from participating. Similarly, most of the educational programs offered by the talent searches also involve substantial tuition and room and board charges. Therefore, they are too expensive for many students who could benefit from them. While such programs have some scholarship money to support students, there are still many more qualified students who never even apply because of the fees involved.

- Talent search does a good job of assessing the abilities of children who are already achieving in school, but it does not help to identify children who are underachieving or who cannot demonstrate their abilities on the off-level tests because of a language difference. Also, it does not identify children who, because of economic disadvantage or other factors, have not had an environment supportive enough to develop their abilities—children who may have the potential to achieve, but who do not yet have a high level of developed talent. These groups of children are often most in need of the services that talent search has to offer, but may initially need remedial work and extra classes to enable them to catch up.

Talent search has been and continues to be a phenomenon within education and the field of the gifted and talented. Of all the identification and program models promoted within the field of the education of the gifted, it is the most sound, having a solid basis of research support behind it. It also has led to a flowering of programs for gifted students and a wider recognition of their special needs.

20

Give Us the Best and Brightest, But . . .
A Historical Review of U.S. National Policy on Education for the Highly Capable

by Clifton D. Wickstrom

The first phrase in the title of this chapter has been a frequently heard cry at many points of public and private crises in the past half century in this country. When Sputnik was launched by the Soviet Union in the late 1950s, the rush was suddenly on to push the highly capable into the sciences and engineering to close the gap and accelerate the nation into the space race. This call was probably sounded at its loudest less than 4 years later, when the newly inaugurated President John F. Kennedy charged a new generation of the highly capable, along with the rest of the citizens of the nation, to step forward and join in the challenges of confronting and conquering a "New Frontier" of social justice, technological excellence, and military capability in this country.

But, the rush to excellence was short-lived, as the multiple challenges of external war, increasing demands for mediation of past racial and economic injustice, gender equity, meeting the needs of the disabled, and other issues commanded the attention of national level decision makers and moved resources to other priorities. In that one brief, Camelot-like moment, there was a flash of attention given to the development of the highly capable as a national resource. But, that moment passed, and, with a few minor, brief exceptions, there has not been any significant effort to reignite the flame at either the national or state level in the United States since that time. Almost a half century has passed, and, as a nation, we still have not owned up to the multifaceted challenge of developing and implementing a clearly coherent set of national policies for educating the youth of this nation often referred to as gifted, highly capable, intellectually talented, multitalented, or uniquely creative.

The call has been heard from time to time since 1961, such as in 1983, when the Reagan Administration's National Commission on Excellence in Education issued the now famous report titled *A Nation at Risk: The Imperative for Educational Reform* (U.S. Department of Education, 1983; cited subsequently as *Nation at Risk*). The report noted "If an unfriendly foreign power had attempted to impose on America the mediocre education performance that exists today, we might well have viewed it as an act of war" (p. 3). It continued, "over half of the population of gifted students do not match their tested ability with comparable achievement in school" (p. 8). The report also noted that "most gifted students, for example, may need a curriculum enriched and accelerated beyond the needs of other students of high ability" (p. 24). Yet, in spite of this now-20-year-old acknowledgement of the need for a major shift in the way that highly capable youth are educated, nothing has significantly changed in terms of national education policy. This has occurred in spite of a flurry of subsequent reports (including two major Carnegie Foundation reports) throughout the 1980s on the need to encourage educational excellence on the part of the highly capable youth.

This is not to say that nothing is being done. In a recent personal communication (May 2, 2002) with Julian C. Stanley, he indicated actions by private agencies and states have been increasing significantly. He noted,

> AP exams are way up. Some schools have more curricular flexibility, and much has been done in the private sector outside of the schools. For example, the surge in distance learning, the huge annual talent searches and the large summer programs conducted by major universities, and the increase in special high schools and early entrance to college programs are making some difference. Even the Intel (formerly Westinghouse) Talent Search has been upgraded greatly.

In the face of this, it remains a question as to why no overriding national policy on gifted education has been forthcoming. The advances that Stanley listed are all the work of private or state, not national, institutes.

There appear to be numerous complex reasons for this. Some are political, some are legal, and some are also nominally cultural. All fall into that rather tangled and complex web of relationships that we call "education policy" in this country. The United States Supreme Court's momentous 1954 decision in *Brown v. Board of Education of Topeka, Kansas* served as the impetus to propel local and national leaders to take steps to ensure equal educational opportunities for all students by recognizing that "today, education is perhaps the most important function of state and local governments" (p. 493). *Brown* ushered in an era of significant, yet incomplete, gains in equal educational opportunities for many children, most notably minorities, females, and students with disabilities.

However, despite the progress that has been made in the struggle for educational equality, many exceptionally able students are not being fully served in spite of Congressional direction in 1994 to accomplish that goal. In education program reauthorization legislation of that year, Congress added this language to the U.S. Code: "National policy is that every citizen is entitled to an education to meet his or her full potential" (20 U.S.C. Section 1221). However, subsequent supportive legislation, regulatory action, and funding have not followed. Aside from commission reports and rhetoric, little has been done at either the federal or state level to offer appropriate programming for gifted and talented children's educational needs. The poor state of gifted education is reflected in the fact that recent federal information on gifted students reported that, in the early 1990s, states spent only 2 cents out of every $100 in education on programs for gifted students (H.R. 490, 107th Cong, 2001). It is without question that national educational leaders and policymakers have not taken sufficient steps to meet the educational needs of gifted children in the United States.

This chapter discusses various reasons for the problem and the many challenges now faced in attempting to meet the educational needs of highly capable students across the entire range of talents and gifts. Section I provides a brief overview of the differing views on the needs of students and also the difference between the idea of educational "equality" and educational "equity" (Benbow & Stanley, 1996) that may be at least a part of the issue at hand. Section II examines some of the historical, political, cultural, legal, and statutory developments in the United States dealing with the rights of gifted students, including the recently passed No Child Left Behind Act of 2001 (NCLBA). Section III provides concluding remarks and some recommendations regarding the future.

I. Meeting the Educational Needs of Highly Capable Students

Program delivery for highly capable students is a contentious issue in the United States. In this self-avowed egalitarian nation,[1] where all citizens are considered to have equal rights under the law (U.S. Department of Education, 1993, p. 5), critics are reluctant to support special programs for gifted students because of the fear and suspicion that intellectualism may lead to elitism. On the other hand, there is the American ideal, most notably reflected in *Brown*, Title IX , the Individuals with Disabilities Education Act (IDEA; Tannenbaum, 1998),

---

[1] In 1840, Alexis De Tocqueville noted in his *Democracy in America*, "The United States is a society with low levels of interest in education and intellect . . . that values equality . . . [and is] uncomfortable with social or intellectual distinctions or with hierarchies that they believe can stand in the way of the success of industrious individuals" (p. 124).

Congressional direction as noted above, and the NCLBA, of helping all to succeed and reach their full potential. The quandary in the lack of any special attention to the education of the gifted remains unanswered. As noted in this chapter, this ambivalent and apparently contradictory perspective is far from resolved, and indeed little is available to help to explain some of the lack of progress in defining a clear and nationally coherent set of policies and programs for the education of the highly capable. This ambivalence can most likely be traced to conflicted misunderstanding of the terms *equality* and *equity*. Although these two words are frequently used synonymously in colloquial or political speech, they have a significant difference in a legal or policy setting. *Equality*, in a legal perspective, means that *all* must receive the same level of protection, service, or consideration regardless of situation. *Equity*, on the other hand, implies that those who are similarly situated, although not necessarily in equal circumstances, will receive similar protection, service, or consideration.

A clarifying set of examples will illustrate the difference. In the case of *Brown v. Board of Education*, the Supreme Court reversed the previously stated view in *Plessey v. Ferguson* (163 US 537, 1896) that "separate but equal" education did indeed provide Black students "equality" of protection and educational opportunity. They held that separate, segregated education was unequal on its face and that it denied students in such circumstances "equal protection of the laws." Similar arguments regarding gender and disabilities have led to major shifts in education opportunities, in both legislation and case law.

However, it is quite legally defensible for people to be treated unequally, but "equitably," in a publicly funded educational setting. A public college or university can quite legally provide a full-tuition scholarship to an athlete, while denying one to an equally academically qualified student who does not participate in athletics. It is understood that the differences in situation provide and allow for defensible differences in treatment based on circumstances, even though public funds are involved. The treatment would be unequal, but is equitable, under the law. I believe that it is likely that highly capable youth can likewise be provided different treatment in a public educational setting because their needs constitute a differing circumstance, much like that of the athlete. Yes, the opportunities would be unequal compared to those for others, but so long as there was no differentiation in this treatment on the basis of race, gender, national origin, or religious belief, the situation would likely be considered equitable and legally defensible. However, this argument has not held sway in most forums where the issue has been debated. Other demands placed on the nation's system of education have commanded the resources of education institutions to the exclusion of the needs of the highly capable.

Even within the gifted education community, the terminology is visibly conflicted. In a recent article in the National Association for Gifted Children's *Education Weekly Commentary*, Tomlinson (2002) used the term *equity* in a way that illustrates the point. She repeatedly referred to the tension between "two bedrock values: equity and excellence" (para. 1). She defined equity "in terms of access to opportunity . . . to excel" (para. 1). Similarly, in a *Roeper Review* article entitled, "Mainstreaming the Gifted: Historical Perspectives on Excellence and Equity," McDaniel (1989) argued for a "program for the gifted in which this educational enterprise is firmly located in the regular classroom—to the maximum degree possible" ("Implications for Contemporary Policy" section, para. 2). He also noted,

> A heterogeneous classroom today may include Asian, Black, Hispanic, and other racial or cultural groups; learning disabled, mentally retarded, orthopedically impaired or other handicapped children; and a wide variety of intellectual and achievement levels, including the gifted. (p. 112)

This is precisely what the legal community would define as equality. I would argue that such access to opportunity must, of course, be equal for all, regardless of how nature and nurture may differentiate that ability to achieve excellence. The pathways to excellence remain obscure, however, and blocked for most highly capable youth in this country because of the combination of low political will and scarce resources committed elsewhere. Also, McDaniel's dream to the contrary, the classroom he describes doesn't exist in any real way. To do so would require either a teacher of superhuman physical and intellectual capabilities, in addition to several specialized academic and educational specialist credentials, or a team teaching staff of at least four specialists, which is far beyond the resource potential of all but the most affluent private institutions. In theoretical terms, it is the ideal; but, in the practical world, few will ever experience this proposed classroom. Indeed, one of the more frequently expressed arguments against providing specialized education for the gifted is the added burden it would place upon the classroom teacher, already coping with multiple Individual Educational Plans (IEPs) for other categories of special needs students.

Regardless of one's attitude toward giftedness, research indicates that highly capable students have unique educational requirements and need special programs, which are not yet being provided (U.S. Department of Education, 1983, p. 24). In addition, it is critical to note the greater potential societal value of high-capability student programs. This is particularly true since many such children not only fail to succeed on their own (Harrington, Harrington, & Karns, 1991), but, indeed, may underachieve (Renzulli, Baum, & Hébert, 1995), experience learning disabilities, and drop out of school (Renzulli & Park, 2000). Similarly, many will not succeed because their potential is cut off or restricted by the lack of creativity or differential options to excel in the traditional school curriculum (Callahan & Kaufman, 1982). In addition, although data have not been tracked consistently (U.S. Department of Education, 1993, pp. 2–3), there are indications that highly capable children from low-income families (Slocumb & Payne, 2000), minority families, or families living in inner-city areas (Hébert, 2000) are in even greater need of better program opportunities than their middle-income or suburban peers because of the greater risk of failure, poor achievement, or underachievement (Harris & Ford, 1991). Failure to meet these opportunity needs may in fact be a policy failure from both equality and equity perspectives.

II. Review of the National Education Policy
for Highly Capable Youth

It is a well-settled legal position that students do not have a constitutionally protected right to receive an education (*San Antonio ISD v Rodriguez*, 411 U.S. 1, 1973) absent a constitutional violation (*Brown*, 1954) or a clear statutory entitlement such as is created in the IDEA. Even so, as noted above, Congress has taken a leadership role in safeguarding the educational rights of minorities, women, and children with disabilities. The history of federal programming for gifted students has been sporadic, however.

The earliest federal program on gifted education was created in 1931 when the United States Department of Education instituted a Section on Exceptional Children and Youth. This program lacked specific legislative or fiscal authority, but laid a foundation for later federal actions regarding the gifted (Zettel, 1982b, p. 51). In the decade following World War II, the threat of Soviet aggression and the spread of communism to China prompted major federal interest in the gifted. This was understood, although unstated, when Congress enacted the National Science Foundation Act of 1950. This historic act "not only directed resources toward the development of the sciences and basic research, but for the first time focused federal attention on the nation's gifted and talented" (Zettel, p. 52). Previously, Congress directed its attention mostly toward higher education of the gifted in basic and applied science areas related to the general welfare (Bok, 1991). However, under this act, programs and projects were geared toward improving the curriculum in schools and encouraging gifted students to seek careers in mathematics and the physical sciences.

The successful launch of the Sputnik satellite in October 1957 led to a swift national-level response, the National Defense Education Act of 1958 (NDEA; Pub. L 85-864). Although the NDEA was not adopted specifically to address the needs of gifted students, its major emphases were on mathematics, science, and foreign languages. This served as a stimulus to the development of programs for the gifted. Furthermore, the Act and the local response elicited by it implicitly made gifted students the prime targets of curricular reforms that were designed to redress underachievement among students who were capable of success (Gallagher, 1988). Consequently, as the 1950s came to a close, there was an increased recognition that, since gifted students had the ability to make significant contributions to the nation's welfare, especially in the essential areas of science and technology, it was vital to develop programs to assist them in achieving their full potential (Russo, 2001).

Even as federal interest in the gifted was evolving, two research studies revealed a decreased interest in programs for the gifted (Zettel, 1982b, pp. 52–53).

This declining interest was exacerbated by anti-intellectualism during and follow-ing the McCarthy Era when "intellectuals" were often viewed with suspicion.[2] For example, discussing President Eisenhower's 1952 and 1956 defeats of Adlai Stevenson, one commentator noted "an alarming fact long suspected: there is a wide and unhealthy gap between the American intellectuals and the common peo-ple" (Zettel, p. 53). Not surprisingly, concern for gifted education policy was quickly overshadowed by the much larger debate over school desegregation during the mid-to-late 1950s and the 1960s.

During the periodic ebbs and flows of support for programs for gifted stu-dents, the much larger and more far-reaching debate over school desegregation came to a head in *Brown v. Board of Education* (1954) and subsequent cases in the federal appellate courts (Russo, Harris, & Sandidge, 1994). Indeed, *Brown* is the cornerstone of all subsequent legal developments ensuring the rights of pre-viously disenfranchised groups. Of particular interest are cases regarding the protection of the rights of students with disabilities, particularly *Pennsylvania Association for Retarded Children v. Pennsylvania* (F. Supp. 1257, E.D. Pa, 1971) and *Mills v. Board of Education* (348 F. Supp. 866, D.D.C, 1972). Consistent with the reasoning in *Brown*, both cases were decided on the basis of constitu-tional principles of equal protection and due process, rather than any specifically defined special entitlement.

Viewed together, these cases stand for two principles that permeate later developments. First, children with disabilities have the substantive due process right to receive a public school education based on their unique, individual needs. Second, students with disabilities are entitled to the protection of procedural due process before they can be classified as being disabled, placed in a nonregular class-room, or transferred to a new placement (Russo, 2001). The precedent has been established that, if a special need or circumstance can be demonstrated, the states must establish programs to accommodate those needs. What is lacking is a clear consensus that high capability constitutes a need requiring such consideration.

One year after the Federal District Court decision in the *Mills* case, Congress enacted Section 504 of the Rehabilitation Act of 1973 (Pub. L.93-112). This was the first major federal law (as amended in 1994) to offer broad-based protection for otherwise qualified individuals with impairments (29 U.S.C. Section794a). Although not originally intended to assist students, Section 504 has had a pro-found impact on schools. The law, as amended, requires that individuals who are

---

[2] Similarly, in 1963, Richard Hofstadter wrote in his book, *Anti-intellectualism in American Life*, "Again and again, it has been noticed that intellect in America is presented as a kind of excellence, as a claim to distinction, as a challenge to egalitarianism, as a quality which almost certainly deprives a man or woman of the common touch" (p. 211). This was particularly true during the McCarthy Era of the early 1950s, when intellectualism was regarded with great suspicion. This anti-intellec-tual bent was obvious in the Presidential politics of the 1952 and 1956 elections, when Democratic Party candidate Adlai Stevenson was twice rebuffed, at least in part because of his image as an intel-lectual "egghead."

otherwise qualified must be permitted to participate in school programs or activities as long as it is possible to do so by means of a "reasonable accommodation." Accommodation was subsequently more fully defined in the Code of Federal Regulations (34 C.F.R. 104.39; Russo, 2001).

In 1975, Congress enacted the Education for All Handicapped Children Act (Pub. L. 94-142), which mandated that all school-age handicapped children in the United States were to have available to them a "free appropriate public education by September 1, 1978" (Zettel & Ballard, 1982, p. 11). Zettel (1982a) has provided a detailed account of the implementation of the act and its variations across the states. The substantive and procedural due-process provisions of the act have been modified and enhanced over the decades since 1975, but the essence of the act remains. The Individuals With Disabilities Education Act (IDEA; 20 USC 1401, et seq.) subsequently replaced it as the most comprehensive federal law protecting the rights of students who have disabilities. Among its provisions, the IDEA, as amended, guarantees all children between the ages of 3 and 21 (20 U.S.C. 1412a, et seq.) with specifically identified disabilities (20 U.S.C. 1403[3]) a "free appropriate public education" (20 U.S.C. 1401[8])[3] in the least restrictive environment that is in conformance with an Individual Education Plan developed for each child.[4] However, in *Board of Education v. Rowley* (1982), the first Supreme Court case reviewing the IDEA, the court held that the act "did not impose any greater substantive educational standard than would be necessary" (p. 192) to provide access to a public education for children with disabilities. The court ruled that the act established a floor of educational opportunity below which public schools could not fall, rather than creating an open-ended continuum maximizing available programs. Given the court's very narrow interpretation of the broadly supported IDEA, it is not surprising that the rights of gifted students are marginal, if not tangential, in educational policy programming to this day (Russo, 2001).

The promise to the gifted of the late 1950s that might have flowered under President Kennedy's leadership (Zettel, 1982b, p. 55) waned under President Johnson's Great Society programs, which emphasized services for the educationally disadvantaged and economically deprived. Although the Elementary and Secondary Education Act of 1965 (ESEA; Pub. L. 89-750) was vital and necessary in looking after the needs of disadvantaged students, it may have hindered

---

[3] The NCLBA amended IDEA to further define the phrase "free appropriate public education" to mean "special education and related services that have been provided at public expense, under public supervision and direction, and without charge; meet the standards of the State education agency; include appropriate preschool, elementary, or secondary school education in the State involved; and are in conformity with the individualized education program (IEP) required under section 1414(d) of this title."

[4] 20 U.S.C. subsection 1401(11), section 1414(d), and 34 C.F.R. 300, subsections 340-350 provide additional detail on IEPs.

development of programs for the gifted. Federal resources that would otherwise have been earmarked for programs for the gifted were diverted to other programs under the auspices of the ESEA (Zettel, 1982b, p. 55). The Johnson Great Society programs promised both "guns and butter" in the political rhetoric. Unfortunately, it turned into "guns *or* butter" in reality. Even though the adoption of the ESEA meant that scant resources were reserved for the gifted, advocates continued to lobby Congress. Two years later, while some funds were allocated for innovative and exemplary programs under the 1967 Amendments to the ESEA (Pub. L. 90-247), very little was spent on programs for the gifted (Russo, 2001).

The lobbying efforts on behalf of the gifted were finally rewarded when versions of a bill were introduced in the Senate and House in January of 1969 (Zettel, 1982b, p. 55). The bill, proposed as a result of the White House Task Force on the Gifted and Talented, was initially defeated, but later won passage as The Gifted and Talented Children's Education Assistance Act, which was passed as Section 806 of the Elementary and Secondary Education Amendments of 1969, "Provisions Related to Gifted and Talented Children" (Pub. L.91-230). President Nixon signed the bill into law on April 13, 1970 (Zettel, p. 58). This law gave the first federal statutory definition of the term *gifted*, called for the development of model programs, and made programs eligible for federal financial assistance under Titles III and IV of the ESEA (see Zettel, pp. 55–62 regarding role of New York Senator Jacob Javits in this regard).

At the outset of the 1970s, the federal government had assumed a much more active role in providing for the educational needs of the gifted. On October 6, 1972, Commissioner of Education Sidney Marland submitted his national assessment of programs for the gifted to Congress. Not surprisingly, the Marland Report urged Congress to provide ongoing support for the development and maintenance of programs for gifted students not only because of their unique needs, but also because the federal government had virtually no role in this process (see Harrington, Harrington, & Karns, 1991, for follow up on this report).

Following the impetus of the Marland Report, three similar bills were introduced in Congress in February 1973. The final bill, signed into law by President Ford on August 21, 1974, as part of the 1974 Amendments to the ESEA (Pub. L. 93-80), called for federal involvement in four major areas. First, it created the Office of Gifted and Talented within the United States Office of Education. Previously, this office had been created administratively and was housed in the United States Bureau of Education for the Handicapped. Second, it called for the creation of a National Clearinghouse for the Gifted and Talented. Third, it made funds available to state and local education agencies along with grants for training, research, and projects for the gifted. Fourth, it authorized an annual federal appropriation not to exceed $12.5 million for programs on the gifted (Zettel, 1982b, p. 61), although the original draft of the bill called for an annual federal authorization of $80 million. It is not surprising that advocates for high capability education were disappointed since this ultimate appropriation amounted to about $1 a year for each eligible student (Karnes & Marquardt, 1997b).

An era of ongoing progress appeared to be on the horizon when the Gifted and Talented Children's Education Act of 1978 (Pub. L. 95-561) became law. This act extended the funding provisions of the Special Projects Act. Unlike the IDEA, which was designed to place children with disabilities in fully inclusive educational settings, the Gifted and Talented Children's Education Act was intended to provide separate programs for gifted students. It provided financial assistance to states to plan, develop, operate, and improve programs for gifted students and allowed the United States Commissioner to provide discretionary funding for such programs (Zettel, 1982b, pp. 61–63).

Unfortunately, the promise of the Gifted and Talented Children's Education Act of 1978 was short-lived. It was repealed in 1981 when President Reagan signed the Omnibus Budget Reconciliation Act (OBRA; Pub. L.97-35, Section 2135), which also closed the Office of Gifted and Talented, eliminated categorical funding from federal sources, and combined authorizations for gifted education and 21 other programs into a single block grant while reducing funding by more than 40% (Zettel, 1982b, pp. 63–64). As a result, the federal government completely suspended its direct involvement in programs for gifted students during much of the 1980s.

Amid concerns of "a rising tide of mediocrity in public education" (U.S. Department of Education, 1983, p. 5), education reform movements swelled to prominence again in the early 1990s. The passage of the Jacob K. Javits Gifted and Talented Students Act of 1994 (Pub. L.103-382) marked the culmination of long-standing efforts by supporters of gifted education. This act, which incorporated many of the recommendations of the Marland Report, reinstated, expanded, and updated earlier programs while offering priority funding for programs to serve gifted students who are economically disadvantaged, speak limited English, or have disabilities (20 U.S.C. 8035[a][1]).

As significant as the Javits Act was, it has three major shortcomings. First, although it provides some modest resources ($10 million in 1992, $21.5 million in 2002), it does not offer enough assistance to help create widespread programs. Second, it does not mandate the creation of programs for gifted students. And, third, it does not include substantive or procedural due process safeguards similar to those available to students with disabilities under the IDEA. Consequently, its good intent aside, the Javits Act can virtually be ignored by states that do not place a priority on programs for gifted children (Russo, 2001).

National policy on gifted education is essentially unchanged at the time of this writing. Beyond the NCLBA, the Second Bush Administration has shown no significant interest in changing education policy at the national level. Quite the contrary, it steadfastly believes in the traditional view that education is a state and local matter, into which the federal government should not tread, unless there is overwhelming national interest. Only in the area of minimal standards of educational achievement, tied to the federal educational assistance programs, is there any ongoing action. Policy on enhanced programs for the highly capable is nonexistent in the current national educational agenda.

III. Recommendations and Conclusions

Advocates, parents, educational leaders, and policymakers, as well as all others who are interested in meeting the needs of highly capable students, might wish to consider the following suggestions. As reflected in *National Excellence: A Case for Developing America's Talent*, Part 3: The Future of Education for the Nation's Most Talented Students, the challenge of meeting the needs of "students with exceptional talent must be shared by many sectors of society and levels of government" (U.S. Department of Education, 1993, Part 3, pp. 2–3).

Addressing this policy void requires action across the whole range of action and policy levels, including national, state, local school district, and the family. First, all advocates for the highly capable must work to ensure appropriate legislative and regulatory action and adequate funding support at the national level. If highly capable students are ever to receive the special education they deserve, then their supporters must demand that Congress strengthen and expand existing federal legislation related to their education. This legislation must include adequate funding support to make the policies viable. It must also include broad definitions of high capability and prescribe the standards for services to be provided, much as the IDEA establishes standards for the education of the disabled.

As Russo (2001) has noted, state legislatures, working in conjunction with their departments of education and colleges of education, must marshal their efforts to meet the needs of all highly capable students. A central goal of cooperation between these key players should be to strengthen certification and licensing standards for all prospective teachers and administrators and define and develop effective delivery programs using both the enrichment and acceleration models. This should assist all prospective educators to better serve the highly capable children with whom they interact. At the same time, schools and colleges of education, in accordance with the standards of appropriate accrediting agencies, should expand existing coursework and field experiences so that all prospective educators can have better exposure to highly capable children and their needs.

Third, at the local school district level, educational leaders should provide professional in-house preparation programs to assist school personnel in identifying and assessing highly capable students. In addition, they must increase their current efforts to provide the highly capable with challenging coursework and other educational experiences to assist them in reaching their full potential. Among the accommodations that educators might consider are adding classes and appropriately enriching assignments for students who might not be able to be afforded a full program of high capability education. School officials might wish to consider bringing in outside experts who can offer workshops to parents of highly capable children. This might be done in conjunction with local, regional, and state associations, as well as local colleges and universities. Julian Stanley adds,

We also need far better articulation of in-school efforts with out-of-school education facilitation, for example, summer academic programs, computer-based distance learning, AP examinations, talent contest participation, early-entrance-to-college residential programs, and college courses taken on a part-time basis while still in high school. (personal communication, May 2, 2003).

Finally, given the key role of parents in the growth and development of their children, advocates should work with school officials and teachers to assist them in nurturing their children's development. As appropriate, parents should attempt to take advantage of the wide range of services that may help them in guiding their highly capable children. Attending classes on effective parenting and child development and working with highly capable children could assist them in enhancing their children's chances for success.

As the nation enters the 21st century and is at the dawn the new millennium, it is time to redress the ongoing inequity of failing to provide equal and equitable educational opportunities for highly capable children. If these children are to reach their full potential, then educational leaders and policymakers need to consider ways to assist in their development for the children's own good and the welfare of the nation. To paraphrase the motto of the United Negro College Fund, wasting any human talent or capability is a terrible thing. It is especially true when that waste involves our greatest potential national asset for the future: the nation's talented children.

[References]

Abelman, R. (1991). Parental communications style and its influence on exceptional children's television viewing. *Roeper Review, 14,* 23–27.

Acton, W. R., & Walker de Felix, J. (1986). Acculturation and mind. In J. Valdes (Ed.), *Culture bound: Bridging the gap in language teaching* (pp. 20–32). Cambridge, England: Cambridge University Press.

Adams, D. W. (1995). *Education for extinction: American Indians and the boarding school experience, 1875–1928.* Lawrence: University Press of Kansas.

Adams, H. (1999). *Tortured people: The politics of colonization* (Rev. ed). Penticton, British Columbia: Theytus Books.

Adler, M. J. (1984). *The Paideia program: An educational syllabus.* New York: Macmillan.

Agresti, A. (1996). *Introduction to categorical data analysis.* New York: Wiley.

Aisenberg, E., & Mennen, F. (2000). Children exposed to community violence: Issues for assessment and treatment. *Child and Adolescent Social Work Journal, 17,* 341–360.

Alfred, T. (2002). Native American political traditions. In J. M. Meyer (Ed.), *American Indians and U.S. politics: A companion* (pp. 15–38). Westport, CT: Praeger.

Allen, R. (2002, May). Collaborative curriculum planning. *ASCD Education Update, 44*(3), 1, 4–5, 8.

Allport, G. W., Vernon, P. E., & Lindzey, G. (1970). *Manual for the Study of Values* (3rd ed.). Boston: Houghton Mifflin.

Althen, G. (1988). *American ways.* Yarmouth, ME: Intercultural Press.

American Association for the Advancement of Science. (1990). *Science for all Americans.* New York: Oxford University Press.

American Educational Research Association, National Council on Measurement in Education, & American Psychological Association. (1999). *Standards for educational and psychological testing.* Washington, DC: American Educational Research Association.

American Indian Education Handbook Committee. (1991). *The American Indian: Yesterday, today, and tomorrow: A handbook for educators.* Sacramento: California Department of Education.

Anderson, D. (2002, October). *Asia's best MBA schools: What you need to know about the region's world-class business schools.* Retrieved December 19, 2003, from http://www.asia-inc.com/September/mba_asias_sep.htm

Andrews, J. F. (1989). Wang Yani and contemporary Chinese painting. In W. C. Ho (Ed.), *Yani: The brush of innocence* (pp. 39–50). New York: Hudson Hills Press.

Apter, A., Reisine, S., Affleck, G., Barrows, E., & ZuWallack, R. (1999). The influence of demographic and socioeconomic factors on health-related quality of life in asthma. *Journal of Allergy and Clinical Immunology, 103,* 72–78.

Archambault, F. X., Jr., Westberg, K. L., Brown, S., Hallmark, B. W., Emmons, C., & Zhang, W. (1993). *Regular classroom practices with gifted students: Results of a national survey of classroom teachers.* Storrs: The National Research Center on the Gifted and Talented, University of Connecticut.

Armas, G. C. (2002, July 18). Study shows dollar value of staying in school. *Palm Beach Post*, p. 2A.

Arnheim, R. (1995). Foreword. In C. Golomb (Ed.), *The development of artistically gifted children* (pp. vii-viii). Hillsdale, NJ: Erlbaum.

Arnheim, R. (1997). Ancient Chinese aesthetics and its modernity. *British Journal of Aesthetics, 37,* 155–157.

Arnold, K. D. (1995). Academically talented women in the 1980's: The Illinois Valedictorian Project. In K. D. Hulbert & D. L. Schuster (Eds.), *Women's lives through time: Educated American women of the twentieth century* (pp. 393–414). San Francisco: Jossey-Bass.

Aronson, J., Lustina, M. J., Good, C., Keough, K., Steele, C. M., & Brown, J. (1999). When White men can't do math: Necessary and sufficient factors in stereotype threat. *Journal of Experimental Social Psychology, 35,* 29–46.

Aronson, J., & Salinas, M. F. (1998). *Stereotype threat, attributional ambiguity, and Latino underperformance.* Unpublished manuscript, University of Texas at Austin.

AsiaWeek.com. (2000). *AsiaWeek.com special report: Asia's best universities 2000: Overall rankings: Science and technology schools.* Retrieved October 20, 2002, from http://www.asiaweek.com/asiaweek/features/universities2000/scitech/sci.overall.html

Association of American Universities. (1997, April 14). *On the importance of diversity in higher education.* Retrieved from February 5, 2004, from http://www.aau.edu/issues/Diversity4.14.97.html

Assouline, S. G. (2003). Psychological and educational assessment of gifted children. In N. Colangelo & G. A. Davis (Eds.), *Handbook of gifted education* (3rd ed., pp. 124–145). Boston: Allyn and Bacon.

Aylward, G. (1992). The relationship between environmental risk and developmental outcome. *Developmental and Behavioral Pediatrics, 13,* 222–229.

Aylward, G. P. (2003). Cognitive function in preterm infants: No simple answers. *JAMA: Journal of the American Medical Association, 289,* 752–753.

Bacani, C. (2000). *Masters of e-commerce.* Retrieved October 20, 2002, from http://www.asiaweek.com/asiaweek/features/mba/index.html

Banks, J. A. (1999). *Introduction to multicultural education* (2nd ed.). Boston: Allyn and Bacon.

Banks, J. A., & Banks C. A. (1996). *Teaching strategies for ethnic studies* (6th ed.). Boston: Allyn and Bacon.

Barbe, W. B. (1954). Differentiated guidance for the gifted. *Education, 74,* 306–311.

Barbe, W. B. (1981). A study of the family background of the gifted. In W. B. Barbe & J. Renzulli (Eds.), *Psychology and education of the gifted* (3rd ed., pp. 302–309). New York: Irvington.

Barnett, L. B., & Durden, W. G. (1993). Education patterns of academically talented youth. *Gifted Child Quarterly, 37,* 161–168.

Bartkovich, K. G., & Mezynski, K. (1981). Fast-paced precalculus mathematics for talented junior-high students: Two recent SMPY programs. *Gifted Child Quarterly, 25,* 73–80.

Bassuk, E., Weinreb, L., Dawson, R., Perloff, J., & Buckner, J. (1997). Determinants of behavior in homeless and low-income-housed preschool children. *Pediatrics, 100*(1), 92–100.

Battle, J. (1999). How the boyz really made it out of the hood: Educational outcomes for African-American boys in fathers-only versus mothers-only households. *Race, Gender, & Class, 6,* 130–146.

Battle, J., & Lewis, M. (2002). The increasing significance of class: The relative effects of race and socioeconomic status on academic achievement. *Journal of Poverty, 6*(2), 21–35.

Baum, S. M., Renzulli, J. S., & Hébert, T. P. (1995). Reversing underachievement: Creative productivity as a systematic intervention. *Gifted Child Quarterly, 39*, 224–235.

Baumgarten, F. (1930). *Wunderkinder: Psychologische untersuchungen.* Leipzig: Johann Ambrosius Barth.

Beach, M. (1988). Family relationships of gifted adolescents: Strong or stressed? *Roeper Review, 10*, 169–172.

Bean, F. D., & Tienda, M. (1987). *The Hispanic population of the United States.* New York: Russell Sage Foundation.

Beane, J. A. (2002). Beyond self-interest: A democratic core curriculum. *Educational Leadership, 59*(7), 25–28.

Bearer, C. (1995). Environmental health hazards: How children are different from adults. *The Future of Children: Critical Issues for Children and Youth, 5*(2), 11–26.

Beck, W. (1928). *Romano Dazzi: Self-development in drawing as interpreted by the genius of Romano Dazzi.* New York: G. P. Putnam's Sons/Knickerbocker Press.

Becker, L. (1980). *With eyes wide open* [Motion picture]. Austin TX: Creative Learning Environments.

Bee, H. (1997). *The developing child.* New York: Longman.

Beer, W. (1987, May/June). Resolute ignorance: Social science and affirmative action. *Society, 24*(4), 63–69.

Benbow, C. P. (1992). Academic achievement in mathematics and science of students between ages 13 and 23: Are there differences among students in the top one percent of mathematical ability? *Journal of Educational Psychology, 84*, 51–61.

Benbow, C., & Stanley, J. (1983). *Academic precocity.* Baltimore, MD: Johns Hopkins University Press.

Benbow, C. P., & Stanley, J. C. (1996). Inequity in equity: How "equity" can lead to inequity for high-potential students. *Psychology, Public Policy, and Law, 2*, 249–292.

Berlin, D. F. (1991). *A bibliography of integrated science and mathematics teaching and learning literature* (School Science and Mathematics Association topics for teachers series No. 6). Bowling Green, OH: School Science and Mathematics Association.

Bernol, E. M. (2002). Three ways to achieve a more equitable representation of culturally and linguistically different students in GT programs. *Roeper Review, 24*, 82–88.

Bernstein, H. T. (1985). The new politics of textbook adoption. *Phi Delta Kappan, 66*, 463–466.

Better Homes Fund. (1999). *America's homeless children: New outcasts.* Newton, MA: Author.

Betts, G. T., & Knapp, J. K. (1981). Autonomous learning and the gifted. In A. Arnold & L. Arnold (Eds.), *Secondary programs for the gifted/talented* (pp. 29–36). Ventura, CA: Office of Ventura County Superintendent of Schools.

Bickel, R., Smith, C., & Eagle, T. (2002). Poor, rural neighborhoods and early school achievement. *Journal of Poverty, 6*(3), 89–108.

Black, M., & Krishnakumar, A. (1998). Children in low-income, urban settings. *American Psychologist, 53*, 635–646.

Bland, L. C., Sowa, C. J., & Callahan, C. M. (1994). An overview of resilience in gifted children. *Roeper Review, 17*, 77–80.

Bleske-Rechek, A., Lubinski, D., & Benbow, C. P. (in press). Meeting the educational needs of special populations: Advanced Placement's role in developing exceptional human capital. *Psychological Science.*

Bloom, B. (Ed.). (1985). *Developing talent in young people.* New York: Ballantine Press.

Board of Education v. Rowley, 458 US 176 (1982).

Bok, D. (1991). What's wrong with our universities? *Harvard Journal of Law & Public Policy, 14,* 305–333.

Boss, P. G., Doherty, W. J., LaRossa, R., Schumm, W. R., & Steinmetz, S. K. (Eds.). (1993). *Sourcebook of family theories and methods: A contextual approach.* New York: Plenum Press.

Bouillion, L. M., & Gomez, L. M. (2001). Connecting school and community with science learning: Real world problems and school-community partnerships as contextual scaffolds. *Journal of Research in Science Teaching, 38,* 878–898.

Bowen, W. G., & Bok, D. (1998). *The shape of the river.* Princeton, NJ: Princeton University Press.

Boyce, L. N., VanTassel-Baska, J., Burruss, J. D., Sher, B. T., & Johnson, D. T. (1997). A problem-based curriculum: Parallel learning opportunities for students and teachers. *Journal for the Education of the Gifted, 20,* 363–379.

Boykin, A. W. (1994). Afrocultural expression and its implications for schooling. In E. R. Hollins, J. E. King, & W. C. Hayman (Eds.), *Teaching diverse populations: Formulating a knowledge base* (pp. 225–273). New York: State University of New York Press.

Bradley, R., Whiteside, L., Mudfrom, D., Casey, P., Kelleher, K., & Pope, S. (1994). Contributions of early intervention and early caregiving experiences to resilience in low-birthweight, premature children living in poverty. *Journal of Clinical Child Psychology, 23,* 425–434.

Brescia, W., & Fortune, J. C. (1988). *American Indian education: Standardized testing of American Indian students.* Charleston, WV: ERIC Clearinghouse on Rural Education and Small Schools. (ERIC Document Reproduction Service No. EDO-RC-88-15)

Breslau, N., Davis, G., Andreski, P., Federman, B., & Anthony, J. (1998). Epidemiological findings on posttraumatic stress disorders in the general population. In B. Dohrenwend (Ed.), *Adversity, stress, and psychopathology* (pp. 319–340). New York: Oxford University Press.

Britsch, G. *Theorie der bildenden Kunst* (E. Kornmann, Ed.). Munich: Bruckman.

Brody, L. E. (2001). The talent search model for meeting the academic needs of gifted and talented students. *Gifted and Talented International, 16,* 99–102.

Brody, L. E., & Benbow, C. P. (1987). Accelerative strategies: How effective are they for the gifted? *Gifted Child Quarterly, 31,* 105–110.

Brody, L. E., & Blackburn, C. P. (1996). Nurturing exceptional talent: SET as a legacy of SMPY. In C. P. Benbow & D. Lubinski (Eds.), *Intellectual talent* (pp. 246–265). Baltimore: Johns Hopkins University Press.

Brody, L. E., & Fox, L. H. (1980). An accelerative intervention program for mathematically gifted girls. In L. H. Fox, L. Brody, & D. Tobin (Eds.), *Women and the mathematical mystique* (pp. 164–178). Hillsdale, NJ: Erlbaum.

Brody, L. E., & Mills, C. J. (1997). Gifted children with learning disabilities: A review of the issues. *Journal of Learning Disabilities, 30,* 282–296.

Brody, L. E., & Stanley, J. C. (1991). Young college students: Assessing factors that contribute to success. In W. T. Southern & E. D. Jones (Eds.), *The academic acceleration of gifted children* (pp. 102–131). New York: Teachers College Press.

Brody, N. (2003). Construct validation of the Sternberg Triarchic Abilities Test: Comment and reanalysis. *Intelligence, 31,* 319–329.

Brooks-Gunn, J., & Duncan, G. (1997). The effects of poverty on children. *The Future of Children: Children and Poverty, 7*(2), 55–71.

Brown v. Board of Education of Topeka, Kansas, 347 U.S. 483 (1954).

Brown, H. D. (1986). Learning a second culture. In J. Valdes (Ed.), *Culture bound: Bridging the gap in language teaching* (pp. 33–48). Cambridge, England: Cambridge University Press.

Brown, H. D. (1994). *Principles of language learning and teaching.* Englewood Cliffs, NJ: Prentice Hall Regents.

Brown, J. H., D'Emidio-Caston, M., & Bernard, B. (2001). *Resilience education.* Thousand Oaks, CA: Corwin Press.

Brown, L. L. (1993). Special considerations in counseling the gifted. *School Counselor, 40,* 184–191.

Brown, S. G. (2000). *Critical literacy in the borderlands.* Albany: State University of New York Press.

Buck, C. (1921). *Mental and scholastic tests.* London: P. S. King & Son.

Buck, L. (1991). Creativity in the retarded. *Empirical Studies of the Arts, 9*(1), 75–95.

Buck, L., Kardeman, E., & Goldstein, F. (1985). Artistic talent in "autistic" adolescents and young adults. *Empirical Studies of the Arts, 3*(1), 81–104.

Buckner, J., & Bassuk, E. (1997). Mental disorders and service utilization among youths from homeless and low-income housed families. *Journal of the American Academy of Child and Adolescent Psychiatry, 36,* 890–900.

Buka, S., Stichick, T., Birdthistle, I., & Earls, F. (2001). Youth exposure to violence: Prevalence, risks and consequences. *American Journal of Orthopsychiatry, 71,* 298–310.

Bukstein, D. (1996). Practical approach to the use of outcomes in asthma: Traveling the road to better asthmatic care. *Immunology and Allergy Clinics of North America, 16,* 859–891.

Burt, C. (1921). *Mental and scholastic tests.* London: P. S. King & Son.

Burton, N. W. (1988). *Young SAT-takers: Two surveys. Survey II: Test-taking history for 1980–81 young SAT-takers* (College Board Report No. 88-1). New York: College Entrance Examination Board.

Cajete, G. A. (1994). *Look toward the mountain: An ecology of indigenous education.* Durango, CO: Kivaki Press.

Callahan, C. M., & Kaufman, J. M. (1982). Involving gifted children's parents: Federal law is silent but its assumptions apply. *Exceptional Education Quarterly, 33,* 50–55.

Calmes, D., Leake, B., & Carlisle, D. (1998). Adverse asthma outcomes among children hospitalized with asthma in California. *Pediatrics, 101,* 845–850.

Campbell, B. M. (1984, December). To be Black, gifted, and alone. *Savvy,* 67–74.

Campbell, D. T., & Stanley, J. C. (1966). *Experimental and quasi-experimental designs for research.* Chicago: Rand McNally.

Campbell, P., & Clewell, B. C. (1999, September 15). Science, math and girls: Still a long way to go. *Education Week,* 50–51.

Carroll, J. B. (1993). *Human cognitive abilities: A survey of factor-analytic studies.* New York: Cambridge University Press.

Carroll, J. B. (1996). A three-stratum theory of intelligence: Spearman's contributions. In I. Dennis & P. Tapsfield (Eds.), *Human abilities: Their nature and measurement* (pp. 1–17). Mahwah, NJ: Erlbaum.

Castellano, J. A. (2003). *Special populations in gifted education: Working with diverse gifted learners.* Boston: Allyn and Bacon.

Castellano, J. A., & Diaz, E. I. (2002) *Reaching new horizons: Gifted and talented education for culturally and linguistically diverse students.* Boston: Allyn and Bacon.

Chen, G. (1990). The compilation of young children's non-intellectual personality inventory. In Cooperative Research Group for Supernormal Children in China (CRGSCC) (Ed.), *Selected works on supernormal children of the last ten years in P.R. China* (pp. 144–150). Beijing: Tuanjie Publishing House.

Chen, G., & Shu, D. (1990). Comparative study on perceptual ability of supernormal and normal children from age 7 to 12. In Cooperative Research Group for Supernormal Children in China (CRGSCC) (Ed.), *Selected works on supernormal children of the last ten years in P.R. China* (pp. 217–219). Beijing: Tuanjie Publishing House.

Chhibber, K. (2002a, April). "The young and the restless"—What does it mean to be young and South Asian in America? *Khabar,* 64–74.

Chhibber, K. (2002b, June). Parenting in America. *Khabar,* 26–38.

Christopher, K. (2002). Single motherhood, employment, or social assistance: Why are U.S. women poorer than women in other affluent nations? *Journal of Poverty,* 6(2), 61–79.

Cicchetti, D., Ganihan, J., & Barnett, D. (1991). Contributions from the study of high-risk populations to understanding the development of emotion regulation. In J. Garber & K. Dodge (Eds.), *The development of emotion regulation and dysregulation* (pp. 15–48). New York: Cambridge University Press.

Clark, B. (2002). *Growing up gifted: Developing the potential of children at home and at school* (6th ed.). Upper Saddle River, NJ: Prentice Hall.

Clark, G. (1993). Judging children's drawings as measures of art abilities. *Studies in Art Education, 34*(2), 72–81.

Clark, G., & Zimmerman, E. (1992). *Issues and practices related to identification of gifted and talented students in the visual art.* Storrs: National Research Center on the Gifted and Talented, University of Connecticut.

Claus, J., & Ogden, C. (1999). *Service learning for youth empowerment and social change.* New York: Lang.

Cohen, L. M. (1990). *Meeting the needs of gifted and talented language minority students* (ERIC Digest #E480). (ERIC Document Reproduction Service No. ED321485)

Cohen, L. M., Ambrose, D., & Powell, W. N. (2000). Conceptual foundations and theoretical lenses for the diversity of giftedness and talent. In K. A. Heller, F. J. Mönks, R. J. Sternberg, & R. F. Subotnik (Eds.), *International handbook of giftedness and talent* (2nd ed., pp. 331–344). Oxford: Elsevier Science.

Cohn, S. J., Carlson, J. S., & Jensen, A. R. (1985). Speed of information processing in academically gifted youths. *Personality and Individual Differences,* 6, 621–629.

Colangelo, N. (1997). Counseling gifted students. In N. Colangelo and G. A. Davis (Eds.), *Handbook of gifted education* (2nd ed., pp. 353–365). Boston: Allyn and Bacon.

Colangelo, N., & Davis, G.A. (1997). *Handbook of gifted education* (2nd ed.). Boston: Allyn and Bacon.

Colangelo, N., & Davis, G.A. (2003). *Handbook of gifted education* (3rd ed.). Boston: Pearson Education.

Colangelo, N., & LaFrenz, N. (1981). Counseling the culturally diverse gifted. *Gifted Child Quarterly, 25,* 27–30.

Coleman, L. J., & Cross, T. L. (2000). Social-emotional development and the personal experience of giftedness. In K. A. Heller, F. J. Mönks, R. J. Sternberg, & R. F. Subotnik (Eds.), *International handbook of giftedness and talent* (2nd ed., pp. 203–212). Oxford: Elsevier Science.

College Board. (2001). *2001 College bound seniors are the largest, most diverse group in history*. Retrieved August 8, 2002, from http://www.collegeboard.com/press/sat/cbsenior/yr2001/pdf/completecbsreport.pdf

College Board. (2002). *The utility of the SAT I and the SAT II for Admissions Decisions in California and the Nation*. Retrieved August 19, 2002, from http://www.collegeboard.com/repository/cbreport20026_10771.pdf

College Board National Taskforce on Minority High-Achievement. (1999). *Reaching the top*. Retrieved August 15, 2000, from http://www.collegeboard.com/repository/reachingthe_3952.pdf

Collier, V. P. (1987). Age and rate of acquisition of second language for academic purposes. *TESOL Quarterly, 21*, 617–641.

Committee on Minority Representation in Special Education. (2002). *Minority students in special and gifted education* (M. S. Donovan & C. T. Cross, Eds.). Washington, DC: National Academy Press.

Coner-Edwards, A. F., & Edwards, J. (1988). The Black middle class: Definitions and demographics. In A. F. Coner-Edwards & J. Spurlock (Eds.), *Black families in crisis: The middle class* (pp. 1–9). New York: Brunner/Mazel.

Cooksey, E. (1997). Consequences of young mothers' marital histories for children's cognitive development. *Journal of Marriage and Family, 59*, 245–261.

Cornell, D. G. (1983). Gifted children: The impact of positive labeling on the family system. *American Journal of Orthopsychiatry, 53*, 322–335.

Cornell, D. G., & Grossberg, I. N. (1987). Family environment and personality adjustment in gifted program children. *Gifted Child Quarterly, 31*, 59–64.

Corwin, M. (2000). *And still we rise*. New York: Morrow.

Corwin, M. (2001). *And still we rise: The trials and triumphs of twelve gifted inner-city high school students*. New York: Harper Perennial.

Cose, E. (1993). *The rage of a privileged class*. New York: HarperCollins.

Cox, M., & Bragal, C. (1985). The representation of spatial relationships in the drawings of ESN (M) and normal children. *Educational Psychology, 5*, 279–286.

Crocker, A. C. (1987). Underachieving, gifted working class boys: Are they wrongly labeled underachieving? *Educational Studies, 13*, 169–178.

Cross, T. (1997). Guiding and supporting the development of gifted children: Part I. *Gifted Child Today, 21*(5), 46–47, 49.

Cross, T. L. (2002). Competing with myths about the social and emotional development of gifted students. *Gifted Child Today, 25*(3), 44–45.

Cross, W. E., Jr., & Vandiver, B. J. (2001). Nigrescence theory and measurement: Introducing the Cross Racial Identity Scale (CRIS). In J. G. Ponterotto, J. M. Casas, L. A. Suzuki, & C. M. Alexander (Eds.), *Handbook of multicultural counseling* (2nd ed., pp. 371–393). Thousand Oaks, CA: Sage.

Csikszentmihalyi, M., & Getzels, J.W. (1988). Creating and problem-finding in art. In F. H. Farley & R. W. Neperud (Eds.), *The foundations of aesthetics, art, and education*, (pp. 91–106), New York: Praeger.

Csikszentmihalyi, M., Rathunde, K., & Whalen, S. (1993). *Talented teenagers: The roots of success and failure*. New York: Cambridge University Press.

Cummins, J. (1981). The role of primary language development in promoting educational success for language minority students. In California State Department of Education, *Schooling and language minority students: A theoretical framework* (pp. 3–49). Los Angeles: California State Department of Education.

Cummins, J. (2000). *Language, power, and pedagogy.* Clevedon, England: Multilingual Matters.

Davison, D. M., Miller, K. W., & Methany, D. L. (1995). What does integration of science and mathematics really mean? *School Science and Mathematics, 95,* 226–230.

Deary, I. J. (2000). *Looking down on human intelligence: From psychometrics to the brain.* Oxford: Oxford University Press.

Daniels, S. (1997). Creativity in the classroom: Characteristics, climate, and curriculum. In N. Colangelo and G. A. Davis (Eds.), *Handbook of gifted education* (2nd ed., pp. 292–307). Boston: Allyn and Bacon.

Delbanco, D. H. (1989). Monkeys in Chinese art and culture. In W. C. Ho (Ed.), *Yani: The brush of innocence* (pp. 27–38). New York: Hudson Hill Press.

Delisle, J. R. (1992). *Guiding the social and emotional development of gifted youth.* New York: Longman.

Denetclaw, W. F., Jr. (2002). *Not so wild a dream.* Keynote address presented at a meeting of the Health Professions for American Indian Students, Boise State University, Boise, ID.

De Tocqueville, A. (1840). *Democracy in America.* Chicago: University of Chicago Press.

Dewey, J. (1902). *The school and society.* Chicago: University of Chicago Press.

Diaz, E. I. (1999). Hispanic Americans. In A. Y. Baldwin & W. Vialle (Eds.), *The many faces of giftedness: Lifting the mask* (pp. 23–44). Toronto, Canada: Wadsworth.

Diaz, E. I. (2002). Introduction. In J. A. Castellano & E. I. Diaz (Eds.), *Reaching new horizons: Gifted and talented education for culturally and linguistically diverse students.* (p. xxii). Boston: Allyn and Bacon.

Diffily, D. (2002). Project-based learning: Meeting social studies standards and the needs of gifted learners. *Gifted Child Today, 25*(3), 40–43, 59.

Dimitriou, A., & Valanides, N. (1998). A three-level theory of the developing mind. Basic principles and implications for instruction and assessment. In. R. Sternberg & W. Williams (Eds.), *Intelligence, instruction, and assessment: Theory into practice* (pp. 149–199). Mahwah, NJ: Erlbaum.

Donahue, P. L., Voelkl, K. E., Campbell, J. R., & Mazzeo, J. (1999). *NAEP 1998 reading report card for the nation and the states.* Washington, DC: U.S. Department of Education, Office of Educational Research and Improvement.

D'Souza, D. (1995). *The end of racism.* New York: The Free Press.

Duncan, G., Brooks-Gunn, J., Yeung, W., & Smith, J. (1998). How much does childhood poverty affect the life chances of children? *American Sociological Review, 63,* 406–423.

Duncan, J., Seitz, R. J., Kolodny, J., Bir, D., Herzog, H., Ahmed, A., Newell, F. N., & Emslie, H. (2000). A neural basis for general intelligence. *Science, 289,* 457–460.

Duncum, P. (1981). Children's spontaneous drawing and environmental influences. *Visual Arts Monographs, 1*(2), 1–22.

Duncum, P. (1984). How 35 children, born between 1724–1900, learned to draw. *Studies in Art Education, 26*(1), 93–102.

Duncum, P. (1986). *Middle childhood spontaneous drawing from a cultural perspective.* Unpublished doctoral dissertation, Flinders University of South Australia.

Durden, W. G., & Tangherlini, A. E. (1993). *Smart kids.* Seattle, WA: Hogrefe & Huber.

Eamon, M. K. (2002). Influences and mediators of the effect of poverty on young adolescent's depressive symptoms. *Journal of Youth and Adolescence, 31,* 231–242.

Ebmeier, H., & Schmulbach, S. (1989). An examination of the selection practices used in the talent search program. *Gifted Child Quarterly, 33,* 134–143.

Education of All Handicapped Children Act (Pub.L. 94-142) (1975).

Educational Policies Commission. (1950). *Education of the gifted.* Washington, DC: National Education Association and American Association of School Administrators.

Elementary and Secondary Education Act of 1965 (Pub. L. 89–750), subsequently amended by legislation in 1969, "Provisions Related to Gifted & Talented Children" (Pub. L. 91-230).

Enersen, D. (1993). Summer residential programs: Academics and beyond. *Gifted Child Quarterly, 37,* 169–176.

Evans, G. W., & Maxwell, L. (1997). Chronic noise exposure and reading deficits: The mediating effects of language acquisition. *Environment and Behavior, 29,* 638–656.

Faltis, C. (1993). From kindergarten to high school: Teaching and learning English as a second language in the U.S. In S. Silberstein (Ed.), *State of the art TESOL essays: Celebrating 25 years of the discipline* (pp. 91–114). Alexandria, VA: Teachers of English to Speakers of Other Languages.

Fatt, J. P. T. (1999). Innovative curricula: Involving the community in novel ways. *Journal of Instructional Psychology, 26,* 151–160.

Feldhusen, J. F. (1998). A conception of talent and talent development. In R. C. Friedman & K. B. Rogers (Eds.), *Talent in context: Historical and social perspectives on giftedness* (pp. 193–209). Washington, DC: American Psychological Association.

Feldhusen, J. F., & Jarwan, F. A. (2000). Identification of gifted and talented youth for educational programs. In K. A. Heller, F. J. Mönks, R. J. Sternberg, & R. F. Subotnik (Eds.), *International Handbook of Giftedness and Talent* (2nd ed., pp. 271–282). Oxford: Elsevier Science.

Feldhusen, J. F., & Treffinger, D. J. (1985). *Creative thinking and problem solving in gifted education.* Dubuque, IA: Kendall/Hunt.

Feldhusen, J. F., & Willard-Holt, C. (1993). Gender differences in classroom interactions and career aspirations of gifted students. *Contemporary Educational Psychology, 18,* 355–362.

Fetterman, D. M. (1988). *Excellence & equality: A qualitatively different perspective on gifted and talented education.* Albany: State University of New York.

Fineberg, J. (1997). *The innocent eye.* Princeton, NJ: Princeton University Press.

Finkelstein, Y., Markowitz, M., & Rosen, J. (1998). Low level lead-induced neurotoxicity in children: An update on central nervous system effect. *Brain Research in Review, 27,* 168–176.

Ford, D. Y. (1992). Determinants of underachievement as perceived by gifted, above-average, and average Black students. *Roeper Review, 14,* 130–136.

Ford, D. Y. (1994). *The recruitment and retention of African American students in gifted education programs: Implication and recommendations* (RBDM 9406). Storrs: National Research Center on the Gifted and Talented, University of Connecticut.

Ford, D. Y. (1995a). *Correlates of underachievement among gifted and non-gifted Black students.* Storrs: National Research Center on the Gifted and Talented, University of Connecticut.

Ford, D. Y. (1995b). Desegregating gifted education: A need unmet. *Journal of Negro Education, 64,* 52–62.

Ford, D. Y. (1996). *Reversing underachievement among gifted Black students: Promising practices and programs.* New York: Teachers College Press.

Ford, D. Y. (1998). The under-representation of minority students in gifted education: Problems and promises in recruitment and retention. *Journal of Special Education, 32*(1), 4–14.

Ford, D. Y. (2003). Equity and excellence: Culturally diverse students in gifted education. In N. Colangelo & G. A. Davis (Eds.), *Handbook of gifted education* (3rd ed., pp. 506–520). Boston: Allyn and Bacon.

Ford, D. Y., & Frazier Trotman, M. (2001). Teachers of gifted students: Suggested multicultural characteristics and competencies. *Roeper Review, 23*, 235–239.

Ford, D. Y., & Harmon, D. (2001). Equity and excellence: Providing access to gifted education for culturally diverse students. *Journal of Secondary Gifted Education, 12*, 141–147.

Ford, D. Y., & Harris, J. J., III. (1990). On discovering the hidden treasures of gifted and talented Black children. *Roeper Review, 13*, 27–32.

Ford, D. Y. & Harris, J. J., III. (1999). *Multicultural gifted education*. New York: Teachers College Press.

Ford, D. Y., Harris, J. J., III, Tyson, C. A., & Frazier Trotman, M. (2002). Beyond deficit thinking: Providing access for gifted African American students. *Roeper Review, 24*, 52–58.

Fordham, S. (1988). Racelessness as a strategy in African-American students' school success: Pragmatic strategy or pyrrhic victory? *Harvard Educational Review, 58*, 54–84.

Fordham, S., & Ogbu, J. (1986). African-American students' school success: Coping with the "burden of 'acting White.'" *Urban Review, 18*, 176–203.

Fox, L. H. (1977). Sex differences: Implications for programs planning for the academically gifted. In J. C. Stanley, W. C. George, & C. H. Solano (Eds.), *The gifted and the creative: A fifty-year perspective* (pp. 113–138). Baltimore: Johns Hopkins University Press.

Fox, L. H., Brody, L., & Tobin, D. (1985). The impact of early intervention programs upon course-taking and attitudes in high school. In S. F. Chipman, L. R. Brush, & D. M. Wilson (Eds.), *Women and mathematics: Balancing the equation* (pp. 249–274). Hillsdale, NJ: Erlbaum.

Fox, S. J. (2000). *Standards-based reform and American Indian/Alaska Native Education*. Paper presented at the National American Indian and Alaska Native Education Research Agenda Conference, Albuquerque, NM.

Frasier, M. M., Garcia, J. H., & Passow, A. H. (1995). *A review of assessment issues in gifted education and their implications for identifying gifted minority children*. Storrs: National Research Center on the Gifted and Talented, University of Connecticut.

Frasier, M. M., Martin, D., Garcia, J., Finley, V. S., Frank, E., Krisel, S., & King, L. L. (1995). *A new window for looking at gifted children*. Storrs: National Research Center on the Gifted and Talented, University of Connecticut.

Frasier, M. M., & Passow, A. H. (1994). *Towards a new paradigm for identifying talent potential* (Research Monograph 94412). Storrs: National Research Center on the Gifted and Talented, University of Connecticut.

Frederickson, R. J., & Rothney, J. W. M. (1972). *Recognizing and assisting multipotential youth*. Columbus, OH: Merrill.

Freedman, E. B. (2002). *No turning back: The history of feminism and the future of women*. New York: Ballantine.

Friedman, R. C., & Gallagher, R. J. (1994). Upstream helping for low-income families of gifted students: Challenges and opportunities. *Journal of Educational and Psychological Consultation, 5*, 321–338.

Gagné, F. (2003). Transforming gifts into talents: The DMGT as a developmental theory. In N. Colangelo & G. A. Davis (Eds.), *Handbook of gifted education* (3rd ed., pp. 60–74). Boston: Allyn and Bacon.

Galindo, E., & Reinhart, B. (1999). *Indian summer V: Student Streamside Northwest Salmon and Steelhead Incubation Project 1999.* Arco, ID: INEEL Technical Publications.

Gallagher, J. J. (1988). National agenda for educating gifted students: Statement of priorities. *Exceptional Child, 55,* 107–114.

Gallagher, J. J. (2003). Issues and challenges in gifted education. In N. Colangelo & G. A. Davis (Eds.), *Handbook of gifted education* (3rd ed., pp. 11–23). Boston: Allyn and Bacon.

Gallagher, S. A., Stepien, W. J., Sher, B. T., & Workman, D. (1995). Implementing problem-based learning in science classrooms. *School Science and Mathematics, 95,* 136–146.

Gardner, H. (1983) *Frames of mind: The theory of multiple intelligences.* New York: BasicBooks.

Gardner, H. (1991). Assessment in context: The alternative to standardized testing. In B. R. Gifford & M. C. O'Connor (Eds.), *Changing assessments: Alternative views of aptitude, achievement, and instruction.* Boston: Kluwer.

Gardner, H. (1993). *Multiple intelligences: The theory into practice.* New York: BasicBooks.

Gardner, H. (1995). Reflections on multiple intelligences: Myths and messages. *Phi Delta Kappan, 77,* 200–209.

Gardner, H. (1999a). *Intelligence reframed: Multiple intelligences for the 21st century reframed.* New York: BasicBooks.

Gardner, H. (1999b). *The disciplined mind: What all students should know and understand.* New York: Simon & Schuster.

Georgia Department of Education, State Board of Education. *160-4-2-.38: Education program for gifted students.* (1998). Retrieved April 21, 2003, from http://www.doe.k12.ga.us/doe/legalservices/rules_db.asp?u_order=NSBA_Code

Getzels, J. W., & Csikszentmihalyi, M. (1976). *The creative vision: A longitudinal study of problem finding in art.* New York: Wiley.

Gibson, S., & Effinger, J. (2001). Revisiting the schoolwide enrichment model: An approach to gifted programming. *Teaching Exceptional Children, 33*(4), 48–53.

Gifted and Talented Children's Education Act of 1978 (Pub. L. 95-561).

Giftedness and the gifted: What's it all about? (ERIC Digest #E476). (1990). Reston, VA: The Council for Exceptional Children, ERIC Clearinghouse on Disabilities and Gifted Children. (ERIC Document Reproduction No. ED321481)

Glasser, W. (1998). *The quality school teacher* (Rev. ed.). New York: HarperCollins.

Goenjian, A., Karayan, I., Pynoos, R., Minassian, D., Najarian, L., Steinberg, A., & Fairbanks, L. (1997). Outcome of psychotherapy among early adolescents after trauma. *American Journal of Psychiatry, 154,* 536–543.

Goldsmith, L. T. (1992). Wang Yani: Stylistic development of a Chinese painting prodigy. *Creativity Research Journal, 5,* 281–293.

Goldsmith, L. T. (2000). Tracking trajectories of talent: Child prodigies growing up. In R. C. Friedman & B. M. Shore (Eds.), *Talents unfolding: Cognition and development* (pp. 89–117). Washington, DC: APA Books.

Goldsmith, L. T., & Feldman, D. H. (1989). Yani: Gifts well given. In W. C. Ho (Ed.), *Yani: The brush of innocence* (pp. 51–62). New York: Hudson Hill Press.

Goleman, D. (1997). *Emotional intelligence: Why it can matter more than IQ.* New York: Bantam Books.

Golomb, C. (1992a). Eytan: The early development of a precociously gifted child artist. *Creativity Research Journal, 5,* 265–279.

Golomb, C. (1992b). *The child's creation of a pictorial world.* Los Angeles: University of California Press.

Golomb, C. (Ed.). (1995). *The development of artistically gifted children*. Hillsdale, NJ: Erlbaum.

Golomb, C. (2002). *Child art in context: Cultural and comparative perspectives*. Washington, DC: APA Press.

Golomb, C. (2003). *The child's creation of a pictorial world* (2nd ed). Mahwah, NJ: Erlbaum.

Golomb, C., & Barr-Grossman, T. (1977). Representational development of the human figure in the familial retardate. *Genetic Psychology Monographs, 95*, 247–266.

Gong, Z., & Cheng, N. (1998). Identification and cultivation of supernormal children: 12 years education reform of experimental class for supernormal children in middle school. In Z. Zha (Ed.), *The mystery of the development of supernormal children: The collection of research on psychological development and education of supernormal children in China in the last twenty years* (pp. 250–265). Chongqing: Chongqing Publishing House.

Gonzales, A. A. (2001). Urban (trans)formations: Changes in the meaning and use of American Indian identity. In S. Lobo & K. Peters (Eds.), *American Indians and the urban experience* (pp. 169–185). New York: Altamira Press.

Gonzalez, J. (2000, February). Gifted minority students left behind. *Cleveland Plain Dealer*, pp. 6–7.

Goodenough, F. L. (1926). *Measurement of intelligence by drawing*. New York: Harcourt, Brace, and World.

Gordon, A. (1987). Childhood works of artists. *The Israel Museum Journal, 6*, 75–82.

Gottfredson, L. S. (1996). Racially gerrymandering the content of police tests to satisfy the U.S. Justice Department: A case study. *Psychology, Public Policy, and Law, 2*, 418–446.

Gottfredson, L. S. (1997). Why *g* matters: The complexity of everyday life. *Intelligence, 24*, 79–132.

Gottfredson, L. S. (2000, July/August). Equal potential: A collective fraud. *Society, 37*(4), 19–28.

Gottfredson, L. S. (2002). *g*: Highly general and highly practical. In R. J. Sternberg & E. L. Grigorenko (Eds.), *The general intelligence factor: How general is it?* (pp. 331–380). Mahwah, NJ: Erlbaum.

Gottfredson, L. S. (2003a). Dissecting practical intelligence theory: Its claims and evidence. *Intelligence, 31*, 343–397.

Gottfredson, L. S. (2003b). *Implications of cognitive differences for schooling within diverse societies*. Manuscript submitted for publication.

Gottfredson, L. S. (2003c). The science and politics of intelligence in gifted education. In N. Colangelo & G. A. Davis (Eds.), *Handbook of gifted education* (3rd ed., pp. 24–40). Boston: Allyn and Bacon.

Gould, J. B., & LeRoy, S. (1988). Socioeconomic status and low birth weight: A racial comparison. *Pediatrics, 82*, 896–904.

Gowan, J. C. (1979). Differentiated guidance for the gifted: A developmental view. In J. C. Gowan, J. Khatena, & E. P. Torrance (Eds.). *Educating the ablest: A book of readings on the education of gifted children* (pp. 190–199). Itasca, IL: Peacock Publishers.

Graham, H. D. (2002). *Collision course: The strange convergence of affirmative action and immigration policy in America*. New York: Oxford University Press.

Granada, A. J. (2002). Addressing the curriculum, instruction, and assessment needs of the gifted bilingual/bicultural student. In J. A. Castellano & E. I. Diaz (Eds.), *Reaching new horizons: Gifted and talented education for culturally and linguistically diverse students* (pp. 133–153). Boston: Allyn and Bacon.

Granada, A. J. (2003). Casting a wider net: Bilingual and gifted education. In J. A. Castellano (Ed.), *Special populations in gifted education: Working with diverse gifted learners* (pp. 1–16). Boston: Allyn and Bacon.

Grigorenko, E. L., Jarvin, L., & Sternberg, R. J. (2002). School-based tests of the Triarchic theory of intelligence: Three settings, three samples, three syllabi. *Contemporary Educational Psychology, 27,* 167–208.

Gross, M. U. M. (1998). The "me" behind the mask: Intellectually gifted students and the search for identity. *Roeper Review, 20,* 167–175.

Hack, M., & Fanaroff, A. (1999). Outcomes of children of extremely low birthweight and gestational age in the 1990's. *Early Human Development, 53,* 193–218.

Hack, M., Flannery, D., Schluchter, M., Cartar, L., Borawski, E., & Klein, N. (2002). Outcomes in young adulthood for very low birth weight infants. *New England Journal of Medicine, 346,* 149–157.

Hadley, A. O. (2001). *Teaching language in context* (3rd ed.). Boston: Heinle & Heinle.

Hale, J. E. (2002). *Learning while Black: Creating educational excellence for African American children.* Baltimore: The Johns Hopkins University Press.

Halfon, N., & Newacheck, P. W. (1993). Childhood asthma and poverty: Differential impacts and utilization of health services. *Pediatrics, 91,* 56–61.

Hall, M. (1996). Full circle: Native educational approaches show the way. *The Journal of Experiential Education, 19,* 141–144.

Halpern, D. F. (1989). The disappearance of cognitive gender differences: What you see depends on where you look. *American Psychologist, 44,* 1156–1158.

Halpern, D. F. (2000). *Sex differences in cognitive abilities.* Mahwah, NJ: Erlbaum.

Hambrick-Dixon, P. (1988). The effect of elevated subway train noise over time on Black children's visual vigilance performance. *Journal of Environmental Psychology, 8,* 299–314.

Hambrick-Dixon, P. (2002). The effects of exposure to physical environmental stressors on African American children: A review and research agenda. *Journal of Children and Poverty, 8(1),* 23–34.

Hanson, C., & Stone, C. (2002). Recruiting leaders to transform school counseling. *Theory Into Practice, 41,* 163–168.

Harrington, J. E., with Harrington, C., & Karns, E. (1991). The Marland Report: Twenty years later. *Journal for the Education of the Gifted, 15,* 31–43.

Harris, C. R. (1993). *Identifying and serving recent immigrant children who are gifted* (ERIC EC Digest #E520). (ERIC Document Reproduction Service No. ED358676)

Harris, D. B. (1963). *Children's drawings as measures of intellectual maturity.* New York: Harcourt, Brace, and World.

Harris, J. J., III, & Ford, D. Y. (1991). Identifying and nurturing the promise of gifted Black children. *Journal of Negro Education, 60,* 3–18.

Hatch, T., & Bowers, J. (2002). A block to build on: Elements of ASCA's national model for school counseling programs. *School Counselor, 39,* 12–17.

Hayes, R. L., & Paisley, P. O. (2002). Transforming school counselor preparation programs. *Theory Into Practice, 41,* 169–176.

Hébert, T. P. (2000). Defining belief in self: Intelligent young men in an urban high school. *Gifted Child Quarterly, 44,* 91–114.

Hejzlar, J. (1987). *Chinese water colors.* New York: Gallery Books.

Heller, K. A., Mönks, F. J., Sternberg, R. J., & Subotnik, R. F. (2002). *International handbook of giftedness and talent* (2nd ed.). Oxford: Elsevier Science.

Hermelin, B. (2001). *Bright splinters of the mind*. London: Kingsley.

Hermelin, B., & O'Connor, N. (1990). Art and accuracy: The drawing ability of idiot savants. *Journal of Child Psychology and Psychiatry, 31*, 217–228.

Hermelin, B., Pring, L., Buhler, M., Wolff, S., & Heaton, P. (1999). A visually impaired savant artist: Interacting perceptual and memory representations. *Journal of Child Psychology and Psychiatry, 40*, 1129–1139.

Herrnstein, R. J., & Murray, C. (1994). *The bell curve*. New York: The Free Press.

Hines, P. L. (2002). Transforming the rural school counselor. *Theory Into Practice, 41*, 192–201.

Hofstadter, R. (1963). *Anti-intellectualism in American life*. New York: Knopf.

Hollins, E. R. (1996). *Culture in school learning: Revealing the deep meaning*. Mahwah, NJ: Erlbaum.

Ho, W. C. (Ed.). (1989). *Yani: The brush of innocence*. New York: Hudson Hill Press.

Hong, D., Zhou, J., Wang, Y., & Xu, Z. (1989). The Chinese adolescent non-intellective personality inventory (CA-NPI) (1988 Edition): Its compilation and application. *Information on Psychological Science, 2*, 13–17.

Horner, M. (1972). Toward an understanding of achievement-related conflicts in women. *Journal of Social Issues, 28*, 157–175.

House, R. M., & Sears, S. J. (2002). Preparing school counselors to be leaders and advocates: A critical need in the new millennium. *Theory Into Practice, 41*, 154–162.

Howley, C. B., & Howley, A. (1995). The origins of anti-intellectualism in U.S. schools. In C. B. Hrabowski, F. A., Maton, K. I., Greene, M. L., & Greif, G. L. (2002). *Overcoming the odds: Raising academically successful African American young women*. NY: Oxford University Press.

Howley, C. B., Howley, A., & Pendarvis, E. D. (Eds.). (1995). *Out of our minds: Anti-intellectualism and talent development in American schooling*. New York: Teachers College.

Huang, L. (1990). Revision of memory sub-test of the Cognitive Ability Test for Identifying Supernormal Children (2nd version). In Cooperative Research Group for Supernormal Children in China (CRGSCC) (Ed.), *Selected works on supernormal children of the last ten years in P.R. China* (pp. 84–95). Beijing: Tuanjie Publishing House.

Indian Education Act of 1972, 20 U.S.C. § 3385 *et seq.* (U.S.C. 2000).

Indian Institute of Technology Bombay. (n.d.). Retrieved December 1, 2003, from http://www.cse.iitb.ac.in/~jee

Indian Self-Determination and Education Assistance Act of 1975, 25 U.S.C. § 450f. (U.S.C. 2000).

Individuals With Disabilities Education Act, 20 USC Section 1401 et seq. (1995).

Jackson, C. M. (1987). *Not to grow is to die: A counseling prototype for the gifted*. Unpublished manuscript, University of Alabama at Tuscaloosa.

Jackson, C. M., Snow, B. M., Boes, S. R., Phillips, P. L., Stanard, R. P., Painter, L. C., & Wulff, M. B. (2002). Inducting the transformed school counselor into the profession. *Theory Into Practice, 41*, 177–185.

Jackson, C. M., Snow, B. M., Phillips, P. L., Boes, S. R., & Rolle, G. E. (1999). Professional school counseling: A new vision at State University of West Georgia. *Georgia School Counselors Association Journal, 1*, 46–51.

Jacob K. Javits Gifted and Talented Students Act of 1994 (Pub. L. 103-382).

Jacob K. Javits Gifted and Talented Students Education Act of 2001, H.R. 490, 107th Cong. [section] 2(a)(8) (2001).

Jacob K. Javits Gifted and Talented Students Education Act of 2001 (Subpart 6–Gifted and Talented of No Child Left Behind ESEA Legislation). (2002). Retrieved May 27, 2003. from http://www.ed.gov/legislation/ESEA02/pg72.html

James, D. W., Jurich, S., Estes, S. (1999). *Raising minority academic achievement: A compendium of education programs and practices.* Washington, DC: American Youth Policy Forum.

Jamison, K. (1993). *Touched with fire: Manic-depressive illness and the artistic temperament.* New York: Free Press.

Janos, P. M., & Robinson, N. M. (1985). Psychological development in intellectually gifted children. In F. D. Horowitz & M. O'Brien (Eds.), *The gifted and talented: Developmental perspectives* (pp. 149–195). Washington, DC: American Psychological Association.

Jensen, A. R. (1987). Individual differences in the Hick paradigm. In P. A. Vernon (Ed.), *Speed of information-processing and intelligence* (pp. 101–175). Norwood, NJ: Ablex.

Jensen, A. R. (1992). The importance of intraindividual variability in reaction time. *Personality and Individual Differences, 13,* 869–882.

Jensen, A. R. (1993a). Why is reaction time correlated with psychometric *g? Current Directions in Psychological Science, 2,* 53–56.

Jensen, A. R. (1993b). Spearman's hypothesis tested with chronometric information processing tasks. *Intelligence, 17,* 47–77.

Jensen, A. R. (1997). The neurophysiology of *g.* In C. Cooper & V. Varma (Eds.), *Processes in individual differences* (pp. 108–125). London: Routledge.

Jensen, A. R. (1998). *The g factor: The science of mental ability.* Westport, CT: Praeger.

Jensen, A. R. (2000). The g factor: Psychometrics and biology. In *The Nature of Intelligence* (Novartis Foundation Symposium 233, pp. 37–47). New York: Wiley.

Jensen, A. R. (2002). Psychometric *g:* Definition and substantiation. In R. J. Sternberg & E. L. Grigorenko (Eds.), *The general factor of intelligence: How general is it?* Mahwah, NJ: Erlbaum.

Jensen, A. R., & Whang, P. A. (1994). Speed of accessing arithmetic facts in long-term memory: A comparison of Chinese-American and Anglo-American children. *Contemporary Educational Psychology, 191,* 1–12.

Jensen, L. (1999). *Developing mathematically promising students.* Reston, VA: National Council of Teachers of Mathematics.

Jencks, C., & Phillips, M. (1998). *The Black-White test score gap.* Washington, DC: Brookings Institution Press.

Johnsen, S. K. (2000). What the research says about curriculum. *Tempo, 23*(5), 25–30.

Johnson, K. (2001). Integrating an affective component in the curriculum for gifted and talented students. *Gifted Child Today, 24*(4), 14–18.

Juberg, D. R., Kleiman, C. F., & Kwon, S. C. (1997). Position paper of the American Council on Science and Health: Lead and human health. *Ecotoxicology Environmental Safety, 38*(3), 162–180.

Kandinsky, V. (1977). *Concerning the spiritual in art* (M. T. H. Sadler, Trans.). New York: Dover. (Original work published 1912)

Kane, T. J. (1998). Racial and ethnic preference in college admissions. In C. Jencks & M. Phillips (Eds.), *The Black-White test score gap* (pp. 431–56). Washington, DC: Brookings Institution Press.

Karnes, F. A. (2000). State definitions for the gifted and talented revisited. *Exceptional Children, 66,* 219–238.

Karnes, F. A., & Marquardt, R. G. (1997a). *Gifted children and the law.* Hattiesburg, MS: Great Potential Press.

Karnes, F. A., & Marquardt, R. G. (1997b). The fragmented framework of legal protection for the gifted. *Peabody Journal of Education, 72,* 166–179.

Kearney, K. (1998). Gifted children and homeschooling: Historical and contemporary perspectives. In S. Cline & K. Hegeman (Eds.), *Gifted education in the twenty-first century* (pp. 175–194). Delray Beach, FL: Winslow Press.

Keith, T. Z., & Cool, V. A. (1992). Testing models of school learning: Effects of quality of instruction, motivation, academic coursework, and homework on academic achievement. *School Psychology Quarterly, 7,* 207–226.

Kerr, B. A. (1985*). Smart girls, gifted women.* Columbus: Ohio Psychology Publishing.

Kerr, B. A. (1990). *Career planning for gifted and talented youth* (Report No. E492). Reston, VA: Eric Clearinghouse on Handicapped and Gifted Children. (ERIC Document Reproduction Service No. ED 321497)

Kerr, B. (1994). *Smart girls two: A new psychology of girls, women, and giftedness.* Dayton: Ohio Psychology Press.

Kerr, B. (1997). *Gender and genius.* Retrieved February 27, 2003, from http://www.wm.edu/education/gifteded/Publications/GenderGenius.htm

Kerr, B., & Colangelo, N. (1998). The college plans of academically talented students. *Journal of Counseling and Development, 67,* 42–49.

Kerschensteiner, G. (1905). *Die Entwicklung der zeichnerischen Begabung.* Munich: Gerber.

Kirst, M. W. (1982). How to improve schools without spending more money. *Phi Delta Kappan, 64,* 6–8.

Kitano, M., & Kirby, D. (1986). *Gifted education: A comprehensive view.* Boston: Little, Brown.

Kläger, M. (1987). Mentally handicapped men and women as artistically productive persons. In *Artists from Stetten: An exhibition by persons with a mental handicap* (pp. 20–38). Stuttgardt: Konrad Wittwer.

Kläger, M. (1992). *Krampus: Die Bilderwelt des Willibald Lassenberger.* Hohengehren: Schneider Verlag.

Kläger, M. (1993). *Die Vielfalt der Bilder.* Stuttgart: Konrad Wittwer.

Kläger, M. (1996). Two case studies of artistically gifted Down-syndrome persons. *Visual Arts Research, 22,* 35–46.

Kläger, M. (2002). *Die Kunst des Christopher Eder in der Stiftung de la Tour.* Hohengehren: Schneider Verlag.

Klee, F. (Ed.). (1964). *The diaries of Paul Klee, 1898–1918.* Berkeley: University California of Press.

Klein, A., & Zehms, D. (1996). Self-concept and gifted girls: A cross-sectional study of intellectually gifted females in grades 3, 5, and 8. *Roeper Review, 19,* 30–34.

Klein, S. P. (2001–2002, Winter). Law school admissions, LSATs, and the bar. *Academic Questions, 15,* 33–38.

Klitgaard, R. (1985). *Choosing elites.* New York: BasicBooks.

Kloosterman, V. I. (1997, Spring). Building a bridge: A combined effort between gifted and bilingual education. *Newsletter of the National Research Center on the Gifted and Talented.* Retrieved August 28, 2003, from http://www.sp.uconn.edu/~nrcgt/news/spring97/sprng972.html

Klug, B. J., & Whitfield, P. T. (2003). *Widening the circle: Culturally relevant pedagogy for American Indian children.* New York: Routledge/Falmer.

Kolitch, E. R., & Brody, L. E. (1992). Mathematics acceleration of highly talented students: An evaluation. *Gifted Child Quarterly, 36*, 78–86.

Koppel, D. (1991, June). What it's like to raise a genius. *Redbook, 51*, 57–58.

Kolloff, P. B. (2003). State-supported residential high schools. In N. Colangelo & G. A. Davis (Eds.), *Handbook of gifted education* (3rd ed., pp. 238–246). Boston: Allyn and Bacon.

Kolloff, P. B., & Feldhusen, J. F. (1981). PACE (Program for Academic and Creative Enrichment): An application of the three-state model. *Gifted Child Today, 18*(3), 47–50.

Korenman, S., & Miller, J. (1997). Effects of long-term poverty on physical health of children in the National Longitudinal Survey of Youth. In G. Duncan & J. Brooks-Gunn (Eds.), *Consequences of growing up poor* (pp. 70–99). New York: Sage.

Kornhaber, M. L. (1994). *The theory of multiple intelligences: How and why schools use it.* Unpublished qualifying paper, Harvard Graduate School of Education, Cambridge, MA.

Kornhaber, M. L., & Krechevsky, M. (1995). Expanding definitions of teaching and learning: Notes from the MI underground. In P. Cookson & B. Schneider (Eds.), *Transforming Schools* (pp. 181–208). New York: Garland Press.

Kranzler, J. H., Whang, P. A., & Jensen, A. R. (1994). Task complexity and the speed and efficiency of elemental information processing: Another look at the nature of intellectual giftedness. *Contemporary Educational Psychology, 19*, 447–459.

Krashen, S. (1982). *Principles and practice in second language acquisition.* New York: Pergamon Press.

Kulieke, M. J., & Olszewski-Kubilius, P. (1989). The influence of family values and climate on the development of talent. In J. L. VanTassel-Baska & P. Olszewski-Kubilius (Eds.), *Patterns of influence on gifted learners: The home, the self, and the school* (pp. 40–59). New York: Teachers College Press.

Kulik, J. A., & Kulik, C. C. (1992). Meta-analytic findings on grouping programs. *Gifted Child Quarterly, 36*, 73–77.

Ladson-Billings, G. (1994). *The dreamkeepers: Successful teachers for African-American children.* San Francisco: Jossey-Bass.

Lark-Horovitz, B., Lewis, H. P., & Luca, M. (1967). *Understanding children's art for better teaching.* Columbus, OH: Merrill.

Larntz, K. (1998). Expert report of Kinley Larntz, Ph.D. Grutter, et al. v. Bollinger, et al., No. 97-75928 (E.D. Mich.).

Leap, W. L. (1993). *American Indian English.* Salt Lake City: University of Utah Press.

Lerner, R. (1998, November). The empire strikes back. *CEO Policy Brief,* 3–23.

Lerner, R., & Nagai, A. K. (2000). Reverse discrimination by the numbers. *Academic Questions 13,* 71–84.

Lerner, R., & Nagai, A. K. (2001a). *Pervasive preferences: Racial and ethnic discrimination in undergraduate admissions across the nation.* Retrieved February 5, 2004, from http://www.ceousa.org/docs/multistate.doc

Lerner, R., & Nagai, A. K. (2001b). *Critique of the Gurin report.* Retrieved February 5, 2004, from http://www.ceousa.org/pdf/Gurin1.pdf

Levine, J., Pollack, H., & Comfort, M. (2001). Academic and behavioral outcomes among the children of young mothers. *Journal of Marriage and the Family, 63,* 355–369.

Li, Z. (1984). A comparative study of the creative thinking of abnormal (supernormal) and normal children aged from 7 to 14. *Journal of Hunan Teachers' College (Philosophy & Social Sciences Edition), 1,* 93–98.

Lilienfeld, D. E., & Stolley, P. D. (1994). *Foundations of epidemiology* (3rd ed.). New York: Oxford University Press.

Lim, L., & Renshaw, P. (2001). The relevance of sociocultural theory to culturally diverse partnerships and communities. *Journal of Child and Family Studies, 10,* 9–21.

Linnemeyer, S. A., & Shelton, J. (1991). Minds in the making: A community resource program. *Roeper Review, 14,* 35–39.

Liu, F. (1980). Some issues of supernormal children. *Child Psychology and Educational Psychology, 4,* 56–60.

Liu, Y., & Zhu, Y. (2001). *Psychological development and education of supernormal children.* Hefei: Anhui Education Press.

Loury, G. C. (2002). *The anatomy of racial inequality.* Cambridge, MA: Harvard University Press.

Lubinski, D., & Benbow, C. P. (1992). Gender differences in abilities and preferences among the gifted: Implications for the math-science pipeline. *Psychological Science, 1*(2), 61–66.

Lubinski, D., & Benbow, C. P. (1995). Optimal development of talent: Respond educationally to individual differences in personality. *Educational Forum, 59,* 381–392.

Lubinski, D., Webb, R. M., Morelock, M. J., & Benbow, C. P. (2001). Top 1 in 10,000: A 10-year follow-up of the profoundly gifted. *Journal of Applied Psychology, 86,* 718–729.

Lupkowski-Shoplik, A., Benbow, C. P., Assouline, S. G., & Brody, L. E. (2003). Talent searches: Meeting the needs of academically talented youth. In N. Colangelo & G. A. Davis (Eds.), *Handbook of gifted education* (3rd ed., pp. 204–218). Boston: Allyn and Bacon.

Luscombe, A., & Riley, T. L. (2001). An examination of self-concept in academically gifted adolescents: Do gender differences occur? *Roeper Review, 24,* 20–22.

Lynch, F. R. (1997). *The diversity machine: The drive to change the White male workplace.* New York: Simon and Schuster.

Lynch, S. J. (1992). Fast-paced high school science for the academically talented: A six-year perspective. *Gifted Child Quarterly, 36,* 147–154.

Maccoby, E. E., & Jacklin, C. N. (1974). *The psychology of sex differences.* Stanford, CA: Stanford University Press.

MacKinnon, D. W. (1962). The nature and nurture of creative talent. *American Psychologist, 17,* 484–495.

Mahoney, A. S. (1995, Summer). Exceptional children require an exceptional approach: Issues in counseling gifted children. *Counseling and Guidance Newsletter, 4*(3), 1–4. Retrieved December 18, 2003, from http://www.counselingthegifted.com/articles/counselingissues.html

Maker, C. J. (1982). *Curriculum development for the gifted.* Rockville, MD: Aspen Systems.

Maker, C. J., Nielson, A. B., & Rogers, J. A. (1994). Multiple intelligences: Giftedness, diversity, and problem-solving. *Teaching Exceptional Children, 27*(1), 4–19.

Maker, C. J., Rogers, J., & Nielson, A. (1995). *The DISCOVER process (grades 3–5).* Unpublished set of instructions, University of Arizona, Tucson.

Mansour, M., Lanphear, B. P., & DeWitt, T. G. (2000). Barriers to asthma care in urban children: Parent perspectives. *Pediatrics, 106,* 512–519.

Mantsios, G. (2001). Class in America: Myths and realities (2000). In P. Rothenberg (Ed.), *Race, class, and gender in the United States: An integrated study* (5th ed., pp. 168–182.) New York: Worth.

Marinova-Todd, S. H., Marshall, D. B., & Snow, C. E. (2000). Three misconceptions about age and L2 Learning. *TESOL Quarterly, 34,* 9–34.

Marland, S. P., Jr. (1972). *Education of the gifted and talented: Report to the Congress of the United States by the U.S. Commissioner of Education and background papers submitted to the U.S. Office of Education,* 2 vols. Washington, DC: U.S. Government Printing Office. (Government Documents, Y4.L 11/2: G36)

Marlow, B. A., & Page, M. L. (1998). *Creating and sustaining the constructivist classroom.* Thousand Oaks, CA: Corwin Press.

Martin, P. J. (2002). Transforming school counseling: A national perspective. *Theory Into Practice, 41,* 148–153.

Matthews, F. N., West, J. D., & Hosie, T. W. (1986). Understanding families of academically gifted children. *Roeper Review, 9,* 40–42.

Matthews, J. (1999). *The art of childhood and adolescence.* London: Palmer Press.

McCaig, N. M. (2002, Spring). Raised in the margins of the mosaic: Global nomads balance worlds within. *International Educator, 11,* 10–17.

McCarthy, C. R. (1998). Assimilating the talent search model into the school day. *Journal of Secondary Gifted Education, 9,* 114–123.

McCarthy, C. (1999). Dual-enrollment programs: Legislation helps high school students enroll in college courses. *Journal of Secondary Gifted Education, 11,* 24–32.

McCarton, C., Brooks-Gunn, J., Wallace, I., Bauer, C., Bennett, F., Bernbaum, J., Broyles, S., Casey, P., McCormick, M., Scott, D., Tyson, J., Tonascia, J., & Meinert, C. (1997). Results at age 8 years of early intervention for low-birth-weight premature infants. *Journal of the American Medical Association, 277,* 126–132.

McClain, L. (1983, July 24). How Chicago taught me to hate Whites. *Washington Post,* pp. C1, C4.

McCluskey, K. W., & Walker, K. D. (1986). *The doubtful gift: Strategies for educating gifted children in the regular classroom.* Kingston, Canada: Frye.

McCormick, M., Gortmaker, S., & Sobol, A. (1990). Very low birth weight children: Behavior problems and school difficulty in a national sample. *Journal of Pediatrics, 117,* 687–693.

McCubbin, H. I., Thompson, A. I., Pirner, P. A., & McCubbin, M. A. (1988). *Family types and strengths: A life cycle and ecological perspective.* Edina, MN: Bellweather Press.

McDaniel, T. R. (1989). Mainstreaming the gifted: Historical perspectives on excellence and equity [Electronic version]. *Roeper Review, 11,* 171–172.

McGuire, T. J. (1992, April). My bout with affirmative action. *Commentary,* 50–52.

McLeod, J. D., & Nonnemaker, J. M. (2000). Poverty and child emotional and behavioral problems: Racial/ethnic differences in process and effects. *Journal of Youth and Adolescence, 41,* 137–161.

McLoyd, V. (1998). Socioeconomic disadvantages and child development. *American Psychologist, 53,* 185–204.

McWhorter, J. H. (2000). *Losing the race: Self-sabotage in Black America.* New York: Free Press.

Meckstroth, E. A. (1991) Guiding the parents of gifted children: The role of counselors and teachers. In R. M. Milgram (Ed.), *Counseling gifted and talented children: A guide for teachers, counselors, and parents* (pp. 95–120). Norwood, NJ: Ablex.

Meisels, S., & Wasik, B. (1990). Who should be served? Identifying children in need of early intervention. In S. Meisels & J. Shonkoff (Eds.), *Handbook of early childhood intervention* (pp. 605–632). Cambridge: Cambridge University Press.

Mendaglio, S. (2003). Heightened multifaceted sensitivity of gifted students: Implications for counseling. *Journal of Secondary Gifted Education, 14,* 72–82.

Ment, L. R., Vohr, B., Allan, W., Katz, K., Schneider, K. C., Westerveld, M., Duncan, C., Makuch, R. (2003). Change in cognitive function over time in very low-birth-weight infants. *Journal of the American Medical Association, 289,* 705–711.

Meriam, L. (1928). The effects of boarding schools on Indian Family Life: 1928. In S. Unger (Ed.), *Destruction of American Indian families* (pp. 14–17). New York: The Association on American Indian Affairs.

Meyer, J. M. (Ed.). (2002). *American Indians and U.S. politics: A companion reader.* Westport, CT: Praeger.

Milbrath, C. (1995). Germinal motifs in the work of a gifted child artist. In C. Golomb (Ed.), *The development of artistically gifted children* (pp. 101–134). Hillsdale, NJ: Erlbaum.

Milbrath, C. (1998). *Patterns of artistic development.* New York: Cambridge University Press.

Milgram, R. M. (Ed.). (1991). *Counseling gifted and talented children. A guide for teachers, counselors, and parents.* Norwood, NJ: Ablex.

Millais, J. G. (1849). *The life and letters of Sir John Everett Millais.* New York: Stokes.

Miller, J., & Davis, D. (1997). Poverty history, marital history, and quality of children's home environments. *Journal of Marriage and the Family, 59,* 996–1007

Miller, L. S. (2000). *Minority high academic achievement patterns and their implications for the gifted and talented education community.* Paper prepared for the National Academies Committee on Minority Students in Special Education and Gifted and Talented Programs. Washington, DC.

Mills, C. J., Ablard, K. E., & Lynch, S. J. (1992). Academically talented students' preparation for advanced coursework after an individually paced precalculus class. *Journal for the Education of the Gifted, 16,* 3–17.

Mills v. Board of Education (348 F. Supp. 866, D.D.C., 1972).

Milner, H. R. (2002). Affective and social issues among high-achieving African-American students: Recommendations for teachers and teacher education. *Action in Teacher Education, 24*(1), 81–89.

Milner, H. R. (2003). Reflection, racial competence, and critical pedagogy: How do we prepare preservice teachers to pose tough questions? *Race, Ethnicity, and Education, 6,* 193–208.

Mohawk, J. (2002). The "disappearing Indian": 20th century reality disproves 19th century prediction. *Native Americas, 19*(1–2), 40–45.

Moon, S. M., Jurich, J. A., & Feldhusen, J. F. (1998). Families of gifted children. In R. C. Friedman & K. B. Rogers (Eds.), *Talent in context: Historical and social perspectives on giftedness* (pp. 61–77). Washington, DC: American Psychological Association.

Moon, T. R. (2002). Using performance assessments in the social studies classroom. *Gifted Child Today, 25*(3), 53–58.

Moon, T. R., & Callahan, C. M. (2001). Classroom performance assessment: What should it look like in a standards-based classroom? *National Association of Secondary School Principals Bulletin, 85,* 48–57.

Morishima, A., & Brown, L. F. (1977). A case report on the artistic talent of an autistic idiot savant. *Mental Retardation, 15*(2), 33–36.

Morris, J. E. (2002). Underrepresentation among ethnically diverse students in gifted education. *Roeper Review, 24,* 59–62.

Munro, D. J. (1969). *The concept of man in early China.* Stanford, CA: Stanford University Press.

Musheno, S., & Talbert, M. (2002) The transformed school counselor in action. *Theory Into Practice, 41,* 186–191.

Nagel, J. (1997). *American Indian ethnic renewal: Red power and the resurgence of identity and culture.* New York: Oxford University Press.

Naglieri, J. A. (1985). *Matrix analogies test.* New York: Psychological Corporation.

National Center for Educational Statistics. (2001). *NAEP data tool.* Retrieved August 27, 2002, from http://www.nces.ed.gov/nationsreportcard/naepdata/getdata.asp

National Defense Education Act of 1958, Pub. L. No. 85-864, 72 Stat. 1580 (codified at scattered sections of 20 & 42 U.S.C. [1994]).

National Research Council. (2000). Communicating and learning. In National Research Council, Board of Children, Youth, and Families, & Institute of Medicine, *From neurons to neighborhoods: The science of early childhood development.* (pp. 124–162). Washington, DC: National Academy Press.

Neihart, M., Reis, S. M., Robinson, N. M., & Moon, S. M. (Eds.). (2002). *The social and emotional development of gifted children: What do we know?* Waco, TX: Prufrock Press.

Neisser, U., Boodoo, G., Bouchard, T. J., Boykin, A. W., Brody, N., Ceci, S. J., Halpern, D. F., Loehlin, J. C., Perloff, R., Sternberg, R. J., & Urbina, S. (1996). Intelligence: Knowns and unknowns. *American Psychologist, 51,* 77–101.

Nez Perce Tribe. (2002). *Two world view curriculum.* Lapwai, ID: Nez Perce Tribal Foundation Two World View Environmental Education Project.

No Child Left Behind Act of 2001 (Pub. L. 107-110) (2002).

O'Connor, N., & Hermelin, B. (1987a). Visual graphic abilities of the idiot-savant artist. *Psychological Medicine, 17,* 79–90.

O'Connor, N., & Hermelin, B. (1987b). Visual memory and motor programmes: Their use by idiot savant artists and controls. *British Journal of Developmental Psychology, 78,* 307–323.

O'Connor, N., & Hermelin, B. (1990). The recognition failure and graphic success of idiot savant artists. *Journal of Child Psychology and Psychiatry, 31,* 203–215.

Office of Ethnic Minority Affairs. (1993). Guidelines for providers of psychological services to ethnic, linguistic, and culturally diverse populations. *American Psychologist, 48,* 45–48.

Ogbu, J. U. (1987). Variability in minority school performance: A problem in search of an explanation. *Anthropology and Education Quarterly, 18,* 312–334.

O'Hearn, C. C. (1998). Introduction. In C. C. O'Hearn (Ed.), *Half and half: Writers on growing up biracial and bicultural* (pp. vii–xiv). New York: Pantheon Books.

Olszewski-Kubilius, P. (1995). A summary of research regarding early entrance to college. *Roeper Review, 18,* 121–125.

Olszewski-Kubilius, P. (2003). Special summer and Saturday programs for gifted students. In N. Colangelo & G. A. Davis (Eds.), *Handbook of gifted education* (3rd ed., pp. 219–228). Boston: Allyn and Bacon.

Olszewski-Kubilius, P., & Grant, B. (1996). Academically talented women and mathematics: The role of special programs and support from others in acceleration, achievement, and aspiration. In K. D. Noble & R. F. Subotnik (Eds.), *Remarkable women: Perspectives on female talent development* (pp. 281–294). Cresskill, NJ: Hampton Press.

Olszewski, P., Kulieke, M., & Buescher, T. (1987). The influences of the family environment on the development of talent: A literature review. *Journal for the Education of the Gifted, 11,* 6–28.

Olszewski-Kubilius, P., Kulieke, M. J., Willis, G. B., & Krasney, N. (1989). An analysis of the validity of SAT entrance scores for accelerated classes. *Journal for the Education of the Gifted. 13*, 37–54.

Omnibus Budget Reconciliation Act of 1981 (Pub. L. 97-2135)

Osborne, J. W. (2001). Testing stereotype threat: Does anxiety explain race and sex differences in achievement? *Contemporary Educational Psychology, 26*, 291–310.

O'Sullivan, C. Y., Lauko, M. A., Grigg, W. S., Qian, J., & Zhang, J. (2003). *The nation's report card: Science 2000*. Washington, DC: National Center for Education Statistics.

Paine, S. (1981). *Six children draw*. London: Academic Press.

Parham, T. A. (1989). Cycles of psychological Nigrescence. *Counseling Psychologist, 17*, 187–226.

Pariser, D. (1987). The juvenile drawings of Klee, Toulouse-Lautrec, and Picasso. *Visual Arts Research, 13*, 53–67.

Pariser, D. (1991). Normal and unusual aspects of juvenile artistic development in Klee, Toulouse-Lautrec, and Picasso: A review of findings and direction for future research. *Creativity Research Journal, 3*, 51–65.

Pariser, D. (1995). Lautrec—Gifted child artist and artistic monument: Connections between juvenile and mature work. In C. Golomb (Ed.), *The development of artistically gifted children* (pp. 31–70). Hillsdale, NJ: Erlbaum.

Paul, R. (1992). *Critical thinking: What every person needs to survive in a rapidly changing world*. Rohnert Park, CA: Critical Thinking Foundation.

Peirce, B. N. (1995). Social identity, investment, and language learning. *TESOL Quarterly, 29*, 9–31.

Pellett, A. (2002, May). Community connections. *National Education Association Today, 22*.

Pennsylvania Association for Retarded Children v. Pennsylvania (F. Supp. 1257, E.D. Pa, 1971).

Perkins, D. (1992). Selecting fertile themes for integrated learning. In H. Hayes Jacobs (Ed.), *Interdisciplinary curriculum: Design and implementation* (pp. 67–75). Alexandria, VA: Association for Supervision and Curriculum Development.

Perkins, D. (1999). The many faces of constructivism. *Educational Leadership, 57*(3), 6–11.

Perleth, C., Schatz, T., & Mönks, F. (2000). Early identification of high ability. In K. A. Heller, F. J. Mönks, R. J. Sternberg, & R. F. Subotnick (Eds.), *International handbook of giftedness and talent* (2nd ed., pp. 179–192). Oxford: Elsevier Science.

Perrone, P. (1986). Guidance needs of gifted children, adolescents, and adults. *Journal of Counseling and Development, 64*, 564–566.

Perrone, P. A., & Pulvino, C. J. (1979). New directions in the guidance of the gifted and talented. In J. C. Gowan, J. Khatena, & E. P. Torrance (Eds.), *Educating the ablest: A book of readings on the education of gifted children* (pp. 190–199). Itasca, IL: Peacock Publishers.

Peters, W. A. M., Grager-Loidl, H., & Supplee, P. (2000). Underachievement in gifted children and adolescents: Theory and practice. In K. A. Heller, F. J. Mönks, R. J. Sternberg, & R. F. Subotnik (Eds.), *International handbook of giftedness and talent* (2nd ed., pp. 609–620). Oxford: Elsevier Science.

Pewewardy, C., & Bushey, M. (1992). A family of learners and storytellers: The American Indian Magnet School. *Native Peoples Magazine, 5*(4), 56–60.

Phenix, P. (1964). *Realms of meaning*. New York: McGraw-Hill.

Piechowski, M. M. (1997). Emotional giftedness: The measure of intrapersonal intelligence. In N. Colangelo and G. A. Davis (Eds.), *Handbook of gifted education* (2nd ed., pp. 366–381). Boston: Allyn and Bacon.

Piskurich, P. (2002). The role of summer programs: Providing support for students, parents, and schools. In J. F. Smutny (Ed.), *Designing and developing programs for gifted students* (pp. 129–137). Thousand Oaks, CA: Corwin Press.

Plessy v. Ferguson, 163 US 537 (1896).

Plucker, J. A. (1996). Gifted Asian-American students: Identification, curricular, and counseling concerns. *Journal for the Education of the Gifted, 19*, 315–343.

Popham, W. J. (2001). *The truth about testing: An educator's call to action.* Alexandria, VA: Association for Supervision and Curriculum Development.

Posner, G. J. (1992). *Analyzing the curriculum.* New York: McGraw-Hill.

Presser, A. L. (1991, July). Article brings discipline charges. *ABA Journal, 77,* 30.

Price, J., & Lento, J. (2001). The nature of child and adolescent vulnerability: History and definitions. In R. Ingram & J. Price (Eds.). *Vulnerability to psychopathology: Risk across the lifespan* (pp. 20–38). New York: Guilford.

Prom-Jackson, S., Johnson, S. T., & Wallace, M. B. (1987). Home environment, talented minority youth, and school achievement. *Journal of Negro Education, 56*(1), 111–121.

Pulliam, J. D. (1987). *History of education in America* (4th ed). Columbus, OH: Merrill.

Pynoos, R., & Eth, S. (1985). Children traumatized by witnessing acts of personal violence: Homicide, rape, or suicide behavior. In S. Eth & R. Pynoos (Eds.), *Post-traumatic stress disorder in children* (pp. 17–44). Washington, DC: American Psychiatric Press.

Rahm, J. (2002). Emergent learning opportunities in an inner-city youth gardening program. *Journal of Research in Science Teaching, 39,* 164–184.

Read, C. R. (1991). Achievement and career choices: Comparisons of males and females. *Roeper Review, 13,* 188–193.

Reese, C. M., Miller, K. E., Mazzeo, J., & Dossey, J. A. (1997). *NAEP 1996 mathematics report card for the nation and states.* Washington, DC: National Center for Education Statistics.

Rehabilitation Act of 1973 (Pub. L. 93–112) (1973).

Rehyner, J. (1992). American Indians out of school: A review of school-based causes and solutions. *Journal of American Indian Education, 31*(2), 37–56.

Reis, S. M., Burns, D. E., & Renzulli, J. S. (1992). *Curriculum compacting: The complete guide to modifying the regular curriculum for high ability students.* Mansfield Center, CT: Creative Learning Press.

Reis, S. M., Hébert, T. P., Diaz, E. I., Maxfield, L. R., & Ratley, M. E. (1995). *Case studies of talented students who achieve and underachieve in an urban high school* (Research Monograph 95120). Storrs: National Research Center on the Gifted and Talented, University of Connecticut.

Reis, S. M., Westberg, K. L., Kulikowich, J., Calliard, F., Hébert, T., Purcell, J. H, Rogers, J., Smist, J., & Plucker, J. (1993). *An analysis of the impact of curriculum compacting on classroom practices: Technical report.* Storrs: The National Research Center on the Gifted and Talented, University of Connecticut.

Rensburger, B. (1984). Margaret Mead: An indomitable presence. In A. L. Hammond (Ed.), *A passion to know: 20 profiles in science* (pp. 37–38). New York: Scribner.

Renzulli, J. S. (1977). *The enrichment triad model: A guide for developing defensible programs for the gifted and talented.* Mansfield Center, CT: Creative Learning Press.

Renzulli, J. (Ed.). (1986a). *Systems and models for developing programs for the gifted and talented.* Mansfield Center, CT: Creative Learning Press.

Renzulli, J. S. (1986b). The three ring conception of giftedness: A developmental model for creative productivity. In R. J. Sternberg & J. E. Davidson (Eds.), *Conceptions of giftedness* (pp. 53–92). New York: Cambridge Press.

Renzulli, J. S. (1988). The multiple-menu model for developing differentiated curriculum for the gifted and talented. *Gifted Child Quarterly, 32,* 298–309.

Renzulli, J. S. (1997). *Interest-A-Lyzer family of instruments: A manual for teachers.* Mansfield Center, CT: Creative Learning Press.

Renzuilli, J. S. (2003). Conception of giftedness and its relationship to the development of social capital. In N. Colangelo & G. A. Davis (Eds.), *Handbook of gifted education* (3rd ed., pp. 75–87). Boston: Allyn and Bacon.

Renzulli, J. S., Baum, S. M., & Hébert, T. P. (1995). Reversing underachievement: Creative productivity as a systematic intervention, *Gifted Child Quarterly, 39,* 224–235.

Renzulli, J. S., & Park, S. (2000). Gifted dropouts: The who and the why. *Gifted Child Quarterly, 44,* 261–271.

Renzulli, J. S., & Reis, S. M. (1991). The reform movement and the quiet crisis in gifted education. *Gifted Child Quarterly, 35,* 26–35.

Renzulli, J. S., & Reis, S. M. (1997). *The schoolwide enrichment model: A comprehensive plan for educational excellence.* Mansfield Center, CT: Creative Learning Press.

Renzulli, J. S., & Smith, L. H. (1979). *A guidebook for developing individualized educational programs for gifted and talented students.* Mansfield Center, CT: Creative Learning Press.

Richert, E. S. (2003). Excellence with justice in identification and programming. In N. Colangelo & G. A. Davis (Eds.), *Handbook of gifted education* (3rd ed., pp. 146–158). Boston: Allyn and Bacon.

Rizza, M. G., & McIntosh, D. E. (2001). Introduction to the special issue: New perspectives in gifted education. *Psychology in the Schools, 38,* 401–402.

Roberts, D. J., Carter, K. R., & Mosley, D. (1982, September/October). A comparison of the perceptions of gifted children and their parents concerning the child's academic, social, and family characteristics.. *G/C/T,* 46–49.

Robinson, A., & Clinkenbeard, P. R. (1998). Giftedness: An exceptionality examined. *Annual Review of Psychology, 49,* 117–139.

Robinson, N. M., Abbott, V. W., & Busse, J. (1996). The structure of abilities in math-precocious youth children: Gender similarities and differences. *Journal of Educational Psychology, 88,* 341–352.

Robinson, N. M., Reis, S. M., Neihart, M., & Moon, S. M. (2002). Social and emotional issues facing gifted and talented students: What have we learned and what should we do now? In M. Neihart, S. Reis, N. M. Robinson, & S. M. Moon (Eds.), *The social and emotional development of gifted children: What do we know?* (pp. 267–289). Waco, TX: Prufrock Press.

Robinson, N. M., & Robinson, H. B. (1982). The optimal match: Devising the best compromise for the highly gifted student. In D. Feldman (Ed.), *Developmental approaches to giftedness and creativity* (pp. 79–94). San Francisco: Jossey-Bass.

Robisheaux, J. A. (2002). The intersection of language, high potential, and culture in gifted English as a second language student. In J. Castellano & E. Diaz (Eds.), *Reaching new horizons: Gifted and talented education for culturally and linguistically diverse students* (pp. 154–174). Boston: Allyn and Bacon.

Rogers, K. B. (1991). *The relationship of grouping practices to the education of the gifted and talented. Research based decision making series.* Storrs: National Research Center on the Gifted and Talented, University of Connecticut.

Rogers, K. B. (2001). *Re-forming gifted education*. Scottsdale, AZ: Great Potential Press.

Rose, L. (1999, Spring). Gender issues in gifted education. *Newsletter of the National Research Center on the Gifted and Talented*. Retrieved February 27, 2003, from http://www.sp.uconn.edu/~nrcgt/news/spring99/sprng994.html

Rosnow, R., Skedler, A., Jaeger, M., & Rind, B. (1994). Intelligence and the epistemics of interpersonal acumen: Testing some implications of Gardner's theory. *Intelligence, 19,* 93–116.

Rostan, S. M., Pariser, D., & Gruber, H. E. (2000). Across time and place: A cross cultural study of early artistic development. Paper presented at the annual meeting of the Jean Piaget Society, Montreal, Canada.

Rushton, J. P. (1997). *Race, evolution, and behavior*. New Brunswick, NJ: Transaction Press.

Russell, T. L., Reynolds, D. H., & Campbell, J. P. (1994). *Building a joint-service classification research roadmap: Individual differences measurement* (AL/HR-TP-1994-0009). Brooks Air Force Base, TX: Armstrong Laboratory, Manpower, and Personnel Research Division.

Russo, C. J. (2001). Unequal educational opportunities for gifted students: Robbing Peter to pay Paul? *Fordham Urban Law Journal, 29,* 727–758.

Russo, C. J., Harris J. J., & Sandidge, R. F. (1994). *Brown v. Board of Education* at 40: A legal history of equal educational opportunities in American public education. *Journal of Negro Education, 63,* 297–309.

Rutter, M., Giller, H., & Hagell, A. (1998). *Antisocial behavior by young people*. New York: Cambridge University Press.

Ryan, F. J., Sweeder, J. J., & Bednar, M. R. (2002). *Drowning in a clear pool: Cultural narcissism, technology, and character education: A primer for secondary education*. New York: Lang.

Sackett, P. R., Schmitt, N., Ellingson, J. E., & Kabin, M. B. (2001). High-stakes testing in employment, credentialing, and higher education: Prospects in a post-affirmative-action world. *American Psychologist, 56,* 302–318.

Sacks, O. (1993, Dec. 27). A neurologist's notebook: An anthropologist on Mars. *New Yorker,* 106–125.

Sadker, M., & Sadker, D. (1985). Sexism in the schoolroom of the '80s. *Psychology Today, 19*(3), 54–57.

Sadker, M., & Sadker, D. (1994). *Failing at fairness: How America's schools cheat girls*. New York: Charles Scribner's Sons.

Saigal, S., Hoult, L., Streiner, D., Stoskopf, B., & Rosenbaum, P. (2000). School difficulties at adolescence in a regional cohort of children who were extremely low birth weight. *Pediatrics, 105,* 325–331.

Salzmann, Z. (1993). *Language, culture, & society*. Boulder, CO: Westview Press.

San Antonio Independent School District v. Rodriguez, 411 U.S. 1 (1973).

Sapolsky, R. (1998). *Why zebras don't get ulcers: An updated guide to stress, stress-related diseases, and coping*. New York: Freeman.

Saracho, O. N., & Gerstl, C. K. (1992). Learning differences among at-risk minority students. In H. C. Waxman, J. Walker de Felix, J. E. Anderson, & H. P. Baptiste (Eds.), *Students at risk in at-risk schools: Improving environments for learning* (pp. 105–136). Newbury Park, CA: Corwin Press.

Saunders, A., & Remsberg, B. (1985). *The stress-proof child*. New York: Holt.

Saville-Troike, M. (1996). The ethnography of communication. In S. McKay & N. Hornberger (Eds.), *Sociolinguistics and language teaching* (pp. 351–382). New York: Cambridge Press.

Sawyer, R. N. (1982). The Duke University program to identify and educate brilliant young students. *Journal for the Education of the Gifted, 5*, 185–189.

School Dropout Prevention and Basic Skills Act of 1990, 20 U.S.C. § 7262 *et seq.* (U.S.C. 1994)

Schwab, J. (Ed.). (1964). *Education and the structure of knowledge.* Chicago: Rand McNally.

Schwartz, L. L. (1991). Guiding gifted girls. In R. M. Milgram (Ed.), *Counseling gifted and talented children: A guide for teachers, counselors, and parents* (pp. 143–160). Norwood, NJ: Ablex.

Selfe, L. (1977). *Nadia: A case of extraordinary drawing ability in an autistic child.* London: Academic Press.

Selfe, L. (1995). Nadia reconsidered. In C. Golomb (Ed.), *The development of artistically gifted children* (pp. 197–236). Hillsdale, NJ: Erlbaum.

Sethna, B. N., Wickstrom, C. D., Boothe, D., & Stanley, J. C. (2001). The Advanced Academy of Georgia: Four years as a residential early-college-entrance program. *Journal of Secondary Gifted Education, 13*, 11–21.

Shade, B. J., Kelly, C., & Oberg, M. (1998). *Creating culturally responsive classrooms.* Washington, DC: American Psychological Association.

Sheffield, G. K. (1997). *The arbitrary Indian: The Indian Arts and Crafts Act of 1990.* Norman: University of Oklahoma Press.

Shepard, L. (1993). Evaluating test validity. *Review of Research in Education, 19*, 405–450.

Sher, B. T. (1993). *Guide to key science concepts.* Williamsburg, VA: College of William and Mary, Center for Gifted Education.

Shi, J. (1990a). Memory and the organization of memory of gifted and normal children. *Acta Psychologica Sinica , 22*, 127–134.

Shi, J. (1990b). Memory and memory monitoring of gifted and normal children. *Acta Psychologica Sinica, 22*, 323–329.

Shi, J. (2002). *Identifying and educating academically gifted children in China.* Invited speech at the International Conference on Education for the Gifted in Science (ICEGIS), Busan, Korea.

Shi, J., & Xu, F. (1998). The developmental trends and issues of study on supernormal children in China. *Acta Psychologica Sinica, 30*, 298–305.

Shi, J., & Xu, F. (1999). *Recognizing gifted children.* Beijing: Esperanto Publishing House of China.

Shi, J., & Zha, Z. (2000). Psychological research on and education of gifted and talented children in China. In K. Heller, F. Mönks, R. Sternberg, & R. F. Subotnik (Eds.), *International handbook of research and development of giftedness and talent* (2nd ed., pp. 757–764). Oxford: Pergamon Press.

Siegel, J., Aneshensel, C., Taub, B., Cantwell, D., & Driscoll, A. (1998). Adolescent depressed mood in a multiethnic sample. *Journal of Youth and Adolescence, 27*, 413–427.

Silverman, L. (1986). Giftedness, intelligence, and the Stanford-Binet. *Roeper Review, 8*, 168–171.

Silverman, L. K. (1993). *Counseling the gifted and talented.* Denver: Love.

Schaefer-Simmern, H. (1948). *The unfolding of artistic activity.* Berkeley: University of California Press.

Simonton, D. K. (1994). *Greatness: Who makes history and why.* New York: Guilford.

Singer, M., Anglin, T., Song, L., & Lunghofer, L. (1995). Adolescents' exposure to violence and associated symptoms of psychological trauma. *Journal of the American Medical Association, 273*, 477–482.

Siren, O. (1963). *The Chinese on the art of painting.* New York: Schocken.

Skrentny, J. D. (2001). *Color lines: Affirmative action, immigration, and civil rights options for America.* Chicago: University of Chicago Press.

Slocumb, P. D., & Payne, R. K. (2000). Identifying and nurturing the gifted poor. *Principal, 79*(5), 28–32.

Smiley, P., & Dweck, C. (1994). Individual differences in achievement goals among young children. *Child Development, 65,* 1723–1743.

Smith, A. D. (1981). *The ethnic revival.* New York: Cambridge University Press.

Smith, E. M. J. (1989). Black racial identity development. *Counseling Psychologist, 17,* 277–288.

Smith, J., Brooks-Gunn, J., & Klebanov, P. (1997). The consequences of living in poverty for young children's cognitive and verbal ability and early school achievement. In G. Duncan & J. Brooks-Gunn (Eds.), *The consequences of growing up poor* (pp. 132–189). New York: Sage.

Sniderman, P. M., & Piazza, T. (1993). *The scar of race.* Cambridge, MA: Harvard University Press.

Snow, B. M. (1990). Seasoned reflections: A dialogue with Clayton A. Morgan. *Journal of Counseling and Development, 68,* 673–676.

Southern, T. W., & Jones, E. D. (1992). The real problems with academic acceleration. *Gifted Child Today, 15*(2), 34–38.

Southern, W. T., & Jones, E. D. (1993). *The academic acceleration of gifted children.* New York: Teachers College Press.

Southern, W. T., Jones, E. D., & Stanley, J. C. (1993). Acceleration and enrichment: The context and development of program options. In K. A. Heller, F. J. Mönks, & A. H. Passow (Eds.), *International handbook of research and development of giftedness and talent* (pp. 387–409). Oxford: Pergamon Press.

Sowell, T. (1993). *Inside American education: The decline, the deceptions, the dogmas.* New York: Free Press.

Squires, W. D. (2001). The impact of elementary education majors' intuitively held beliefs on reading instruction. *Dissertation Abstracts International, 62*(08), 2732A.

St. Germaine, R. (1995). *Drop-out rates among American Indian and Alaska Native students: Beyond cultural discontinuity. ERIC Digest.* (ERIC Document Reproduction Service No. ED3888492)

Stahl, L. (2003, January 9). *Leslie Stahl's notebook.* Retrieved December 1, 2003, from http://www.cbsnews.com/stories/2003/01/09/48hours/main535897.shtml

Stanley, J. C. (1979). The study and facilitation of talent for mathematics. In A.H. Passow (Ed.), *The gifted and the talented: Their education and development* (pp. 169–185). Chicago: University of Chicago Press.

Stanley, J. C. (1983). Introduction. In C. P. Benbow & J. C. Stanley (Eds). *Academic precocity: Aspects of its development* (pp. 1–8). Baltimore, MD: Johns Hopkins University Press.

Stanley, J. C. (1989a). A look back at educational non-acceleration: An international tragedy. *Gifted Child Today, 12*(4), 60–61.

Stanley, J. C. (1989b). Guiding gifted students in their academic planning. In J. L. VanTassel-Baska & P. Olszewski-Kubilius (Eds.), *Patterns of influence on gifted learners: The home, the self, and the school* (pp. 192–200). New York: Teachers College Press.

Stanley, J. C. (1991a). An academic model for educating the mathematically gifted. *Gifted Child Quarterly, 35,* 36–42.

Stanley, J. C. (1991b). A better model for residential high schools for talented youth. *Phi Delta Kappan, 72*, 471–473.

Stanley, J. C. (1994). Gender differences for able elementary school students on above-grade-level ability and achievement tests. In N. Colangelo, S. G. Assouline, & D. L. Ambroson (Eds.), *Talent development, Vol. 2: Proceedings from the 1993 Henry B. and Jocelyn Wallace National Research Symposium on Talent Development* (pp. 141–148). Dayton: Ohio Psychology Press.

Stanley, J. C. (2000). Helping students learn only what they don't already know. *Psychology, Public Policy, and Law, 6*, 216–222.

Stanley, J. C., Benbow, C. P., Brody, L. E., Dauber, S., & Lupkowski, A. E. (1992). Gender differences on eighty-six nationally standardized aptitude and achievement tests. *Talent Development, 1*, 42–65.

Stanley, J. C., Keating, D. P., & Fox, F. H. (1974*). Mathematical talent: Discovery, description and development.* Baltimore: Johns Hopkins University Press.

Stanley, N. V. (1996). Vygotsky and multicultural assessment and instruction. In L. Dixon-Krauss (Ed.), *Vygotsky in the classroom: Mediated literacy instruction and assessment* (pp. 133–148). New York: Longman.

State Policy Documentation Project. (2001). *State policies regarding TANF work activities and requirements.* Retrieved February 5, 2004, from http://www.spdp.org/tanf/work/worksumm.htm

Steele, S. (1990). *The content of our character.* New York: St. Martin's Press.

Steele, C. M. (1997). A threat in the air: How stereotypes shape the intellectual identities and performance of women and African Americans. *American Psychologist, 52,* 613–629.

Steele, C. M. (1999, August). Thin ice: "Stereotype threat" and Black college students. *Atlantic Monthly, 284*(2), 50–54.

Steele, C. M., & Aronson, J. (1995). Stereotype threat and the intellectual test performance of African Americans. *Journal of Personality and Social Psychology, 69,* 797–811.

Stephens, E. (1998, February 16). State studies ways to revamp gifted programs. *Atlanta Business Chronicle,* p. 1.

Stephens, K. R., & Karnes, F. A. (2000). State definitions for the gifted and talented revisited. *Exceptional Children, 66,* 219–38.

Sternberg, R. J. (1985). *Beyond IQ: A triarchic theory of human intelligence.* New York: Cambridge University Press.

Sternberg, R. J. (1993). *Sternberg triarchic abilities test (STAT).* Unpublished test.

Sternberg, R. J. (1997). *Successful intelligence.* New York: Plume.

Sternberg, R. J. (2000). The theory of successful intelligence. *Gifted Education International, 15,* 4–21.

Sternberg, R. J. (2002). Intelligence is not just inside the head: The theory of successful intelligence. In J. Aronson (Ed.), *Improving academic achievement: Impact of psychological factors on education* (pp. 227–244). San Diego, CA: Academic Press.

Sternberg, R. J., Castejón, J., Prieto, M. D., Hautamäki, J., & Grigorenko, E. L. (2001). Confirmatory factor analysis of the Sternberg Triarchic Abilities Test in three international samples: An empirical test of the triarchic theory of intelligence. *European Journal of Psychological Assessment, 17,* 1–16.

Sternberg, R. J., Ferrari, M., Clinkenbeard, P., & Grigorenko, E. L. (1996). Identification, instruction, and assessment of gifted children: A construct validation of a triarchic model. *Gifted Child Quarterly, 40,* 129–137.

Sternberg, R. J., Grigorenko, E. L., Ferrari, M., & Clinkenbeard, P. (1999). A triarchic analysis of an aptitude-treatment interaction. *European Journal of Psychological Assessment, 15*, 1–11.

Sternberg, R. J., & Williams, W. M. (Eds.). (1998). *Intelligence, instruction, and assessment: Theory into practice*. Mahwah, NJ: Erlbaum.

Stevenson, H. W. (1998). Cultural interpretations of giftedness: The case of East Asia. In R. C. Friedman & K. B. Rogers (Eds.), *Talent in context: Historical and social perspectives on giftedness* (pp. 61–77). Washington, DC: American Psychological Association.

Stormont, M., Stebbins, M. S., & Holliday, G. (2001). Characteristics and educational support needs of underrepresented gifted adolescents. *Psychology in the Schools, 38*, 413–423.

Storti, C. (1989). *The art of crossing cultures*. Alberta, Canada: Intercultural Press.

Storti, C. (2001). *The art of crossing cultures* (2nd ed.). Alberta, Canada: Intercultural Press.

Strang, R. (1952). Guidance of the gifted. *Personnel & Guidance Journal, 31*, 26–30.

Stumpf, H., & Jackson, D. N. (1994). Gender-related differences in cognitive abilities: Evidence from a medical school admissions testing program. *Personality and Individual Differences, 17*, 335–344.

Stumpf, H., & Stanley, J. C. (1996). Gender-related differences on the College Board's Advanced Placement and Achievement Tests, 1982–1992. *Journal of Educational Psychology, 88*, 353–364.

Stumpf, H., & Stanley, J. C. (1997). The gender gap in Advanced Placement Computer Science. *College Board Review, 181*, 22–27.

Sully, J. (1910). *Studies of childhood*. London: Appleton.

Suskind, R. (1998). *A hope in the unseen: An American odyssey from the inner city to the Ivy League*. New York: Broadway.

Swain, C. M. (2002). *The new White nationalism in America*. Cambridge, MA: Cambridge University Press.

Swisher, K. (1994). American Indian Learning Styles Survey: An assessment of teacher knowledge. *Journal of Educational Issues of Language Minority Students, 13*, 59–77.

Tan, L. (1993). *A case study of an artistically gifted Chinese girl: Wang Yani*. Unpublished master's thesis, Concordia University, Montreal.

Tannenbaum, A. J. (1983). *Gifted children: Psychological and educational perspectives*. New York: Macmillan.

Tannenbaum, A. J. (1992) Early signs of giftedness: Research and commentary. *Journal for the Education of the Gifted, 15*, 104–133.

Tannenbaum, A. J. (1998). Programs for the gifted: To be or not to be? *Journal for the Education of the Gifted, 22*, 3–36.

Terman, L. M. (1925). *Mental and physical traits of a thousand gifted children: Genetic studies of genius, Vol. I*. Stanford, CA: Stanford University Press.

Terman, L., & Oden, M. (1935). *The promise of youth: Genetic studies of genius, Vol. III*. Stanford, CA: Stanford University Press.

The 2002 student guide: Participating in the Midwest Talent Search. (2002). Evanston, IL: Center for Talent Development, Northwestern University.

Thernstrom, A. (2000, July/August). Race-based programs and good schooling. *Society 37*, 44–46.

Thernstrom, S., & Thernstrom, A. (1997). *America in Black and White*. New York: Simon and Schuster.

Thernstrom, S., & Thernstrom, A. (1999, June). Reflections on *The Shape of the River*. *UCLA Law Review, 46*, 1583–1631.

Thompson, P. M., Cannon, T. D., Narr, K. L., van Erp, T., Poutanen, V-P, Huttunen, M., Lönnqvist, J., Standertskjöld-Nordenstam, C. G., Kaprio, J., Kheldy, M., Dail, R., Zoumalan, C. I., & Toga, A.W. (2001). Genetic influences on brain structure. *Nature Neuroscience, 4,* 1253–1258.

Thorndike, E. L. (1913). The measurement of achievement in drawing. *Teachers College Record, 14*(5).

Ting-Toomey, S. (1999) *Communicating across cultures.* New York: Guildford Press.

Title IX of the Education Amendments of 1972, Pub. L. No. 92-318, 86 Stat. 235,373–75 [codified as amended at 20 U.S.C. [section] 1681–1968 (1994)].

Tomlinson, C. A. (1995). *How to differentiate instruction in mixed-ability classrooms.* Alexandria, VA: Association for Supervision and Curriculum Development.

Tomlinson, C. A. (1999). *The differentiated classroom: Responding to the needs of all learners.* Alexandria, VA: Association for Supervision and Curriculum Development.

Tomlinson, C. A. (2000). *Differentiation of instruction in the elementary grades* (Report No. ED443572). Champaign, IL: ERIC Clearinghouse on Elementary and Early Childhood Education.

Tomlinson, C. A., (2002, November 6). Proficiency is not enough. *Education Weekly Commentary, 22*(10), 36, 38. Retrieved September 1, 2003, from http://www.nagc.org/Policy/tomlinsonarticlenov62002.htm

Treffert, D. A. (1989). *Extraordinary people. Understanding "idiot savants."* New York: Harper & Row.

Treffinger, D. J. (1986). Fostering effective independent learning through individualized programming. In J. S. Renzulli (Ed.), *Systems and models for developing programs for the gifted and talented* (pp. 429–460). Mansfield Center, CT: Creative Learning Press.

Tsosie, R. (2002). Tribal membership and "Indian status": Federal Indian law in the post-Martinez world. *Native Americas, 19*(1& 2), 18–23.

Tyler-Wood, T. L., Mortenson, M., Putney, L. D., & Cass, M. A. (2000). An effective mathematics and science curriculum option for secondary gifted education. *Roeper Review, 22,* 266–269.

U.S. Bureau of the Census. (2000). *Preliminary estimates of weighted average poverty thresholds in 1999.* Washington, DC: U.S. Department of Commerce.

U.S. Department of Education, National Commission on Excellence in Education. (1983). *A nation at risk: An imperative for educational reform.* Washington, DC: U.S. Government Printing Office.

U.S. Department of Education, Office of Educational Research and Improvement. (1993). *National excellence: A case for developing America's talent.* Washington, DC: U.S. Government Printing Office.

U.S. Department of Education. (1994). *Javits gifted and talented students education program: Grants projects abstracts, 1992–1993.* Washington, DC: Author.

U.S. Department of Education, Office of Educational Research and Improvement. (1998). *Talent and diversity: The emerging world of limited English proficient students in gifted education.* Washington, DC: U.S. Government Printing Office. Retrieved August 29, 2003, from http://www.ed.gov/pubs/TalentandDiversity

Valdez, S., & Waseta, D. (2000). *Four directions: An indigenous model.* Retrieved December 3, 2001, from http://www.4Directions.org

Vandrick, S. (1997). The role of hidden identities in the postsecondary ESL classroom. *TESOL Quarterly, 31,* 153–157.

VanTassel-Baska, J. (1983). Profiles of precocity: The 1982 Midwest Talent Search finalists. *Gifted Child Quarterly, 27,* 139–144.

VanTassel-Baska, J. (1985). The talent search model: Implications for secondary school reform. *National Association of Secondary School Principals Journal, 69*(482), 39–47.

VanTassel-Baska, J. (1989). Profiles of precocity: A three-year study of talented adolescents. In J. L. VanTassel-Baska & P. Olszewski-Kubilius (Eds.), *Patterns of influence on gifted learners: The home, the self, and the school* (pp. 29–39). New York: Teachers College Press.

VanTassel-Baska, J. (Ed.). (1990). *A practical guide to counseling the gifted in a school setting* (2nd ed.). Reston, VA: Council for Exceptional Children.

VanTassel-Baska, J. (1992). *Effective curriculum planning for gifted learners.* Denver: Love.

VanTassel-Baska, J. (1994). Development and assessment of integrated curriculum: A worthy challenge. *Quest, 5,* 5–15.

VanTassel-Baska, J. (1995). *Comprehensive curriculum for gifted learners* (2nd ed.). Boston: Allyn and Bacon.

VanTassel-Baska, J. (1996). Contributions of the talent-search concept to gifted education. In C. P. Benbow & D. Lubinski (Eds.), *Intellectual talent* (pp. 236–245). Baltimore: Johns Hopkins University Press.

VanTassel-Baska, J. (1998). *Excellence in educating gifted and talented learners* (3rd ed.). Denver: Love.

VanTassel-Baska, J. (2003). *Curriculum planning and instructional design for gifted learners.* Denver: Love.

VanTassel-Baska, J., Avery, L. D., Little, C. A., & Hughes, C. E. (2000). An evaluation of the implementation of curriculum innovation: The impact of the William and Mary units on schools. *Journal for the Education of the Gifted, 23,* 244–272.

VanTassel-Baska, J., Bass, G. M., Ries, R. P., Poland, D. L., & Avery, L. D. (1998). A national pilot study of science curriculum effectiveness for high-ability students. *Gifted Child Quarterly, 42,* 200–211.

VanTassel-Baska, J., & Brown, E. (2000). An analysis of gifted curriculum models. In F. A. Karnes & S. M. Bean (Eds.), *Methods and materials for teaching the gifted* (pp. 91–131). Waco, TX: Prufrock Press.

VanTassel-Baska, J., Johnson, D., & Avery, L. D. (2002). Using performance tasks in the identification of economically disadvantaged and minority gifted learners: Findings from Project STAR. *Gifted Child Quarterly, 46,* 110–123.

VanTassel-Baska, J., Johnson, D. T., Hughes, C. E., & Boyce, L. N. (1996). A study of the language arts curriculum effectiveness with gifted learners. *Journal for the Education of the Gifted, 19,* 461–480.

VanTassel-Baska, J., & Little, C. A. (Eds.). (2003). *Content-based curriculum for high-ability learners.* Waco, TX: Prufrock Press.

VanTassel-Baska, J., Zuo, L., Avery, L. D., & Little, C. A. (2002). A curriculum study of gifted student learning in the language arts. *Gifted Child Quarterly, 46,* 30–44.

Vasari, G. (1959). *Lives of the most eminent painters, sculptors, and architects* (Gaston Du C. De Vere, Trans.). New York: Modern Library. (Original work published 1559)

Venugopal, A. (2003, June 20). Homegrown champions. *India Abroad,* pp. M2-M3.

Viola, W. (1936). *Child art and Franz Cizek.* Vienna: Austrian Red Cross

Vygotsky, L. S. (1978). *Mind in society.* Cambridge, MA: Harvard University Press.

Walker, J. J. (1982). The counselor's role in educating the gifted and talented. *The School Counselor, 37,* 351–358.

Wang, S. (1987). *Wang Yani: Pictures by a young Chinese girl.* Munich: Prestel Verlag.

Wang, X. (1990). A comparative study on analogical ability-figural and verbal analogy. In Cooperative Research Group for Supernormal Children in China (CRGSCC) (Ed.), *The selected works of supernormal children of the last ten years in P.R. China* (pp. 230–234). Beijing: Tuanjie Publishing House.

Wang, X., & Lu, Z. (1990). A report on the compilation of the non-intellectual personality inventory for identifying supernormal children in primary school. In Cooperative Research Group for Supernormal Children in China (CRGSCC) (Ed.), *The selected works on supernormal children of last ten years in P.R. China* (pp. 151–160). Beijing: Tuanjie Publishing House.

Ward, V. (1980). *Differential education for the gifted.* Ventura, CA: Office of Ventura County Superintendent of Schools.

Watley, D. J. (1969) Career progress: A longitudinal study of gifted students. *Journal of Counseling Psychology, 16,* 100–108.

Watson, J., Kirby, R., Kelleher, K., & Bradley, R. (1996). Effects of poverty on home environment: An analysis of three-year outcome data for low birthweight premature infants. *Journal of Pediatric Psychology, 21,* 419–431.

Webb, J. T., Meckstroth, E. A., & Tolan, S. S. (1982). *Guiding the gifted child.* Columbus: Ohio Psychology Press.

Weinreb, L., Goldberg, R., Bassuk, E., & Perloff, J. (1998). Determinants of health and service use patterns in homeless and low-income housed children. *Pediatrics, 102,* 554–562.

Weis, L. (1985). *Between two worlds: Black students in an urban community college.* New York: Routledge/Kegan Paul.

Werckmeister, I. K. (1977). The issue of childhood in the art of Paul Klee. *Arts Magazine, 52*(1), 138–151.

Westberg, K. L., Archambault, F. X., Dobyns, S. M., & Salvin, T. J. (1993). *Technical report: An observational study of instructional and curricular practices used with gifted and talented students in regular classrooms.* Storrs: The National Research Center on the Gifted and Talented, University of Connecticut.

White, W. (2002). *The gifted curriculum.* Unpublished manuscript.

Whitehurst, G., & Fischel, J. (2000). Reading and language impairments in conditions of poverty. In D. Bishop & L. Leonard (Eds.), *Speech and language impairments in children: Causes, characteristics, intervention and outcome.* (pp. 53–71). Hove, East Sussex, England: Psychology Press.

Wilson, B. (1974). The super-heroes of J. C. Holz. *Art Education, 27*(8), 2–9.

Wilson, B. (1976). Little Julian's impure drawings: Why children make art. *Studies in Art Education, 17*(2), 45–61.

Wilson, B., & Wilson, M. (1976). Visual narratives and the artistically gifted. *Gifted Child Quarterly, 20,* 432–447.

Wilson, B., & Wilson, M. (1977). An iconoclastic view of the imagery sources in the drawings of young people. *Art Education, 30,* 4–12.

Wilson, B., & Wilson, M. (1979). Figure structure, figure action, and framing in drawings of American and Egyptian children. *Studies in Art Education, 21,* 33–43.

Wiltshire, S. (1987). *Drawings.* London: Dent.

Wiltshire, S. (1989). *Cities.* London: Dent.

Wiltshire, S. (1991). *Floating cities.* New York: Summit Books.

Winner, E. (1989). How can Chinese children draw so well? *Journal of Aesthetic Education, 23*(1), 41–63.

Winner, E. (1996). *Gifted children: Myths and realities.* New York: BasicBooks.

Winner, E. (2000). The origins and ends of giftedness. *American Psychologist, 55,* 159–169.

Wolf, D. P. (1988). From endpoints to repertoires: Some new conclusions about drawing development. *Journal of Aesthetic Education, 22*(1), 17–34.

Wolf, D. P. (1994). Development as the growth of repertoires. In M. B. Franklin & B. Kaplan (Eds.) *Development and the arts* (pp. 59–78). Hillsdale, NJ: Erlbaum.

Wong-Fillmore, L. (1991). When learning a second language means losing a first. *Early Childhood Research Quarterly, 6,* 323–346.

Wulff, O. (1927). *Die Kunst des Kindes.* Stuttgardt: Ferdinand Enke.

Xin, H. (Ed.). (1990). *Gifted education.* Beijing: People's Education Press.

Yzaguirre, R. (2001, April). Census shows disparity in education of Latino children. *Hispanic Magazine,* 104.

Zettel, J. J. (1982a). Implementing the right to a free appropriate public education. In J. Ballard, B. A. Ramirez, & F. J. Weintraub (Eds.), *Special education in America: Its legal and governmental foundations* (pp. 23–40). Reston, VA: Council for Exceptional Children.

Zettel, J. J. (1982b). The education of gifted and talented children from a federal perspective. In J. Ballard, B. A. Ramirez, & F. J. Weintraub (Eds.), *Special education in America: Its legal and governmental foundations* (pp. 51–64). Reston, VA: Council for Exceptional Children.

Zettel, J. J. & Ballard, J. (1982). The Education for All Handicapped Children Act of 1975 (Pub. L. 94-142): Its history, origins, and concepts. In J. Ballard, B. A. Ramirez, & F. J. Weintraub (Eds.), *Special education in America: Its legal and governmental foundations* (pp. 11–22). Reston, VA: Council for Exceptional Children.

Zha, Z. (1983). A three-year longitudinal study of supernormal children. In Cooperative Research Group for Supernormal Children in China (CRGSCC) (Ed.), *Monograph of study on supernormal children* (pp. 1–22). Xining: Qinhai Publishing House.

Zha, Z. (1984). A comparative study of the analogical reasoning of 3- to 6-year-old supernormal and normal children. *Acta Psychologica Sinica, 16,* 382–390.

Zha, Z. (1986). A five-year study of the mental development of supernormal children. *Acta Psychologica Sinica, 18,* 123–131.

Zha, Z. (1993). *Psychology of supernormal children.* Beijing: People's Education Press.

Zhang, L. (1987). A comparative study on observation ability between supernormal and normal children age 3–6. *Acta Psychologica Sinica, 19,* 214–218

Zimmerman, E. (1995). It was an incredible experience: The impact of educational opportunities on a talented student's art development. In C. Golomb (Ed.), *The development of artistically gifted children* (pp. 135–170). Hillsdale, NJ: Erlbaum.

Zito, J., Safer, D., DosReis, S., & Riddle, M. (1998). Racial disparity in psychotropic medications prescribed for youths with Medicaid insurance in Maryland. *Journal of the American Academy of Child and Adolescent Psychiatry, 37,* 179–184.

Zimpher, N. L., & Ashburn, E. A. (1993). Countering parochialism in teacher candidates. In M. E. Dilworth (Ed.), *Diversity in teacher education: New expectations* (pp. 40–62). San Francisco: Jossey-Bass.

Zsensun, Z., & Low, A. (1991). *A young painter: The life and paintings of Wang Yani—China's extraordinary young artist.* New York: Scholastic.

Zuriff, G. (2002a, Winter). Inventing racism. *The Public Interest,* 114–129.

Zuriff, G. (2002b, August). Is racial and ethnic diversity educationally beneficial? *The World and I,* 271–287.

[Index of Names]

[About the Authors]

[Editors]

Diane Boothe is professor and chair of the Department of Curriculum and Instruction at the State University of West Georgia. She served as the first director of the Advanced Academy of Georgia, a full-time university residential program for gifted and talented high school students. Her research areas include gifted education, cultural diversity, and second language acquisition. She has published and been featured as the keynote and plenary speaker at international and national conferences in these areas. She has served as the president of Georgia Teachers of English to Speakers of Other Languages (TESOL), chair of the Higher Education Interest Section for TESOL International, and, for 10 years, as the editor of the *TESOL in Action Journal*.

Julian C. Stanley is professor *emeritus* of psychology in the Department of Psychology and Brain Sciences of Johns Hopkins University. In 1971, he founded the Study of Mathematically Precocious Youth (SMPY) at Johns Hopkins. It has grown into four regional programs that cover the whole country: the Center for Talented Youth (CTY) at Johns Hopkins, the Talent Identification Program (TIP) at Duke University, the Center for Talent Development (CTD) at Northwestern University, and the Rocky Mountain Talent Search (RMTS) at the University of Denver. Prior to 1971, Dr. Stanley was a research methodologist and psychological statistician; he was also president of the American Educational Research Association, the National Council on Measurement in Education, two divisions of the American Psychological Association, and several other organizations. He is a member of the National Academy of Education, Phi Beta Kappa, Phi Delta Kappa, and other groups. He is the author, coauthor, editor, or coeditor of 14 books and 550 articles, reviews, technical notes, and letters to editors. Currently, he is senior consultant at the Center for Talented Youth.

[Contributors]

Linda E. Brody directs the Study of Exceptional Talent and codirects the Diagnostic and Counseling Center at the Johns Hopkins University Center for Talented Youth (CTY). Her research interests focus on special populations of gifted students, particularly the highly gifted, gifted females, and twice-exceptional students. She has published numerous articles in professional journals and has coedited two books: *Women and the Mathematical Mystique* and *Learning Disabled Gifted Students: Identification and Programming*. She also supervises the publication of *Imagine*, an award-winning magazine for academically talented students. Linda has extensive experience counseling gifted students and their parents, and she has also taught graduate courses in gifted education at Johns Hopkins for many years.

Jaime A. Castellano is a nationally recognized leader in the areas of identifying, assessing, and serving historically underrepresented students—Hispanics, the poor, and other culturally and linguistically diverse students—in gifted education programs. As a staff member of Florida Atlantic University, Lynn University, and Arizona State University, Jaime's experience includes teaching graduate courses in educational leadership, gifted education, assessment and evaluation, curriculum and instruction, and multicultural education. He is currently the secretary of the Special Populations Division of the National Association for Gifted Children (NAGC) and the chairperson of the Special Interest Group in Gifted Education for the National Association for Bilingual Education (NABE). His two books, *Reaching New Horizons: Gifted Education for Culturally and Linguistically Diverse Students* (2002) and *Special Populations in Gifted Education: Working With Diverse Gifted Learners* (2003), have been widely accepted in the field. He is also the author of several articles and continues to consult with school districts across the country on gifted education for underrepresented gifted students.

Donna Y. Ford is a professor at The Ohio State University College of Education. She teaches all courses in gifted education and focuses her teaching, research, and writing on recruiting and retaining diverse students in gifted programs; reversing underachievement among gifted Black students; developing multicultural curricula for gifted students; and promoting healthy, positive racial identities in gifted diverse students. She is the author of *Reversing Underachievement Among Gifted Black Students* (1996) and *Multicultural Gifted Education* (1999). She consults with school districts nationally and has written many articles on gifted Black students.

Claire Golomb is a professor of psychology (*emerita*) at the University of Massachusetts at Boston. She has written extensively on the development of child art and on children's imaginative development. She is the author of *Young Children's Sculpture and Drawing*, *The Child's Creation of a Pictorial World*, and *Child Art in Context: A Cultural and Comparative Perspective*, and she is the editor of *The Development of Artistically Gifted Children*.

Linda S. Gottfredson is a professor at the University of Delaware School of Education and affiliated faculty in the University Honors Program. Her research focuses on individual and group differences in abilities and interests and their implications for schools, employers, vocational counselors, and health care providers. She also writes frequently on the socio-political dilemmas that intelligence differences create in democratic societies. She teaches measurement in the

Elementary Teacher Education program and interdisciplinary colloquia for honors students.

Tarek C. Grantham is an assistant professor in the Department of Educational Psychology at the University of Georgia. He teaches courses in the Gifted and Creative Education Program, and his research focuses on motivation, mentoring, and underrepresentation among culturally diverse youth in gifted programs, particularly Black students. Dr. Grantham serves on The Diversity Task Force and Education Commission of the National Association for Gifted Children, which provide leadership for researchers, practitioners, and parents in meeting the needs of gifted students.

C. Marie Jackson is a counselor education faculty member at State University of West Georgia. She has a master's in counseling from Jacksonville State University and a doctoral degree in counselor education from the University of Alabama. She has experience in public schools as a teacher, psychometrist and a school counselor, K–12. She has been program leader for school counseling training programs in three university settings. In addition to her school counseling credentials and experience, she is a Licensed Professional Counselor and a Nationally Certified Counselor, having worked in a psychiatric hospital outpatient setting as a therapist.

Arthur R. Jensen is professor *emeritus* of educational psychology in the Graduate School of Education, University of California, Berkeley. During the 40 years of his tenure at Berkeley, he was a prolific researcher in the psychology of human learning, individual differences in cognitive abilities, psychometrics, behavioral genetics, and mental chronometry, and his activity has continued since his official retirement in 1994. His work, published in seven books and some 400 articles in scientific and professional journals, has placed him among the most frequently cited figures in contemporary psychology.

Beverly J. Klug is an associate professor of education at Idaho State University, where she teaches classes in literacy and multicultural education. Her research interests include literacy development for underrepresented populations and the developmental processes of becoming teachers who are sensitive to the needs of all students. She has published widely and presents regularly to organizations concerning the education of ethnically diverse populations. She is coauthor of *Widening the Circle: Culturally Relevant Pedagogy for American Indian Children* (2003). Dr. Klug is a member of the Idaho State Department of Education's Indian Education Committee, contributing to the knowledge base on the needs of American Indian peoples in Idaho. In addition, she has served for the last 4 years in the position of Partnership School university liaison to the Ft. Hall Elementary School located on the Shoshone-Bannock Indian Reservation, working directly with teachers and students to improve educational opportunities for all.

Mindy Kornhaber is an assistant professor in the College of Education at The Pennsylvania State University. Her research focuses on the questions: How do institutions and the policies surrounding them enhance or impede the development of human potential? How can institutions enhance individual potential to a high level and on an equitable basis? She has most recently authored (with Edward G. Fierros and Shirley A. Veenema) *Multiple Intelligences: Best Ideas from Research and Practice.*

Jonna Kwiatkowski is an associate research scientist at the Center for the Psychology of Abilities, Competencies, and Expertise (PACE) at Yale University. Her main research interest is creativity, which she has explored through cognitive, neurophysiological, as well as educational research. Within the PACE Center, Jonna works on refining triarchic assessments tools, specifically for Project Rainbow, which is focused on developing assessment tools as potential supplements to the SAT, and the Transitions in the Development of Giftedness project, which is focused on investigating current definitions of giftedness within school districts and providing research-based guidelines for realigning gifted identification practices to better match the skills required for success beyond school years.

Robert Lerner is commissioner of the National Center for Education Statistics, U.S. Department of Education. Previously, he ran a statistical consulting business, Lerner & Nagai Quantitative Consulting. He received his Ph.D. in sociology from the University of Chicago and was assistant director at the Center for the Study of Social & Political Change, Smith College. He has taught at Syracuse University, Smith College, and Johns Hopkins University. He is coauthor of several books and numerous articles. The positions taken in his contribution are solely his own. They do not reflect the views of the National Center for Education Statistics, the U.S. Department of Education, or any other agency of the federal government.

H. Richard Milner is an assistant professor in the Department of Teaching and Learning at the Peabody College of Vanderbilt University. Dr. Milner teaches courses focusing on curriculum theory and development, as well as the social and philosophical aspects of education. His research interests concern curriculum and professional development; academic achievement and resilience among African American students; and learning opportunities for students of color. Among other academic journals, Dr. Milner's work has appeared in *Teaching and Teacher Education, Race Ethnicity and Education, The Journal of Curriculum and Supervision,* and *Theory into Practice.*

Althea K. Nagai is an independent statistical consultant. She received her Ph.D. in political science from the University of Chicago. She was a researcher at the Center for the Study of Social & Political Change, Smith College, and also taught there. She is coauthor of three books and many articles.

Paula Olszewski-Kubilius is the director of the Center for Talent Development at Northwestern University. She has worked at the Center for more than 20 years, during which she has conducted research and published widely on issues of talent development, particularly the effects of accelerated educational programs and the needs of special populations of gifted children. She has designed and conducted educational programs for learners of all ages, as well as workshops for parents and teachers. She is active in national- and state-level advocacy organizations for gifted children. She currently serves as the editor of *Gifted Child Quarterly* and formerly was a coeditor of the *Journal of Secondary Gifted Education*. She has served on the editorial advisory board of the *Journal for the Education of the Gifted* and *Gifted Child International* and was a consulting editor for *Roeper Review*.

Margarete Parrish is an assistant professor of social work at the University of Maryland School of Social Work in Baltimore. She teaches courses in the foundation and clinical curricula. She has worked extensively with disadvantaged youth, especially those with traumatic injuries and medical complications. She has published in the areas of urban violence, youth suicide, and Munchausen Syndrome by Proxy.

Judith A. Rance-Roney is assistant professor of secondary education at the State University of New York at New Paltz. She teaches in the TESOL teacher education program (Teaching English to Speakers of Other Languages) and educational studies. Her major research area is in teaching English language learners with special needs, including service to students with learning disabilities and to students with high intellectual ability. She has received a U.S. Department of Education Secretary's Award for her programs in adult education, literacy, and TESOL, and she is the author of numerous articles in those areas. She is currently on the advisory board for NCLE, the National Clearinghouse for ESL Literacy Education.

Sally M. Reis is a professor and the department head of the Educational Psychology Department in the Neag School of Education at the University of Connecticut, where she also serves as principal investigator of the National Research Center on the Gifted and Talented. She was a classroom teacher in public education, as well as an administrator, before coming to the University of Connecticut. She has authored more than 130 articles, 11 books, 40 book chapters, and numerous monographs and technical reports and worked in a research team that has generated more than $35 million in grants in the last 15 years. Her research interests are related to talent development in all children, as well as special populations of gifted and talented students, including students with learning disabilities, gifted females, and diverse groups of talented students who are often underserved.

Joseph Renzulli is a professor of educational psychology at the University of Connecticut, where he also serves as director of the National Research Center on the Gifted and Talented. His research has focused on the identification and development of creativity and giftedness in young people and on organizational models and curricular strategies for differentiated learning environments and total school improvement. A focus of his work has been on applying the pedagogy of gifted education to the improvement of learning for all students. His most recent books include the second edition of *The Schoolwide Enrichment Model*, *The Multiple Menu Model for Developing Differentiated Curriculum*, and *Enriching Curriculum for All Students*. Dr. Renzulli was recently designated a Board of Trustees Distinguished Professor at the University of Connecticut, and, in June 2003, he was awarded an Honorary Doctor of Laws Degree from McGill University in Montreal, Canada.

Beheruz N. Sethna is professor of business at the University of West Georgia and its president. He is the first person of Indian origin to become president of a U.S. university and the first of any ethnic minority to become president of an IHE (non-HBCU) in Georgia. Remaining active in teaching and scholarship, he considers among his highest honors being elected Honors Professor of the Year (1999) and being the faculty advisor for the student research team winner at Big Night and at the National Social Sciences Association (2003). His research areas include gifted education and business. He was associated with the start of the Texas Academy for Leadership in the Humanities, and later he started the Advanced Academy of Georgia, a full-time residential program for gifted youth of high school age. He is the author or coauthor of more than 55 papers and *Research Methods in Marketing and Management* (1984).

Jiannong Shi is a professor of psychology at the Institute of Psychology, Chinese Academy of Sciences. He focuses his research in the field of giftedness and creativity, theoretically and practically. Based on his natural perspective on giftedness, he developed a bio-socio-psycho model to guide gifted education and creativity cultivation in kindergarten, primary, and secondary schools in China. He authored or coauthored *Discovering Gifted Children* and *Developmental Psychology of Gifted Children* and nine other books in the field of child development and education, as well as more than 70 journal articles, book chapters, and conference presentations since 1990. He is currently a director of five projects in the field of gifted education, giftedness, and creativity. He serves as a director of the Center for Supernormal Children at the Institute of Psychology, Chinese Academy of Sciences, and president of the Asia-Pacific Federation of World Council for Gifted and Talented Children.

Brent M. Snow is a professor and chair of the Department of Counseling and Educational Psychology at the University of West Georgia. For 13 years, he was a faculty member in both the Department of Psychology and the Department of Applied Behavioral Studies at Oklahoma State University. Prior to his work at O.S.U., he was on the faculty at the University of Idaho, where he received his Ph.D. Most recently, he has served as the principal investigator/project director of the Transforming School Counseling initiative/grant funded by the Wallace Reader's Digest Fund. In 2002, his department was honored by the Education Trust as a pioneer, advocate, and national leader in transforming school counseling in both universities and public schools.

Robert J. Sternberg is IBM Professor of Psychology and Education and director of the Center for the Psychology of Abilities, Competencies, and Expertise (PACE) at Yale University. He was also was the 2003 president of the American Psychological Association. Sternberg is the author of more than 950 journal articles, book chapters, and books, and has received more than $18 million in government and other grants and contracts for his research. The central focus of his research is on intelligence, creativity, and wisdom, and he also has studied love and close relationships, as well as hate. This research has been conducted in five different continents. Sternberg is most well known for his theory of successful intelligence, investment theory of creativity (developed with Todd Lubart), theory of thinking styles as mental self-government, balance theory of wisdom, and for his triangular theory of love and his theory of love as a story. His most recent theory is the WICS theory of leadership.

Joyce VanTassel-Baska is the Jody and Layton Smith Professor of Education at the College of William and Mary in Virginia, where she has developed a graduate program and a research and development center in gifted education. Dr. VanTassel-Baska has published widely, including five recent books and over 260 monographs, book chapters, and articles in refereed journals. She also serves as the editor of *Gifted and Talented International*.

Clifton D. Wickstrom is a professor and faculty advisor at the Union Institute and University, Sacramento, California Center. He is a graduate of Stanford University, the University of Alaska, and Berne University, and has also attended the University of Southern California. His areas of research interest are in research and analytical methods, systems of public organizational governance, national policy on gifted student education, and assessment of educational program effectiveness. Recent publications include coauthoring an article in the *Journal of Secondary Gifted Education* and two articles in *Georgia TESOL in Action*.

Jinghua Zhai is a superintendent in the Beijing Yumin Elementary School. She has been engaged in the education of gifted children for more than 10 years. When she was promoted to the superintendent in 1997, she set up the philosophy for running the school that education must be student-oriented and give the first priority to student cultivation. The school was awarded Community Recognized Successful School for their education program. She is a concurrently a member in the Elementary & Middle School Textbook Review Committee of the National Department of Education. She is also a representative of the Beijing People's Congress and a professor in the Beijing West City Education Institute.